T0373497

DEPLORABLE

DEPLORABLE

The Worst Presidential Campaigns from Jefferson to Trump

Mary E. Stuckey

THE PENNSYLVANIA STATE UNIVERSITY PRESS
UNIVERSITY PARK, PENNSYLVANIA

Library of Congress Cataloging-in-Publication Data

Names: Stuckey, Mary E., author.
Title: Deplorable : the worst presidential campaigns from Jefferson to Trump / Mary E. Stuckey.
Description: University Park, Pennsylvania : The Pennsylvania State University Press, [2021] | Includes bibliographical references and index.
Summary: "Explores the use of anti-democratic language in US presidential elections, using examples detailing the political, economic, and cultural elements that make such appeals more likely"—Provided by publisher.
Identifiers: LCCN 2021021664 | ISBN 9780271091761 (cloth)
Subjects: LCSH: Presidents—United States—Election—History. | Democracy—United States—History. | Rhetoric—Political aspects—United States—History.
Classification: LCC JK524 .S88 2021 | DDC 324.973—dc23
LC record available at https://lccn.loc.gov/2021021664

Printed in the United States of America
Published by The Pennsylvania State University Press, University Park, PA 16802–1003

The Pennsylvania State University Press is a member of the Association of University Presses.

It is the policy of The Pennsylvania State University Press to use acid-free paper. Publications on uncoated stock satisfy the minimum requirements of American National Standard for Information Sciences—Permanence of Paper for Printed Library Material, ANSI Z39.48–1992.

CONTENTS

ACKNOWLEDGMENTS

In some ways, this book started more than a decade ago, when I published *Defining Americans*, a book about the processes of inclusion and exclusion in US presidential rhetoric. This book might be considered that volume's shadowed twin, focusing as it does on the bleaker elements of our history. Both books focus on how the narrative of our nation slowly winding its painful way toward a fuller realization of national ideals is an inaccurate and unproductive one, allowing Americans—especially white Americans—to ignore the ways oppression is built into the very fabric of the country and influences every interpretation of those ideals. In this book, I want to do two things: draw attention to the structural elements that make exclusionary discourse and policy more likely and focus on the recurring themes that animate that discourse. The United States survived deplorable elections in the past. It would be nice to learn from them as well.

I had a great deal of help conceptualizing this project. In no particular order, I'm grateful to John Murphy, Bob Hariman. Leslie Harris, Kirt Wilson, Paul Stob, Allison Prasch, Steve Browne, Abe Khan, Erina MacGeorge, Denise Solomon, Jim Dillard, Angela Ray, Ann Burnette, Stephen Heidt, Rob Mills, Ryan Neville-Shepard, Meredith Neville-Shepard, Lynn Goodnight, Tom Goodnight, David Cheshier, David Zarefsky, Brandon Inabinet, Lisa Corrigan, Zoe Hess Carney, the Rhetorichicks, individually and collectively, Victoria Sanchez, and everyone else who listened to me spout off about this project at conferences, over lunches, and in the hallways of Sparks. In addition, Jim Dillard and Steve Browne read and commented on chapters and made them smarter, for which I thank them both.

Books like this are sometimes tricky to research. So my deepest thanks to Penn State's College of Liberal Arts and the Department of Communication Arts and Sciences for the funding, time, and travel that made that research and this book possible. Pennsylvania State University (PSU) librarian Eric Novotny provided important help in accessing newspaper accounts of early elections. The archivists who staff the presidential library system are always supremely helpful. Thanks to Paul M. Sparrow, Kirsten Strigel Carter, Virginia Lewick, Matthew Hanson, and Sarah Navins at the FDR Presidential Library; to Jason Schultz, Nicholas Herold, and Melissa Heddon at the Nixon Library; to Debbie Wheeler and the archival staff at the George H. W. Bush Library; to Heath Robinson and Amy Allen at the University of Arkansas, which houses papers relevant to the 1992 Clinton campaign; and to Bob Clark and Tom Rosenbaum at the Rockefeller Archive Center. Tom was an insightful, caring, and kind person—as are so many archivists. He will be missed. And Bob, thanks again and always for everything.

I'm extremely grateful to Ryan Peterson at PSU Press, whose kindness is matched only by his professionalism and acumen. I've worked with a lot of copyeditors in my day, and all of them have made my work better. None of them have done so as graciously and effectively as Dana Henricks, who has my deepest gratitude. I'm also grateful to Brian Beer, Cate Fricke, Janice North, Laura Reed-Morrison, and Kendra Boileau, whose work was and always is consistently exemplary. I love working with PSU Press for very good reasons. I'm also grateful to Diane Heith and Angela Ray, whose careful reading and scholarly insights made the book smarter. Thanks also to Scott Bennett and PSU's graduate school for helping to make production possible and the book more affordable.

Some of the material in chapter 4 appears in "Complicit Civility and the Politics of Exclusion: Nixon's Southern Strategy and Rockefeller's Response," *Western Journal of Communication*, forthcoming, and some of the material in chapter 5 is in "The Presidency and Fracturing of American Political Identity," in *The Rhetorical History of the United States*, vol. 10, *The Fragmentation of Liberalism* (East Lansing: Michigan State University Press, forthcoming). Some material in the afterword also appears in "'The Power of the Presidency to Hurt': The Indecorous Rhetoric of Donald J. Trump and the Rhetorical Norms of Democracy," *Presidential Studies Quarterly* 50 (2020): 366–91, https://onlinelibrary.wiley.com/doi/abs/10.1111/psq.12641, and in "The Rhetoric of the Trump Administration," *Presidential Studies Quarterly*, forthcoming.

Last but never least, I'm grateful to my friends and family, especially to Maren, Jim, and Laura, who offered many insights and ideas and more than a few good laughs every week; Denise and Erina, the best happy hour companions a person could ask for; Linda and Chuck, who are always there for me, and with whom I have seen any number of fabulous places; Jennifer, who knows more than she realizes; Beth, who always has hope; my brother Steve and his wife, Carolee, who are always interested; my niece and nephews, who are the future; and my mother, who doesn't like to be told she is amazing (even though she is), and to whom this book is lovingly dedicated.

INTRODUCTION
Deplorable Elections, Despicable Discourses

In 1828 Andrew Jackson, the famously violent hero of the Battle of New Orleans, won the presidential election and defeated incumbent John Quincy Adams, son of the second president. This was the second time the two contended in a presidential campaign. The first time, Adams emerged the victor, and, predictably, Jackson did not take his defeat well, declaring the result a "corrupt bargain," and claiming he had been robbed of victory. He had a point—he won the popular vote in 1824 but lost the election in the House through the machinations of Henry Clay, who then became Adams's secretary of state. The rematch four years later was unsurprisingly bitter, characterized by personal insults, wild accusations, double dealing, and heated controversy circulated over a nastily partisan press. Adams, for example, relying on old rumors about Jackson's willingness to execute militia members accused of desertion in 1815, accused Jackson of willful murder. Jackson, equally willing to circulate rumor, asserted that while serving as ambassador to the Russian court Adams had supplied an American woman's sexual services to the tsar. Rhetorically, then, the election pitted a corrupt elitist against a brutal backwoodsman; the clear loser was the developing American democracy. That election is remembered as one of the ugliest in US history but is also treated as a sad relic of a more colorful past rather than as part of a lasting national pattern.

The framers of the US Constitution shared an understanding of democracy as based on rational, careful deliberation. They used this standard to exclude those they considered incapable of democratic citizenship—white men without sufficient property, women, enslaved people, and, often, American Indians. But they did not themselves live up to the standard they set as they frequently governed by insult, invective, and the occasional duel. Since the founding it has become commonplace to assume that elections meet some standard of decorum and to express surprise at the perceived lapses in the civil tradition of the world's most influential democracy.

But American elections are often full of personal attacks, trivialized presentations of issues, the exploitation of the politics of fear, and other kinds of appalling elements, all of which are generally considered bad for the health of a democratic republic. Over time, the US political system has proven itself to be both fragile and resilient, susceptible to its citizens' worst instincts and capable of reaching for their loftiest goals.[1] Recent elections seem to tilt the nation in both directions at once. This, too, is a recurring theme in American national politics. This book offers a discussion of how and why antidemocratic discourses surface in some elections and not in others.

The chapters proceed chronologically, with particular attention to specific themes that tie the individual elections together and help us understand the ways in which certain conditions and the choices candidates and parties make lead to the worst kinds of politics. I consider "deplorable" elections to be those in which a variety of despicable discourses not only circulate but gain purchase among the mass public. But all elections in US political history can be understood as being, in some sense, deplorable. I use the word here as a nod to Hillary Clinton's notorious characterization of Donald Trump's supporters as a "basket of deplorables" during the 2016 campaign.[2] That characterization registered dismay at the approval those supporters offered for Trump's norm-breaking rhetoric and seemed to implicitly argue that there was something new and unusual about its appearance in national politics. I use it to mark the ways that this kind of behavior is more common than we want to believe. There is nothing new or unusual about dangerous and antidemocratic campaign rhetoric. I use "deplorable," then, in the same way we talk about good art or obscene art—we know it when we see it. Deplorable elections are those in which the candidates, their campaigns and spokespeople, and sometimes the media, rely on rhetoric that is misleading, dishonest, petty, bigoted, and malicious. Not only is this rhetoric inappropriate to democratic politics, and surely unbecoming for a future head of state, but it is also despicable.

Throughout the book, I call rhetoric "despicable" as a shorthand for language that is undemocratic, even antidemocratic. More specifically, it excludes specific members of the public, encourages authoritarian procedures for dealing with national problems, and/or actively works against the national democratic project representing the higher ideals of American national identity, by which I mean that they run counter to aspirations for an inclusive and just polity. I treat "despicable discourse" as a synonym and shorthand for antidemocratic and exclusionary language. That language is not always the same; the shape of despicable discourse is melded to its political moment. But it is always exclusionary; it always treats politics as a competition between citizens rather than a means of providing community between and for them. Resentment is thus always in evidence and is often exploited by candidates. Furthermore, deplorable discourse is often rooted in political nostalgia, evoking an Edenic past that has been perniciously disrupted. It also tends to delegitimate political opposition, suppressing debate on important issues and also seeking to suppress the vote. And finally, the parameters of national identity are always restricted when deplorable discourse is deployed as a political tool.

In focusing on this language, I am not also, in most cases, interested in the motives and character of those who use it. Candidates use the political language that is available to them. Such use can be quite intentional and can be intended to specifically exclude its targets. But it can also be less thoughtfully produced, more a matter of cultural norms and the discourses that prevail at any given moment. This does not allow the candidates to escape responsibility for their language. It does spread that responsibility more widely. To the extent that political exclusions are permitted in a culture, they will be reflected in and deepened by the language of political elites.

Given the problematic nature of our founding documents, which themselves contain elements of despicable discourse—the Constitution, for instance, instantiates slavery without ever mentioning the word, and the Declaration contains language excoriating indigenous peoples as "savages"—I don't want to claim that the nation was founded on the principles I associate with the higher ideals of democracy. But both those documents also contain ideas that facilitated arguments against slavery and for more inclusion. Democratic principles have been present since the founding, and Americans continue to reach for them today. These ideals have always been present in contradictory and contentious ways, and the nation's ability to enact its ideals has often conflicted with the self-interest of ruling elites and those who support them. In some ways, what follows can be read as a chronicle of national failures, rendered in hopes of learning from them.

I focus on public discourse because it is in our public conversations that the limits and possibilities of our politics are most obvious. I concentrate on elections because they are moments that allow the capture of deplorable discourses as they circulate nationally. Antidemocratic discourses are always present in US politics; elections allow us to zero in on the ways in which they are widely shared and contested. Certainly, other kinds of political events feature such discourses—you can find them in debates over legislation, in hearings on political nominees for federal office, and so on. But elections entail a kind of sustained attention and participation by the mass public that other events do not offer as consistently across history. And once an election has been won because of this language, that language may insinuate itself into the political culture more broadly, proving to be a continuous, rather than an episodic, threat to the nation's democracy.

Even though elections require choices between candidates, this project is less about judging the merits of specific candidates than highlighting the conversations surrounding them. Which is to say that I call an election deplorable not because of who won but because of the public conversations that took place in the course of that election. The effort is not about deciding which candidates or which political parties are more or less wedded to despicable discourse but about determining what kinds of things make despicable discourse rise to the surface of political life. The distinction between a deplorable election, then, and one that does not fall into that category is that in a deplorable election, candidates facilitate despicable discourse; in nondeplorable elections, they do not. The 2008 election is not on my list of deplorable elections, for instance, because John McCain pushed back against claims that Barack Obama was un-American, but 2016 is on my list because Donald Trump actively argued that Hillary Clinton was unqualified on the basis of her gender.

Not every deplorable election is included in the book—I started this chapter with 1828, but I don't treat it at length elsewhere, for example. As I noted earlier, a case could be made for almost every election, and the absence of an election from the analysis here is not an argument that the election wasn't deplorable or that despicable discourse didn't circulate—such discourse obviously did circulate, for instance, in 2008. I chose elections that I considered to be the clearest examples of what I am trying to argue, not the only examples. Readers are welcome to play along at home by thinking about the ways other elections might fit into the conversation.

I also think that despicable discourse is both episodic and cumulative. By this I mean that it circulates in individual elections and recurs across time—many of the same arguments present in the nineteenth century about immigration and nonwhites reappeared in both the twentieth and twenty-first centuries. The United States is not, in other words, on some trajectory of greater inclusion but instead makes progress toward inclusion and then pulls back from it. There is no rigid, cyclical pattern to these reappearances, but it is quite clear that earlier iterations of despicable discourses resurface later. It is also true that at least since 1968 there is an additive quality to these discourses. If one candidate uses despicable discourse, and the next candidate of their party chooses not to, the discourse will probably recede, at least for a while. But if a candidate uses such language, and then the next one in line does so as well, and as audiences and parties form around the appeals present in that rhetoric, it becomes much more difficult to force it off to the margins. Recognizing this fact, the book includes three chapters and an afterword that deal with despicable discourse as it has evolved since 1968.

Most of the voices you will hear are from men, and most of those men are white. This is emphatically not because those whose voices you rarely hear lacked agency or because they did not argue against these discourses. It is because I concentrate on the exclusionary discourses themselves, and in general those who have traditionally been excluded from the nation's power are the targets, not the purveyors, of exclusion. Like the problem of racism more generally, the problems associated with despicable discourse are problems made by white people, so those are the voices you hear in this book.

Most of the rhetoric you will hear comes from political candidates and their most prominent surrogates. In locating that rhetoric, I use secondary sources and the *New York Times* for early elections and archives as well as public records for more recent ones. The *Times* did not always have the prominence it currently enjoys, but it is a consistent and detailed record of the elections in question. Campaign records are not always preserved in archives; there are extensive sources for the ones included here, however, and the voices of the candidates and the details of their strategies are illuminated in those records.

Yet deplorable elections do not depend solely on candidates, although they are the focus of the book. Candidates and their surrogates, of course, facilitate undemocratic language. But the public must be open to those appeals, and other elites must at least tacitly allow them, or they would not circulate with authority. Deplorable elections are more likely when political institutions are weak; when economic conditions are bad; when white voters suffer from real or imagined status anxiety; and when candidates focus attention on race, class, and gender, and on fearmongering more generally. When these elements align in certain ways, it becomes more likely that undemocratic language will find a receptive audience.

THE MAKINGS OF A DEPLORABLE ELECTION

For despicable discourse to circulate widely, the system must be open to it. Several things contribute to such systemic fragility. These are moments when the relationship of the people to the institutions that govern them shift. When institutions seem to fail, as they did, for example, in 1824, new leadership and new institutional forms feel necessary. Because both political institutions and those who occupy them lack legitimacy, a space opens for new or previously ignored possibilities. At the same time, elites who hold power under the old rules, and often because of those rules, threatened with the loss of that power, can reach out for ways to preserve the status quo. Not all those ways are either inclusive or democratic. The first requirement for a deplorable election, then, is that the contemporary institutional arrangements must have reached a certain point of fragility. For example, 1964 is not a deplorable election, despite some of the excesses of the Goldwater campaign, but 1968 is, because events between Johnson's 1964 landslide and the 1968 campaign created a crisis of systemic legitimacy.

A moment of crisis is not enough to create a deplorable election, however, because there is always more than institutional politics involved. When a fragile political system must cope with a difficult moment in the nation's economy, the chances of a deplorable election grow. Economic tensions, which may be rooted in either real suffering or the fear of it, often bring up questions of class and labor. They also generate and increase tensions between the nation's urban and rural citizens. A resilient system can manage those tensions, while a fragile one cannot. When economic tensions appear, politics can more readily seem to be a zero-sum game in which the prosperity of some citizens is understood as coming at the expense of other citizens. Politics is then understood not as a cooperative effort among citizens but as a contest between them. When that happens, despicable discourse is more likely. The 1932 election, for example, had the potential to be deplorable, but it wasn't, because a cooperative frame was both available to the candidates and accepted by the public. But the 1924 election took place amid growing tensions between rural and urban citizens, and those tensions were exacerbated by the role of the Ku Klux Klan in the election, marking it as antidemocratic in the clearest way possible.

Deplorable elections are more likely when immigration is an important issue. Even though in some ways immigration is an economic issue, I treat immigration as different from the economy because in the contest between capital and labor, between rural and urban, between rich and poor, economic conflict is internal and pits citizens against one another. In the case of immigration, the conflict occurs between those who are already here and those who are more recently arriving. In this case, some of the economic tensions may be lessened by a shared ideological interest in opposing an increase in unassimilated residents, while other tensions may be exacerbated by opposing views on immigration. In either example, the composition of political coalitions becomes less stable, more unpredictable. And in that unpredictability, despicable discourse finds an opening. In 2008, for example, immigration was an issue, but it was not a wedge issue. By 2016, however, immigration was both a wedge issue and one concerning which overtly racist rhetoric was circulated.

These kinds of tensions are always and inevitably accompanied by questions of race. Racial inequity is constitutive of American politics, and no discussion of the less savory elements of our national politics can exclude race as a factor.[3] When the political system loses its legitimacy, the place of those deemed less than fully "American" becomes more tenuous. Only a strong and legitimate political system can make advances in racial equity. But these advances often contribute to a loss of systemic legitimacy. When African Americans are seen to be advancing "too quickly," or to be making "illegitimate" claims on the system, the racism that simmers below the national surface will be explicitly articulated and will be attached to a major party candidacy. I do not classify 1948 as deplorable because the Dixiecrat revolt was confined to an unsuccessful third party. But I do classify 1992 as deplorable because Bill Clinton's treatment of Jesse Jackson and Sister Souljah and the way the campaign domesticated Hillary Clinton indicate the ways in which tacitly discriminatory politics had developed bipartisan appeal.

Overtly bigoted appeals are normally associated with third-party or losing candidates—one thinks of the Dixiecrats in 1948, of George Wallace in 1964, or of Pat Buchanan in 2000, for instance. But deplorable elections require more than one unheeded voice; they involve the active participation or the tacit approval of one or both major party candidates. If the major parties refuse to advance despicable discourse, and especially if they actively combat it, this rhetoric will be shoved to the shadowed corners of our politics. When they endorse such discourse, it becomes central to our politics.

Those discourses often grab hold when candidates master new media technologies. Many of these elections feature the addition of a new kind of communication, which appears to facilitate less restrained political content. Because they unsettle the communicative environment, new communication technologies also unsettle norms and behaviors. Appeals that seem "uncivil" or otherwise inappropriate when delivered through one medium may be more acceptable when delivered over another. In such unsettled spaces, exclusion often finds room to flourish. It mattered that the battle over an anti-Klan resolution at the Democratic Convention in 1924 was heard over the national airwaves. Cable television made Clinton's comments on Sister Souljah more publicly available than they would otherwise have been. And Donald Trump's ability to control the media agenda was instrumental to his political success.[4] For an election to be considered deplorable, despicable discourse must circulate; such circulation depends on media technologies and, as we see in the more contemporary chapters, on media norms and practices, such as their tendency to fragment audiences, rely on horse-race coverage (the tendency of the media to focus on the politics of an issue or event rather than the substance), and focus on candidate personality rather than policy and issues. One way we might chart elections can be seen in table 1.

TABLE 1 The Elements of a Deplorable Election

Nature of Campaign	Status of System	State of Economy	Media	Issues	Discourse	Example
Traditional	Resilient	Distribution of benefits seen as equitable	No change	Wedge issues not dominant	Campaigns accept legit-imacy of opposition	1956
Anti-democratic elements	Fragile—third parties often begin to appear	Distribution of benefits seen as either equitable or inequitable	Beginnings of new technology	Wedge issues present	Some exclu-sionary/delegit-imating rhetoric	1964
Deplorable	Precarious—third parties often present	Distribution of benefits seen as inequitable	New technol-ogy or new use of old technology	Wedge issues involving race, class, gender dominant	Exclusionary /resentment/ nostalgia/divi-sion—ques-tions of national identity central	2016

For example, 1952 is the kind of election we think of as "normal." The system was widely understood as legitimate, even fair; distribution of benefits was understood as paralleling appropriate political hierarchies; political advertising was beginning to become important, but it was used in similar ways to existing media forms; both parties generally accepted the political parameters of the New Deal, and the election didn't turn on wedge issues; and, finally, the candidates were respectful of one another, and neither offered delegitimating discourses. By 1964, however, there were signs of both stability and change; there were indications that despicable discourse might be welcome, but there were also factors that worked against such discourse. The cohesion of the Republican Party had begun to falter. Conservatives opposed to the New Deal were increasingly hostile to the Republican mainstream and to Democrats. But the economy was expanding, and strains caused by the tension between Johnson's War on Poverty and his war in Vietnam were not yet being felt. Television was becoming increasingly important to national campaigns but was still used in largely traditional ways, conveying largely traditional messages. Goldwater and his supporters offered some divisive rhetoric based on race and other wedge issues. But he lost decisively, and there was pushback to such campaigning both from within and from outside Republican ranks. By 2016, though, this stability was all but gone. Republicans were no longer objecting to the use of divisive language or wedge issues but had been increasingly relying on both for decades. That use was eased by the affordances of new media, especially social media. It found a receptive audience in those afflicted with racism and by "economic anxiety." Economic benefits were increasingly understood as unequal. The weaknesses of the political system meant that the Republican Party was unable to stop Donald Trump, the purveyor of some of the most despicable discourse in US history.

As these examples indicate, a fragile political system (made more so by economic tensions that implicate both continuing and aspirational citizens), the surfacing of race, gender, and/or class as explicit issues, the presence of candidates willing to plumb the depths of our political discourse (and the technologies allowing them to do so) combine to create moments that are both dangerous to democracy and important to our understanding of how to protect democratic and republican forms of governance.

THE TARGETS AND PATHWAYS OF DESPICABLE DISCOURSES

These structural elements explain why white voters are more susceptible to exclusionary language at some moments. But those exclusions are aimed at certain targets and take specific paths because those targets and paths are deeply embedded in the national political culture. So here I briefly discuss the history of national dependence on racism, resentment, and political nostalgia more generally, how those fit into the ways we understand politics, and the role of political celebrity. I weave together these various and disparate strands in order to establish the ways in which deplorable politics is connected to American national political traditions as matters of ideology and political practice, to argue that they are connected to how Americans think and act politically, and to insist that changing the way citizens conduct themselves communally is not a simple matter of removing specific political actors or electing members of a particular political party.

It's Always About Race

Politics in the US have been dominated, to greater or lesser degrees, by questions of race since before the founding.[5] Many of the issues that divided participants in the Constitutional Convention in 1787, for example, were about protecting slavery. Political compromises since the founding have all too often also centered on the maintenance of racial hierarchies.

Preserving slavery was, of course, the price of union before the Civil War, and race was a central issue in reunion following it. The New Deal was passed only because Franklin Roosevelt capitulated to Southern power—in his twelve years in office, he never signed a single civil rights bill. The election of the nation's first African American president created a vicious and sustained racial backlash. The need to maintain racial hierarchies while pretending that no such hierarchies exist has structured much of American national political history and has dominated its understanding of national identity.[6]

The narrative of the nation fighting to always come closer to its founding ideals is a comforting, if mistaken, one. Those ideals were tainted from the beginning by a commitment to slavery and human inequality. But even if we are to accept that as a necessary element of the times, the fact remains that there have been only limited and sporadic efforts to address systemic inequities. As Ibram X. Kendi points out in his magisterial history of racism in the United States, racism is not merely the product of hate and ignorance, and thus subject to correction through education.[7] Instead, racist ideas have been produced by the need to justify racist policies. The causal chain begins with discrimination and proceeds through practice to ideology. In other words, needing to justify a political economy based on slavery, racism was invented. Racism is the product of racist policy; policy is not the product of racism. By privileging white people at the expense of people of color, the nation created a system that depends on that racial hierarchy. That dependence has bred racist ideologies.

Historically, the nation has been envisioned as white, but a particular kind of whiteness has dominated that vision. On the one hand, there is "an embrace of the common man, the working stiff, the forgotten rural American," who is understood as the backbone of the nation.[8] This person is white by default. And while he (it is generally a "he") holds a valorized place in the national imagination, he also receives very little political power. The gap between the place he thinks he occupies and the way he is actually treated has consequences for our communal life, as it feeds directly into the politics of resentment.[9]

Political Resentment and Political Nostalgia

The United States has always been a rather resentful polity. The American Revolution was authorized by a declaration of grievances against

Great Britain. The list of those grievances was long; the resentments they expressed were born out of a sense of outraged entitlement. White Americans tend to believe that they have earned their place in the world, that it is not assigned to them. Therefore, that place should be commensurate with the amount of work they do—this is one of the precepts of both American Exceptionalism and the American Dream.[10] When the reality doesn't meet those expectations, resentment is a natural response.

One of the great myths of US politics is that politics plays out in a classless society. Lacking a formal aristocracy, this myth encourages Americans to believe, means that the United States also lacks immutable social hierarchies. But in fact, the United States has, and as Nancy Isenberg informs us, has always had, its share of "waste people," those who are excluded from the capacity to live the American dream.[11] The presence of these people serves as a reminder that economic inequalities persist. One way of managing that has been to naturalize these inequities by disparaging those who suffer most from them. Perhaps especially in a two-party political system, there is a tendency to understand opportunities and privileges as zero-sum, to regard the political pie as finite. When the political system, which is celebrated as the most democratic system in the world, yields results that are less than democratic, citizens blame first the system and then one another. Resentment thus operates multidirectionally—the poor resent those who keep them impoverished; those better off resent the poor for draining "their" resources. Both kinds of resentments can be activated and mobilized by political leaders and can be wielded to sustain or to undermine the political system.[12]

Historically, many political movements and associations have been forged out of this resentment. The Sons of Liberty who operated during the American Revolution are one example. Members of the American Party (better known as the Know-Nothings) were motivated by resentment of immigrants and Catholics during the 1850s. The Ku Klux Klan, originally aimed at African Americans in the years following the Civil War and amid Reconstruction, in later iterations grew to express resentment against immigrants, elites, and urban dwellers in general. These resentments are often articulated as economic and are often explained as products of economic insecurity, but the correlation between the strength of such movements and actual economic distress is weak.[13]

Political resentment is often accompanied by a pernicious sort of nostalgia. Resentment of others is premised on scapegoating them for unwelcome change.[14] It is the choice to point at others in blame rather than to the future in hope. Resentment is mired in the past. In politics, nostalgia is not merely memory; it remakes the past, creating an experience of equality or privilege where none existed. And it authorizes a sense of loss for what was once possible and is no longer. The need to restore what was lost can be a powerful motivator for political resentment because it is so often presented not as merely lost but as taken away.

There is a partisan angle to the politics of resentment. Corey Robin, for instance, argues that conservatism is a "rhetoric of loss and hopeful recovery."[15] By focusing on the loss side of this equation, conservatives are able to understand themselves as perpetually powerless, always defending that which is disappearing, constantly besieged. It is a form of what Timothy Meiley calls "agency panic," fear of powerlessness and resentment.[16] Especially active since the end of World War II, agency panic fuels conspiracy theories and reinforces a specific view of the self—one that depends on the ability to make choices. The more people see their choices as taken over by technologies and governmental forms beyond their control, the more likely it is that they will feel agency panic. And that makes them more susceptible to nostalgic rhetoric and its accompanying politics of resentment. Conservative rhetoric, therefore, tends to rely on and appeal to outsiders, those who feel displaced in the present. They succeed politically by "broadening the circle of discontent," by spreading resentment.[17]

Often this resentment spreads as one group is seen as taking the entitlements belonging to another. It operates through scapegoating, often also associated with the rhetoric of nostalgia. Historically, African Americans, indigenous peoples, and other nonwhite citizens and immigrants have been the most popular scapegoats of white resentment. Resentment thus works through what Carol Anderson calls "white rage."[18] Aimed primarily at African Americans, white rage works not openly, as through organizations like the Klan, but more insidiously, through courts, legislatures, and bureaucracies. It is triggered by fears of Black advancement. To use Arlie Russell Hochschild's metaphor, some white people feel as if they have been standing patiently in line, ever hoping that it would soon be their turn. But it never gets to be their turn because there are "line cutters," people who have worked less hard, waited less patiently, but who are being awarded privileges and opportunities that those ahead of them in line have not received.[19] It doesn't matter than this understanding isn't confirmed by empirical evidence. Nor is it important that those perceived as "line cutters" have their own histories of exclusion and despair. What matters is that white citizens are being encouraged not to see the political problem as one of generalized inequities, but as a specific kind of inequity, with specific groups of citizens as the appropriate targets for resentment. This process has a lot to do with the way we think about politics.

Political Cognition

While we often seem to prefer politics grounded in reason and logic, there is evidence that this is not an accurate description of how our political brains operate. The human brain works not in a linear fashion, but through specific kinds of associative logics, "bundles of thoughts, feelings, images, and ideas."[20] Activating citizens' emotions through narratives and imagery is a potent form of persuasion and motivation. Our partisan allegiances, for instance, are emotional, formed early in life and associated with identities as much as policy preferences. Politics is as much about how we feel as it is about what we think. And how we feel influences how we think.

The less we know about a social group or set of ideas, the more dependent we are on media portrayals of that groups or set of ideas.[21] As John Hope Franklin noted in his essay on *Birth of a Nation*, a large part of the power of the depictions of African Americans in that film was tied to the way they were conveyed through the new medium of motion pictures.[22] Mediated narratives must reduce the context of depictions and narrow the frame; they always present a limited view of political reality. Different media have different ways of doing this, which means they will all limit the frames in different ways. This, of course, is true not just for news stories about crime, or fictionalized narratives about suburban families, but also for how members of political groups are figured by political leaders. Successful leaders turn these media practices to their own political advantage. This ability does not always lead them in the direction of the national interest if we understand that to mean a more inclusive and democratic polity.

I am not arguing here that the human susceptibility to narrativized imagery is necessarily bad, nor am I arguing that reason-based arguments are inherently superior or more politically reliable than those grounded in emotion. Both logic and emotion are prone to manipulation. Sound logic can be emotionally compelling and emotionally compelling ideas can be logical. It is worth noting, however, that arguments about difficult things—and all political arguments are about difficult things—are often couched in ways that allow us to overlook what is really at stake and focus on some other, often more palatable element. It becomes perfectly possible for someone to favor a policy with racist outcomes while denying that it is about race at all. Arguments about social justice fare better when those stakes are an explicit part of the conversation. Because Americans are embedded in structures of systemic racism, all Americans are racist in some senses, many of them unconscious. Ethical appeals on race highlight conscious values, the ones humans choose to live by, rather than activating predilections of which people may be only dimly aware.[23]

This is partly because of the way humans order thought. Kenneth Burke argues that to think is to order things hierarchically.[24] The kind of hierarchies one prefers may well be associated with one's partisanship.[25] To put this in the language of cognition, liberals and conservatives rely on different associative schemas when forming political judgments. Dannagal Goldthwaite Young, for example, notes that members of political parties prefer different kinds of humor, a finding that has implications for other forms of communication as well.[26] This makes creating arguments that are similarly understood, much less similarly valued, by members of both groups very difficult.

It is worth noting, however, that the nation's political tradition has a long history of connecting certain ideas. Immigrants are often referred to, for instance, through metaphors of disease, infestation, and contagion.[27] Such metaphors develop and sustain a belief that immigrants are somehow always inherently suspect. If these metaphors were restricted to a single period of time, it would be possible to argue that this misapprehension had little impact beyond its immediate context. But this is not how politics works. Metaphors from one era recirculate in another. These ways of understanding the political world take root in communities; political attitudes persist over time and across generations, making political change difficult.[28] But cultures have critical junctures, moments when choices can be made overt, and change can happen. Making choices at these moments narrows options for the future—a community that chooses white supremacy at such a moment will find it ever more difficult to choose to upend that hierarchy moving forward.[29] Attitudes can soften or decay and can be changed in response to specific events. Understanding those moments of critical juncture is especially key in understanding the state of our national politics. Currently, this seems to turn on spectacle and celebrity.

Political Celebrities, Celebrity Politics, and the Media

Spectacle has always been important in American politics, and politicians as far back as George Washington and Thomas Jefferson made good use of spectacle in advancing their political goals.[30] Just as consistently, politics relying on spectacle have earned the condemnation of those who cherish a conception of democratic politics as based on rationality and logical argumentation, and who deplore the supposedly trivial nature of celebritized politics.

Theodore Roosevelt was probably the nation's first modern celebrity politician, as we currently understand that phrase.[31] His policies, adventures, and even the exploits of his children were widely covered by a media increasingly dependent on mass circulation. His example points to the important connection between political leadership and media coverage. Successful political leaders have always been able to use the available means of communication to craft and circulate their messages. As Roosevelt's example illustrates, the more open politics becomes, the more "the people" are encouraged to participate, the more important mass media also become, as leaders must circulate their messages more widely and to ever more diverse audiences. These efforts have always been accompanied by fears among the privileged that politics was being "dumbed down" to the lowest common denominator, that if politicians reached out to the general public, politics itself would be increasingly demeaned as its participants grew in number. In the current moment, such fears have reached a fever pitch. Lauren A. Wright, for example, convincingly argues that celebrities have a persuasive edge when it comes to politics, possessing as they do name recognition, a popular following, and experience at motivating large publics, and that this edge is bad for our politics, as celebrities lack expertise and may be poorly suited for responsible political leadership.[32]

While I do not necessarily share these suspicions of the mass public as always bad for politics, I do believe that how the media cover political processes and how they explain citizen participation in those processes matter a great deal, influencing how citizens respond to politics.[33] When political leaders use oppositional rather than communitarian frames, for example, that has the potential to affect the way people perceive politics. When the media pick up those frames and amplify them through the kinds of horse-race coverage that characterizes most media election narratives, that potential increases. This dynamic generally produces less than admirable election coverage.

Media norms influence both public understandings of politics and the ways candidates and office holders conduct themselves. Once C-SPAN began to cover Congress, for example, congressional behavior changed in response to the presence of cameras, and members give impassioned speeches to an empty chamber, because the audience that concerns them is not in the nation's capital but at home. It is an interesting element of deplorable elections that purveyors of despicable discourses are often more entrepreneurial in adapting to developments in media technologies. Consideration of those developments and the ways they contribute to the circulation of such language play a role in the chapters to follow, although the media tend to wink in and out of the discussion rather than forming a consistent through line. Technological change is always important in that it unsettles the communicative environment, which may facilitate despicable discourse; it is not responsible for the appearance of that discourse.

These various elements—a national commitment to structural and systemic racism, resentment and political nostalgia, the templates forming the ways Americans think about politics and the political world, and dependence on political spectacles—have all been present since before the founding. They were part of the conversation as Americans learned what it meant to be citizens of a republic. They provide the targets and the paths for despicable discourse. And they mean that changing American politics is not merely a matter of changing personal or party leadership. Change is not only about reforming national institutions. Changing US politics will require those changes, to be sure. But it will also require changing the political culture in which US parties, leaders, and institutions are embedded. To make that possible, Americans must first understand that culture and its history. It means white Americans will have to overcome their fear of others.

A FEW WORDS ABOUT THE POLITICS OF FEAR

More than anything else, antidemocratic rhetoric depends on creating and magnifying fear in its audience. If white voters do not fear others, they will not exclude them. It is both easy and conventional to deplore the politics of fear, but I want to be careful about what I mean when I write about such politics. Humans, as well as members of other species, rely on alarm calls for both self-protection and the protection of others. We should understand the ability to alert others to impending danger as both evolutionarily necessary and morally responsible.[34] For such alerts to be morally responsible, though, the danger must be real. This is easy to measure if you are an impala and there is a lion nearby. When it comes to making judgments about the politics of fear, however, the terrain quickly becomes more difficult.

It is entirely possible, for example, that a white, native-born, conservative person's politics may lead them to sense imminent danger to the republic when the number of immigrants increases. Their sense of danger may be heightened if those immigrants come from Africa or the Middle East rather than from Northern Europe. That sense may persist despite empirical evidence that immigrants from these places do not cause identifiable harm to the nation because such evidence depends on the definition of "identifiable harm"—which could be measured by instances of terrorism or crime, for example. But if the person in question is really worried about some ineffable definition of "American" national identity, then it does not matter to them that these immigrants do not engage in terrorism or commit crimes. They are worried about protecting something they understand as "their" culture. And so they may communicate alarm, alerting those who share their politics that their sense of shared community is being threatened.

Such alarms are politically potent.[35] Fear appeals create both attitudinal and behavioral changes. So persuasive are such appeals, in fact, that people react to arguments about threats with the same intensity as to experiences of actual threats.[36] When it comes to politics, rather than say health-related messages, though, these appeals are likely to resonate differently among different groups. It is easy to suppose that one's politics aren't relevant to how one responds to news of an impending hurricane or influence one's decision about quitting smoking in response to an ad campaign featuring pictures of diseased lungs. It is equally easy to imagine that one's political beliefs are strongly related to how one responds to messages about immigration or an asserted relationship between crime and race.[37]

There are at least two kinds of fear. The easiest to deal with is primal fear, one's response to an immediate danger, such as the recognition of an impending car crash. That response is visceral and short-lived. It does not normally have important implications for politics. The second kind of fear, however, is less urgent, more cognitive. It is a response to attacks on abstractions that are important to a person, such as their values. Fear appeals grounded in the supposed threats others present to us range from FDR's declarations that the Nazis imperiled human civilization or environmentalists' claims that climate change represents a danger to human survival to racist assertions about the "mongrelization" of the white race or Donald Trump's repeated contention that migrants from south of the border threaten to contaminate the polity.[38] Evaluating such arguments depends on both their empirical validity (assuming validity can be measured) and on one's political beliefs and preferences.

Consequently, making judgments about fear appeals in politics is tricky. It isn't fair to argue that fear appeals are ethical when they flag fears I personally find reasonable (white supremacist violence, for example, or climate change) and are unethical when alerting citizens to fears I personally find unwarranted (immigrants from the Middle East, for instance). And it is reasonable, in a book on politics, to allow fears concerning threats to culture and political organization to weigh as much as fears about the continued existence of the species. I flag fear appeals as fear appeals whenever I see them. Because this book is about despicable discourses, I generally focus on examples of fear appeals that I find worrying, by which I mean that they serve antidemocratic ends. Statements like "racists are bad for democracy," and "immigrants threaten the nation," are both fear appeals. I treat such appeals as despicable discourse when they appear in political speech in ways that undermine what I understand to be the broader national democratic project. By this I mean when such appeals are used to segment the polity, and to turn citizens against one another on the basis of ascriptive rather than ideological terms, I deem that discourse despicable. When the terms used to define threats to democracy turn on a lack of patriotism rather than a lack of agreement on basic values, I deem that discourse despicable. It is not despicable discourse to argue that violent white supremacists are dangerous to democracy. It is despicable discourse to claim that Muslims are dangerous to democracy, or that Republicans are by definition unpatriotic or unprincipled. It is not despicable discourse to state that a specific politician is engaging in unethical politics and to provide evidence for that claim. It is despicable discourse to allege that a particular political actor is incapable of acting on political principle because their principles disagree with yours. Because fear appeals are typically understood as attempts to frighten people into compliance, I treat discourse as despicable when it seems to me that citizens are being encouraged to surrender agency. Discourse that motivates citizens to turn to the government for protection from threats is more likely to be classified here as despicable than rhetoric that empowers citizens.

These definitions are slippery and depend very much on the context in which the language in question is embedded. I strive to be consistent in how I treat these ultimately unclassifiable appeals. I maintain as my standard a sense of what contributes to a healthy and robust democracy and democratic community and what undermines these things. Such a standard is necessarily subjective, and readers are welcome to disagree with specific instances of interpretation.

THE ELECTIONS: THE TABLE OF CONTENTS

Many elections fit my criteria for deplorable elections—a depressing number of them, in fact. As the case of 1828 indicates, not every deplorable election could be included. In choosing the elections for this book, I concentrated on the time period following the birth of mass politics and pay specific attention to those following the Civil War. I chose elections because of how well they highlight various elements of despicable discourse, so that every chapter adds to understanding rather than repeating themes already discussed. It is an illustrative, not an exhaustive, list. In every case, despicable discourse was present to some degree in the previous election and that election constitutes part of the context for the election I am talking about. These elections are, again, not isolated and discrete moments when such discourse rose and fell but are instances when it attained a sufficient level of prominence to be amenable to sustained analysis.

Creating Citizenship in a Republic, 1800/1840/1852: These early elections form the first chapter and the broad context for the more detailed discussions to follow. They come at moments when the nation was figuring out what it meant to be a citizen of a republic rather than the subject of a crown and are moments when citizenship was under stress. The 1800 election, the first of the newly created party system, was rancorous to an extreme and featured conflict between Federalists John Adams and Alexander Hamilton as well as between Democratic Republicans Aaron Burr and Thomas Jefferson, and then also between Adams and Jefferson. The 1840 election, which pitted Martin Van Buren, "The Little Magician," against "Tippecanoe and Tyler too," was one of the first to include mass means of persuasion. "The log cabin campaign" is also widely considered to be a model of the trivialization of political campaigns. Less famously, it also centered on issues of race. Finally, in the last gasp of the Whig party, in 1852 Winfield Scott lost to Democrat Franklin Pierce. This election revealed a nation divided on sectional rather than political lines as the politics of slavery destroyed the legitimacy of the political system as well as the national political parties. The stories of these elections reveal both the institutional and deeply personal nature of deplorable elections—they are contests between people as well as ideas. These elections tell us that deplorable elections have always been with us and provide a baseline of judgment for the rest of the book.

Looking Backward During the Nation's Centennial, 1876: One of the most disputed elections in US history, the election of 1876 is often compared to the 2000 election. It was the last election featuring the "bloody shirt" and was characterized by bitter accusations, electoral fraud, and violence. This election featured a massive infusion of money from railroad interests, adding to the already fraught racial and sectional politics of the day. The election results were contaminated by the ways the news of those results was spun by political operatives, and the actual decision came months after Election Day. The electoral drama was finally ended by the "corrupt bargain" that put Rutherford B. Hayes (often contemporaneously called "Rutherfraud") in office and led to the end of Reconstruction.

Introducing the Politics of Fear to the Twentieth Century, 1924: The 1924 Democratic Convention, meeting in Madison Square Garden, was attended by so many members of the KKK that it became known as the "Klanbake." The convention barely managed to avoid nominating the Klan's preferred candidate and was unable to pass a resolution condemning the Klan. At the same time, the populist tide continued in the West, personified by Robert La Follette and William Jennings Bryan. Calvin Coolidge, one of the most unpleasant figures in US presidential history, won in a three-way contest characterized by bitter racial and class arguments. This election features some of the most well-known American orators; the fact that a man known mostly for his refusal to speak emerged victorious is only one of the many ironies of this campaign.

The Veneer of Civility: The Subtle Politics of Racism, 1968: Richard Nixon defeated Hubert Humphrey in one of the most painful American elections, featuring the assassinations of civil rights leader Martin Luther King Jr. and presidential candidate Robert F. Kennedy. It was also the first election to rely on what has become known as the "dog whistle," or the use of subtle, rather than overt, appeals to racism. Richard Nixon's "Southern strategy" mobilized both the South and elements of the North by appealing to the "politics of resentment," which have become a staple in our electoral history. Four years earlier, liberal Republican Nelson A. Rockefeller went to the Republican National Convention and implored the delegates there to repudiate the politics of the far right; he was booed off the stage and blamed for Goldwater's defeat. In 1968, despite his belief in the iniquity of such politics, he remained silent. Deplorable elections are made possible because of the acquiescence of elites; that point is driven home in 1968.

The Southern Strategy Goes Bipartisan, 1992: The contest between George H. W. Bush, previously associated with the racist "Willie Horton" ads in 1988, and Bill Clinton, known in some circles as "America's first Black president," sheds some bipartisan light on contemporary deplorable elections.[39] Clinton's campaign included a willingness to include racial and gendered appeals in a campaign ostensibly dedicated to inclusion. It provides evidence that despicable discourse, while subtle, had become an important element of national campaigns, and that the inclusion of some groups—such as blue-collar workers—often seems to come at the expense of others—such as racial minorities and women. This campaign also featured accusations of sexual misconduct and echoed the problems Gary Hart faced four years earlier. This election illustrates a new context for judging candidates and elections, one that begins to mark racism and sexism as deplorable.

It Doesn't Get More Deplorable Than This, 2016: In 2016, a woman became the nominee of a major party for the first time in US history. At the same time, the long-simmering subtexts of anti-immigrant, racist, and misogynistic appeals became explicit in the rhetoric of Donald Trump. The election was one in which routines of political campaigns were upended by new forms of mediated communication, influence over those forms by the interference of a foreign government, and a generalized sense that the political system was broken. The question of whether the system will prove resilient or not remains an open, and important, question.

Or Maybe It Does: Brief Thoughts on 2020: The Trump administration was tumultuous and controversial, marked by strong resistance to the president and his policies as well as by adamant loyalty to him and his policy preferences. The president himself was a polarizing figure whose rhetoric was marked by attempts to divide rather than to unite the nation. His conduct as president led to his impeachment and acquittal on charges of obstruction of Congress and abuse of power in early 2020, actions that formed one element of the context for the 2020 campaign. That campaign took place amid a global pandemic that substantially weakened the US economy and, as of Election Day, had caused the deaths of over two hundred thousand Americans. Through it all, Trump relied on incendiary rhetoric and appeals to his base while denying responsibility for either the economic situation or the persistence of the pandemic. Characterized by divisive discourses by the president, 2020 may present a significant turning point in the history of deplorable elections.

CHAPTER 1

CREATING CITIZENSHIP IN A REPUBLIC, 1800/1840/1852

In Lin Manuel Miranda's depiction of the election of 1800 in his hit musical *Hamilton*, he emphasizes all of the ways that election was particularly fraught: the discord between Alexander Hamilton and President John Adams, Aaron Burr's decision to directly campaign for office, and Jefferson's reaction to that challenge. All these elements made for compelling drama on stage and were no less interesting in real life. By 1840, the torchlight parades, log cabins filled with whiskey, and sloganeering indicated the importance of mass participation in electoral politics and demonstrated how easily that participation could devolve into a kind of mass display of political trivia to the exclusion of pressing national issues. In 1852, as those issues became ever more divisive, the role of regionalism in national politics came to the fore, and the nation wallowed in nostalgia, preferring discussion of past glory to decisions about current policy. These were not the only difficult elections during the early republic, nor were they the only ones in which despicable discourses circulated. But in their combination of the elements that create deplorable elections, focusing on them helps set the frame for the chapters to follow.

System fragility makes deplorable elections more likely. When citizens don't trust the system or the people who manage it, electoral stakes become frighteningly high. If the political system is understood as strong and legitimate, citizens are more likely to believe that it can withstand the election of a party or candidate they find noxious. But if the system is understood as lacking legitimacy or even as weak, such parties and candidates may be seen as threatening the nation itself. In the early republic, the system was extraordinarily fragile. No one knew what it took to sustain it and so no one could correctly identify threats. In addition, only a very limited number of people had either political power or political influence, and in the tight networks that thus developed, personal animosities were inevitably conflated with political differences. This personal element impeded the development of a system based on laws and not on personalities, even as those individuals sought such a system.

Americans in these early years felt the burden of their efforts in representative government, often arguing that the future of democracy depended on the "American experiment." They thus felt acutely events such as the French Revolution (1789) and, closer to home and in some ways more threatening, the Haitian Revolution (1791). The example of France either indicated the potential of a global advance of democracy or presaged the dangers of democracy disintegrating into violence, anarchy, and, with the arrival of Bonaparte, despotism, depending on where one stood politically. Those like Jefferson, with an affinity for France, found their commitment to order questioned, while those like Hamilton, who looked to Great Britain, were thought to skew too far toward monarchism for comfort. If the success of US democracy meant finding a balance between those positions, it was not easily achieved.

The Haitian Revolution caused a different set of problems, much less openly discussed but important nonetheless. A slave uprising that led to the establishment of an independent state, free of slavery and explicitly opposed to colonialism, sent shock waves throughout the Atlantic world.[1] The very presence of Haiti as a nation challenged notions of Black inferiority upon which US politics increasingly depended. Slaveholders felt the threat symbolized by Haiti most acutely, but it unsettled white Americans of all political stripes. "Racial segregation," as John Hope Franklin tells us, as well as other forms of "discrimination, and degradation are no unanticipated accidents in this nation's history. They stem logically and directly from the legacy that the founding fathers bestowed upon contemporary America."[2] That legacy was baked into the Constitution. Contending with it in the face of global events has required acts of conciliation, protest, and reform, all of which left the basic structure largely untouched.[3]

American politics thus developed in a context of global colonialization, insurrection, and revolution. The fight for territory controlled much of the nation's thinking for its first century, as Americans sought to make territorial claims that could be recognized by European powers as legitimate. This required specific kinds of arguments concerning the displacement of indigenous peoples.[4] Westward expansion took some pressure off the nation as it developed economically, benefiting some and leaving others behind. That expansion created other kinds of pressures, implicating members of indigenous nations as they negotiated with, accommodated, opposed, and fought those encroaching on their lands.

The politics of expansion also and inevitably meant the politics of slavery. Constitutional forms having given the South considerable power, Southerners did not hesitate to use it in defense of their "peculiar institution." Compromise after compromise and negotiation after negotiation all ended in the same place: the price of union was the acceptance of, and often the endorsement of, slavery. This was a price white Americans outside the South became increasingly resentful about paying. This resentment wasn't necessarily a matter of endorsing emancipation and was almost never a matter of wanting to guarantee African American equality. It often involved questions over the rights of free white labor. Slavery, race, and capitalism circled and embraced one another in complicated ways during these years.

Cultures make choices. Once those choices are made, they narrow the options going forward, making change, especially major change, very difficult.[5] This provides cultures with stability. It also makes inclusion in a polity premised on specific exclusions hard to achieve. When cultures undergo stress—caused by system fragility, economic constriction, influxes of new immigrants, and so on—members of exclusionary cultures (and make no mistake—all cultures are to some degree exclusionary) are likely to depend on those long-standing and familiar patterns of exclusion. Even in—and maybe especially in—contexts where it may feel like progress has been made, cultural relapses are all too likely, making it especially important to understand these cultural patterns as they were formed.

This chapter sets the stage for understanding the deplorable elections that follow. In it, I argue that these years set the terms and conditions of citizenship in the United States, often in exclusionary ways, and always providing for the specific exclusion of African Americans, women, American Indians, and others. Under these conditions, even when US politics maintains an overt veneer of inclusion and democracy, exclusion and resentment lurk. And when the system becomes fragile, when pressures stemming from economic challenges, and/or cultural fears of immigration or Black progress reach a certain point, those lurking exclusions and resentment erupt. This chapter thus focuses how those things came to constitute our understanding of citizenship, as Americans strove to establish their independence from Great Britain and make a place for their new nation in a world that in their understanding was dominated by Europe and convulsed by global conflict.

Specifically, these elections teach three lessons about how the American polity was created and developed in ways that help create deplorable elections. First, because political power was at first restricted to so few people, there is, in times of political tension, a tendency to conflate policy and personality. This means that politics can become personalized, and that when it is, it is very easy to move from "I disagree with this person" to "this person represents a danger to the republic." This second position is one kind of despicable discourse I associate with deplorable elections. Second, democracy means mass participation. As the franchise expanded and more white men were included in the polity, leaders had to find ways to animate the public, stir enthusiasm, and mobilize the electorate. Not all these ways equally benefit the democratic project and the tendency of leaders to position themselves as "of the people," especially when such claims are deceptive, are among the least productive. Third, despicable discourse is often found, as the first two lessons reveal, in the kinds of arguments that circulate during an election. But it can also be located in how leaders seek to suppress or sidestep important arguments. Under some conditions, political silence can be as despicable as political speech. In what follows, I detail these lessons through the examples of three US presidential elections: 1800, 1840, and 1852.

PERSONALIZING POLITICS IN 1800: ADAMS VS. HAMILTON VS. JEFFERSON VS. BURR

The US in 1800 was a different place than it had been during the revolution. The population had doubled; the nation now contained over five million souls. It was still largely rural. Only a quarter of the nation lived in cities with over one thousand people. One in six Americans was enslaved. The institution was legal everywhere except Vermont and Massachusetts. The nation was also home to about 150,000 free Blacks.[6] Politicians in the early republic were also aware of the conflict between their founding principles and the persistence of slavery. Nearly all the Founders were also slave owners who believed that the perpetuation of slavery was required if the Union was to survive. Most argued that the institution was a necessary evil if they argued about it at all. The tendency was to bury the issue, to treat it as an understood, if unarticulated, element of the national union. They agreed on the necessity of protecting slavery and had plenty of other things to argue about.

Into 1800

Since the battle at Yorktown functionally ended the revolution, Americans had tried government under the Articles of Confederation, which emphasized the rights of states but failed to provide for the common defense, a common currency, or a system of managing revenue. The Constitution that followed attempted to remedy some of these issues while also allowing for the retention of strong state governments. The American system of federalism was thus a complicated admixture of unspecified power, floating among and between the different institutions of the federal government, and between that government and those of the various states. This system was, for its first years, held together largely because of loyalty to George Washington and to the revolutionary cause.[7] During Washington's administration, however, the fissures that created the first American party system developed. There were a number of catalysts fomenting the conflict. The Constitution was only a decade old, and people didn't trust it yet; no one was quite sure how it might work in the absence of Washington. Some, like Jefferson, feared the power given to the executive. Others, like Adams, were leery of the power granted to the Senate.

The burgeoning conflict over the best locus of power was important, as the national government was a lot more powerful than it had been under the Articles of Confederation. Fears that the "American experiment" might be lost to the recurrence of monarchy were both real and deep. So any move that could be interpreted as grasping for personal power or as attempting to secure power to the national government was regarded with suspicion. The development of a national bank and the suppression of Shay's Rebellion, an armed uprising in Massachusetts set off by increased taxation in the face of a debt crisis, both seemed to indicate the potential for tyranny in the new system.[8] The events of the French Revolution caused concern on the other end of the political spectrum. Rather than fearing too much federal power, the French example raised fear that the people, if given too much power, would use it unwisely, and that the nation would descend into violence, anarchy, and even despotism.[9]

Alexander Hamilton offered his thoughts on the logics behind the French Revolution in the infamous *Reynolds Pamphlet*, writing:

> The spirit of Jacobinism, if not entirely a new spirit, has at least been clothed in a more gigantic body and armed with more powerful weapons than it ever before possessed. It is perhaps not too much to say, that it threatens more extensive and complicated mischiefs to the world than have hitherto flowed from the three great scourges of mankind, WAR, PESTILENCE, and FAMINE. To what point it will ultimately affect society it is impossible for human foresight to pronounce; but there is ground to apprehend that its progress may be marked with calamities of which the dreadful incidents of the French Revolution afford a very faint image. Incessantly busied in undermining all the props of public security and private happiness, it seems to threaten the political and moral world with a complete overthrow.[10]

Hamilton feared not just the effects of the French Revolution on international politics, as dire as those effects might be. He also feared the contagion of the "spirit of Jacobinism," which had the potential to infect US domestic politics. That spirit, in his view, threatened not merely the political world but the moral world as well. For Federalists like Hamilton, politics was a deeply moral enterprise. The structures of government were the outward display and bulwark of inner morality. The moral health of the people depended on the forms of government. Arguments over those forms were thus consequential.

These tensions deepened under the Adams administration as the president sought, largely unsuccessfully, to keep them from breaking into open conflict. After winning the 1796 election, Adams reached out to Jefferson hoping for a united national government. He did not get it. What he got instead was a refusal from Jefferson and his supporters to work with him and, consequently, a cabinet full of Jefferson's most ardent opponents. These fissures were deepened by events in Europe; the seemingly endless war between England and France threatened always to draw the United States into its maw. Adams, seeking to avoid such entanglements, agreed to a peace with the British, irritating the Jeffersonians, and attempted one with the French, equally irritating members of his own faction. His efforts to secure peace at home ended with what was widely considered inappropriate use of federal power manifested in the creation of the "Additional Army" and the hated Alien and Sedition Acts, passed amid fears of war with France, and limiting freedom of speech and the activities of "foreigners" in 1798. In response, Jefferson authored the Kentucky and Virginia Resolutions, which criticized the Acts and also made a pitch for the primacy of states.

By the end of Adams's first term, then, the Federalists under Adams were exercising what could easily be interpreted as monarchial power, authorizing a standing army, and suppressing dissent. Republicans, under Jefferson, were arguing for states' rights but were doing so in ways that could easily be understood as threatening disunion. As the election of 1800 loomed, the fate of the nation seemed increasingly to be at stake. Consequently, the level of political and personal animosity was high.[11] Return to monarchism seemed as likely as descent into anarchism. As historian A. Roger Ekrick writes:

> Not for another sixty years would electoral politics exhibit such urgency or the stakes of a presidential campaign bulk so large. At issue in the minds of Americans in this bitterly polarized contest

> was nothing less than the survival of their infant republic. Absent was the comfort of George Washington's commanding presence. Unheeded were his pleas for national unity. Americans clashed over the scope and administration of government, the roles of leaders and followers—indeed, over the very words and meaning of the Constitution. The race became a battle for the country's soul, whether the people would continue to accept the guidance of a paternalistic class determined to establish the supremacy of the federal government or place their trust instead in representatives striving to protect and advance liberties won in the Revolution—"friends of the people," rather than "fathers of the people."[12]

This distinction is important, revealing as it does the two possibilities available to people trying to determine what it meant to be a citizen of a republic rather than a subject of a crown. At issue was not just the role of the government but the question of who got to decide what kinds of power would be exercised and by whom. Some people were considered ill-suited for a role in governance. African Americans, whether free or enslaved, women, those without enough property to ensure the kinds of independence and autonomy required for citizenship, and, in most places, indigenous peoples were all liable to exclusion. These extensive exclusions aside, there was still a great deal to divide the developing political parties. Federalists were unabashed defenders of elite rule backed by a strong central government. Republicans were equally vehement supporters of rule by the majority of those admitted to be "the people" and thought their rights to be made most secure not by the concentration but by the diffusion of political power to the states and localities. The election thus turned on important questions of power and citizenship, and how these were to be best translated into the institutions of government.

The Election

As the election approached, Republicans stood united in opposition to Adams, the Federalists, and all their works. The Federalists, on the other hand, were divided into two factions. So-called "High Federalists," like Alexander Hamilton, sought strong, centralized power and deeply distrusted the mass of the people. The more democratic Federalists, like John

Adams, also preferred a strong central government but deeply distrusted the elitism of the High Federalists. So deep were the divisions among the Federalists that one Pennsylvania essayist argued that it was not a two but a three-party election, in which only one party could be trusted:[13]

> For we know well, that, as many of the two divisions of the federal party are *republicans*; so all the republican party are friends of the federal government. Those for whom we now act, lay no claim to *exclusive republicanism*; but they will not permit certain of their opponents to retain a pretension to *an exclusive attachment to the Constitution of the United States*. It is the desire of the republican interest, that the real enemies of representative government may be thoroughly known. We do not wish . . . to excite an unlawful and anarchic *"hatred and animosity"* to destroy the opponents of our representative governments. The republican party only wish the people and governments to be well informed who are, in truth, the enemies of the Constitution. They desire that the governments of the union and the states may enforce the laws against them. The republicans are utterly averse to *persecuting*, even the enemies of representative government through the medium of an *irreligious* and *barbaric* spirit of "hatred and animosity" nor will they be betrayed into such a conduct by the example of those infuriated federalists, whose long known violence is announced by the Massachusetts member of congress, to have at length divided their party.[14]

This essayist, obviously a Republican, was in effect arguing that the Federalists were enemies of representative government. They wanted, the author implied, to secure all power to the federal government and to dominate the states and thus also the people. These Federalists were attempting, through oppressive measures like the Alien and Sedition Acts, to undermine and corrupt the nation's governing institutions. Political actors, in the process of creating a party system, were increasingly conscious of the importance of policy to their electoral fortunes.[15] The pretense maintained by Washington of letting high office come to potential officials was gone. Offices were now explicitly sought by those who wanted to occupy them in the name of saving the republic from those who would undermine it. This kind of discourse delegitimates political opposition and is dangerous to representative government.

Such discourse wasn't circulated by Republicans alone. Federalists were equally concerned about Republican intentions. The Virginia and Kentucky Resolutions were, in Hamilton's words, a "regular conspiracy to overthrow the government."[16] He recommended that "the government must not merely defend itself but must attack and arraign its enemies"[17] and requested a well-publicized congressional report on Jefferson's excesses. He didn't get such a report, but he also didn't need it. These years saw the development of a viciously partisan press, which, along with the frequent publication of pamphlets and broadsides, ensured that elite opinions on every event in national politics were well and widely circulated. Hamilton in particular "practiced a hard-edged style of politics, savaging his foes in newspapers and pamphlets while aggressively advancing his plans behind the scenes."[18] Despicable discourses were circulating widely, both publicly and privately.

As the election began to more clearly turn on a contest between Adams and the Federalists on one hand and Jefferson and the Republicans on the other, Hamilton was caught in the middle, loathing both men. Preferring the Federalist position, and fearing that Adams couldn't win reelection, Hamilton schemed to replace him with Charles Pinckney. This scheme had the potential to split the party between Adams and Hamilton loyalists as Hamilton forced Federalists to choose between their party and its ostensible leader. While the Federalists feuded, the Republicans worked together, united by the goal of replacing any and all Federalists with Republicans.

These battles were not, by any means, hidden from the mass public or confined to the nation's capital. They all took place in the pages of an increasingly partisan press. Some papers even included party labels in their mastheads. These papers were funded by the parties, carried partisan messages, and often conflated news and editorial commentary. They were widely understood as tools of the parties and contributed to building partisan organizational structures.[19] The Federalists, more divided than the Republicans, had a small advantage in this aspect of the contest over public opinion, as they controlled the majority of the nation's newspapers and broadsides. "Jefferson was more active than Adams in circulating partisan messages but Adams was president and enjoyed all the advantages incumbency brings," which included communicative as well as other political benefits.[20] So important were the nation's papers that, a foreign visitor claimed, "the opinions of all classes arise entirely from what they read in their newspapers; so that *by newspapers the country is governed*."[21] Those newspapers circulated elite fears of the consequences of their opponents' potential victory, exacerbating concerns about the fate of the new republic among members of the public.

The presidency was decided not by a general vote on a single election day but by a series of statewide elections that determined the composition of state legislatures and thus the composition of the Electoral College, which those legislatures appointed. The presidential election, to the extent that something like a presidential election occurred, was a lengthy, drawn-out process across the states in a rolling order. Because of the different natures of the states, different issues mattered differently in different states.

In Pennsylvania, for example, religion was quite important. In Virginia, on the other hand, the main argument was over whether electors would be chosen in district or statewide elections. And in New York, the contest turned on Aaron Burr's brilliant and effective political machine.[22] Overall, as one historian of the era notes, "the campaign of 1800 was conducted both at the level on which issues were discussed and alternatives provided and at the level where parties appealed to the emotions, prejudices, sectional attachments, and selfish interests of the voters."[23] The election was fought on a variety of different fronts, and many of them turned ugly.

Adams was attacked both for policy reasons and for personal ones. In terms of policy, Adams was criticized for undermining the separation of powers by bending Congress to his will and passing legislation like the Alien and Sedition Acts by slim margins, and for relationships with both France and Great Britain.[24] These were perfectly legitimate concerns, legitimately expressed. There is nothing here to indicate that 1800 was a deplorable election. Such indications, however, were plentiful when it came to the more personal attacks. High Federalists thought Adams was temperamentally unfit to be chief magistrate. They considered him egotistical, capricious, and dangerous to a system that demanded personal and political balance. Historian James Roger Sharp writes, "Adams suffered similar abuse with charges that he was incompetent, 'quite mad,' and a monarchist and a warmonger. The Alien and Sedition Acts, voters were reminded, were stark examples of Adams's treachery and his willingness to violate American civil liberties."[25] Note the way in which these criticisms conflated the personal and the political. His contemporaries claimed Adams was a poor executive because his personal failings led him to make political misjudgments. The distinction between personality and policy disappeared. These personal failings were so severe, his opponents argued, that they threatened the republic both domestically and internationally.

An author from New Jersey made his concerns about Adams clear:

> When we reflect on the precarious tenure by which we hold our liberties; when we consider the artifices which have been displayed by foreign influence, to bring us back to a state of vassalage, we cannot but commiserate the fortune of misguided Americans, and reject the wiley [*sic*] agents who have endeavored to effect our ruin. . . . We have been told by Mr. Adams that "the finger of Heaven points to war"—but we differ from our present chief magistrate, and discredit the declaration. . . . The People of America are averse to carnage. They revolt from the bloody conflict, and are resolved to cherish the blessings of peace, while they disdain the intrigues of foreign despots. . . . The common resorts of wicked men are *violence* and *distraction*. We pray you to avoid the snares of the *cunning* and the *corrupt*, and to guard yourselves with temper becoming sober men, and worthy of freemen.[26]

This author, deploring the Alien and Sedition Acts as well as what they considered to be saber rattling in the president's conduct with France, essentially accused Adams of what we now think of as "wagging the dog," or creating a foreign crisis to distract citizens from domestic problems. Then as now, it was considered unethical political behavior and dangerous to a free people.

In October 1800, Hamilton publicly broke with Adams in a lengthy treatise arguing that Adams was unfit for office. Historians characterize the treatise as "fifty-four pages of unremitting vilification"[27] that "read like one long rant."[28] In it, Hamilton cited the "great and intrinsic defects in his character, which unfit" Adams for any high office, referred to Adams's "vanity," his "distempered jealousy," his "extreme egoism," and his "ungovernable temper," which was "given to hasty and 'premature' decisions" as well as "ill humors and jealousies."[29] Again, note that the problems mentioned here are all related to Adams's temperament, which were considered to lead to inimical policies.

Hamilton was even nastier in private. He wrote to Theodore Sedgwick that "*most* of the *most influential men* of [the Federalist] . . . party consider him as a very *unfit* and *incapable* character."[30] Hamilton then placed himself firmly in what we might now call the "#NeverAdams" camp of the Federalist party, writing, "I will never be responsible for him by my direct support—even though the consequence should be the election of *Jefferson*."[31] Politicians in the early republic were greatly concerned with issues of character, which for them referred more to a person's public persona than to their private actions. But in and around 1800, the distinction between public and private blurred. Hamilton's personal affairs were a matter of public debate. Jefferson's private conduct, as we will soon see, inched into the election as well. And Adams's personal foibles and insecurities were deemed to be at the root of poor policymaking. The nation's first partisan election, then, was also the first in which attacks on candidate character were conflated with attacks on their policy preferences.

Adams was not the only candidate who suffered from this conflation. Sharp writes, "Jefferson, it was charged, was a Jacobin, a Francophile, and a libertine unfit and unreliable to defend his country against France. A civil war would surely follow if he were to be elected."[32] He was, some went so far as alleging, "an immoral and godless man who would order the confiscation of Bibles."[33] He was accused of having fathered an illegitimate child with an enslaved woman,[34] of lacking faith in God, and of lacking allegiance to the nation. His love for France, it was argued, would inevitably bring that nation's turmoil and violence to the United States.[35] But most despicably, he was attacked for his religion, or lack thereof. He was accused, over a wide variety of media, of deism, atheism, and opposition to religion in general. The language of these accusations was often as intemperate as the accusations themselves. In a nation dedicated to democratic forms, condemning a candidate as unpatriotic delegitimates that candidacy. Condemning candidates because of their views on religion does the same thing. These attacks constitute despicable discourse, for they seek to place candidates beyond the limits of democratic politics on the basis of their presumed lack of patriotism or religion.

The unpopular Adams, however, suffered more at the hands of his attackers than did Jefferson, who had legions of dedicated defenders. One contemporaneous author condemned the attacks on Jefferson as "written by the pen of his enemies, conceived in malignity and malevolence, under the powerful influence of party feeling and political resentment."[36] Those attacks, the author argued, show "him to be the worst of men, an enemy to his God, an enemy to his country, an enemy to the human race."[37] Attacks such as the one specifically referenced, the author argued, "cannot long deceive, since it fully betrays the jealousy, fear and anger of its authors—jealousy, of his unrivaled talents; fear, that on his elevation to the Presidency, every germ of monarchy and aristocracy in our country will dissipate at the electrical touch of his republican virtues; and anger, that notwithstanding all their distractions and efforts, he continues to possess the unshaken and undiminished confidence of the great body of the American people."[38] Jefferson, the essay continued, was "a man of pure, ardent, and unaffected piety; of sincere and genuine virtue; of an enlightened mind and superior wisdom; the adorer of our God; the patriot of his country; and the friend and benefactor of the whole human race."[39] If politics turned on the use of adjectives, surely this essay would have sealed the election for Jefferson.

Jefferson was defended by another author as religious in a better-than-conventional sense: "But there is evidence of the real piety of Mr. Jefferson. Our duty to Almighty God, and our duty towards our neighbor, are *the sum of true religion*. By performing those high duties, we may expect the esteem of good men, and hope for the favor of heaven."[40] This same author also noted that while Jefferson abolished religious discrimination in Virginia, Adams had not done the same in Massachusetts. By implication then, Jefferson was actually a better Christian than the indisputably Christian Adams.

All of this furor finally resulted in an outcome no one wanted. Federalists, hoping to prevent a Jefferson victory and divided in their opinions on the merits of Adams, were unable to muster a majority in the Electoral College. Republicans, determined to elect Jefferson, nonetheless all cast both of their electoral votes for Jefferson and his designated running mate Aaron Burr. But because there was no formal mechanism for distinguishing between presidential and vice-presidential candidates, the electoral vote was a tie and the election itself was thus sent to the House of Representatives for a decision. Federalists, not numerous enough to earn a victory for their party, nevertheless had enough votes to decide the contest between Burr and Jefferson.

Republicans responded with what political scientist Mel Laracey calls "apocalyptic" rhetoric, arguing that the republic was doomed if anyone other than Jefferson was chosen.[41] "The simmering arguments over just how 'democratic' the new republic should be, and, by extension, how directly connected presidents were to 'the people' and the 'national will,' had exploded into the open,"[42] Laracey notes, because of the arguments Republicans were making that Jefferson should be president as he best represented the people. Jefferson's paper, the *Intelligencer*, predicted dire consequences if Jefferson was not chosen by the House: "Faction after faction will rise up. None can long retain the support of the people, because the power of all will be illegitimate. The despot of today may kneel tomorrow to a wretch whom he had consigned to a loathsome jail. Property will change as rapidly as power, and some warrior will become master of everything."[43]

The matter was complicated by Burr's unexpected refusal to withdraw in Jefferson's favor. Instead, he opened negotiations with Federalists, which made Republicans angry at both the Federalists, who entertained Burr's advances, and Burr, who offered them. One historian describes the situation: "From December 1800 until late February 1801, the Union teetered at the verge of collapse as a result of political tensions fueled by sectional jealousies as well as almost paranoid fears of foreign influence and domestic sedition. Federalists and Republicans were willing to believe that their opponents were capable of virtually any action, no matter how treacherous or violent, in order to gain or retain power."[44] This belief often manifested in despicable discourse, which undermines faith in the legitimacy of political disagreement. In a healthy system, one's party should be able to lose an election without causing fears about the fate of the republic. Fomenting such fear undermines representative government.

Hamilton, who had once argued that "unity alone can save us from the fangs of Jefferson,"[45] now wrote to Gouverneur Morris, "*Jefferson* ought to be preferred to *Burr* as the 'lesser of two evils.'"[46] Burr, in Hamilton's view, "is in every sense a profligate; a voluptuary in the extreme, with uncommon habits of expence [*sic*]. . . . His very friends do not insist on his integrity."[47] Further, "No mortal can tell what his political principles are," and "he is of a temper bold enough to think no enterprise too hazardous and sanguine enough to think none too difficult."[48] For Hamilton, Burr thus represented an unquestioned danger to the republic. He lacked political principle and the restraint that adherence to principle required. He represented everything that made democracy dangerous, and in condemning Burr, Hamilton made his reservations about democracy clear: "Discerning men of all parties agree in ascribing to him an irregular and inordinate ambition . . . he knows well the weak sides of human nature, and takes care to play in with the passions of all with whom he has intercourse. By natural disposition, the haughtiest of men, he is at the same time the most creeping to answer his purposes. Cold and collected by nature and habit, he never loses his object and scruples no means of accomplishing it."[49] Hamilton, once a "#NeverAdams," was equally a "#NeverBurr," writing, "It will be impossible for me to reconcile with my notions of *honor* or policy, the continuing to be of a Party which according to my apprehension will have degraded itself and the country" by supporting Burr's candidacy.[50]

On Jefferson, Hamilton wrote, "I admit that his politics are tinctured with fanaticism, that he is too much in earnest in his democracy. That he has been a mischievous enemy to the principal measures of our past administration, that he is crafty & persevering in his objects, that his is not scrupulous about the means of success, nor mindful of truth, and that he is a contemptible hypocrite."[51] Despite these manifest defects, Jefferson was, in Hamilton's view, still to be preferred to Burr because he would be "temporizing" rather than violent and "he will not go beyond certain limits."[52] The Federalists eventually decided to follow Hamilton's advice, and on February 11, 1801, the House started voting in an election that lasted for nearly a week, ending with Jefferson's election on the thirty-sixth ballot on February 17, 1801.

I dwell on Hamilton's writing here because it is indicative of the dilemma faced by the Federalists. They did not like either Jefferson or Burr, and they found both to be wanting in appropriate political principles. But in Burr they saw a man who was willing to bend principle to personal ambition. Jefferson they understood as more willing to abide by at least something that resembled principle, and more likely to subordinate his personal ambition to those principles. In deciding between these two unsavory choices, Federalists based their decision not on the avowed policy positions of either man but on the examples of public and private character they could construe from their past behavior and present conduct. And in this conflation between personality and policy, these early American politicians laid some of the groundwork for deplorable elections to come.

By this I mean that this election displayed and legitimated two elements of deplorable elections and despicable discourse. First, they made the character of the candidate very much the issue. As these men invented the first American party system, they could have made allegiance to clearly defined party positions the centerpiece of that system. Instead, they focused on the personalities of the people involved. Policy was there too, of course. But in emphasizing things like Adams's presumed instability, Jefferson's presumed irreligiosity, or Burr's unrestrained ambition, they also subordinated party cohesion to personal loyalty. In doing so, they legitimated a certain kind of politicking that would later contribute to eruptions of despicable discourse.

Second, the various actors in this election all treated their opponents as if opposition itself was a problem. Democracy depends on all participants acknowledging the legitimacy of political opposition within an overall context of faith in pervasive loyalty to the nation and its values. Instead, in 1800 both sides of the dispute acted as if the election of the other side would mean the imminent destruction of American democracy. They had reason to fear this, given events in France and Haiti. But they could have tempered those fears instead of exploiting them. The tendency to delegitimate political opposition is one of the core elements of despicable discourse, and it dates back to the nation's first election.

In this context, it is worth noting that the nation still managed a peaceful transfer of power from one party to another. There was, then, in 1800, at least some evidence of the strength of the American experiment in democratic government. There was, however, also evidence of the potential to undermine that experiment. Adams lost for many reasons. One of them was the disproportionate strength given to Southern states in the Electoral

College by the US Constitution. If the election had been decided by the popular vote, or if the three-fifths compromise had not been enacted, that election might well have had a different outcome. As it was, 1800 led to some sixty years of dominance by Jefferson's Republican party or its successor. And that dominance meant the protection of slavery and the white supremacist ideology on which it depended. In the refusal of the nation's leaders to grapple with that fact lay the seeds of campaigns that trivialized and/or ignored important constitutive issues. The election of 1840 is one example of such elections.

TRIVIALIZING POLITICS IN 1840: TIPPECANOE AND TYLER TOO

Several developments between 1800 and 1840 are worth noting. First, the partisan press developed from weekly or monthly editions into more regular daily and weekly forms. At the same time, and as national literacy increased and mass circulation became more important, sensationalism, especially resting on forging connections between race, poverty, and crime, characterized the news. This change in emphasis necessarily affected national politics, as views of the cities and how life there was lived increased white fears and demands for protection from mysterious, threatening, and racialized others. The fact of urbanization itself mattered politically, as cities grew, as increasing numbers of immigrants found homes there, and as they began to feel increasingly cosmopolitan and divorced from rural localities.

The national economy also went through a series of convulsions as technological advances and internal improvements changed the nation from one that was understood as relying on yeoman farmers with all their supposed virtues, and the subsistence agricultural they represented, to a market economy in which tariffs and trade became one of the key points of contention. Various Panics dotted the economic landscape. The Panic of 1837 in particular had consequences for the 1840 election, for it indicated the potential weakness of the Democratic Party and lessened the legitimacy of the political system in place since Andrew Jackson's election.[53]

That election helped create a popular presidency, in which the president not only spoke for the people, as a Jefferson was thought to do, but came from them and represented them in ways that would have been abhorrent to the aristocratic Jefferson.[54] With this popularized presidency came changes in the party system as well. The franchise was broadened to include more white men, and elites were increasingly opposed to parties representing the "common man" in various forms. By the 1840s, this system was weakening, and the decade saw the creation of various other parties, the most important of which was the Liberty Party, formed by abolitionists.

Parties weren't the only legacy of Andrew Jackson, whom political historian Kenneth O'Reilly characterized as "arguably the only chief executive in American history not to consider slavery a moral evil."[55] A slave owner himself, Jackson prevented abolitionists from using the US mail and signed off on the gag rule, and he began what would become a lengthy process among Democratic presidents of demonizing abolitionists as dangerous to the republic. As much as Jackson had delegitimated abolitionism and abolitionists, both remained on the national scene, and calls for the end of slavery increased during these years, as did Southern recalcitrance on the matter of slavery. But these ideas were also increasingly a matter of dispute. Former president John Quincy Adams took on both slavery and the question of executive power in his defense of the *Amistad* mutineers; abolitionism was appearing to make inroads in the US Supreme Court.[56] By 1840, in other words, slavery and abolition were increasingly contentious topics.

Both the vagaries of the national economy and the arguments over slavery were intimately connected to the demands for western expansion. Historian Ronald Takaki writes:

> The development of the cotton export sector depended on the appropriation of Indian lands and the expansion of slavery. The major cotton-producing states—Alabama, Mississippi, and Louisiana—were carved out of Indian territory. Tribe after tribe in the South were forced to cede their lands to the federal government and move west of the Mississippi River. Eleven treaties of cession were negotiated with these tribes between 1814–1824; from these agreements the United States acquired millions of acres of lands, including one-fifth of Mississippi and three-quarters of

> Alabama. . . . But as the market revolution buttressed the institution of slavery and the westward expansion into Indian territory, the very boundlessness of this racial and ethnic diversity generated a need to reinforce interior borders.[57]

Jackson had demanded Cherokee removal; his presidency did not end the demands for indigenous land. As the nation required more and more land, Indian nations were pushed into each other's territory, increasing intertribal conflict as well as exacerbating conflicts between Indians and whites. The fact that indigenous people did not recognize collective identities as "Indians" but relied on tribal ones meant that alliances and conflicts among and between Indian nations and among and between Indian nations and the United States were in a constant state of flux, negotiation, and violence. It is not surprising that following Jackson, a large number of US presidents earned their national reputations as "Indian fighters," including William Henry Harrison, "Old Tippecanoe" himself, hero of the battle of Fallen Timbers in 1794, and victor over Tecumseh's legendary confederacy. Pitting him against incumbent Martin Van Buren, who seemed unable to bring the endless war against the Florida Seminole to a satisfactory conclusion, was intentional and effective.[58] The connection between the demand for land that could accommodate slavery, Southern dominance of national politics, and making national heroes and presidents out of those made famous for killing Indians was a keystone of American politics.

In this racialized political context, the United States' first minstrel shows appeared, and they began attracting large audiences of European immigrants, native whites, and sometimes even Blacks. These shows provided a "normalizing shield" for white supremacy.[59] And through the vehicle of entertainment, they helped train newly arrived immigrants in the politics of white supremacy, teaching many of them that their claim to whiteness was both contingent and dependent upon the exclusion of African Americans and the removal of Indians.

President Van Buren articulated what was clearly majority opinion on the "Indian Question" in an 1840 message to the Senate, writing, "the removal of the New York Indians is not only important to the tribes themselves, but to an interesting portion of western New York, and especially to the growing city of Buffalo, which is surrounded by lands occupied by Senecas. To the Indians themselves it presents the only prospect of preservation. Surrounded as they are by influences which work for their destruction, by temptation they cannot resist and artifices they can not counteract, they are rapidly declining, and, notwithstanding the philanthropic efforts of the Society of Friends, it is believed that where they are they must soon become extinct."[60] Note that the "city of Buffalo" is not depicted as encroaching on Indian territory, but as uncomfortably "surrounded" by lands "occupied" (but not, apparently, owned) by members of the Seneca nation. Van Buren then flips the narrative, arguing that it is the Indians who are surrounded, in their case by the temptations of civilization, and whose extinction is thus inevitable if they are not removed from their homes and sent west. The pretense here of concern for the "vanishing Indian" as a means of taking Indian land had already been long established and was widely accepted by non-Indian Americans.[61] It is also worth noting that as late as the 1840s, indigenous people were still living (as they are today) in their local communities as far east as New York. Removal was a slow and uneven process, but the idea that Indians were no longer present even as they continued to reside in states and localities had a powerful hold on the white American imagination. It was a fiction allowing them to make "legitimate" claims on Indian lands.

In this context, one might imagine that the 1840 election would be characterized by discussion over policies such as the best principles guiding western expansion, or the most appropriate way to contend with the increasingly difficult issues of slavery, or the best ways to manage a diversifying economy. It was not. Partly, this was due to the political process itself. From 1796 until 1824, congressional caucuses chose presidential candidates; those candidates then owed a certain allegiance to their party in Congress. But in 1824, Andrew Jackson won both the popular and the electoral vote. This majority was not enough, however, and that election, decided in a "corrupt bargain" in the House of Representatives, put John Quincy Adams in the White House. Jackson, enraged by this result, became the first candidate to (unsuccessfully) demand the abolition of the Electoral College. The 1824 election meant the demise of "King Caucus," as presidential politics felt the push for more democratization. Starting in 1832, parties shifted to national nominating conventions. This generally meant a long, drawn-out process, especially for the Democrats, who required their nominees to earn a two-thirds majority of delegates.[62] The inception of national nominating conventions theoretically meant that parties went into the general election with a consensus. In practice, it meant that potentially divisive issues were suppressed or ignored in the interests of party unity. Those issues continued to fester and often erupted, as we will see in later chapters.

Still, the impulse for more democracy meant there was high voter engagement, given what was still a fairly limited franchise. Mass rallies and other kinds of events were important sources of political information. There was a lot of public correspondence, which appeared in national as well as state and local newspapers. Material and popular culture were significantly political. The Whigs, famously the more elitist of the two parties, took the lead in democratizing the presidential campaign, increasing the amount and content of public electioneering.[63] They did so by relying not on images of elite candidates protecting the people's interests but on a very public display of "Tippecanoe and Tyler too," who ran a campaign based on log cabins and hard cider. The log cabin referenced Harrison's ostensibly humble origins, and the hard cider indicated the ways he remained close to "the people."

By 1840, then, there were a number of issues needing sustained national attention. But the political system was structured in ways that discouraged such attention, requiring consensus that incentivized suppression of controversial topics. The fissures starting to open among various constituencies didn't break along party lines—party leaders thus could not exploit them for partisan gain and tended to avoid them for fear of fracturing an increasingly fragile partisan consensus. Campaign historian Mark R. Cheathem writes:

> At stake in the 1840 presidential election was the future of the political party system. Democrats had formed their party identity during the 1828 campaign and early in Jackson's first administration they possessed a political ideology based on the Jeffersonian principles of limited government and the will of the people. A Van Buren victory would further strengthen the Democrats and seemed likely to, if not scatter the Whigs, at least make them a permanent minority party for the near future. The Whigs, on the other

> hand, had initially organized as an anti-Jackson party, bringing together disparate individuals of factions who agreed on opposing Old Hickory but not necessarily much else. By 1840, the Whigs were the party of social morality and progressivism; that year's presidential campaign offered the first legitimate opportunity for the Whigs to articulate a focused political agenda and to begin building a stable voting base led by their presidential choice.[64]

There were risks involved in bringing a focused agenda to the political forefront; the Whigs chose to avoid them in favor of developing a particular image of Harrison and attacking a caricatured image of Van Buren. A campaign that could have relied on issues instead became one of the more trivial contests in US history, in which the logic of party dominated the political landscape.

On the Whig side, there were a number of potential candidates in 1840, including such luminous names as Henry Clay, Daniel Webster, Winfield Scott, and William Henry Harrison. The Whigs were in the middle of a generational and ideological shift, although these candidacies reveal the extent to which that remained unclear at the time. Men such as Thurlow Weed and Horace Greeley were increasingly loud voices in party councils, and Webster and Clay were starting to look and sound anachronistic. Campaign technologies were changing, and the oratory of a Webster or Clay was ill-suited to mass rallies and torch-light parades. Politics was still entertainment, but the nation's taste in entertainment, as in politics, was changing. Increasingly, as the politics roiling around the issue of slavery were taking hold, national tickets had to balance Northern and Southern interests; this generally meant that the "slave power" needed to be represented in some fashion on the presidential ticket. So the Whigs chose famed Indian fighter Harrison, from Ohio, a former slave owner from an antislavery state, balancing his presence with that of John Tyler, a former Democrat who favored nullification, the specious legal theory that a state has the power to invalidate a federal law. Tyler's views were, to say the least, inconsistent with mainstream Whig doctrine, but Whig leaders hoped those views would solidify party challenges to the current administration.

The Democrats had fewer choices and a narrower set of acceptable views. They easily nominated incumbent Martin Van Buren, the famed

"Little Magician," who had served as Jackson's vice president. Ideological consistency was becoming increasingly important to the Democrats, and they became the first nominating convention to adopt a party platform, a set of ideas to which all candidates were expected to adhere. Consistent with their Jeffersonian roots, they espoused limited government, innocuously favored a "sound economy," predictably opposed both internal improvements and a national bank, ominously argued that abolitionists were endangering the "stability and permanency of the union," and, somewhat surprisingly, advocated fairly liberal naturalization policies.[65]

As is so often the case in deplorable elections, there were third parties roaming the political landscape. The Anti-Masons lingered on, nominating Harrison but choosing as his vice-presidential nominee the redoubtable Daniel Webster. There was by 1840 significantly less hostility to the Anti-Masons as they dwindled in power and influence. Potentially more threatening was the new Liberty Party, dedicated to the destruction of the "slave power." Arguing that slavery was both a moral and a political evil, members of the Liberty Party did not engage in the kind of mass organizing that was occupying the Whigs and the Democrats, but their presence in the campaign was a sign both of the weakening legitimacy of the political system, as affiliated with the iniquitous slave system, and of the increasingly important role that affiliation was playing in national politics.[66] The stain of slavery was spreading, and containing it was preoccupying those involved in both major parties.

Discussion of the national economy should have dominated the national campaign, and it was one of the prime foci of Whig argumentation, to the extent that the campaign actually involved argumentation. More frequent were accusations that Van Buren was tyrannical, manipulative, and monarchial. Presidential and candidate nicknames indicate affection, as nicknames generally do. In the early 1800s, appellations such as "Old Hickory," which summoned up Jackson's immutable strength of will, or "Old Tippecanoe," which called to mind Harrison's valor against the Indians, were similarly useful politically. Van Buren, however, suffered under his plethora of nicknames. Titles such as "Martin Van Ruin," "King Matty," or the "Little Magician of Kinderhook" referenced not his equality with the masses but his willingness to feed off them, to manipulate them, to serve his interests rather than theirs.[67]

The Whigs based their campaign on contrasting Harrison to Van Buren, relying on Harrison's military career and on his purported connection to that mysterious entity, "the people." The depiction of Harrison as a "common man" centered on his claim to "log cabin" origins and an affection for hard cider. Such campaigning lent itself to spectacle, and spectacle there was. "Both sides made their case via 'cultural politics,' or political activities that took place outside formal party organization and the act of voting. What sounded and looked like entertainment—things such as music, public events, and cartoons—held important political meaning in the first few decades of the United States' existence."[68] The Whigs, lacking a platform, depended on other means of messaging, relying on large public events such as rallies and parades. Harrison himself made a number of public speeches, personally involving himself in the campaign in unprecedented ways. Whigs added other innovations as well, including processions, banquets, mass meetings, and assorted kinds of political memorabilia.[69] One event for Harrison included a banner that read "Harrison and Tyler—vox populi, vox dei," meaning "the voice of the people is the voice of God."[70] Valorizing the voice of the people was the new Whig mantra.

This message wasn't conveyed only by the candidate or in mass rallies. Increasingly during these years, newspapers were important sources of political information, and they expanded in influence and circulation throughout the decade.[71] Both major parties also relied on the relatively new form of the campaign biography in their bids to prove that their candidate was closer to the people. Interestingly, it was the more conservative Whigs who made the most innovative use of campaign technology, and who made the best use of women as quasi-political actors, active campaigners who couldn't vote themselves. While the Democrats maintained existing hierarchies on the campaign trail, Whigs had women speakers, circulated pamphlets written by women, and involved women in meaningful roles throughout the campaign.[72]

There were plenty of issues at stake in this election, and both campaigns studiously avoided discussing them, not least because their coalitions lacked consensus. They avoided discussion of slavery most of all, but they also elided conversations about a national bank, the national economy, western expansion, and foreign policy. The Whigs concentrated their efforts on discrediting Van Buren as an elitist snob living the high life at public expense. David B. Ogdale, for example, speaking at a "Great Meeting of Merchants" in New York, "exhorted those present, if they had property, to keep the Loco Focos [a derogatory name for Democrats] from power, for by them property would be prostrated—if they loved their country, to save it from that Loco-focoism which would ruin the country. . . . He believed that from what he had seen, that there was an effort making by our opponents to inflame the worst feelings of our citizens. He had noticed their processions and martial music, and their banners, on which were inscribed 'VICTORY OR DEATH'—as much as to say, we will defeat you or die for it."[73] This kind of hysteria is an example of despicable discourse. In an election in which the actual issues facing the country took second place to the politics of spectacle, that spectacle would be, almost by necessity, hyperbolic. That hyperbole was then used as evidence for the unprincipled intentions of the opposition.

Yet these claims were made with no small degree of hyperbole themselves. At a New Jersey Whig convention, for instance, J. W. Miller argued, "You have all marked and formed a definite opinion respecting the series of intrigues by which the present Administration has crept into power, and of the unblushing fraud by which that power has been exercised. . . . To insure a continuance of this system of speculation and default, this monopoly of misbegotten power and fraudulent wealth, it became necessary to sow dissension, to cultivate hatred, malice, and distrust, to destroy the holy bonds of society itself, and arm neighbor against neighbor, community against community."[74] The Van Buren administration in this accounting was not principled but mistaken. Instead it was depicted as based on fraud, dedicated to self-interest, and prone to dividing the nation by inflaming the worst sort of passions. It was exactly the kind of regime the framers feared and was therefore illegitimate. Democrats, less hyperbolic in this instance, contented themselves with ridiculing the Whig candidate, calling him "an old Granny," and suggesting that he would be an inactive chief magistrate at a time when vigorous administration was required.[75]

Van Buren, as president a fairly infrequent campaigner, made his case from the president's chair. In the midst of a serious economic downturn, Van Buren, like Harrison, avoided discussion of such issues, preferring to rely on bromides and vague statements of national happiness and contentment. He began his fourth annual message, for example, this way: "Our devout gratitude is due to the Supreme Being for having graciously continued to our beloved country through the vicissitudes of another year the invaluable blessings of health, plenty, and peace. Seldom had this favored land been so generally exempted from the ravages of disease or the labor of husbandman more amply rewarded, and never before have our relations with other countries been placed on a more favorable basis than that which they so happily occupy at this critical conjuncture in the affairs of the world."[76] Given the economic and social turmoil convulsing the nation, this opening, while fairly standard for annual messages, is complacent to the point of insulting those who were suffering from the depression or otherwise occupied with the nation's pressing problems. In a political context of large amounts of campaign and political communication, rhetoric of this kind would have traveled widely and in largely unflattering ways.

All this public electioneering increased both interest in the campaign and participation—even, as in the case of women, among those denied a formal role as voters in the proceedings. But it came at a price, for the tone of the campaign was as low as it had been in years if not decades. As one might expect in a campaign waged primarily on personal attributes, there was a palpable increase in the number of personal attacks. Campaign communication was characterized by pandering, sloganeering, and deception.[77] In short, it had all the earmarks of a modern deplorable election.

In the end, Harrison and Tyler won 234 of the available 294 electoral votes, winning the popular vote by a margin of 146,000 in an election in which 2,400,000 votes were cast. Harrison became the oldest man ever elected to the presidency, at the age of sixty-seven. His enjoyment of the office was brief, however, for he gave the longest inaugural in presidential history, caught pneumonia, and died about a month into his administration. Tyler's succession to the White House was a disaster for the Whigs and didn't do the country much good either. Tyler was a states' rights advocate at a time when that position was becoming anathema to those who owed allegiance to the Whigs. He was eventually, if unsurprisingly, expelled from the party.

The portents in 1840 were clear. Sectionalism was an increasing problem. The question of whether to expand the nation and the price of doing so was looming ever larger. The issue of how to manage the nation's economy was a matter of tension, marking both sectionalism and expansion with its concerns. That election, however, did nothing to help resolve these issues. Instead, Southerners became ever more recalcitrant in their commitment to and defenses of slavery. Indeed, that commitment and those defenses tied Southerners together in ways that had previously been difficult to achieve. John Hope Franklin writes that during the 1840s "the pressures of sectional conflict were causing southerners to minimize the physiographic variations within their section, the differences in the economic and social status of the people, and the several disagreements in political allegiances and philosophies. Committed to perpetuating a system of servitude increasingly condemned by the rest of the Western world, southern whites began to think of themselves as having a common set of values, common problems, common dangers, and common aspirations that set them apart from other Americans. Inevitably, they came to believe also that they had a common and distinctive history."[78]

Evidence for this claim is not hard to find. The members of the Republican convention in Virginia, for example, urged unity in the face of Whig assaults on the South, publishing an address from the convention to "the people of Virginia" that argued, "By union and concert of action, we may avert the evils we have too much a cause to apprehend from the election of a Federal Whig to the Presidency; we may indelibly impress upon our system the doctrine of the States Rights Republican school, and we may bring back the Government, in all its departments, to the principles asserted by Taylor in his Resolutions, and by Madison, in his Report."[79] They reaffirmed their commitment to the principles of the Virginia and Kentucky Resolutions and warned that a Whig president would endorse not only a national bank but an iniquitous tariff policy and "wasteful and extravagant expenditures of the public money, upon gigantic schemes of internal improvement." Worse, "there is too, another circumstance which ought to bind southern men to him by indissoluble ties. We allude to the stand he has taken against the insane and mischievous designs of the Abolitionists, from the very commencement of that fearful excitement." For Southerners, there was nothing good to be apprehended from the election of a Whig president and much to fear. Such a president, instead of combatting the "insane and mischievous" actions of abolitionists might endorse them.

That sense of separateness made solving the sectional crisis ever more difficult, and it is part of what makes this election an important precursor to modern deplorable elections. Such rhetoric depended on dividing the nation, not endeavoring to see in it a united people with the same commitment to the national interest. Opponents were characterized as insane, mischievous, and therefore untrustworthy at best and disqualified to be president at worst.

At the same time, and for connected reasons, following the 1840 election, there was a remarkable growth in expansionist sentiment in the United States.[80] Questions of expansion, of course, brought with them questions related to whether slavery would be expanded with the nation and whether the prevailing view of American national identity would be expanded as well. The war with Mexico exacerbated the sectional crisis, raising questions about who to incorporate into the nation and under what terms.

The election of 1840 was singularly unproductive in terms of helping the nation manage these connected difficulties. But elections aren't deplorable because of their results, although I would argue that deplorable elections also often lead to unproductive results. They are deplorable because of the kinds of discourses that circulate during the election. In this case, the election reveals important aspects of what makes some US elections deplorable. First, as in 1800, there was an emphasis on the personality of the candidates. Image dominated campaign discourse. This is not, in and of itself, necessarily a problem. Images can be a kind of shorthand for policy, making both candidates and policies more accessible to a broader range of citizens. In this case, however, the image was less a shorthand for policy and more a distraction from it. The attention paid to hard cider and log cabins was important, perhaps, to the kinds of mass mobilization the election required. But it was deceptive.

Nancy Isenberg argues that among elites, dating back to colonial times, there's been a conception of the United States as a trash heap, a place where the "disposable people" could be sent.[81] She also argues that an important shift occurred in 1840, the "moment when the squatter morphed into the colloquial common man of democratic lore."[82] That is, as the nation expanded the franchise and became more inclusive of white men, political discourse shifted in ways that began to accept, if not valorize, some of the white men who had previously been excluded. As these people became important to electoral success, candidates sought to forge connections with them. Harrison, however, was no common man. Despite the spectacle attending his campaign, regardless of the amount of hard cider he imbibed, and independent of his supposed upbringing in a log cabin, Harrison was a member of the American elite. Son of William Harrison, delegate to the Continental Congress and a signer of the Declaration of Independence, and himself a member of the House of Representatives, a territorial governor, and a senator, Harrison was the privileged scion of a privileged family. That in itself is no bar to arguments for democratic leadership, of course. Plenty of wealthy people have advocated for those less privileged. But Harrison was not making those arguments. He was instead presenting himself as if he was, by nature, a more democratic alternative to a presumably monarchial "King Matty," a nickname that conveys both presumed elitism and contempt for his incapacities. This isn't an argument for better policy on behalf of the nation's underserved. It's an image aimed at their political manipulation. Elections like this taught American politicians that the masses could be mobilized. It also taught them that such mobilization did not depend on making arguments about the people's best interest.

There were plenty of issues deserving open debate in 1840, and there were enough differences of opinion on those issues to makes such discussion both possible and important. But because those differences threatened to fracture increasingly fragile party coalitions, both parties chose to suppress such debate, focusing instead on the kinds of spectacle new technologies made possible. The mobilization of the electorate through such spectacle came at a price. That price grew steeper as the major parties became ever more invested in suppressing conversations about expansion, race, and the nature of American national identity.

THE POLITICS OF SILENCE IN 1852: SLAVERY AND DISUNION

In presidential scholar Stephen Skowronek's terms, Franklin Pierce is a disjunctive president, presiding over the death of a party system. Disjunctive presidents are affiliated with doomed regimes and lack the legitimacy and the resources to govern. Even given the fact that this category is rife with presidential failure, Skowronek calls Pierce "perhaps the most colossal failure in presidential history."[83] Pierce governed during an all but impossible time, and he proved himself to be entirely unequal to that task. He was left a legacy of unsolved issues and made no progress on solving any of them.[84] The issues that roiled about in the 1840 election continued to agitate the nation and played important roles throughout the 1840s. As a response to the lack of government action, the 1840s were characterized by reform movements, as temperance, education, "the Indian problem," women's rights, and abolition consumed increasing numbers of the nation's citizens. The nation's people, wanting to see action on a variety of fronts that seemingly paralyzed the nation's government, were organizing to pressure the government into legislative activity. Instead, the government prosecuted a controversial war with Mexico that increased dissatisfaction with the functioning of the political system. That war's conclusion gained the US enormous territory and the problem of deciding what to do with it. The decade of the 1840s was, in many ways, dedicated to the idea of Manifest Destiny, the presumably God-given right to govern the continent. Premised on the idea that white Americans were more civilized, and thus also morally superior to those already inhabiting the West, Manifest Destiny demanded that the nation claim, occupy, and control those territories.

This mandate, of course, served specific kinds of ideological functions for the nation, giving those with the resources to do so both land and the kind of independence that had long been associated with the privileges of citizenship. Less discussed was the cost. There were those left behind in the nation's crowded cities, those who were trapped in economic circumstances that didn't allow them to follow the dictate to "go west," and those who were already living in those "vacant" lands, and whose often violent dispossession became required so that others could access their land and their resources. The movement west was fraught with difficulty for the nation's citizens. And it was fraught with pain and death for those not considered citizens, especially the continent's indigenous peoples and its enslaved people.

As the nation expanded, Southerners demanded that slavery expand as well. Recognizing that the confinement of slavery would eventually mean its end, slave owners and their allies fought hard to secure the extension of their "peculiar institution" even as opponents of slavery, for the same reason, fought to prevent that extension. Ibram X. Kendi summarizes the moment this way: "When General Zachary Taylor began his tenure as the twelfth US president in 1849, Free Soilers were demanding slavery's restriction, abolitionists were demanding the closure of the slave market in Washington, DC, and enslavers were demanding the expansion of slavery and a stricter fugitive slave law to derail the Underground Railroad and its courageous conductors."[85] These demands whipsawed the federal government, which, because of the power of the Southern states and the willingness of those states to threaten disunion, meant unsatisfactory compromise after unsatisfactory compromise, and a system that was increasingly seen by all parties as lacking moral authority and political legitimacy.

For Southerners, the protection of slavery increasingly demanded extreme measures. They demanded enforcement of the noxious Fugitive Slave Act, which required the return of enslaved persons who had escaped to the North; they continued to refuse abolitionist literature to travel through the US mail; they required gag orders in Congress on the question of slavery. Demanding that their rights be protected, they were ever more willing to trample the civil liberties of others. At the same time, it is important to remember that not all of those who were opposed to slavery did so out of their concern for the enslaved population. Many of them were more concerned about slavery's effects on white labor, for instance. Few white Americans were willing to concede even the possibility of African American equality much less to advocate for African American rights. As the slavery issue finally broke apart the Whig party along sectional lines, for example, former Whigs moved variously to the Free Soil Party and from there to the new Republican Party or, as was often the case for Southerners, became Democrats. No political parties could create or sustain a national mandate. Ominously, party differences became identified with regional differences, and the line between them hardened.

The movement between these various party configurations was neither quick nor easy. As the Whigs collapsed, third parties appeared, including parties dedicated to prohibition, to nativism, and to the protection of "free soil" for white labor. Creating a viable coalition among these various interests was no simple task. The Democrats had a somewhat easier time. Looking less for a national coalition and more to single-mindedly protect slavery, they increasingly narrowed their political view to that one issue.

The question of slavery arose in two different but related contexts. First, there was considerable overt and explicit discussion of slavery itself. Southerners, having since the days of John C. Calhoun decided that slavery was not a necessary evil but a positive good, depended on an affirmative defense of the institution's benefits, relying on widely accepted notions of white supremacy to make their case. Northerners, agreeing with the premise but not with its conclusion, increasingly considered slavery a moral stain on the nation and argued that for the country to fulfill its God-given mission in the world, slavery had to be ended. It was an issue that admitted no compromise, although the country's political leaders crafted one unsatisfactory compromise after another.

Second, the slavery issue, and the issue of free white labor that impinged on it, appeared as both text and subtext in debates over national expansion. Residents of slave states wanted to see new territories open to slavery. Those interested in protecting free white labor were equally insistent that slavery be banned from those territories. The "common man," so central to the 1840 election appeared again, this time as the hero and victim of the national narrative.[86] Northerner opponents of slavery argued that slave labor prevented poor whites from making the progress that they otherwise might. Southern defenders of slavery argued that the real problem was "wage slavery" as it occurred in the industrialized north.

The arguments about incorporating new territories was complicated by the nation's endemic racism. While the West held a kind of idealized fascination for Americans, it was also a place, as borders always are, of unnamed terrors and liminal spaces. Adding new territory seemed on the one hand to present a set of enticing opportunities. On the other hand, those new territories were occupied by Mexicans, Indians, and other people who were regarded with suspicion by many whites. Incorporating them, especially as citizens, could in the eyes of white Americans both dilute and endanger the country's "racial stock."[87]

Slavery was thus the pivotal question both for the nation and for this election. But it wasn't the issue overtly before the electorate, as the candidates focused on the past glories of the Mexican-American War and the possibilities of expansion it provided. Slavery threatened to tear both major parties apart, rendering them into merely regional entities. Consequently, both major parties subsumed discussions of slavery into conversations about expansion. They were abetted in this effort by the presence of the Free Soil Party, whose commitment to protecting the rights of white labor in the West was absolute. Their efforts were complicated by the presence of other third parties: the Union Party, which represented Southerners disaffected by the Whig party; the Know-Nothings, who brought nativism into an already toxic mix of racism and territorial greed; the Southern Rights Party, an offshoot of the Democrats in the South and advocates of secession; the Temperance Party; and the Liberty Party, which I mention only because it was so small and yet so determined (so few members came to its national nominating convention that they had to convene three times before achieving a quorum). The presence of these small parties indicates the increasing lack of system legitimacy. Rather than building workable coalitions among the variety of interests animating national politics, advocates of those interests were fracturing into small subsets, each unlikely to be able to influence politics on a national scale.

The various parties dealt with this complicated set of issues in a way that sheds light on the character of deplorable elections throughout our history: they chose to bury the issues under the veneer of discussion about the glories of the past and the possibilities of expansion. Each of the major parties was walking on the same eggshells. Consequently, their platforms were practically indistinguishable. The 1852 election was, as such elections tend to be, a contest of personalities. Winfield Scott, the eventual Whig nominee, had distinguished himself as a general in the Mexican-American War, despite his unflattering nickname, "Old Fuss and Feathers." Staunchly opposed to slavery, Scott was a candidate very likely to divide what remained of the Whig Party rather than unite it across sectional lines. Unsurprisingly, a group of Southern Whigs, refusing to endorse Scott's candidacy, nominated their own slate of candidates, ensuring Scott's inability to win in the South.

He was nominated in a convention sharply divided between supporters of Millard Fillmore, who, it was argued by his supporters, had saved the Union by brokering the Compromise of 1850. Opponents more successfully claimed that the compromise had ceded far too much to the South in exchange for far too little. The disputes between the two factions were characterized by the *New York Daily Times* as constituting a "very warm canvass," as Fillmore was as fervently supported by the South as he was opposed by the Northern delegates.[88] The *New York Daily Times* noted that "the real grounds of difference as to Mr. Fillmore's nomination, are unquestionably, in their origin, sectional; though they do not necessarily rest solely upon sectional collisions on measures or principles."[89] The *Times* made clear its view on the possibilities of sectional strife impacting the national election:

> The Whigs of the North have no desire to renew the strife upon them, and will gladly avoid all controversy and agitation concerning them, if they are allowed to do so. If, however, the Whigs of the South refuse thus to allow the subject of slavery to remain untouched—if they insist on thrusting it again into the agitation and issues of a presidential contest—and if they demand such a nomination as will inevitably renew the agitation, and again throw open all the controversies now happily settled, they ought not to be allowed to do it under any misapprehension of the inevitable result.[90]

That is, in the view of the *Times*, the Compromise of 1850 had done its work and the issue of slavery was settled; there was no productive way to continue agitating on that score. Continued insistence on slavery as an important issue would cost the Whigs the presidency and might cost the nation its union. "This Union," another *Times* contributor agreed, "was not made for the fanatics of either section; nor is the public mind to be swayed by such influences."[91] For these representatives of what passed for the contemporaneous political center, the Union was safe only upon the middle ground between the slave power and the abolitionists.

Democrats opposed Scott with their own distinguished general, Franklin Pierce of New Hampshire. A Northern Democrat and a war hero, the party hoped he would be able to maintain a national coalition. The road to his nomination is instructive. The Democrats in 1852 had a choice among four main contenders. Least important was William Macy, the favorite son from New York, present as a possibility only because of the power of his home state. There was also Lewis Cass of Michigan, who was backed by Northerners who supported the Compromise of 1850, in hopes that this time, a compromise on the issue of slavery would hold. James Buchanan of

Pennsylvania was popular in the South and was a firm advocate for their rights. Stephen A. Douglas, senator from Illinois, was favored by expansionists and especially by the railroads, who saw in his candidacy a chance to open the West. This slate of candidates, many of them accomplished politicians, revealed the fissures and possibilities in 1852. Some states, like New York, had enough power, given the logic of the Electoral College, to at least get their local interests a hearing. But in an election that would be dominated by national issues, the local was increasingly losing ground. In 1852 the complex set of regional interests, pitting the North against the South with the West having a role either as coalition member or as spoiler was infinitely more important.

Pierce won the nomination (on the forty-ninth ballot) less because of his own capacities and more because of his ability to serve as a compromise candidate mediating a Northern presence with the protection of Southern demands. It is telling that his campaign ceded to Buchanan's people the right to name Pierce's vice-presidential nominee (they chose William R. King, a strong unionist who died of tuberculosis forty-five days into his term as vice president). The *Times* approved the choice, noting, "The Democratic nomination is everywhere received with the entire acquiescence of the party. It will, beyond all question, thoroughly unite its hitherto disordered ranks, and be supported with harmony and energy. . . . The ticket has a northern and a southern face."[92] The Democrats, in other words, had done what the Whigs had failed to do—they had come up with a compromise ticket at a political moment in which compromise was the most important thing in politics.

The Whigs, however, were in fact trying to present themselves as the campaign of national unity. Announcing the creation of a party newspaper dedicated to the campaign, they declared, "The direct object of the CAMPAIGN TIMES will be to promote the permanent ascendency of Whig principles, by aiding the election of the Whig Candidate for the Presidency. . . . It will endeavor, by fair argument and unquestioned facts, to convince the public judgment, that the interests of the Country and the advancement of Republican Liberty on which the hopes of humanity rest, require the permanent establishment, in our National Councils, of those great principles of Government and of Political Economy which are represented and advocated by the Whig Party of the Union."[93] Newspapers at the time were of course, importantly partisan. But the invention of a paper devoted solely to the election, and at that, devoted solely to the promotion of one party, was an innovation. It was an effort to broaden the appeal of the Whig Party, and to engage citizens in its efforts.

Both Scott and Pierce were opposed by New Hampshire's John P. Hale, nominee of the Free Soil Party. A former congressman and senator, Hale was an ardent opponent of slavery and expansion—he had opposed, for example, the Mexican-American War. He had little chance of winning the election, but his presence helped draw votes away from Scott and the Whigs. A similar function was served by the nominee of the American Party, better known as the "Know-Nothings." Nativist to the core, members of the Know-Nothing Party equally opposed immigrants and Catholics. They nominated the ailing Daniel Webster without his knowledge or approval and, when Webster died, replaced him with Jacob Broom, whose grandfather had signed the Declaration of Independence.

One might think that the plethora of parties and candidates would have led to a vigorous campaign marked by high levels of voter interest and participation. If so, one would be disappointed. The 1852 election had very low turnout—fewer men voted than in any election since 1836. This is one marker of a deplorable election—when the parties seek to suppress rather than encourage debate over important issues, when they are so preoccupied with hiding from the issues that they collide in the political center, when issues are elided instead of faced, and personalities rather than policy constitute the relevant dividing lines, then there is a better than even chance that the election will be deplorable. Despicable discourse is largely found in what kinds of arguments circulate. It can also be found in the refusal to circulate important arguments. Democrats, in fact, offering their opinion of the Whig platform, noted that "the real Platform of every party is to be found in its CANDIDATES," explicitly refusing to engage issues in favor of personalities.[94]

Indeed, the *New York Daily Times* was adamant on the question of the destructive power of what we would now call single-issue politics: "One-ideaism is in every form of manifestation a mischievous abstraction. Allow the object of its devotion to be ever so meritorious, it detaches its votaries from every other worthy object, and precludes the possibility of general usefulness."[95] For the *Times*, at least, neither slavery nor abolitionism should be allowed to dominate the national agenda, for concentration on that one issue prevented voters from seeing all the other issues that united the nation and prevented the political system, based on a complicated set of compromises and trade-offs, from functioning as it was meant to do.

Yet the system was out of balance, as the *Times* itself admitted: "The great body of the American people, hitherto intent on the duty of perfecting and maintaining their free institutions, and developing and augmenting their usefulness towards the security and advancement of the happiness and interests of society, must meet, as they are able, the efforts of a class to force a sectional interest into a controlling position in our Government.... In the long run, slavery must ever lose in all these attempts to fortify itself by expansion. By spreading its blight over an increased area it weakens its original strong-holds, without acquiring a compensating strength in the new."[96] For the author of this piece, the Constitution was at least potentially an antislavery document, promoting the freedom and independence of all Americans. The American people were correctly occupied in pursuing the freedoms and perfecting the institutions that guaranteed them. The South threatened this entire way of life and this entire ideological regime by demanding the protection of slavery. The author explicitly noted the connection between slavery and national expansion and did so in ways that both opposed the expansion of slavery and threatened its demise whether it expanded or not. The essay unsurprisingly concluded, "We are decidedly hostile to all agitation on the subject."[97] Southerners, busily trying through gag orders to silence abolitionists, had, in this author's opinion, better be silent themselves.

They were not, however, silent. Instead they engaged in a "venomous crusade against General SCOTT,"[98] accusing him of swindling, of "making false entries of disbursements, and supporting them by forged vouchers... a life time devoted to his country passes for nothing with them."[99] With one war hero campaigning against another, one way to unlevel the playing field was to denigrate the war record of the opposition. It is the kind of unsupported accusation that otherwise empty campaigns are prone to engage in, the kind of unsupported accusation that constitutes despicable discourse.

This tactic didn't work with every audience. At least one citizen argued that he supported Scott because he was willing to uphold the Compromise of 1850 and the Fugitive Slave Law; it was this spirit of compromise that was required in such difficult times.[100] In coming to this decision, this Southerner had to negotiate complicated questions relating to national, sectional, and party loyalty, and what each of these might mean for his understanding of citizenship. All elections are of course about national identity. Deplorable elections make such questions central in ways that force choices upon citizens who otherwise may not have seen choices as required.

Other citizens similarly rejected their exclusion from the nation on the basis of their vote. A group of self-identified "Irish Voters," for instance, announced their support for Scott "because he has proved himself the friend of his country and all its citizens, no matter on what soil they were born, or from what nation they came."[101] For these voters, Scott was worthy of support because of his willingness to advocate an inclusive version of citizenship. He was unwilling to endorse discrimination either on the basis of national origin or religion.[102]

Despite these avowals of support for Scott, Pierce won in a landslide. Scott won only Kentucky, Tennessee, Massachusetts, and Vermont. Daniel Webster, who, it should be remembered, was dead, earned a fair share of the vote in Georgia and Massachusetts, indicating either a great deal of residual affection for the famous orator or a certain dissatisfaction with living candidates. Stephen Skowronek assessed the election this way: "On the surface, the Democrats' electoral strategy in 1852 was a stunning success. Pierce carried 27 of the 31 states, for a hefty 250 out of 296 electoral votes. In the process the Democratic party claimed huge majorities in both houses of Congress. But as with many other electoral college landslides, support for Pierce was more apparent than real, and his victory anything but a mandate for action."[103] It was a remarkably destructive election. Scott's commitment to antislavery destroyed the Southern wing of the Whig party; at the same time, the Whig's proslavery platform undermined the party's Northern wing. It is unsurprising that the party did not long survive the campaign.

Because the campaign did not require discussion of the major issues facing the country—indeed, because the parties actively suppressed any such conversation—Pierce entered office with no mandate to lead, no potential way forward. He spent his term trying to avoid action that would further divide the nation and ended by failing in even that goal. Lacking the ability or the will to deal with the country's most pressing problems or the ideological assumptions undergirding them, he was unable to prevent the slow slide into civil war.

CONCLUSION: LESSONS FROM THE EARLY REPUBLIC

One of the assumptions of this chapter is that racism and white supremacy are deeply embedded in our national institutions and in our national culture. Opposition to racism and white supremacy are as well, but they play a comparatively minor role in the discourse of the major party candidates over time. Because the nation is built on a structure authorizing white supremacy, and because that structure is itself so rarely openly interrogated, issues of race and racism are generally suppressed, ignored, or denied. Racism was baked into the early republic and into the institutions created by and developed since the founding. These elements, rarely openly discussed by white candidates during national elections, continue to emerge at moments of national tension.

We can see from these early examples not only that deplorable elections are made more likely by the national refusal to acknowledge the unstated premises of the political system but that it is somewhat surprising we don't see more of them. This is perhaps because in general the system works well enough for enough of the nation's privileged citizens, enough of the time. Mostly, the ability of white voters to focus on personality distracts them from the inherent inequalities of the system. Mostly, the trivialization of national political campaigns and the centrality of spectacle in them allow white voters to treat politics as a sideshow and reduces their belief that as citizens they have the capacity and the responsibility to effect political change. And mostly, the ability to suppress long-simmering issues in order to protect system stability has led to a fear of change and a resistance to discussions about the roots of the nation's most venerated political documents among many white people. Americans are taught to revere those documents and the white, often slaveholding men who authored and signed them. Questioning them becomes a marker of disloyalty rather than an integral act of citizenship. As a result, white citizens become invested in national myths and in the restricted views of nation and national identity embedded in them. Those myths long sustained the nation. They are also exclusionary, ignoring as they do the ways that the nation was founded on the removal and genocide of indigenous peoples, the labor of enslaved people, and the tenets of white supremacy. The more discourse in any election evokes them, depends on them, and circles them with an aura of nostalgia, the more likely it is that this discourse will be despicable. Those investments are most likely to appear, often in ugly ways, during moments of national stress, and they find form in the despicable discourses of deplorable elections.

CHAPTER 2

LOOKING BACKWARD DURING THE NATION'S CENTENNIAL, 1876

The United States celebrated its centennial with an election that tore the country apart and made citizens question both the integrity and the viability of their political system. A toxic combination of personal ambition, bitter partisanship, and sectional animosity helped create a situation in which the only real question was whether the frauds perpetrated by the Republicans were necessary antidotes to the violence and intimidation of the Democrats.[1] The election took place in an environment of high partisanship and relatively weak party organizations; party leaders themselves were largely unable to control their own operations, and there was a noticeable absence of central direction.[2] Despite the parties' weakness, partisanship remained strong, as citizens found not just policy but personal identity in their party identification. This in turn meant that there was a kind of political frenzy operating in the nation, and the intemperate nature of political identification wasn't being controlled or channeled by the parties. Consequently, like many deplorable elections the stakes appeared very high, as if the future of American democracy itself was at stake.

We like to believe that in the years between the end of the Civil War and the beginning of the Great War that the United States was at peace. In fact, it was a time of almost unremitting violence. Immediately following the war the US military continued to have a strong presence in the South as an army of occupation, dedicated to maintaining order and protecting both the rights and the lives of the newly freed and enfranchised African Americans there. Other troops were available for two important purposes. First, they were beginning to be deployed to repress the increasingly violent labor uprisings that characterized the beginning of the Gilded Age. Second, they were sent west, and the national government prosecuted a number of "Indian Wars" aimed at eliminating indigenous title to land and, often, at eliminating native peoples altogether. Western emigration helped to siphon off some of the pressures in the East wrought by immigration and financial crises, but it came at a price as the settlement of the frontier was a complicated mixture of negotiation, accommodation, encroachment, and genocide.

The ongoing violence of US society helped to create and was exacerbated by a cultural obsession with manliness and masculinity.[3] The war culture of the time focused strongly on the "manly" virtues; victory strengthened the belief in the North that those virtues were important. In the South, defeat hardened the need to demonstrate "appropriate" kinds of masculinity. The fragility of these norms was apparent in the resistance that met both the enfranchisement of African Americans and the efforts of women to gain the vote. Citizenship is always a matter of cultural and political negotiation; those negotiations, when it came to the cases of both women and Black men, took place in a context where white masculinity was the default.[4] "Good" citizens in this era were those who demonstrated supposedly manly virtues, who exercised power and self-control, and who were strong rather than weak. These virtues tended to be associated with the North, as victors in the war, rather than the South, and white Southerners fought against cultural perceptions of effeminacy as they struggled to regain control over their lives and governments. As during many historical moments of great change, the display of control over one's life and environment became an illusive cultural imperative and facilitated scapegoating of already marginalized citizens as causes of change and as ineligible for citizenship on the grounds of supposed weakness.

At a moment when the nation was trying to move forward, both parties were looking backward. Republicans, invested in their glorious past as opponents of slavery and victors in the Civil War, continued to rely on those themes. Democrats looked even further back, to the days of their past glory when Andrew Jackson took on the National Bank and spoke for a kind of rural populism. Nostalgic appeals often lead to elections dedicated to preventing rather than managing change, and under such circumstances, the blame for unwanted change falls on those least advantaged by the status quo and perceived as fomenting that change, the kind of despicable discourse that characterizes deplorable elections.

RACE, REBELLION, AND RECONSTRUCTION

The 1876 election is often considered the last contest of the Civil War, and the war and its consequences loomed over the entire election in several important ways. First, there was the question of lingering sectional division. The aftermath of the war left white Southerners bitter, exhausted, and impoverished. They responded by attaching themselves fervently to the ideology of the "Lost Cause" and to sectionalism more generally.[5] As part of this attachment, white Southerners continued to resist efforts at incorporating African Americans into the polity and insisted on maintaining the structures of white supremacy. The more they resisted, the more Northerners despised them. At the same time, Northern will to continue efforts at Reconstruction waned in the face of that resistance; committed to freeing the slaves, Northerners were much less committed to protecting the civil rights of the newly freed.

The second important element of the 1876 election, then, was Reconstruction itself. Reconstruction began as an ambitious effort to reengineer the political economy of the South and to instantiate a new regime based on something that looked like racial equality. It was both a political and an economic matter, aimed at changing the way labor in the South was organized.[6] Given the endemic racism and commitment to white supremacy, it is not surprising that it did not have a greater effect; it is notable that any such effort was made at all.

Reconstruction passed through several phases in the years following the Civil War but was marked by a diminishing commitment to changing the political culture and economic structures of the South. The questions animating Reconstruction had to do with the place African Americans would hold in the politics and economy of the South. On one end stood the Radical Republicans, who sought equality for the newly freed slaves. As Charles Sumner (R-MA) put it, "Ceasing to be a slave, the former victim has become not only a man, but a citizen, admitted alike within the pale of humanity and within the pale of citizenship. As a man he is entitled to all the rights of man, and as a citizen he becomes a member of our common household with equality as the pervading law."[7] The idea of including African Americans on an equal footing in a "common household" was abhorrent to the nation's white supremacists. They stood on the other end of the continuum, seeking, through whatever means necessary, to deny freed men and women their constitutional and human rights.

As Reconstruction worked its way through congressional and presidential forms, laws and policies designed to provide and protect those rights were all too often administered in ways that contravened those intentions. In general, both the debates over these laws and the policies themselves were premised on firmly entrenched notions of Black inferiority. For example, the Bureau of Refugees, Freedmen, and Abandoned Land, normally called simply the "Freedmen's Bureau," was established in 1865 under the Department of War, with a mission of helping those newly freed from slavery. The Freedmen's Bureau was woefully underfunded, and its programs were, more often than not, restricted.[8] Oliver Howard (who later founded Howard University) ran the bureau, and he tried to provide African Americans with the requisite skills for life in this era, but Southern resistance to African American education was as strong as resistance to enfranchisement. Having established the bureau, Congress seemed unwilling to allow it to fulfill its mandate and cut back both its mission and its funding.[9]

Congress was not alone in curtailing the capacity of the federal government to challenge the political and economic importance of white supremacy. Decisions made by the US Supreme Court in the *Slaughterhouse Cases* (1873) and later in *Santa Clara County v. Southern Pacific Railroad Company* (1886) mitigated the power of the Fourteenth Amendment and provided corporations with more rights than they accorded to African Americans.[10]

On the local level, states passed a series of Black Codes, designed to curtail the exercise of rights and especially aimed at locking African Americans to specific places, limiting their ability to negotiate their labor and sinking them deeply into debt.[11] Culturally, claims of Black inferiority were supported by the new theories of social Darwinism and by scientific racism more generally.

Black rights were surely at stake. But Republicans also saw in the South the potential to profit, both financially and politically, from a reorganized South. They took power in ways that were both democratic and autocratic.[12] Seeing the freedmen as political assets, they did not necessarily accord them full representation politically or economically. But any gains made by African Americans were too many gains for Southerners steeped in a culture of white supremacy, and white Southerners resisted, often violently. As that resistance continued, the less support there was in the North for sustained efforts in the South.[13]

Another important element of the context leading up to the 1876 election is the fact of Southern resistance to efforts at changing the politics, economy, or culture of the South. That resistance came in a variety of forms, the most visible of which was the creation of the Ku Klux Klan. This first iteration of the Klan traces its origin to the end of the Civil War, when six Confederate veterans founded it as a fraternal organization. It quickly morphed, however, into a series of locally based terrorist cells, dedicated to the preservation of white supremacy and the suppression of African American civil and economic rights.[14] Klan violence was localized and often ad hoc. It revealed a dedication to white supremacy, the willingness to use force to protect its hierarchies, and the weakness of Reconstruction governments to combat it or to keep citizens safe in the face of it.[15] The KKK sought to undermine, through violence and threats of violence, electoral processes and the commitment to democracy that underpin them.[16]

Two examples illuminate the workings of violent white supremacy during these years. In 1873, during the "Colfax Massacre" in Colfax, Louisiana, some two hundred whites, including members of the KKK, "shot, bayoneted, and burned to death 'at least 105 African Americans.'"[17] Of the ninety-eight white leaders, only nine were even arrested. While scores of courageous African Americans testified, the jury, after many weeks' deliberation, convicted precisely one person and found itself unable to reach verdicts on the others. The Republican government proved itself powerless to either protect the Black citizens of Colfax or to provide justice for them. A year later, white Democrats in Mississippi impeached and removed the state's African American lieutenant governor and filed impeachment charges against the state's governor, who fled the state.[18] President Ulysses S. Grant did nothing because he was afraid any action would cost the Republicans the governorship of Ohio and endanger Republican chances in the upcoming presidential election.[19] As these examples—and the many more like them—illustrate, the period between slavery and Jim Crow was, to say the least, unstable. There were certain possibilities for the extension of civil and economic rights, but there was also violent resistance to them. It was, in C. Vann Woodward's words, "a time of experiment, testing, and uncertainty—quite different from the time of repression and rigid uniformity that was to come toward the end of the century. Alternatives were still open and real choices had to be made."[20] The choices that were made were all too often ones that limited rather than extended the rights of freed women and men.

The politics of white supremacy were thus very much at issue during the 1870s. As ever, those politics extended into economics as well, the fourth important element of the political context. The protection of white labor had been very much part of at least some arguments in favor of abolition, and as the Gilded Age began and Black agricultural labor continued to be the subject of the harshest kind of repression in the South, industrial labor faced its own kind of repression in the rest of the country. The Knights of Labor was founded in 1869, signaling the beginning of labor organizing on its own behalf. Strikes, some of them violent, many of them violently opposed, were soon to follow.[21]

With developing labor issues also came questions of how to manage the economy, and one of the biggest issues of the era revolved around how the nation's currency would be managed. "Greenbackers," usually members of the debtor class, wanted to see the country continue to rely largely on paper currency, or "greenbacks," backed solely by the US government. Such currency was not tied to the value of gold or silver, and its fluctuating value favored farmers and made debts easier to pay. Greenbackers were opposed by those in the creditor class, who wanted to see the country return to a system of limited paper money tied to the value of bullion—variously gold or silver. Both parties faced internal conflicts over this issue, which demanded a fair amount of finesse in party platforms and throughout the campaign.

The money issue was complicated by the fact that the West, home to many Greenbackers, was increasingly becoming a site of national attention. Many people, dislocated by the war, began to move west, seeking land and opportunity. These they sometimes found. But that finding came at a cost. As indigenous nations were pushed further west by non-Indian settlement, they encroached on land held by other nations, increasing intratribal conflicts even as the conflicts between various nations and the federal government escalated.[22] While such conflicts had been a constant feature of US history since the 1600s, the period between the Civil War and the Massacre at Wounded Knee, South Dakota, in 1890 saw them move across a vast terrain with equally sweeping consequences. Even as the 1876 election began, Colonel George Armstrong Custer was wending his way toward the Greasy Grass (Little Big Horn); he would die there just weeks before Election Day.

This was a lot to manage, and President Grant, whose administration is yet another element of the 1876 election's political context, is widely considered to have done a fairly poor job of such management.[23] Grant did what he could regarding Reconstruction but lacking Northern support in general and congressional support in particular he was limiting federal efforts in the South well before the election. His responses to the sporadic outbreaks of violence were also limited and largely ineffectual. At least one of his problems was that the material resources needed to actually take control of the South far exceeded the political will or constitutional authority to accomplish that goal.

He had other problems too. His administration was plagued by scandal—first there were revelations about illegal contract manipulations by the Union Pacific Railroad known as the Crédit Mobilier scandal; while those occurred under the Johnson administration, Grant couldn't escape the taint.[24] Worse, his administration was directly responsible for the illegalities of the notorious "Whisky Ring," a conspiracy launched by members of the Grant administration to rob the government of excise tax. The federal government was rotten with corruption; Republicans had been in power for sixteen years and wielded that power largely through intricate systems of patronage. Those inside the system were expected to pay for the privilege of having a federal job, and the party routinely collected campaign funds from federal employees. Those workers were expected to serve both their partisan masters and the special interests who operated through them. The civil service was run by parties at the behest of those interests, and the federal government served the "public interest" only at the margins. The 1876 election was the last gasp of the Civil War and the first breath of the Gilded Age, awash in old animosities and developing allegiances that would control the country from the nation's centennial into the new century.

In short, the most important problem facing the nation as it reeled into the 1876 election was race, but racial issues implicated all kinds of other issues. The question of whether and how to protect the rights of seven hundred thousand newly freed people also involved questions of what the postwar economy would look like, how both agricultural and industrial labor would be organized, what was to be the role of women in the aftermath of a war fought on the basis of equality, how to reincorporate the South into the nation, and what to do about the indigenous people in the West and the land they occupied. Race and the rights of freed men and women became synecdoches for the questions of how the nation was to be politically, economically, and socially constructed. And upon the heads of African Americans was laid the burden of all the anxieties and tensions that accompanied those questions.

The short version of the 1876 election is that Republican Rutherford B. Hayes faced off against Democrat Samuel Tilden in an election characterized by fraud and, in some places, violence. Hayes lost the popular vote but, through the machinations of a New York party official, managed to be declared the victor in the press. The legal outcome depended on vote counts in several disputed states and these counts depended on the rules set for litigating those disputes. After months of wrangling, it was widely believed that a "corrupt bargain" was struck, whereby Hayes won the presidency and agreed to withdraw the remaining federal troops from the South, thus ending Reconstruction. It was one of the closest elections in years and was characterized by memories of treason and accusations of corruption, most of it generated by the Republicans. The election tainted Hayes's presidency and undermined public faith in the integrity of the electoral system. Despicable discourse, exclusionary and antidemocratic, circulated widely, marking 1876 as "the most degrading election in the history of the republic."[25]

Managing the Nominations

Stable political systems manage nominations in a fairly routine manner. In the 1870s, that process included many state conventions, each of which sent delegations to the national nominating conventions. Those delegations were either free to vote as they pleased or were "instructed" by their state conventions to vote a certain way. It was common for delegations to nominate "favorite son" candidates on the first ballot, and then to negotiate their votes for other candidates in exchange for planks protecting that state's interests in the party platform. This process was governed by elites and was reasonably predictable underneath the surface chaos. But in 1876 both parties were riven by sharp internal conflicts among elites leading the Republicans to choose a compromise candidate and leaving the Democrats with a candidate many in their party supported only tepidly.

Convening in the Queen City: The Republicans in Cincinnati

The Republicans met at a moment when party imperatives were beginning to shift away from those associated with the war and toward those we now associate with the Gilded Age. As a result of that shift, the party's dominance over national politics was questioned and their electoral logic centered on the issue of how to maintain that dominance. As historian Keith Polakoff put it:

> Most Republicans no longer supported Radical Reconstruction. The Republican governments in the South had been weak and sometimes corrupt. Many of them had already passed into history. The wartime tariff and the greenback currency, on the other hand, were still very much in evidence; still a source of extreme discomfort to many eastern Republicans. The Grant administration itself, repeatedly rocked by revelations of corruption in high official places, had become a subject of enduring controversy. All of these tensions within the party were aggravated when a severe economic recession in 1873 brought in its wake a dramatic Democratic

> victory in the congressional elections a year later. The organization's ability to preserve its ascendancy within the national government was suddenly at stake.[26]

The Republicans had been governing since 1860. For much of that time the South had been excluded from participating. Once the war ended, restrictions on the Southern white vote continued to operate. But by 1876 most former Confederate white men were able to vote; it was unlikely in the extreme that they would vote for Republicans. The white Republicans who did exist in the South were either newly arrived (known to locals as "Carpetbaggers") or Union men ("Scalawags"). They worked with African American Republicans to restructure the institutional politics of the South, with varying degrees of short-term success. These governments were usually weak and sometimes corrupt. Without the support of the federal government, they were doomed, and as efforts at Reconstruction waned, those governments began to fall back into Democratic control, endangering the Republican Party's chances for success in the national election.

That success was further endangered by the corruption of the Grant administration and by the growing controversy over currency. Consequently, Republicans had to find a reform-minded candidate, sound on party doctrine, and untainted by the pervasive corruption of the Grant administration. Going into election season, Republican reformers didn't have a specific candidate in mind, but they knew that they didn't want Maine congressman James G. Blaine, who was tainted by scandal having to do with the Union Pacific railroad. Sadly for reformists, Blaine continued to be one of the frontrunners for the nomination.

The nomination task was complicated by the fact that there was a series of nomination conventions in the states, which produced delegates that were committed, in varying degrees, to a number of candidates.[27] These processes were importantly democratic in that they encouraged a great deal of participation. But they were also importantly undemocratic in that immigrants and the poor were often at the mercy of urban machines. In 1876, several of these conventions on both sides of the partisan aisle led to "uninstructed" delegations, which meant that the nominations were pretty much up for grabs going into the national nominating conventions. This level of uncertainty is one of the flags indicating the potential for a deplorable election—strong political systems tend to yield predictable candidacies and the parties have little difficulty uniting behind them. This was not the case in 1876.

Making things even more difficult, amid all the state conventions there were a number of other conventions as well. Each had their own views about the nominations, and each, in their own ways, served notice to the Republicans that their national dominance was being threatened by the potential for splinter parties. Members of the Greenback Party met in Indiana, for instance, in an assembly the *New York Times* called both "communistic" and a "farce."[28] According to the *Times*, the convention was sparsely attended and favored policies that were so far left as to be outside the pale of US politics. The Greenback Party reveals the extent to which economic dislocations were an important subtext to the election. Farmers and debtors were suffering and feeling displaced. Their anxiety and anger were in search of an outlet.

A few months after the Greenbackers convened, a group of African Americans met in Nashville, reaffirmed their allegiance to the Republican Party, and passed resolutions disavowing "any desire to cherish ill-feeling toward the old slave-owning elements of the South, but extend[ing] the olive branch to them and ask[ing] them to protect the colored people against mobs, assassinations, outrages, and violence."[29] Even the allegiance of at least some African Americans to the Republican Party was wavering in the face of that party's inability to protect them from the violence spinning out of the South.

Finally, just prior to the Republican National Convention, the Republican Reform Club, a sort of precursor to the Mugwumps and Progressives, met. Their preferred candidate was Benjamin H. Bristow, who attained his reputation through breaking up the "Whisky Ring," but other candidates, including Hayes, were also "received favorably."[30] Reformers prepared an address to the Convention, which read in part:

> We believe that the people wish to keep the Republican Party in power only upon condition that a new Federal administration shall fulfill the promises which were given by the Republican National Convention of 1872. Without pausing to argue whether they do

> demand something more, certainly they will insist upon nothing less. One of these promises committed the Republican Party to a speedy resumption of specie payments; and another committed it to a thorough reform of the civil service. But the only measure that has been enacted toward fulfilling the first promise is a statute which pledges the honor of the nation to redeem its paper currency with specie on the first of January, 1879; and the second promise, after some beneficent experiments, has been openly, willfully, and totally broken by Congress and the President.[31]

Like the African Americans who met in Nashville, white reformers were willing to stick with the Republicans—under certain conditions. But the party was being put on notice by important constituencies that if it couldn't protect its members, and if it didn't fulfill its promises, that allegiance could find itself shifting to a third party. Remember, the presence of small parties and unincorporated groups are themselves an indication of political weaknesses in the major parties and the potential for a less stable political environment.

That any shift in allegiance would be to a third party and not the Democrats was clear; Greenbackers might move to the Democrats if they could be satisfied on the currency question, but neither African Americans nor reformers were likely to trust the Democrats. Reformers wrote:

> We believe that a great majority of the people deeply and justly distrust the motives which animate the Democratic Party and the influences which guide it; that they are not reasonably hopeful of reform at its hands, and that they always will be reluctant to confide the Federal Government to any party which is controlled by men who assailed the Union themselves or sympathized with its assailants. Nor is this distrust inconsistent with fraternal feeling to our fellow citizens who were recently in rebellion. But it is neither honest nor prudent to speculate upon imputation of disloyalty for Republican success.[32]

That is, the reformers had no particular reason to trust the Democrats, but they wanted to see a campaign run on the current issues facing the country, not on "imputations for disloyalty"—imputations that they themselves made. Even those who deplored the use of the past in the present election were trapped by that past, so deep were the scars left by the war.

Reformers, though, were wavering in their allegiance to the Republicans—they wanted to see currency restored to the gold standard, and they wanted civil service reform. They wanted the violence in the South to stop. If Republicans couldn't be trusted to provide these outcomes, they would look elsewhere (as they soon would; the Mugwumps defected from the Republicans in 1884, helping to elect Grover Cleveland, and the Progressive Party formed in 1912). These kinds of arguments, from constituencies as diverse as the Republican reformers and Greenbackers, indicate the degree to which the current party system was becoming unstable. In the midst of such instability, despicable discourse becomes more likely as committed partisans make increasingly fraught arguments and demand increasingly strict loyalty to increasingly weak parties.

This phenomenon can be seen through the candidacy of Speaker of the House James G. Blaine (R-ME). Blaine supported the franchise for African Americans but stopped well short of supporting many other initiatives associated with Radical Republicans. Blaine was able, popular, and the clear frontrunner for the nomination. Or he was, until a scandal broke. Blaine had previously been the subject of some whispers of scandal—it was widely believed that he had sold some bonds that later proved to be essentially worthless to a railroad—the bonds thus acting as a screen for what was actually a bribe. The rumors reached a high enough pitch to warrant a congressional investigation. That investigation appeared to be going in Blaine's favor until a clerk named James Mulligan claimed to have letters from Blaine to a business associate named Warren Fisher, which proved the accusations true. Blaine met with Mulligan and was either given (as he claimed) or stole (as Mulligan asserted) the letters in question. Blaine refused to give the "Mulligan letters" to Congress, and public opinion turned against him. He responded by loudly proclaiming his innocence on the House floor, accused the Democrats of launching an unwarranted partisan attack on his good name, read carefully selected passages from the letters that seemed to prove his innocence, and got the chair of the investigatory committee to apologize. While it appeared that his candidacy was perhaps saved, he then fainted on the church steps one Sunday morning, generating some sympathy for the events having affected his health, some suspicion that he had fainted in order to obtain that sympathy, and some fear that his health was no longer strong enough to allow him to serve as president.[33]

Although seriously damaged by these events, by the time the Republican convention opened, Blaine was still the frontrunner. He was opposed, in every possible sense of the word, by Roscoe Conkling, one of New York's senators. Famed orator and agnostic Robert Ingersoll nominated Blaine in what is widely considered to be among the highlights of the convention and one of the better nomination speeches in history. In it, he laid out the logic governing the Republican nomination. Republicans, Ingersoll argued, demand "a man of intellect, a man of integrity, a man of well-known and approved political opinion. They demand a statesman. They demand a reformer."[34] Republicans were full of demands according to Ingersoll, and they all amounted to a demand for James G. Blaine: "Our country, crowned with the vast and marvelous achievements of its first century asks for a man worthy of its past—prophetic of her future; asks for a man who has the audacity of genius; asks for a man who is the grandest combination of heart, conscience, and brains beneath the flag." In this passage Ingersoll was relying both on the Republican connection to patriotism and an appeal to expertise—Ingersoll argued that Republicans possessed men of intelligence and talent, men who could be trusted to carry the nation forward.

But curiously, the nation's demands, and the imagery used to convey them, were all backward looking. Ingersoll, for instance, famously referred to Blaine as "an armed warrior . . . a plumed knight." He concluded his brief address by arguing that "in the name of the great Republic, the only republic that ever existed upon this earth; in the name of all her defenders and of all her supporters; in the name of all her soldiers living; in the name of all her soldiers who died upon the field of battle; and in the name of those who perished in the skeleton clutch of famine at Andersonville and Libby, whose sufferings he so eloquently remembers, Illinois nominates for the next president of this country, that prince of parliamentarism, that leader of leaders—James G. Blaine." Here Ingersoll relied on the same themes that had been winning elections for the Republicans for a decade. He lauded the Union; he reminded voters that the South had caused a bloody Civil War, the effects of which were still being felt; and he did so in archaic imagery, depicting "armed warriors" and "plumed knights." It depended on the past, both in content and in imagery, and offered startling little for the future. This is not despicable discourse. It doesn't delegitimate, it doesn't exclude. But its dependence on nostalgia provides an indication that there is potential at this moment for such discourse.

The Republicans' immediate future held very little for Blaine.[35] Blaine and Conkling had a history of antagonism; their rivalry split the convention and opened the door for the eventual nominee, Rutherford B. Hayes. Hayes was the perfect compromise candidate. He had a history of siding with Radicals but as a Republican governor of Ohio with a Democratic legislature, he moved more to the center. As he ran for reelection as governor, he grounded that campaign not in big national issues but in the more local issues of religion in the schools where his strong anti-Catholicism helped him. It didn't hurt that the Republicans had decided to meet on Hayes's home turf, in Cincinnati.[36] The *New York Times* summarized the new nominee in exactly the terms that won him the nomination, writing, "It is admitted that he has no positive merit as a nominee, but it is asserted that it is a negative which Republicans want this year; if a great deal cannot be said in favor of Hayes as a presidential candidate, nothing whatever can be said against him, either as a private citizen or as a public man."[37] Hayes had nothing going for him except that he had nothing going against him.

Frederick Douglass's speech to the convention was equally revealing of the tenor of the times. He said, "You have emancipated us. I thank you for it. You have enfranchised us, and I thank you for it. But what is your emancipation—what is your enfranchisement? What does it all amount to, if the black man, after having been made free by the letter of your law, is unable to exercise that freedom; and after having been freed from the slaveholder's lash, he is to be subject to slaveholder's shot gun?"[38] Like the African Americans who met in conference in Nashville earlier that spring, Douglass here was concerned less with the past than with the present and the future and he was getting very few answers about whether those would be managed in a way that provided for the security and safety of African Americans.

The need for "preservation" rather than progress was underlined by Theodore M. Pomeroy (R-NY). "The late war," he asserted, "was not a mere prize-fight for national supremacy. It was the outgrowth of the conflict of irreconcilable moral, social, and political forces. Democracy had its lot with the moral, social, and political forces of the cause which was lost; the Republican Party with those that triumphed and survived. The preservation of the results of that victory devolves upon us now."[39] The point was to preserve; such preservation was, he declared, the "mission of the manhood of the Republican Party." This speech interestingly combined the need to prevent the ascension of the South to national office, the need to protect Northern power, and the association of both of those with gendered tropes. The North didn't just have a mission, it had a "manly mission," one in which the masculinity of the Republicans was at stake. This reveals just how fraught the moment was—and how norms of masculinity get used as lenses through which such moments are understood. It also, of course, revealed the Republican strategy for the upcoming election, one that would be based in reminders of the South's rebellion and defeat.

That strategy was purveyed by all the convention speakers and by the newspapers associated with the Republican Party. One of the defining elements of contexts that facilitate deplorable elections is the rise of new kinds of media, which unsettle the communicative environment. In this case, the newspapers were strongly partisan; they adopted and circulated the party line. The *New York Times*, for example, stressed the unity of the Republicans, noting in particular that those who didn't earn the nomination accepted that outcome with good grace and in a public display of "manliness."[40] According to the *Times*, unlike the South, even in defeat, Northerners and Republicans retained their manly virtue. Hayes's nomination was evidence of Republican patriotism-as-masculinity in the view of the *Times*, which emphasized his army career, the wounds he received in the recent war, and his bravery in general.[41]

Other outlets, similarly partisan, were similarly fulsome in their praise. Vermont's *Burlington Free Press* wrote, "The Cincinnati Convention has fairly justified the confidence reposed in it. It has given the party a pure, strong and safe ticket," and its *Rutland Herald* called the nominations "excellent." New York's *Troy Times* opined, "The ticket, as it stands, may be considered invincible." The *Chicago Post*, somewhat less enthusiastically, argued that "the ticket is "conspicuously judicious." The *Philadelphia North American* was pleased with the news of the nomination, writing, "The nomination of Rutherford B. Hayes is one of which the Republican Party will never be ashamed."[42] These reports reflected two things: First, the kind of reporting we see in this election begins to reveal an interest in what we now call "horse-race coverage," or the tendency of the media to read politics through the frame of who is "winning" and who is "losing" in any given election or policy debate. Horse-race coverage fixates on the politics of a given policy more than on its substance. The emphasis in these reports is on the "strong and safe" nature of the ticket, on its supposed invincibility, not on the party's platform. It is an indication of where the press as an institution is headed—they are increasingly mass-market commodities, and selling papers to large numbers of people is the prime goal. As news moves from an elite to a mass commodity, changes in the way political news is covered become increasingly evident. Second, and relatedly, Northern press reports were consistently full of fulsome praise for Hayes. One subhead, for a story on his character, for example, reads, "Not One Touch of Vanity."[43] The character of the candidates was becoming more important to the press than the policies for which that candidate stood. This interest isn't confined to the candidates alone, either—it is notable in this regard that the *Chicago Tribune* carried profiles of Hayes's wife and children.[44]

But policy did matter, and much of the policy espoused by the Republicans was noxious. Hayes had won reelection as Ohio governor at least in part because of his focus on the "school issue," the need for Ohio schools to be kept free of the "taint" of Catholicism. He planned to rely on similar bigotry to help him gain the White House. "The day after his nomination he wrote of the approaching contest: 'The interesting point is *to rebuke the Democracy by a defeat for subserviency to Roman Catholic demands*.' It need not be thought that Hayes himself was necessarily a bigot; but he certainly intended to exploit the bigotry of others."[45] That he could count on this bigotry is not in question. It was also reflected in the party platform. A fairly routine example of its kind, the Republican platform had only one controversial plank: "It is the immediate duty of congress fully to investigate the effect of immigration and importation of Mongolians on the moral and material interests of the country."[46] While the passage of the infamous Chinese Exclusion Act, banning the immigration of Chinese workers, was still six years away, the Republicans were already acknowledging and beginning to rely upon growing anti-Chinese sentiment, adding racial to their already prominent religious exclusionary tendencies.

By the end of the Republican convention, several things were clear: their candidate was going to reflect their party ideology well and project an image of stolid worth; the party was going to finesse the question of corruption in its ranks by stressing Hayes's manly virtue; it was also going to stoke sectional animosity by waving "the bloody shirt," wallowing in memories of the war; and it was going to inflame other bigotries as well, making arguments about the nefarious nature of Catholics and "Mongolians," who were to be presented, as were Southerners, as threats to the Union and to a specific version of national identity. They were going to circulate despicable discourse.

Meet Me in St. Louis: The Democrats

The Democrats, practically destroyed by the Civil War, remained noticeably weak until the Panic of 1873 revived their fortunes. Their time in the political wilderness ensured that they lacked politicians of experience, making their choices among candidates somewhat easier than those facing the Republicans. They were, as a result, generally united around Samuel Tilden, who had built a reputation as a reformer by bringing down Tammany Hall's Boss Tweed. But Tilden had baggage of his own when it came to a national election. First, his battle with Tweed and Tammany created problems for him in his home state of New York, whose thirty-five electoral votes could well determine the victor.[47] A Northern Democrat, Tilden had once been a member of the Free Soil Party. Considering himself a Jeffersonian, he was a believer in states' rights but not an ardent defender of slavery. He supported the controversial Wilmot Proviso that would have banned slavery from the lands gained in the Mexican-American War and had generally taken positions indicating loyalty to the Union in the years before the war. But as a Democrat his loyalties were suspect throughout the war and to Republicans were still suspect a decade later.[48]

Democrats were tired of those suspicions, which became a powerful motive for intraparty unity. As historian Roy Morris Jr. described the emerging Democratic coalition:

> Northern Democrats, who had seen their patriotism and loyalty consistently impugned since the Civil War by Republican accusations of Copperheadism, wanted to strike back at their flag-waving

> accusers. Small farmers, shopkeepers, and humble working men and women, who had seen their life savings swallowed up by the Panic of 1873, wanted to lash out at the physical instruments of their suffering—the bankers, brokers, and financiers who controlled and exploited the nation's wealth behind a miserly bulwark of high tariffs, high taxes, and hard money. Southern Democrats, who had lost the flower of a generation on Civil War battlefields, and then returned home to find their state governments dominated by carpetbaggers, scalawags, and former slaves, wanted to reclaim their old way of life. And honest, hardworking Democrats on both sides of the old Mason-Dixon line, who had endured eight years of unparalleled corruption at the very seat of power, wanted simply to throw the rascals out—not as a function of political reform, but as an expression of personal disgust.[49]

Some Democrats were tired of accusations of disloyalty and wanted their view of the nation treated as equally acceptable as its opposing view. Some were motivated by economic anxiety, and others by fear that their cultural values were being lost to the illusion of progress. Others were motivated by racism. And some were motivated by a desire to root out corruption. Of course, these motives were not mutually exclusive but coexisted in a complex compendium of fears and aspirations.

Fears and aspirations, however, aren't a program. And while the Democrats didn't have a lot to argue over, argue they still did. The main site of dispute was not about policy but about personality, as Tildenites and Conkling supporters squared off both in and outside of the convention hall. The *New York Times*, no supporter of the Democrats, had this to say: "Thanks to Tammany and an unlimited supply of bad whisky, this has been one of the most exciting days that ever preceded a National Convention. In every sense it has been exciting, and in many disgraceful, not only to the Democratic Party, but to the nation, for it unfortunately happens that the Democrats are part of the nation. There has been unlimited drinking; there have been brawls, fisticuff encounters, and men crazed with liquor roaring themselves hoarse for and against Tilden in such a manner that nobody understood much of what they said."[50] The implicit argument, of course, was that the Democrats were nothing more than a group of brawling drunkards, unfit to govern the nation. They were, indeed, barely, and only "unfortunately," part of the nation themselves. There was implicit bigotry operating here as well, as it was generally the Tammany men who were accused of overindulging—and Tammany was associated with operating a big city machine, which of course meant the Irish and other immigrants.[51]

If Conkling supporters were depicted as drunks, Tildenites were figured as guilty of corruption. The *Times* argued, "That Tilden had the majority of the Convention was due solely to the fact that a great deal of time and perhaps some money had been expended in convincing the Democrats that he is inevitable."[52] Here, the Republicans, viewed through the lens of one of their more important newspapers, had clearly decided that they were going to meet charges of corruption in their ranks by reminding voters of Tilden's ethical problems: the *Times* asserted, "The tiger that has tasted blood never stops till he gets more, and there seems to be every probability that those who know of Mr. Tilden's liberality will continue to support him as long as there is any chance of their securing a part of the money which he gained in his numerous little railroad transactions. The stockholders of the Alton and Terre Haute Railroad Company have contributed not a little to the Tilden campaign in St. Louis."[53] Tilden was depicted here as a small man who engaged in "numerous little" acts of corruption. He relied on those acts to support his campaign, but even those were framed not as large but as "not a little." Size is ever associated with masculinity; Tilden was too small and insignificant to govern even as the exclusion of women from politics was naturalized. The Republicans thus styled the Democrats as too tainted for governance—one candidate was associated with the unsavory immigrant and lower classes and the other with the unsavory elements of the upper classes. Both were considered too ill-disciplined to govern. If they needed another disqualifying factor, they found it in the Democrats' Confederate past, which, of course, was treated as not actually past. The *Times* reported, "The Convention then adjourned until 2 P. M. and the band striking up 'Dixie,' the old rebellion air, it so stirred the Democratic heart that they had to repeat it."[54] Republicans, it seemed, were harping on the war because the Democrats were unwilling to concede defeat in any real sense and still clung to Confederate symbols and ideologies. They were thus a danger to the nation.

Tilden was finally nominated, and as the *Times* opined, "He was supported from the first by all the political wire-pullers and tricksters and by the railroad corporations and great monopolies of the country. They all recognized in him a kindred spirit and consequently they made him their candidate."[55] If the Democrats remained the party of the Confederacy, Tilden was the nominee of the special interests. To Republicans he represented both disunion and greed. He could not succeed on his own but needed the support of the railroad money and the "wire-pullers and tricksters." Dishonest himself, he depended on the dishonesty of others as well.

Lest one suspect that this kind of delegitimating and thus despicable discourse was all on the Republican side, it should be noted that Democrats were not shy about making claims about Republicans and their lack of fitness for high office during their convention. Representative Samuel S. Cox (D-OH), for instance, referred to the "profligacy, robbery, ringdom, and the rake-helly brood of ragged-rascaldom" that had been "loose in this country since the war."[56] He then added this bit of crowd-pleasing rhetoric:

> They say that because of their inordinate expenditures we will cut down the Army. Well maybe we might do without the Army after the November election. . . . They say we will break up the Navy. Well, what does our Navy do? Protect our commerce—commerce ruined by bad taxation and worse tariffs, out of existence [Applause]. I think the Navy might rest a little while. Good! But what else would we stop—the Indian Bureau? [Laughter and applause]. Spotted Tail and Crazy Horse, they might be let loose on the plains. Let them, if they would stop their raids, turn the border men loose and they would end these contractors' wars very soon [Applause]. But we might stop the internal revenue system a while. Well, I would like to make the crooked parties straight. [Applause].[57]

Here we have the kind of "red meat" often offered to nominating conventions. Cox implied that ending Army appropriations would be considered no bad thing by the Democrats; surely those in the South wouldn't miss the Army. He accused the Republicans of such dire financial mismanagement that the navy, too, whose job was not to protect the nation's borders but its commerce, "could rest a little while." More interestingly, he argued that the Indian Bureau, a famously corrupt agency, could be ended. Its main goal was apparently the prevention of Indian "raids" and could be better accomplished by letting the "border men" loose on Indian nations, with the presumption that those nations would not long survive, that the border men would do what Custer and the Army had failed to do. This was, of course, a fairly direct advocacy of genocide—in retaliation for the deaths of Custer and his men—an advocacy his audience rewarded with applause.[58]

Like the platform that attacked the Republicans "for corruption, extravagance, and lack of leadership,"[59] Cox's speech similarly implied that the Republicans should not be allowed to continue occupying the White House. They were committing the Army to the wrong places, occupying the South instead of pacifying the West; they were responsible for a weak economy; they were corrupt; and they needed to be replaced with the Democrats. Much of this is, of course, standard campaign rhetoric. But it becomes despicable discourse because of its willful erasure of the problems that continued in the South and its hearty embrace of the violence in the West. To ignore the homicidal violence of one region and encourage genocidal violence in another is hardly the stuff of a strong democracy. Republicans actively circulated despicable discourse. Democrats tacitly endorsed it. There is not much to admire on either side.

Into the General Election

As the two parties headed into the general election, there was agreement on the one side that the Democrats were treasonous and violent. They engaged in corruption when they could, and they lacked the appropriately "manly" character for leadership, falling prey instead to effeminacy, brawling, and drunkenness. There was agreement on the other side that the Republicans were a party dedicated to self-aggrandizement at the expense of the common people. Committed to a corrupt system, they lacked the ability to truly reunite the nation. Neither of these discourses offered a view of their opponents as legitimate contenders for the presidency. Both indicated that the fate of the Union was bound up in the destruction of their opponents. The general election, therefore, was conducted amid a welter of despicable discourse centering around suspicions concerning the patriotism of the disputants and fears about the consequences of losing the election. That discourse was almost entirely issued from the Republicans. Tilden and the Democrats tried to display the kinds of civility that the North seemed to demand. They made accusations of Republican corruption but, keenly aware of their own vulnerability in that quarter, did so with a relative lack of venom. Tilden's adherence to the political high ground did him little good. Republicans mounted a shrill defense of their years of depression and scandal. That defense rested on two pillars: the bloody shirt, which recalled the past, and fearmongering about the future should the Democrats win.

Waving the Bloody Shirt

Democrats may have been heartily tired of having their allegiance to the Union questioned, but Republicans had been winning national elections on that issue for years and were not likely to give it up easily. As a matter of policy, there were perhaps good reasons to prefer a Republican to a Democratic president. Certainly, however weak the Republican commitment to Reconstruction was, it was, for those advocating equal rights for African Americans, preferable to the Democratic commitment to abrogating those rights. But that wasn't the argument the Republicans made. Instead, as Hayes wrote, they were determined that "our main issue must be *it is not safe to allow the rebellion to come into power*."[60] This "issue," colloquially known as "waving the bloody shirt," or appeals by which Northerners were urged to "vote as they shot," was, first and last, not an actual issue but a distraction, a way of avoiding the actual issues facing the nation. Waving the bloody shirt allowed Republicans to avoid discussion of the Grant administration scandals and focus attention on the sins of the Democrats.

Once committed to this strategy, Republicans were unrelenting in its use. Robert Ingersoll, for instance, thundered, "At the time the Republican Party came into existence, slavery was not satisfied being local but endeavored to use its infamous leprosy, as it were, for pushing it into every territory of the United States. Recollect the condition of the country at the time. Boats went down the Mississippi River loaded with wives torn from their husbands, with children torn from the breasts of their mothers, while the same men who did this are now standing for Tilden and Reform [Great applause]."[61] Ingersoll here harkened back to the prewar Northern rhetoric, warning of the dangers inherent in the "slave power," adding to it the pathos of appeals to the destruction of families under the rule of that power. He asserted that nothing had really changed; the "same men" who perpetrated such villainy against enslaved families must be prevented from governing, or the disease they continued to carry, their "infamous leprosy," would infect the nation.

Ingersoll was not alone. New York's Stewart L. Woodford, for instance, said:

> I believe that the people, after full deliberation, will decide that, as in the old struggle for the arrest of slavery, and as in the following struggle for the suppression of treason, so now in the hour when pressing questions of finance and labor demand brave and wise settlement, the Republican Party may again be safely trusted. As in 1856 it had the humanity to resist slavery; as in 1860 it had the manhood to defy the threat of secession; as in 1861 to 1865 it had the courage to crush rebellion; so now it has the wisdom and nerve to meet the new questions that arise [Applause].[62]

Woodford deftly combined the themes of the Republican campaign here. The Republicans had been on the right side of history before; they had shown the requisite manliness in the face of great moral issues, and so they could be trusted to be appropriately manly now. Note the ways "manhood," "humanity, "courage," and "wisdom" are all conflated; they stand as markers of one another. To possess one of these traits is to possess them all. Lacking any one of them is to lack them all.

Samuel Tilden, of course, was not a Southerner and might be expected to be immune from any charges of disloyalty to the Union and its values. But he was a Democrat, and therefore potentially a "Copperhead"; his allegiances were and continued to be suspect. As New York senator Chauncy M. DePew put it shortly before Election Day:

> In 1860, Gov. [*sic*] Tilden published the ablest argument in [*sic*] behalf of the Calhoun doctrine of States Rights that I have ever read. In it he argued that this Government is not a Federal Union, but a Federative Agency; and that a State can snap the tie of federation as

> a nation would break a treaty. . . . When Samuel J. Tilden was arguing that this Republic was a federated agency Rutherford B. Hayes was offering his life to prove it be a federal Union! When Samuel J. Tilden was proving the Union soldier to be a trespasser, Rutherford B. Hayes was trespassing wherever an enemy of his country could be found! When Samuel J. Tilden, as a member of the Democratic National Convention in Chicago, was declaring the war a failure, Rutherford B. Hayes lay upon his back, shot almost to death with wounds, to prove the war an absolute success![63]

Elections are always about comparisons. In this case, DePew asserted that the choice facing the country was whether they wanted as president someone who argued against the Union or someone who fought for it. The emotional freight of this argument, placing one man away from battle and the other in the thick of it, supported the implicit claim that the superior president would be the one who had demonstrated his willingness to sacrifice for the nation.

The *Times* weighed in on this as well, initially arguing that Tilden didn't adequately support the Union during the war.[64] Later, the paper added heat to that claim, calling Tilden a "tool of the slave power" and an outright secessionist:

> In 1860, Mr. Tilden, who had for years been one of the most supple and pliant tools of the slave power, distinguished himself by extraordinary efforts to prevent the election of Mr. Lincoln. He attacked every idea and principle upon which the Republican Party was founded, as false in theory, as wrong in morals, and certain to be most disastrous in their results. He asserted the right of the slave-holder to take his human chattel into any of the Territories of the United States, and was preeminently the champion of that hideous system whose triumph in this country would have been the end of all liberty, of all humanity, of all progress, of all that characterizes a Christian civilization.[65]

After quoting from a letter authored by Tilden, the *Times* concluded, "There cannot in the whole of Calhoun's works be found a more concise and terse statement of the right of each State to secede at will from the Union." Tilden had advocated for the right of secession. He had opposed Lincoln and had defended slavery. His morals and his judgment were therefore questionable. He was not, therefore, suited to be president.

Republicans continued to wave the bloody shirt because it worked. Those who fought for the Union were unwilling to hand its government over to those who had seceded from it. Hayes wrote James G. Blaine, clearly enunciating the Republican strategy: "Our solid ground is a dread of a solid south, rebel rule, etc., etc. . . . it leads people away from 'hard times' which is our deadliest foe."[66] Hayes thus explicitly, if privately, acknowledged that the bloody shirt was employed as a distraction, taking national attention away from the fact of a faltering economy. It wasn't a serious issue; by questioning the patriotism of the opposition candidate without any evidence of disloyalty, this amounts to despicable discourse.

Dire Consequences

As in most deplorable elections, one of the main themes is a lack of respect for one's interlocutors. Opponents are not merely mistaken, they are evil, out to destroy the very fabric of democracy. Robert Ingersoll, for instance, depicted the Democrats in animalistic terms: "The Democratic Party, with the hungry, starving, eyes of wolf, has been looking in at the national Capitol and scratching at the doors of the White House for sixteen years [Laughter]. Occasionally, it has retired to some congenial eminence and lugubriously howled about the Constitution [Cheers and laughter]."[67] The Democrats were not worthy opponents, equally dedicated to national ideals and merely possessed of a different sense of how to reach toward those ideas. They were depicted here as the wolf at the door, slavering for power, which they would use for dishonest ends.

Republicans argued that Southerners in general and Tilden in particular lacked principle. The *Times* asked, "What have Mr. Tilden and Mr. Hendricks in common so far as their professions or associations go? Why should they be on the same ticket, except for the purpose of deceiving each other's followers?"[68] It is possible, if not probable, that the logic of putting two men with some disagreements on the same ticket was indeed to paper over some fissures within the party and hold the Democratic coalition together. This is, in fact, one of the basic functions of a presidential / vice presidential ticket: to help build an electoral coalition. But here the *Times* portrayed this not as competence at the routine business of politics but as deception.

According to Republicans, Democrats were not only deceptive but dangerously violent. One piece of Republican propaganda, purporting to be a Democratic circular, announced a "CARNIVAL OF BLOOD! Republicans to be Massacred at the Polls!" as part of "Tilden's Desperate Plan to Carry a Solid South!"[69] The circular, claiming to be a secret document meant only for Democratic eyes, announced a plan to win the election by force of arms. Democrats were encouraged to "evade Grant's minions as much as you can, but let your unerring bullets pierce the breasts of ravenous carpet-baggers and scallawags [*sic*]." This circular offered "proof" that the Democrats, guilty of having taken up arms against the United States after one electoral defeat, couldn't be trusted not to do so again. As Ingersoll argued, "There are plenty of men in the South who fought against the Government and who were satisfied with the arbitration of the war, and who laid down their arms and are Union men today. I want the Government to protect them too [Applause]. As a general rule, however, the population of the South is turbulent, and the best men cannot control it, and men are shot down for opinion's sake. It ought to be stopped."[70] Ingersoll argued that too many Southerners, and too many Democrats, remained loyal not to the Union but to the slave power. They were "turbulent" and would erupt into violence in its defense, and they would actively work against the national interest—in secret, as the circular claimed, or in the open, as Ingersoll and others argued.

The country needed stability amid the welter of change and, according to Republicans, Hayes was the more stable candidate. Jonathan Norcross of Georgia, for example, argued that the best interests of the nation and even of the South would be best served by Hayes's election: "All matters on the South will be quieted down. Under his administration, capital and immigration will flow to the South to help build up our waste places. Under him we shall know precisely what to expect. We shall know that there shall be no violent changes to the policy of the Government; there will be no working up of another rebellion, or something else equally bad and dangerous to our interests. But let Samuel J. Tilden be elected and the Democratic Party installed in power then fear and trembling will take possession of every man."[71]

That "fear and trembling" was largely due to the behavior of Democrats as a party. But Tilden as a candidate also came in for more than his fair share of despicable discourse. The *Chicago Tribune*, for instance, wrote of Tilden that he was "weazoned, and shrimpled, and meanly cute. There is nothing about the man that is large, big, generous, solid, inspiring, powerful, or awakening. He's a small, lazy, odorous, ungainly, trickling stream, winding along and among the weeds that have grown up a long the track of a great river, long since dried up. He is as cold as 32 below zero. O that face!—that left eye!—that mouth!"[72] Note here that the imputations of size and masculinity are obvious. Tilden was being depicted as dangerously effeminate; even his sexuality was suspect. Cartoonist Thomas Nast often depicted him in a dress. The Democrats as a party suffered in the Republican portrayal from an excess of masculinity—they were prone to violence and thus couldn't be trusted. Their candidate on the other hand, suffered from a deficit of masculinity—he had been a tool of the slave power, and was now a tool of the party. He didn't have the manly virtues required for democratic governance.

This gendered language both denigrated Tilden as too effeminate for national leadership and denigrated women as entirely unsuited for political participation as well. In searching for ways to argue against a white male candidate, opponents found rhetorical resources in descriptions of those already excluded. This justified and naturalized the exclusion of women from politics. Antidemocratic discourses often operate in this kind of circular fashion, reinforcing existing exclusions and using those exclusions as warrants to condemn others.

There were plenty of important issues in 1876. The question of how to incorporate formerly enslaved people and other African Americans into the polity loomed large. So did the question of how to manage the nation's finances and its currency. Equally important were questions of modernization and how to develop the nation's infrastructure. The role of corporations like the railroads was very much at issue and played an important, if implicit, role in the election. But like the role of the railroads, other important issues went equally undiscussed as the campaign itself was mired in the despicable discourses centering on corruption, treason, and delegitimating the opposition. Republican attacks were instrumental in keeping the election as close as it was. They continued their efforts after the election was over.

The Election and Its Aftermath

The election itself was almost unbearably close. On Election Day, eight and a half million voters went to the polls; at least two million more people than had voted four years earlier. At the end of the day, Democrats held seventeen states and 184 electoral votes; Republicans held eighteen states and 166 electoral votes. Three states (Florida, Louisiana, and South Carolina), with a combined total of nineteen electoral votes were undecided. In every one of those states, Republican governors held office. There was evidence of fraud in all of the disputed states. In South Carolina, in fact, more adult males appeared to have voted than actually lived in the state.[73] While most historians agree that Hayes probably won in South Carolina and Louisiana, they also agree that Tilden most likely won both the popular vote and Florida, giving him 188 electoral votes to Hayes's 181, and earning him the presidency.

But Republican actions prevented any such conclusion. Upon hearing how close the election returns were in those states, Republicans William Chandler of New Hampshire and John C. Reid, the managing editor of the *New York Times*, contacted Republican officials in contested states and told them to hold their states for Hayes. His telegraph to those officials read, "With your state sure for Hayes, he is elected. Hold your state."[74] Republican officials in South Carolina, Louisiana, Florida, and Oregon were thus each convinced that Hayes's election depended upon them alone. They acted accordingly, and in the party's interest rather than in the national interest.

As the disputes wore on, the *Times* became impatient and angry at what the editors there understood as Democratic intransigence:

> We regret to observe in Democratic papers generally threats of refusal to submit to a decision which should declare Rutherford B. Hayes elected president. The line of reasoning adopted is this—The three disputed States in the South were claimed for Tilden hence they should be counted for Tilden. The Returning Boards in the three states are Republican, hence they are composed of dishonest scoundrels. It is the intent of the Returning Board to perpetrate gross frauds in the interest of Hayes, hence a return giving these states to Hayes must be fraudulent. "The people will

> not submit." Mr. Hayes has not been legally elected. He shall not be inaugurated. If the Republicans persist in inaugurating him, "war will follow." Such is the line of talk adopted by Democratic journals generally. . . . There were threats in 1860 that Mr. Lincoln should not be inaugurated. There were threats at the same time that the South should not be "coerced" into the Union. We all know what came of those threats.[75]

The *Times* had things a little backward. It was Republicans who were busy rigging the election—the *Times* was practicing a kind of proactive defense, attacking the Democrats for behavior in which they were engaged. Yet the threats of violence and war were real, and so was the possibility that the Union could not survive this conflict.

Resolving the electoral vote took months and occurred amid justified accusations of fraud, bribery, threats, and irregular practices of all kinds.[76] Finally, it all came down to Florida. As one summary of the events has it: "The first vote tallies showed Hayes the victor by just 43 votes, but a recount had Tilden victorious by 94 votes. The Republican-controlled returning board disallowed enough ballots to deliver the state to Hayes by about 1,000 votes, and this action, as it had in Louisiana and South Carolina, had the added effect of overturning the gubernatorial result and awarding the office to the Republican candidate. Further complicating the situation, the Florida Supreme Court threw out these results and awarded the governorship to Democrat George Franklin Drew, who promptly announced that Tilden, not Hayes, had won Florida."[77] There was no easy way out of the mess thus created, and now more than the presidency was at stake because as votes got disallowed the consequences rippled down the ballot to state offices.

The parties in Congress agreed to appoint a joint commission to litigate the various disputes. Democrats argued justice would be better served by investigating what happened within each state. Republicans argued that any such investigation violated the Constitution and the right of individual states to determine their own electors. Both sides had reasonable arguments to make—Democrats believed that there had been sufficient skullduggery to warrant an investigation of the entire electoral process. Republicans argued that the commission had no such power, and, somewhat ironically, that they needed to respect the rights of the states.

The deliberations of the joint commission took months, during which the nation was convulsed in a partisan frenzy.[78] The election was finally brought to a close in a conference held, ironically enough, in the Wormley Hotel, owned by an African American whose property was the site of a deal that would materially harm African Americans. On February 26, 1877, a group of Hayes's intimates met there with representatives of Southern interests. Those meetings eventually led to an agreement that Republicans would abandon their claims to establish governments in South Carolina and Louisiana, ceding those states to Democrats, and the Democrats in turn would abandon Tilden's claim to the presidency. In other words, Democrats ended their claim to the presidency in exchange for renewed control over Southern state governments. The Republicans abrogated their responsibilities to African Americans in the South and ceased their efforts at party building there in exchange for a peaceful ascension to the presidency. Republicans retained control, such as it was, of the federal government, and the Democrats hunkered down in defense of their capacity to control their local and state governments. That deal, immediately castigated as a "corrupt bargain," was in many ways not much more than a recognition of the actual state of affairs. Northerners had already conceded that Reconstruction was essentially dead; the price of the presidency was merely making that fact publicly indisputable. But the symbolism of the conference and its contribution to resolving the crisis were unmistakable.

The consequences of this bargain, whether it was corrupt or not, were grave and far-reaching. The gravest and most far-reaching of these consequences was borne by African Americans, for the end of Reconstruction meant the immediate institutionalization of racial segregation and abuse of African Americans in the South. There were no Republican governments left below the old Mason-Dixon line, the army was gone, and African Americans were left to the dubious mercies of resentful white supremacists. Making matters worse, the national government was now committed to a policy of indifference toward the fate of African Americans and of reconciliation with an accommodation toward the white South.

The Army, freed from its responsibilities in the South, was used to suppress labor unrest in other parts of the nation. White laborers, just beginning to organize and defend their rights, were on the receiving end of state-sponsored violence designed to keep them quiescent and at the mercy of the "robber barons" who would soon dominate the nation's Gilded Age. At the same time, the opening of the West continued to promise wealth and opportunity for those able to settle there. The Battle of the Greasy Grass (Little Big Horn) reverberated around the nation, justifying an onslaught of terrible, if intermittent, violence in the West that lasted until the Massacre at Wounded Knee on December 29, 1890 ended the Indian Wars.

This violence was unleashed and authorized by cultural practices easily discernible in the despicable discourses of 1876: the prevalence of graft and corruption that rotted the government and mitigated against fair treatment, the reluctance of politicians to recognize change for what it was and manage it rather than relying on nostalgic rhetoric evoking the past, and the increasing lack of legitimacy accorded the political system as a whole. All of these were connected, and all of them found expression in the ceding of government to corporations and the raiding of western land. The Gilded Age was about to begin.

CONCLUSION: THE CONSEQUENCES OF THE CORRUPT BARGAIN

All of the elements contributing to a deplorable election were present in 1876. The political system had only dubious legitimacy. The South, having voluntarily left the Union, spent years on probation after it was defeated in the ensuing war. Newly enfranchised African Americans contended with newly reenfranchised Southern whites, and, largely because of often-violent assaults on the former, Republican governments in the South were returned to the latter. The party systems themselves were threatened by widespread dissatisfaction with Reconstruction, endemic corruption, and continued economic woes. Their weakness was manifested in the rise of the Greenbackers, the prominence of the Reform Republicans, and the partisan restlessness of African Americans.

Many white citizens were also worried about both economic and social conditions. Whites were fearful that their status as emblematic Americans was being threatened by the newly freed people on one hand and the increasing immigration of "Mongolians" on the other. These fears were heightened by the Panic of 1873 and its accompanying dislocations. Many of those who were able to emigrated west, into a complicated blend of races and nations, adding to the political and military turmoil across the continent.

All of these issues were multivalenced and complicated. They were, also increasingly conveyed to the nation through a hyperpartisan press, which took up and circulated the most inflammatory claims made by the parties. Because of the political economy in which that press was embedded, creating a need for mass circulation, the press was becoming increasingly sensationalized. The newspaper wars between Joseph Pulitzer and William Randolph Hearst that sparked an era of "yellow journalism," the "clickbait" of its day, were only a decade away; the early signs of that journalism are apparent in this election.

All the factors were there: system instability and party weakness; economic and status anxiety among whites; the need to deal overtly with questions of internal race relations in particular and, to a lesser extent, questions of immigration as well; the rise of new media technologies that unsettled the communicative environment; and practices that widened the circulation of despicable discourses. The 1876 election, widely perceived as the last battle of the Civil War, resulted not in a victory for the Union but in a nasty sort of stalemate. Thousands of unrepentant Confederates returned to power in the South, the North essentially gave up attempting to protect African American civil rights, and the Democrats were denied, at least for the moment, national power. Hayes did not singlehandedly end Reconstruction. That process had been underway when the Supreme Court undermined federal intervention in the South through the *Slaughterhouse Cases* and in *US v. Cruikshank*. Hayes's predecessor failed to protect Reconstruction as well; in 1875 Grant began to withdraw troops from the South and refused to intervene in a violent Mississippi election. Congress, too, played a role; in 1877 it blocked a military appropriations bill, making the further withdrawal of troops a foregone conclusion.

But the election had other kinds of consequences. Within a decade, just 10 percent of the population held almost 75 percent of the nation's wealth.[79] The robber barons built mansions and businesses that repressed the nation's labor and hoarded its resources. As Jack Beatty writes, "Gilded Age politics induces pertinent despair about democracy. Representative government gave way to bought government. Politicians betrayed the public trust. Citizens sold their votes. Dreams faded. Ideals died of their impossibility.

Cynicism poisoned hope. The United States in these years took on the lineaments of a Latin American party-state, an oligarchy ratified in rigged elections, girded by bayonets, and given a genial and historical gloss by its raffish casting."[80] This quotation overstates the degree to which the United States was actually characterized by representative government prior to the Gilded Age, but nevertheless the point is an important one. During the Gilded Age, the nation's commitment to white supremacy remained the animating force of US politics. The very real issues of economic inequality increasingly manifested as cultural resentment of African Americans, immigrants, and labor. That resentment was channeled everywhere except against the elites amassing huge profits. Those resentments festered until they erupted again in the election of 1924.

CHAPTER 3

INTRODUCING THE POLITICS OF FEAR TO THE TWENTIETH CENTURY, 1924

The convention was in chaos. Party leaders couldn't agree on the platform, on the candidates, or on anything else. The anger and division had been building for at least four years, and when it erupted in New York's Madison Square Garden in the summer of 1924, it couldn't be contained. According to historian Robert K. Murray, the Democratic National Convention "was certainly the most acrimonious and bitterly fought event in the Democratic party's modern history. It involved more arguments, aroused more passion, left more wounds, and shed more political blood than any other single incident. During its sixteen days and 103 ballots, the party virtually committed suicide."[1] Venerated leaders were booed off the stage; fistfights broke out among the delegates and in the gallery; rules were challenged; debate was often impossible. So bitter were the arguments at the convention that democracy itself seemed at risk of breaking down entirely.

National nominating conventions are usually moments of celebration—occasions when the party leaves the contention over platforms and candidates behind and joyfully reunites in the face of a common opponent. Party officials exult in their harmony and parties that are unable to convincingly stage a performance of unity are often parties that lose in the fall's general election. And so it was in 1924; the Democrats lost to Republican incumbent "Silent Cal" Coolidge in a bitter three-way race. The campaign turned on a toxic stew of arguments over immigration; religion and morality; race; science, and its role in what can only be called the contemporaneous culture wars; the stench of political scandal left over from the Harding administration; and an insurgency from the Western Progressives in response to economic dislocations produced by US involvement in the Great War. The newly revitalized Ku Klux Klan loomed over this political miasma and exerted enormous influence throughout the country. The Klan's presence at Madison Square Garden was a chief cause of the Democrats' troubles. The very nature of US democracy seemed to be at stake, and, as is so often the case when political stakes are high, political discourse reached for new lows.

This chapter tells the story of the 1924 election, focusing on its descent into chaos at Madison Square Garden, the Democrats' attempts to recover from that suicidal debacle, and the ways in which despicable discourse was mobilized by all the candidates in their efforts to win the White House. I begin with a brief history of the era, placing the election in context. I then turn to the Democratic National Convention and to the general election that followed. The 1924 election is a classic example of a deplorable election, demonstrating what can happen when a system without much legitimacy meets a moment in which economic benefits seem inequitably distributed. Such moments may have the potential to bring out the best in our politics. In this case, at least, democratic norms and values were tested and sometimes failed.

THE PERILS OF NORMALCY

The 1920 election was the first after the conflagration of the Great War. Woodrow Wilson, who had led the nation into war on the basis of high ideals, found himself unable to control the terms of peace and foundered his way out of office in 1921. His successor, Republican Warren G. Harding, promised the nation a "return to normalcy," capitalizing on nostalgia for the days prior to the Great War. Such nostalgic appeals are often precursors for and elements of despicable discourse, for they harken back to some mythical time when life was somehow better, before it was infected with whatever ills characterize a present moment. Such ills are easily, and thus frequently, associated with specific people, at whose door the burden of change is laid. The 1920s were no different.

The political system itself tenuously maintained its legitimacy in 1920 but that legitimacy became shakier with each ensuing election—the party system and ideological alignments of the 1920s were shattered by the rise of the New Deal coalition in the 1930s. The portents of that impending change were clear in the 1920s, characterized by a contrast between staid leadership and an increasingly agitated public. As one Coolidge biographer put it, "Harding and Coolidge had benefitted from the calming images they had projected for the American public. They had also been the beneficiaries of adverse reaction to the coldness and stubbornness of Woodrow Wilson, the identification of the Democrats with liquor at a time of high dry sentiment; the outrage of nationalists and of hyphenate groups like Irish-Americans at Wilson's foreign policies, and what Arthur S. Link has called, 'the fragmentation of the progressive movement.'"[2] The 1920 Republican campaign was awash in nostalgia. But it also signaled coming changes. Economically, the nation mostly prospered. The automobile was increasingly important, as were telephones, radio, and movies. The opening of King Tutankhamun's tomb in 1923 caused an international sensation. Skyscrapers began to dominate urban skylines and women got the vote. People talked about Freud and went to church in increasing numbers. But the twenties tended to roar only in the cities; rural America was characterized by a stubborn priggishness. Rural citizens deplored the licentiousness of the cities, often personified by the new freedom accorded to women, the increase in immigration that they perceived as diluting national values and commitments, and the slackening devotion to a Protestant God.

The nation was split on foreign policy as well. When the Democrats fared poorly in the 1918 congressional elections that year, the ensuing Republican strength in Congress meant that the fight over US participation in the League of Nations promised to be an ugly one. Wilson risked his health, if not his life, on a failed public campaign in support of the League. Failing, it was left to Harding to sign the final treaties ending the war.

That triumph, however, was short-lived. Elected in 1920, by 1921 the Harding administration was drowning in scandal. First, and most famously, there was the Teapot Dome scandal, named for the oilfields sold by Bacon Fall, Harding's interior secretary, to private oil companies without going through the mandatory bidding process.[3] That was followed by similar revelations concerning the management of Veterans' Affairs and the Attorney General's office. The scandals seemed to be everywhere at once, making Washington, DC, appear permeated by misconduct.[4] Corruption was a relative thing, of course. It is worth noting that during these years, senators were loyal both to their states and to the industries that dominated them. The assumption was that these interests had a right to a seat at the legislative table; it was only a short step from there to ensuring one in the executive branch as well, however obtained. The argument that the government had been taken over by special interests was an increasingly important one and contributed to the government's shaky legitimacy.

Democracy had its troubles away from Washington as well. After the war, as African American troops returned to the Jim Crow South, violence there escalated.[5] As violence in the South increased, African Americans left for Northern cities in what has become known as the Great Migration. The comparative freedom of this environment allowed for the flowering of African American intellectual, social, and artistic life known as the Harlem Renaissance on the one hand and triggered white rage and retaliation on the other.[6] But its urban context aside, for many African Americans, life in the North wasn't all that different from life in the Jim Crow South. They faced the same hatred on one side of the Mason-Dixon line as they had on the other.

In short, in some parts of the country, women and African Americans were more assertive, and liberalism in general was on the rise. As liberating and hopeful as the decade was for some people, for others it brought a sense of loss, as the values to which they adhered seemed under attack and the world as they knew it seemed to be drastically changing in ways they didn't endorse. They fought back in ways that were repressive and that revealed their anger at changes they could neither fully understand nor control. And so the Ku Klux Klan rose again, the nation approved Prohibition, feared communism and engaged in a Red Scare, and cheered on the Palmer Raids, federal efforts to capture and deport leftists, especially those of Italian heritage and those from Eastern Europe. All of these were accompanied and energized by despicable discourses, turning some citizens against others.

Prohibition, for example, went into effect in 1920. According to historian Douglas Brinkley, it was strongly supported by "provincial, rural, Protestant Americans" because "to them, Prohibition had always meant more than drinking. It represented the effort of an older America to maintain its dominance in a society in which they were becoming relatively less powerful. Drinking, which they associated with the modern city and with Catholic immigrants, became a symbol of the new culture they believed was displacing them."[7] That sense of displacement was important to the decade as a whole; it manifested in other ways as well.

The Great War, ostensibly fought to "make the world safe for democracy," wasn't doing that at home. Immigration had slowed during the war; the war's aftermath brought a wave of xenophobia to the United States. In the wake of that xenophobia, in 1921 and again in 1924 Congress passed and the president signed legislation that sharply restricted immigration to the United States. Conceived as a response to fears of Jewish immigration, these various laws changed the ways the United States managed immigration.[8] By 1924, immigration from Asia was prohibited, and immigration from elsewhere was proscribed in accordance with the presumed desirability of immigrants from specific regions and nations.

Unsurprisingly, the national distrust of immigrants was expressed in other ways as well: a Red Scare and the accompanying Palmer Raids; a rise in religious fundamentalism, accompanied by anti-Semitism and anti-Catholicism; a (related) increase in support for Prohibition; and, most worrying, a resurgence of white supremacist terrorist groups like the Klan. These phenomena were all related, and they were all conveyed through the same kinds of rhetoric—discourse that fomented fear about the decay of morality in American public and private life.

For example, the film *Birth of a Nation* premiered in Woodrow Wilson's White House to the loud acclaim of the president himself. It also set off a series of protests in various US cities. With the avowed goal of presenting a version of the South that would commend itself to the rest of the country, the film also resuscitated the image of the Klan for many white Americans.[9] Within the decade, the Klan was present in every state in the Union.[10] Racism was a key component of the Klan's appeal, but that appeal stretched beyond racism to encompass cultural and status anxieties, both of which were major issues following the Great War. White working-class people were threatened by the rapid increase in urbanization, the influx of immigrants to the cities, and the cultural politics those things represented.

> This "second Klan" as it has been called, took pride in its namesake and its commitment to white supremacy. But it differed from its parent. It was stronger in the North than in the South. It spread across the Mason-Dixon Line by adding Catholics, Jews, immigrants, and bootleggers to its list of enemies and pariahs, in part because African Americans were less numerous in the North. Its leaders tried to prohibit violence, though they could not always enforce this ban. Unlike the first Klan, which operated mainly at night, meeting in hard-to-find locations, the second operated in daylight, and organized public events.[11]

This second Klan attained a level of public respectability that is hard to fathom at this distance; grounded in the ostensible protection of "Americanism," it had a veneer of decency over its resentment.

It was also masked by a certain populism—the KKK was anti-elite as much as it was anti-immigrant, and it opposed foppish intellectuals from the "big city" who were thought to sneer at their rural cousins. In opposing modernity, in other words, the second Klan found a route to national support. That the 1920s iteration of the Klan was national, not merely regional, presented serious problems for its opponents, because Klansmen were deeply embedded in local, state, and national offices in the South, West, and Midwest.[12] Attacking the Klan meant potentially losing the support of those who were both party and Klan members. This was more of a problem for Democrats than for Republicans, for many of the Klan's precepts, in fact, were strikingly similar to those professed by the Democratic Party in general. Even more important, the KKK was a lower-class, rural phenomenon. This meant that opposing the Klan deepened the division between urban Democrats and their rural colleagues, threatening to widen schisms within the party.

Both parties struggled with the intersection of culture and politics; the intersection of economics and politics also created new problems and exacerbated existing tensions. As early as 1919, labor began to agitate for better working conditions and higher wages. It also began to organize itself into trade unions. These moves were resisted by management; labor agitation and managerial violence became endemic. In 1920, aggravated both by labor unrest and by anti-immigrant hysteria, the nation voted the Republicans back into the White House. But Republicans weren't significantly more united than the Democrats—agreeing on the need for restrictive immigration policy and dedicated to damning the Democrats for leading the nation into war, they could agree on little else, as class and regional differences fractured both party coalitions.[13]

The increasing weakness of the political system was manifested too in the possibilities for leadership from outsiders to the world of professional politics. Henry Ford, for example, dipped his toe into the political waters. His claim to fame rested on his reputation as a giant in American industry, and also on his campaign against "international Jews."[14] That campaign included the publication of the *Protocols of the Elders of Zion*, a notoriously anti-Semitic document. His campaign ultimately came to nothing, but the possibility that such a person might achieve high national office is itself revealing of the fragility of the system.[15]

In the aftermath of the Great War, both the world and the nation were changing, and many Americans responded to those changes with a combination of fear and anger. The United States was not alone in finding 1924 tumultuous. In spring of that year, Mussolini took power in Italy and Hitler's party dominated the elections in Munich. Between the Red Scare fomenting fears of Communism on the left and the rise of authoritarian regimes on the right, democracy seemed under siege worldwide. Despite the belief, very strong at the time, that the United States existed in a world apart, events at home were often swirled by the same currents as those roiling in other nations.

Over all this incipient chaos presided the benign image of "Silent Cal" Coolidge, who ascended to office through the death of the scandal-ridden Warren G. Harding in 1923. Unwilling to reveal anything about himself, Coolidge nevertheless mastered the use of both radio and newsreels. He worked hard at public relations, and while he had no soaring vision for what the presidency could be, he conveyed a middling vision of who he, as president, was. Most importantly, Coolidge never used the power of the presidency—such as it was in those years—to engage in the cultural battles occurring across the country. He accepted Prohibition as he accepted the pervasiveness of the Klan; contesting neither, he maintained a conservative and passive stance on the social issues beginning to churn across the nation.

The 1924 election opened in a context that seemed both stable and tumultuous, a breeding ground of despicable discourse. The nation was riven by divides between its urban and rural citizens, reflected in conflicts over Prohibition, immigration, women's rights, and the Klan. Labor was increasingly dissatisfied, farmers increasingly nervous. The "New Negro," rejoicing in the Harlem Renaissance and dedicated to asserting their dignity in the face of the continuing horrors inflicted on African Americans, was offering hope of racial progress even as the violence of Jim Crow in the South and race riots in the North undermined any such hope. The legitimacy of the national government had been severely damaged by scandal and its ability to cope with these burgeoning problems was limited by the unwillingness of those in power to offer a way of managing change. The growing national tensions were largely ignored by both parties, at least until the Democrats met in Madison Square Garden in late June 1924.

A TALE OF TWO CONVENTIONS

Party conventions are usually raucous affairs, full of riotous goodwill, often fueled by an overabundance of celebratory spirits. In 1924, this was not the case for either major party. The Republicans met in decorous amity, convened with staid calm, and exited without any excitement but the loss of Wisconsin senator Robert La Follette, who became the Progressive's candidate alongside Democrat Burton Wheeler, senator from Montana. Progressives thus had a foot in each party, a circumstance that tended to confuse rather than clarify the exact positions of the candidates. For Progressives and Republicans, however, the conventions were not noteworthy affairs; nothing of the kind could be said for the Democrats.

A Quiet Convention: The Republicans

The Republicans met in Cleveland in a convention characterized by its lack of drama and largely overshadowed by the news of the Leopold and Loeb trial in Chicago, featuring two male students from the University of Chicago who had hoped to commit the "perfect crime."[16] Coolidge, whose introversion helped distance him from the Harding administration's scandals, easily won the nomination, and the party managed to bury their positions on the most pressing and controversial issues within an incredibly long platform.[17] Having managed to disguise the biggest potential rifts within the party, Republicans accepted the defection of La Follette with equanimity. Their campaign, as portrayed by the convention, was dedicated to demonstrating their capacity for stable and honest leadership.

Their keynote was offered by Congressman Theodore Burton (R-OH).[18] Understanding that the Harding administration scandals were likely to loom large in November, Burton both scapegoated and excused Harding for those scandals: "A nation bowed in grief mourns his death," the congressman intoned, "the whole world mourned him as a lover of peace and good will. If ever he made those mistakes which mortals must make, it was because of the kindness of his heart, because of a noble mind which thought no ill of any friend or foe but reposed trust in everyone." Harding was thus made singularly responsible for the administration's failings but was also excused for them as they were best understood as the result of a kind heart and too-trusting nature. The corruption associated with Harding should not, Burton implied, be properly thought of as an administration or a Republican problem.

Burton then engaged in the standard credit claiming of such occasions, welcoming women to their first convention as voters and celebrating the Republican peacemaking after Wilson's failure to obtain Senate ratification for the peace treaty. Much of the speech laid out the grounds on which Republicans preferred to wage their fall campaign: immigration and farm policy. The latter of these was an effort to forestall the Progressive insurgency; the former was an accomplishment that Burton chose to celebrate. He said, "Two immigration acts have been passed. While we recognize invaluable benefits to our country from the infusion of immigrants from other lands who have added variety and strength to our national life, we have come to realize that the number landing on our shores has been too large for proper assimilation. The so-called melting pot has boiled over." This is a standard description of contemporaneous mainstream views on immigration. Whites in this era were largely in agreement that immigrants are good, so long as they come from the "right" countries and seek to assimilate. Their contribution is additive to the preexisting national identity, unable to change its core. That national identity must be protected, and large numbers of immigrants threaten it, for they hinder the goal of assimilation and threaten to pollute the nation.

None of this is personal, Burton pointed out: "The adoption of policies for the exclusion of Japanese immigrants by no means implies any claim of their inferiority, but rests upon essential differences, notably in standards of living." He argued that the threat to American national identity resides in the difference of other cultures; those cultures are not inferior, but they nonetheless must be prevented from altering the US political culture or joining its body politic. For Burton, it is unfortunate, but necessary. The Republicans, according to their keynoter, were proud defenders of a specific—and exclusionary—definition of the nation. He made this claim through discussion of immigration, which was uncontroversial, rather than summoning the KKK, which was not. This allowed Republicans to stake their ground on the nature of patriotism and Americanism without having to enter the contentious waters that would shortly engulf the Democrats. It also laid bare the kind of exclusionary politics that characterized the United States in 1924.

Burton positioned Republicans as defenders of tradition in other areas as well, for they were willing to "extend liberality to the last degree in the enactment of legislation which will aid the farmer, but it cannot respond to impracticable theories or accept measures which will only aggravate the situation." In a swipe at La Follette and the Progressives, Republicans avowed themselves firmly on the farmer's side but unwilling to engage in any socialist experiments. Republicans were already positioning La Follette and the Progressives as "extremists" and therefore as a priori unacceptable. Here, as in immigration policy, Republicans understood themselves as defenders of the status quo; change would be fought, inclusion denied.

The speech and its premises were well received by Republicans both inside and outside of the convention hall. There was widespread relief at the idea that the scandals could so easily be laid to rest and that their candidate had been untainted in any real way by them. Republican governance was portrayed as steady and calm, just what a postwar nation needed. In short, their convention was singularly lacking in drama and interest—it went exactly as planners hoped it would. The same could not be said for the Democratic meeting in New York City.

A Klanbake in New York City: The Democrats

Two weeks later, the Democrats met in Madison Square Garden. Given the scandals associated with the Harding administration, Democrats should have been able to use the convention to frame themselves as a more competent, less corrupt alternative to the Republicans. Instead, they appeared contentious, feckless, and unstable. The existing partisan organization was beginning to shift, making both parties vulnerable, but the vulnerability was more strongly felt by the Democrats than the Republicans—their coalition depended on uniting Northern urban centers with Southern conservatives and Midwestern farmers. The tensions between urban political machines and rural voters were thus particularly painful for them.

By 1924, there were three important divisions within the Democratic Party: Eastern and Northern Democrats, largely urbanized, predominantly white ethnics, and those opposed to Prohibition; Westerners, who supported Prohibition and were pro-farmer; and Southerners, who tended to be fundamentalists, endorsed Prohibition, and favored the Klan. When the convention divided into two main camps, these factions also divided internally, making things even more confusing. Prohibition and the Klan served as condensation symbols for the complicated mix of issues and beliefs disrupting the Democratic coalition. One's position on the Klan, for instance, didn't merely flag a commitment to racial politics but to cultural and economic ones as well; the wet/dry division was equally if not more important.[19] Those issues thus took on an emotional significance that seemed disproportionate but that really reflected the entirety of an individual's politics.[20] When single issues come to dominate a political discussion in this way, the chances of despicable discourse escalate because compromise involves not a single issue but the entirety of one's political identity.

Navigating such moments requires skilled political leadership, and this the Democrats did not have in 1924. What they had instead was a series of flawed candidates, each of whom commanded the loyalty of one of the party's factions, and none of whom had any strength across factions.[21] The fight centered, as such fights so often do, on procedure; in this case the two-thirds rule, requiring candidates earn at least two-thirds of delegates' votes rather than a simple majority, which caused so much trouble in 1876.[22] It virtually guaranteed a deadlocked and protracted convention.

Of the many contenders for the presidential nomination, two are worth noting here: William McAdoo, who was tainted by his involvement in the Teapot Dome scandals and was the favorite candidate of the Klan, and New York governor Al Smith, who represented the urban, white ethnic voters of the party. He was strongly, even virulently, opposed by KKK supporters.[23] In a letter from one Smith campaign official to another, for example, the author noted, "I was confidentially but frankly informed that the Ku Klux [*sic*] feeling was so strong [in Arkansas] that every other candidate suggested would be preferred to our Governor."[24] Similarly, a Georgian noted that the hometown paper, the *Atlanta Journal*, would likely support Smith if nominated, but that the Georgia delegation "are mostly Clansmen," making that nomination more difficult.[25]

Battle lines were drawn long before the convention, and animosities between the two camps hardened early. McAdoo, for instance, campaigned hard before the convention, which earned him both delegates and animosity. He united the Klan and pro-Prohibition forces, a fact that worked both for and against his candidacy. Most importantly, McAdoo had defeated Oscar Underwood of Alabama, a dedicated opponent of the Klan and of its prominence in national political life. Authoring an editorial in the *New York Times*, Underwood first railed against the growing influence of "organized bodies of men" in national politics, whose interests ran counter to those of the "unorganized majority," and then wrote:

> And we are approaching an era in our national life where secret organizations are seeking control of the Government. From their secret council chambers these organizations will issue their decrees to those whom they have elected to office, and in that way, the course and destiny of the whole people of the United States will be determined. If this new Government of class and Klan were ruled only by sincere motives of the highest patriotism to achieve that which is best for all the people of the United States, the new oligarchy to be set up in place of a representative Government would not be so disastrous as it will be when men swayed by racial and religious prejudice are directing its course.[26]

The emphasis here is on the secrecy of the Klan; he contrasts the KKK with the open and transparent workings of a democratic government. In this view the Klan was not only secret but also oligarchic; again, the implicit argument is that it is also undemocratic. This was a risky argument for the time as KKK members were elected officials in nearly every state. Underwood was arguing that even when these people followed the dictates of democratic governance by running for office, their secret agenda was to undermine democracy. The Klan attained much of its prominence during these years through an overt association with patriotism; Underwood was disassociating them from exactly that value.

It is also notable that while Underwood cited "racial and religious prejudice," it is religious prejudice that most concerns him in this editorial. Like most Southerners of the time, and most white people nationally, Underwood's problem with the KKK was not primarily that it practiced racial violence. But religious prejudice was an altogether more difficult matter. Again, Underwood had to walk a fine line between fighting the Klan and upholding the kinds of values that both the KKK and most Democrats believed in. But he showed courage in attacking the Klan at all. Underwood vowed to make the Klan the issue of the convention and its platform,[27] a plan that proved disastrous for the party and didn't do Underwood much good either.[28]

Klansmen, in fact, represented a fairly small percentage of delegates to the convention, but their influence was disproportionate to their numbers, at least in part because of the attention given to them by the media. Furor first erupted over the site of the convention—fundamentalists, Klansmen, and members of groups like the Anti-Saloon League united in their disdain for New York City as a haven of vice and depravity.[29] New Yorkers responded as one might imagine, with boisterous bouts of catcalling and other vocal expressions of disdain, and the cultural politics of the convention got ugly. Interestingly, the intractable mood of the delegates was exacerbated by the presence of (white) women—newly enfranchised, they took their responsibilities seriously and resisted compromise. The contention spread beyond the convention, and beyond its host city—encouraged by the KKK, Protestant ministers across the country began to sermonize against Al Smith and his candidacy, putting both direct and indirect pressure on convention delegates.

The keynote, by Senator Pat Harrison (D-MS), was notable for its emphasis on corruption and its silence on the most pressing issues animating the convention.[30] "Forty-eight years ago," he said, invoking the deplorable election of 1876, "in the city of St. Louis, the hosts of Democracy met in convention to dedicate themselves to purging corruption from the public service. We meet today for a rededication to the same purpose. There was corruption then; there is a saturnalia of corruption now." The Democrats, of course, lost in 1876. Perhaps Harrison hoped that by reminding the delegates of that debacle they would find a way to unite against the Republicans. At the very least, Harrison reminded them of the nature of their shared opposition: "The corner stone of the Republican Party is special privilege, and today its grip is more firmly tightened and its place more secure than at any time in its long history." This perfidy was the result, Harrison argued, of choice. The Republicans had been given the opportunity to mend their ways in 1920, and they had failed to do so. He said:

> The American people have taken the measure of this Administration. It may have been able to free itself from sectional identity and to have looked beyond the sky lines of New England. It might have heard the groans of the distressed farmers of the West and sympathetically responded. It might have sought markets and removed the tariff jams in the channels through which our surplus products move. It might have visualized world conditions and courageously assumed the part befitting a great nation. It might have reduced living costs, redeemed pledges to the soldier, followed a definite domestic program and adopted a broad and statesmanlike foreign policy, but even then, it would have availed it nothing with its carnival of corruption.

There are a lot of interesting arguments here. First, he refers to "the skyline of New England," apparently equating the whole region with its urban centers and eliding the fact that much of New England was deeply rural. Depicting Republicans as the party of the urban North falsely restricted their base and constituency. He deepened that claim by immediately referring to the "groans of the distressed farmers," which he claimed Republicans ignored and whose interests they damaged through their tariff policies.

Republicans, he charged, also abrogated the role of the United States abroad, ignored the needs of the nation's veterans, and were, as evidenced by their corruption, dedicated only to their own interests, not to the national interest. Surely, he implied, the Democrats could unite to defeat such a perfidious party. The problem was that Harrison focused primarily on the Republican Party and the issue for the Democrats was within their own party. He gave them reasons to oppose the Republicans; that they already did. He failed to give them any reasons for working together as a unified party; those they sorely needed.

The convention's mood, already bad, worsened once candidates began to be nominated. Underwood was nominated first, in a speech that attacked the Klan, likening them to the Know-Nothings, an analogy that enraged delegates, who erupted into pandemonium. Once order was (briefly) restored, McAdoo was nominated, to chants of "Mac, Mac, McAdoo!" and "Ku, Ku, McAdoo!" The issue of the Klan, which threatened to fatally split the party, was out in the open. Amid the noise and contention, there was a brief lull as Senator Joseph Robinson (D-AR) was nominated. Al Smith's name was then put before the convention, and New Yorkers responded with a sustained demonstration, clapping and cheering. So bad were relations between the candidates that McAdoo's supporters took the demonstration personally, assuming that it was intended to belittle their candidate.[31] Both the floor and the galleries erupted into bedlam, and the day's activities howled to a close. The next day was marginally less chaotic, although six more people were nominated and there were numerous seconding speeches given in support of both McAdoo and Smith. The final nominee was the unpretentious and relatively obscure John Davis of West Virginia, former ambassador to Great Britain and Wilson's Solicitor General.

Rather than explicitly fighting over candidates, the convention chose to fight over the issues represented by those candidates, and the Platform Committee deadlocked over planks concerning Prohibition, the League of Nations, and the Klan. Of these, the last was the most contentious. People like Underwood wanted the convention to directly and explicitly condemn the KKK and all its works. Others, like the venerable William Jennings Bryan, argued that doing so only gave the noxious organization more power and visibility. There were also those who argued that condemning the Klan meant political suicide because of its strength in the

South and Midwest, regions the Democrats needed for victory in the fall. If nothing else, the fight over the platform and the question of whether it should contain an anti-Klan plank revealed both the national power wielded by the KKK and its deep connection to the national Democratic Party. McAdoo, of course, was firmly against any such plank, a fact that helped cement the association between candidates and issues.[32]

The draft platform included a bland endorsement of "constitutional freedoms" and did not mention the Klan; a minority report condemned it with the by now predictable result of mayhem on the convention floor and in the galleries.[33] As the convention took up the question of the KKK, its mood went from bad to worse. Then William Jennings Bryan took the stage, in a moment that one would have predicted would galvanize the convention.[34] His argument regarding the minority report was interrupted several times by boos and catcalls. He responded to the dissension in the gallery by saying, "You do not represent the future of our country."[35] The convention was now clearly at war with itself, and the battle was being waged on terms that went beyond the definition of candidates and issues for one election and went instead to the future identity of the Democratic Party. Such high stakes were not likely to ease the inflamed passions of the delegates.

Delegates began voting on the platform at 11:35 p.m., at which point the convention descended into confusion and riot; there were arguments, fistfights, and brawls.[36] Some delegations were so internally divided that accurate vote counts were impossible, and states voted not as blocs but as fractions of blocs.[37] Delegates screamed, and those in the galleries yelled. All of it was carried over the radio, affording citizens across the country a front-row seat as the Democrats self-destructed.[38] Finally, Franklin D. Roosevelt, whose appearance on behalf of Al Smith constituted both his return to politics after being afflicted with polio and the only highlight of the convention, called for adjournment, and peace was restored as the arena emptied.[39] In what has to have been a massive understatement, the *New York Times* informed the nation that "Negroes Are Disappointed" by the convention's inability to condemn an organization that regularly inflicted unspeakable violence upon them.[40]

The next day, Smith and McAdoo remained the frontrunners and they remained dedicated to the principle that they would defeat one another at all costs. They and their supporters refused to withdraw. They refused to compromise. They refused to do anything but holler at each other. Ballot after ballot ensued with no real change until the delegates, in a final fit of exhaustion, finally nominated John Davis on the 103rd ballot, and the convention ended, on July 9, after twenty-three sessions. The convention set a number of records, none of them salubrious—it was the longest convention on record and the one with the most ballots. It was the most expensive and yielded the longest platform. At least sixty people received votes for the nomination at some point during the convention. The delegates fought over religion and over the Klan; they fought equally fiercely, if less overtly, over Prohibition and its attendant cultural politics. And they fought one another with a deep and abiding bitterness.

Davis's main virtue seemed to be his lack of connection to any of the controversies tearing the party apart. But he also had no ability to unite the party in the face of those controversies, although the party implausibly attempted to celebrate his nomination as evidence of unity.[41] His running mate, brother of the redoubtable William Jennings Bryan, added nothing but a loose connection to history to the ticket. Still, the Republicans had small problems of their own, as La Follette led the Progressives against them, and there was some hope that the Democrats might ride the corruption issue into the White House.

Both conventions contributed to the deplorable nature of the general election. The Republicans did so by burying the question of the Klan and refusing to speak out against it while simultaneously encouraging anti-immigrant discourses based on racist premises. The Democrats did so much more actively, circulating direct defenses of the Klan and launching personal and personalized attacks on opposing candidates. Cultural politics were very much in evidence, and they were fought over with a clear lack of respect for alternative understandings of the nation and in ways that deepened national divisions. These discourses are despicable because they encouraged exclusion and work against democratic norms and procedures. They continued to circulate despicable discourse in the general election.

THE GENERAL ELECTION

The general election took place amid speculation that a three-way race might throw the election into the House.[42] Democrats hoped that the Progressive/Republican split might yield them a victory, much as Theodore

Roosevelt's Bull Moose campaign had helped elect Wilson in 1912. Republicans, on the other hand, argued that the threat of a House-decided election was all the more reason to support their party.[43] From whatever party's perspective one looked at it, the fact of a three-way race affected the electoral calculus of all the participants. They were all willing to encourage whatever degree of democracy was most likely to lead to a victory for their party. Principle was often lost in the electoral melee.

The West Revolts: "Fighting Bob" La Follette

The Progressive Party formed officially in March 1924, and it was clear from the beginning that Wisconsin senator Robert "Fighting Bob" La Follette was their preferred candidate.[44] That convention was so enamored of their candidate that the delegates adjourned without bothering to pick a vice presidential nominee, happy to leave that choice in La Follette's hands. For a party that claimed to be inclusive, this decision seems incongruous, to say the least. They were not enacting the kind of transparency and democratic debate that they made the basis of their campaign. His choice of running mate created problems as well. He picked Montana senator Burton Wheeler, who left the Democratic Party to run with La Follette. This put the Progressive Party in an odd space between the two major parties but with no discernible identity of its own. The *New York Times* caustically responded:

> In consenting, after saying he would ne'er consent, to accept the Vice Presidential nomination on Senator La Follette's ticket, Senator Wheeler is outlining for himself political action which in anyone else he would denounce as insincere and self-condemnatory. He declares himself still a Democrat, but proposes to do all in his power to defeat his party. He announces that he will support the re-election of Senator Walsh in Montana, yet Senator Walsh will be fighting the La Follette party as well as the Republican. . . . If Senator Wheeler were not a pure-minded man of simple nature, he would find immense difficulties in going through with the plan to which he has committed himself. But as it is, all that he will need to do will be to fall into a sublime fury about Wall Street and the predatory interests. That will be the sufficient disproof of inconsistency or hypocrisy on his part.[45]

At least part of the *Times*'s objection to Wheeler's defection was that they worried about the increase in "the number of blocs and groups and factions" when the public interest was better served by adherence to two-party rule.[46] Their response was to discredit the third party as an enterprise and its candidates as worthy of consideration.

Luckily for La Follette, the print media were not the only available outlet for his views. He became the first presidential candidate to deliver a political speech exclusively over radio. But his content was less than helpful, for he wavered on the most important cultural issues of the day. He tried on the one hand to dismiss the Klan, calling it "an unimportant issue," but on the other pronounced himself "unalterably opposed to the evident purposes of the secret organization known as the Ku Klux Klan as disclosed by its public acts."[47] It is hard to parse being "unalterably opposed" to something that "unimportant," and La Follette looked inconsistent at best and poorly pandering at worst. For its part, the Klan resented his association with socialists and called La Follette "a danger to the nation."[48] La Follette was similarly unclear on his position concerning Prohibition, a fact that earned him only opponents and no allies. Similarly, he supported immigration restrictions "for economic reasons" but stood against quotas, a position that seemed untenable and satisfied no one.

As his stance on immigration indicates, La Follette's main concern, and the driving force of his campaign, was economic. Specifically, he worried about "the control of government and industry by private monopoly."[49] This position gave him the qualified support of Samuel Gompers and the American Federation of Labor (the AFL was officially nonpartisan and thus unable to explicitly endorse a candidate).[50] But the Progressives still hoped that bringing labor into their fold could result in a deadlocked election, their best hope for victory.[51] In general, a strategy that calls for stalemating one's opponents is not an obviously winning one; it depends more on attacking and undermining than on making a positive case for one's own candidacy. And so his campaign lacked an inner coherence except on economic issues. Much of his campaign talk was rambling, incoherent, and bitter. His overall campaign was described in the *New York Times* as flailing against his opponents.[52]

In one of his more famous addresses, he launched an attack on the Supreme Court and, through it, on the two major parties as well.[53] He said, "The campaign in which we are now engaged witnesses a conflict between two principles of government as old as human history. In all ages and in all lands men have lived who have denied both the right and the capacity of the people to be the masters of their own government. From the dawn of civilization down to the present hour men have sought to make government an instrument for securing, and extending, special privileges destructive of the liberties, happiness, and prosperity of the masses." La Follette thus cast himself as the implausible hero of a world historical battle for the rights of the masses and cast the two major parties in the roles of villains.

Those villains did not work alone but were abetted by powerful governmental institutions, in this case, the United State Supreme Court. La Follette asserted that the Court had engaged in blatantly undemocratic actions, such as the infamous *Dred Scott* decision, which denied the humanity of enslaved persons. For La Follette, that case illustrated the Court's elitist tendencies and condemned the entire national government as complicit in those tendencies. The Court, he declared, is "on the side of the wealthy and powerful and against the poor and weak." Given that the two major parties were equally complicit in this scenario, the only solution was the election of a third party and consequently changes to the Constitution itself. If nothing else, this argument would have contributed to the decreasing legitimacy of those parties and of the system without materially adding to La Follette's. As a practical matter in a campaign context, it gave his opponents the ability to plausibly claim that La Follette was against the Constitution, thus labeling him un-American. Democratic nominee John Davis, for instance, argued La Follette "would destroy the Constitution, upset the system of checks and balances, eliminate the power of the courts, and undermine the law."[54]

This kind of exchange is notable as an example of the kind of despicable discourse that circulates in a deplorable election. These candidates were not content to argue or disagree with one another on policy or even personal differences. They actively sought to delegitimate the candidacies of their opponents. Both La Follette and Davis argued that the election of the other would be not merely misguided but inimical to American democracy itself. When arguments like this are made in a time of system stability, they perhaps do not do much damage. When they are made at a time like this, when the system is fragile and the party coalitions themselves are weakening, the consequences for the stability of the system are much greater.

La Follette's campaign engaged in similar discourse with his opponents on the right as well. His running mate, Burton Wheeler, for example, once attacked Coolidge by addressing an empty chair, indicating his contempt for a president largely absent from the hustings. Wheeler also accused both major parties of having "gone mad" in their fear of La Follette, further attempting to disassociate the major parties from a capacity for proper leadership.[55] And they tried to associate Coolidge with the nation's most inimical forces, as in this piece of campaign communication:

Kool Klammy
Kal Koolidge
Kant Kondemn the
Ku Klux Klan. You
Kan Kill the Kruel
Ku Klux by Kanning
Kunning Kwiet Kal.[56]

It is one thing to refuse to condemn the KKK, and Coolidge's refusal to do so is one of the reasons I consider 1924 a deplorable election. But to imply, as La Follette's campaign does here, that Coolidge endorsed the KKK is an example of the kind of despicable discourse that circulates during such elections. Such indirect sloganeering was common: there were billboards, for example, telling the nation to "Keep Kool with Koolidge."[57] If La Follette had credible evidence that Coolidge was a member of, or even a supporter of, the KKK, it would be perfectly reasonable to include that information as part of a campaign opposing him on those grounds. But this kind of argument by association implies that claim without making it. It is a visual and phonetic accusation, made without evidence and intended to undermine a candidate through indirection.

The 1924 election marks the high tide of the Klan's resurgence. Scandals involving its leadership and the kind of attention it received during the election helped to mitigate its national power. In part, then, this kind of indirect argument may have helped discredit the Klan. Rather than treating it as a respectable sort of civic organization, as it had been functioning in many places, indirect smears through associative arguments helped to stain the KKK as a less-than-desirable organization. But there are better ways to make this argument, ways that work through a direct and clear defense of democratic values and norms and place entities like the KKK outside of those values and norms. The La Follette campaign wasn't especially well run, and it wasn't especially effective. But it more than did its part to circulate despicable discourse.

In direct contrast to the Democrats, Coolidge was a model of boring decorum, famously dour. Alice Longworth Roosevelt characterized him as "weaned on a dill pickle."[58] As we have seen, having dispensed any potential opposition early, he won the Republican nomination easily.[59] The *New York Times* somewhat tepidly assessed his presidency by noting his "absolute mastery of his party" and his inability to work with Congress, two things they had a bit of trouble reconciling. Nonetheless, they concluded that "he will be a formidable candidate."[60] For a candidate who made a point of avoiding the campaign trail, he was, somewhat surprisingly, an effective campaigner. By his own account, "With the exception of the occasion of my notification, I did not attend any partisan meetings or make any purely political speeches during the campaign."[61] Despite pleas from his own party and challenges from his opposition, he remained largely silent.[62] He chose instead to execute what we would now call a "Rose Garden strategy," staying in the White House and visibly governing while pretending that neither the policies being pursued nor the visibility given them were in any way political.

Despite his assertion of political inactivity and silence, he did manage to make his voice heard. A book of his speeches, for example, titled *The Price of Freedom*, was published during the campaign. He was famous for his photo ops, which were used to create a very particular, if somewhat misleading, image of the president as a working farmer, emblematic of New England rural virtue.[63] Indeed, his use of media created some criticism of him. For example, Frank M. Kent of *The American Mercury* had this to say: "Not in the memory of anyone now living has there been a President who leaned so heavily on this newspaper tendency to praise and protect, who profited by it so much, who would shrivel so quickly if he lost it, as Calvin Coolidge. And there have been few Presidents less gracious and more unappreciative of it."[64] Kent attributed Coolidge's political success to media norms and incentives. Because of those incentives, Kent argued, "The weak and watery utterances of a passive and pallid little man, torn by indecision and doubt, become the forceful and vigorous talk of a red-blooded resolute two-fisted, fighting executive, thoroughly aroused and determined."[65]

In addition to his book and photo ops, Coolidge was on the radio all the time. For a man renowned for his silence, he made extensive use of radio throughout his presidency, and radio helped him maintain his popularity with the public. Here we see the connection between deplorable elections and the use of emerging media technologies. A candidate like La Follette used radio sporadically and as a sort of afterthought while spending most of his time on the stump. Coolidge, as president and as candidate, availed himself of developing media norms and practices to craft the kind of image that helped him succeed politically. His voice, and the kinds of discourse circulated by that voice, had a power and reach denied to less media-savvy opponents.

When Coolidge did speak, he defended the current system and attacked the pretensions of a third party. In his speech accepting the party's nomination, for example, he said, "Very early in their search for a sound method of self-government the American people discovered that the only practical way to secure responsible political action was by the formation of parties, which they adopted because reason pronounced it the most promising and continued practice found it the most successful."[66] Embedded in his defense of the party system, of course, is also an attack on La Follette as a third-party candidate. Two parties were good enough for the Founders, he implied, and their judgment ought to be respected.

Coolidge also offered a defense of his administration, arguing with a noticeable lack of modesty that "perhaps in no peacetime period have there been more remarkable and constructive accomplishments than since March, 1921." He noted the ratification of peace treaties; specified other foreign-policy successes; referred to the "tremendous savings" occasioned by his budget policies, and its associated "revival of industry"; and then turned to the subject of immigration. He lauded the new immigration restrictions and argued, "I should have preferred to continue the policy of Japanese exclusion by some method less likely to offend the Japanese. Restricted immigration is not an offensive but a defensive action. It is not adopted in criticism of others in the slightest degree, but solely for the purpose of protecting ourselves. We cast no aspersions on any race or creed, but we must remember that every object of our institutions of society and

Government will fall unless America be kept American." Coolidge declares that it would have been nice to exclude the Japanese without also offending them, as if exclusion was ever possible without offense. To tell an entire nation of people that they were not to be allowed to immigrate to the United States because that nation needed to be protected from them is, by definition, offensive. Yet it was perfectly possible for politicians like Coolidge to make such statements, secure in the knowledge that they would go unchallenged. The bland assumption that the nation had an exclusionary definition of national identity that had to be protected was widely accepted at the time and is exactly the kind of discourse that makes this a deplorable election.

In this passage the president also declared his intention of protecting and defending American institutions. La Follette considered these institutions complicit in antidemocratic action. Coolidge agreed with him to the extent of connecting institutional practices to national identity. He, however, made the implicit claim that they exemplify democracy and must be protected from contagion. Here, of course, he echoed Burton's arguments made at the convention. Like Burton, Coolidge argued that there is no malice in the exclusion of certain immigrants, it was merely an ideological necessity. They both claimed that there was something that was called a pure sense of Americanism, and that identity was, by definition, connected to whiteness. The claim that others could be excluded without also making negative judgments about those others was, to say the least, specious. It is exactly this kind of casual racism that helps to mark this discourse as despicable.

Coolidge and La Follette may have agreed that US institutions and US national identity were connected. This did not stop Coolidge's running mate, who took on most of the rhetorical burdens of the campaign, from attacking La Follette for his radicalism. As during the convention, the Republicans had three goals: to defend themselves against charges of endemic corruption, to defend their policies, and to protect themselves against any negative consequences from La Follette's insurgency. They generally ignored the Democrats as irrelevant to their chances for reelection. They concentrated their efforts on the Progressives, whom they castigated as threats to the Constitution and American democracy generally.[67] Dawes, for example, asserted that "with a platform drawn by one man, designed to soften as much as possible the apprehensions as to what the movement really means, an attempt is made to induce those who are patriotic at heart to join the Socialists and other diverse elements opposing the existing order of things, in a mobilization of extreme radicalism. A man is known by the company he keeps."[68] Dawes thus argued first that La Follette is duplicitous; he is trying to soften the perception of his campaign and is doing so in an implicitly dishonest way. He then separated the La Follette campaign from "those who are patriotic at heart," casting his patriotism into question. He underlined the final sentence with a reference to socialist Eugene Debs, who had endorsed the Progressives, making an argument for guilt by association, and arguing that socialism is something one should, in fact, feel guilty for being associated with. In the aftermath of the nation's Red Scare, of course, this belief was widely shared, like the casual racism referred to earlier. And, as in the case of that casual racism, grounding a campaign in the presumed biases and fears of the citizenry instead of offering inclusive versions of democracy is part of what makes this discourse despicable.

Unlike his famously silent running mate, Dawes was ever present on the campaign trail, giving over one hundred speeches and traveling over fifteen thousand miles in the course of the campaign.[69] In the KKK stronghold of Maine, he said, "Government cannot last if that way, the way of the Ku Klux Klan, is the way to enforce the law in this country. Lawlessness cannot be met with lawlessness if civilization is to be maintained."[70] Here, though, the implicit argument is that KKK violence was a response to lawlessness, not a violent means of protecting white supremacy. It relied on the fiction that the Klan was an effort to maintain order in the face of African American lawbreaking. Notably, after this single speech, he was told to stop attacking the KKK, and he did.

He castigated La Follette for his association with "Red radicalism,"[71] and historian Robert Ferrell describes one occasion as posing a binary choice between Coolidge and the country and the dangers of socialism: "'Where do you stand?' he shouted, his Hoover collar shaking. 'With President Coolidge on the Constitution with the flag, or on the sinking sands of socialism?'"[72] All campaigns are composed of binaries. Not all campaigns need to question the patriotism of one's opponents. Doing so is engaging in despicable discourse.

The Republicans were happy to denounce La Follette and socialism; they were less inclined to speak out against the Klan. One scholar quipped, for example, that "Coolidge went after black voters with the sort of energy that caused him to spend half his presidency in bed."[73] Coolidge refused to use his position or his platform to condemn the Klan. African Americans repeatedly asked the president for a statement and didn't get one despite the publicity the requests received.[74] The president of the United States refused to issue a statement of any kind condemning a white supremacist organization that perpetrated systematic violence on American citizens.

As president, he did speak on race, in June of 1924 at Howard University.[75] In that speech, he offered exactly the kind of white supremacy that was widely accepted in white circles at the time. He first commended the members of his audience on their progress since they "were brought here from the restrictions on their continent."[76] Slavery, it appears, was a beneficent practice, a "probation," allowing those enslaved to escape the supposed barbarism of Africa. He argued, "In such a view of history of the Negro race in America, we may find the evidences that the black man's probation on this continent was a necessary part in a great plan by which the race was to be saved to the world for a service which we are now able to vision and, even if somewhat dimly, to appreciate."[77] Echoing the kind of claims used by proslavery advocates prior to the Civil War, Coolidge here depicts slavery not as a moral stain upon the American democratic project but as a means for the salvation of the people enslaved, as a positive good. Coolidge admitted that it was an "ordeal," but it was one that saved the slaves from "the tragic fate which has befallen many aboriginal peoples when brought into conflict with more advanced communities."[78] Note the use of the passive voice here. Those "more advanced communities" are not understood here as colonizers who invaded, displaced, and murdered the "aboriginal peoples." Fate is discussed as a neutral force that simply caused things to happen without the volition of the people involved. Those "advanced communities" are thus absolved from any responsibility for these tragic events. Similarly, the violence accompanying that conflict is all but erased: "If some of its members have suffered, if some have been denied, if some have been sacrificed, we are able at last to realize that their sacrifices were borne in a great cause."[79] The suffering, denial, and sacrifice are all figured as contingencies. If they happened, they were in the service of a worthy end.

Agency for the horrors of slavery was displaced from the white people who perpetrated those horrors. Agency for solving the problems of racism, however, was placed squarely on African Americans. Coolidge said, "Racial hostility, ancient tradition, and social prejudice are not to be eliminated immediately or easily. But they will be lessened as the colored people by their own efforts and under their own leaders shall prove worthy of the fullest measure of opportunity."[80] African Americans, themselves the victims of slavery, racial hostility, and social prejudice, were responsible for ending these practices; those guilty of them bore no responsibility.

Overall, then, Republicans, like Progressives, participated in despicable discourse throughout the election. They condemned their opposition as un-American and dangerous to the constitutional order. They defended the exclusion of Japanese immigrants and African Americans and refused to condemn the KKK in any systematic way. And while they urged voters to "Keep Cool with Coolidge," they also warned that it was "Coolidge or Chaos," putting the politics of fear front and center. In all of these ways, the Republicans helped make 1924's contest a deplorable election.

From Bad to Worse: The Democratic Campaign

The Democrats had so thoroughly destroyed themselves at their convention that neither the Republicans nor La Follette paid them much attention during the fall campaign, concentrating their fire on one another and ignoring the Democrats almost entirely. Consequently, Democrats spent much of the fall trying to be noticed and arguing that they still had a chance at victory. Both Davis and his running mate, Charles Bryan, spoke frequently and to attentive audiences. But no one was disposed to trust the country to a party that couldn't manage a convention. The Democratic campaign was like that of the Progressives in that their best hope was a stalemate that led to an election by the House. Democrats needed the Progressives to do well enough to hurt the Republicans but not so well that they damaged the Democrats. They thus concentrated their main fire on the Republicans and only incidentally attacked La Follette.

Davis's most important speech of the election was delivered at Sea Girt, New Jersey, in August 1924.[81] In it, he condemned the Republicans for preying on the American body politic: "In 1921, like a flock of unclean birds hastening to the feast, it gathered from the four winds and descended upon the city. The Little Green House in K Street was set up for sinister purposes, as yet but partly disclosed. Its occupants and their friends soon proved that they lacked neither zeal nor appetite."[82] For Davis, as for La Follette, the Republicans were best understood as a species of carrion birds, ready to pick off what tasty bits they could before the corpse of American democracy rotted completely.

To support this claim, Davis enumerated the various scandals that plagued the Republican administration, connecting them to Coolidge through paralipsis, adding emphasis to a claim by pretending not to make it: "We Democrats are making and will make no campaign of personalities, nor shall I speak with disrespect of any occupant of the Presidential Chair. I am glad to believe that the high office has never been untruthfully held. We have, however, the President's own authority for the statement that, 'the only practical way to secure responsible political action is by the formation of parties.' We agree, and assert further that the only way to secure good government is to hold political parties responsible."[83] In other words, he was perfectly willing to make this a campaign of personalities, to speak of the president with disrespect, and to believe that he shared in the corruption of the Harding years. He just didn't want to accept the responsibility for doing any of these things.

This was, of course, routine stuff. The real import of his speech came in his attack on the KKK. He said, "If any organization, no matter what it chooses to be called, whether Ku Klux Klan or by any other name, raises the standard of racial and religious prejudice or attempts to make racial origins or religious beliefs the test of fitness for public office it does violence to the spirit of American institutions and must be condemned by all those who believe as I do in American ideals."[84] He could not have been more clear. The KKK was doing violence not only to its direct victims but also to national institutions. It therefore merited condemnation. The attack on the Klan came as something of a surprise, especially given the KKK's strength in New Jersey.[85] It was the kind of political courage that could at least partially redeem 1924 from being a completely deplorable election. In my view it doesn't, because like Dawes's statements in Maine, there was no follow-up. The claim was made and then dropped in the interest of political expediency. When political expediency for all parties and participants lies in the direction of exclusion and racism, the whole gestalt of the election is deplorable.

Given that the KKK had played such a prominent part in the Democratic convention, this election could have been rendered less deplorable had the candidates in the general election made direct and explicit arguments in favor of democratic norms and values. But they all avoided, as much as possible, any direct engagement with the religious issue, the KKK, or even Prohibition. Instead, they accused one another of endangering the Constitution and threatening American values. They had opportunities to make the election less deplorable; they generally failed to take them.

Like the Progressives, Democrats did attack the Republicans, mostly on the grounds of the Harding administration's scandals. And again, the fact of a critique of poor administration is not by itself deplorable. But to argue that poor administration is the result of lack of patriotism is an effort to discredit not the policies but the fact of the opposition. It's not the kind of appeal that supports democratic processes. One piece of campaign literature, for example, urged veterans to vote for Davis because "the oil reserve of the United States navy, the first line of the nation's defense, bartered away by a bribe-taking Republican cabinet member, the Veterans' Bureau looted of millions appropriated for disabled men by a crooked director and a coterie of grafting Republican patricians."[86] Like that of the Progressives, if less stridently so, the Democratic campaign hinged on the corruption of the Republicans and on connecting that corruption to an overall ethos of "special privilege." The argument, in his harshest form, was that the Republicans had betrayed the nation's trust.[87] It is perfectly reasonable to argue that corrupt officials should be replaced. That argument doesn't have to be accompanied by claims that members of an entire political party lack patriotism.

Like Republicans, Democrats engaged in scapegoating where Progressives were concerned. Democrats argued that the Progressive campaign was evidence of the danger of increased political unrest and indicated that reelecting Coolidge might increase political instability.[88] Given the recent Red Scare, and the tensions revealed at their convention, to Democratically inclined audiences, at least, these fears may well have seemed very real. If nothing else, they would have encouraged the Democratic faithful to remain in the party and abjure the temptations of defecting to the Progressives.

These appeals added to the deplorable nature of the election by circulating the same kinds of despicable discourse we have seen from the other parties. But they did the Democrats very little good. Democratic inability to manage a convention left considerable room for doubt on the question of whether they should be allowed to run the national government. A postelection analysis parsed the Democratic loss as a result of three main factors: first, Davis had little support in the West, which opened the door for La Follette's campaign. That campaign also hurt the Democrats with labor, as La Follette attracted the support of the AFL. Second, the "disloyalty of the Klan Democrats" in states like Montana, Missouri, and Kentucky meant that "a number of important states" went to Coolidge. Finally, Democrats were plagued by a lack of party discipline and a poorly run campaign.[89] Democrats lost much of their important labor constituency to La Follette. They lost much of their midwestern support to Coolidge, at least partly because of his willingness to abide the Klan. They lost the support of many mainstream partisans to their inability to manage a convention. Going into the general election, Democrats had little to lose and a great deal at stake. They had little to lose because their chances of electoral victory were minimal. There was much at stake because while the party could sustain one loss at the polls almost any appeals made in almost any terms threatened to alienate part of their coalition, further imperiling their future. They engaged in lowest-common-denominator rhetoric and circulated despicable discourse.

When it was all over, incumbent Calvin Coolidge earned 382 electoral votes and 54 percent of the popular vote, John Davis managed 136 electoral votes and 28.8 percent of the popular vote, and Robert La Follette eked out 13 electoral votes with 16.5 percent of the popular vote. Voter turnout was low, and yet the Republicans earned the largest plurality in history. It was a thoroughly deplorable election, in which despicable discourse circulated widely and freely by all three parties. It introduced and legitimated the politics of fear in the twentieth century.

CONCLUSION: THE POLITICS OF FEAR

The argument of this book is that certain elections, characterized by weak political institutions, unfair economic conditions, status anxiety, and the salience of race, class, and/or gender issues facilitate the circulation of despicable discourses and lead to deplorable elections. By those standards, 1924 clearly fits into the category. This election was also characterized by the presence of a new kind of mass media, as radio played a major role in the circulation of campaign communication. Radio made it possible for the entire nation to witness the events in Madison Square Garden; it allowed Coolidge to avoid facing the voters in person; it allowed for comparatively rapid circulation of news. Radio wasn't responsible for making 1924 deplorable, but it circulated despicable discourses and did so nationally and quickly.

The election itself is also not solely responsible for those discourses. They were already widely circulating throughout the polity. The various pieces of legislation that restricted immigration, for instance, were passed before the election and the discourses justifying them were evident long before the campaign itself began. Similarly, well before the parties met to nominate candidates, the KKK had attained a sort of dreadful civic respectability. If anything, the election itself contributed to the Klan's loss of that respectability. The candidates chose to attack one another's patriotism and commitment to national values because those ideals had been under increasing pressure from multiple sources since the end of the Great War. But elections bring these already circulating discourses into sharp focus.

This chapter is about the politics of fear not only because of the role played by the Klan, which specialized in fear, but also because of the ways that all the candidates made certain kinds of fear appeals part of their campaigns. Voters were told to fear the Progressives because they posed a threat to the Constitution; they were told to fear the Supreme Court because it posed a threat to the poor and defenseless; they were told to fear the corruption and elitism of the major parties. All elections are choices and all campaigns tend to pose those choices in stark terms. But the terms posed by this deplorable election tended to delegitimate the opposition, not merely to disagree with it.

One of the criteria for a deplorable election is that the major parties either participate in or refuse to condemn the use of despicable discourse and by these criteria, 1924 is a tricky entry into the category, because Davis and Dawes both did speak against the Klan. Yet both also did so only once, and upon receiving pressure to silence themselves, they did so. Those single statements earned a fair amount of attention, but they were not concentrated and principled defenses of those the KKK victimized. They tended instead to justify the terms under which the Klan gained prominence while criticizing the specific practices of the KKK. The terms of debate, rooted in white supremacist notions of national identity, tended to reinforce rather than challenge those notions. The prominence of the KKK throughout the election validated the presence of bigoted speech in the national conversation. It gave that bigotry a national endorsement. Equally, it endorsed a rabid patriotism and belief in "Americanism," narrowly defined.

The turmoil of the election was soon dissipated. Very little political energy went toward anything that might be considered political reform, and even less went toward dealing with the religious, regional, ethnic, or class conflicts that divided the nation. Coolidge had, in Walter Lippmann's terms, "a genius for inactivity."[90] Under Coolidge, the nation devoted itself to making profit. These were the years where the casual bigotry of the wealthy Buchanans was immortalized in *The Great Gatsby*, where great wealth was attained at the cost of traditional moral and social values, and during which Fitzgerald and Hemingway wrote of the "Lost Generation," those Americans damaged by the Great War and its aftermath.

The 1924 election made the damage done to the polity by the Great War and the technological changes that followed it apparent. The tensions and fissures that animated that election continued to widen until the party system itself faced realignment in the 1930s. The election and its aftermath did little to reduce those tensions or heal the wounds in the nation. They did circulate and legitimize discourses that exacerbated rather than mitigated those tensions and wounds. And so the tensions continued to tighten and the wounds continued to fester.

CHAPTER 4

THE VENEER OF CIVILITY: THE SUBTLE POLITICS OF RACISM, 1968

Richard M. Nixon walked into the meeting in Atlanta an unwelcome front-runner for the Republican presidential nomination. He walked out with the nomination all but guaranteed, having locked up the votes of the Southern conservatives under the leadership of Senator Strom Thurmond (R-SC).[1] With Nixon's nomination in 1968, power within the Republican Party had shifted from the moderate strongholds in the East and upper Midwest to the conservatives in the West and South. The governing logics of the party had also shifted, and those logics were very much on display in Miami. During that meeting, Nixon essentially told Thurmond that as president he would relax the federal pressure for school desegregation—logically, that meant all desegregation.[2] In exchange, Thurmond agreed to campaign for Nixon, undermining the Wallace campaign. Nixon and his party tied their electoral futures to the prevention of racial progress and to the circulation of despicable discourse.

In the 1968 general election, conservatives faced a choice between Nixon, who had a reasonably moderate record on race, and George Wallace, whose record on race was anything but moderate. Republicans also faced a choice. They could condemn the explicit and implicit racism of the Wallace campaign, as Nelson A. Rockefeller had condemned what he called the "extremism" of Barry Goldwater in 1964, and run from the center, potentially risking a loss as catastrophic as the one they experienced then. Or they could steer a different course, one that ceded the explicitly racist vote to Wallace but made a bid for the votes of those who wanted to protect white supremacy but were uncomfortable with the strident racism that had been on display in the opposition to civil rights in the South. That second strategy required two things: a candidate willing to make coded appeals to those white voters and a party willing to pretend that what they were doing was neither racist nor exclusionary. It was a choice to rely on political fictions to win high political office. That was the choice they made. In doing so, they inaugurated a new kind of despicable discourse, one that hid its exclusionary aspects under a veneer of inclusion.

It was a consequential choice in other ways as well. It enabled Republicans to drive a wedge through the heart of the New Deal coalition, an unlikely amalgam of Southern conservatives and Northern African Americans and liberals that had voted solidly Democratic since the 1930s.[3] The New Deal coalition was held together by a combination of legacy politics and the Democratic commitment to economic policies. Race threatened to destroy its consensus, to do for the domestic politics of the Democratic Party what the Vietnam War was doing to the nation's foreign policy consensus.[4] The 1968 election thus marked a pivotal moment in American politics, one that hastened the erosion of the Democrats' political dominance and ushered in a politics based on a kind of conservative populism in which the government itself was increasingly seen as the progenitor of the nation's problems rather than a source of solutions to them. Undermining the federal government's role in national politics also meant undermining the possibilities for building a more just and equitable nation, for that effort relied on federal institutions.

This pivot was neither quiet nor peaceful; 1968 stands out as one of the nation's most turbulent years, concealing the largely conservative nature of national politics under a sense of revolutionary and threatening change. It was a year of conservative backlash against the civil rights movement and liberal backlash against a foreign policy consensus that led to the support of colonialism and war. These phenomena were visible across the nation's politics. They were especially clear in the success of George Wallace, whose candidacy was evidence that some Americans remained comfortable with overt claims to white supremacy. But it also allowed other Americans to envision racially exclusionary politics as abnormal, as the sole province of the KKK and the South.[5] Yet white supremacy was neither abnormal nor confined to the South, and Wallace's campaign laid that fiction bare. After Wallace declared that the University of Alabama would remain segregated in 1963, for example, he got "more than one hundred thousand congratulatory telegrams. He said, 'They all hate black people, all of them. They're all afraid, all of them. Great God! That's it! They're all Southern! The whole United States is Southern!'"[6] Five years later, Nixon's campaign staff agreed. In a memo written to Nixon from aide Jim Keogh, Keogh noted, "Sherm Unger adds by telephone that the remarks you made to White Plains last night about home rule and citizen participation in government would be received very well in Charlotte."[7] The same arguments that swayed voters in North Carolina were working in New York. While the national fictions confined strident racism to the South and pictured it as a last gasp of resistance among a few poorly educated whites there, resistance to the policy entailments of civil rights was national, and so was the violence associated with that resistance. Historian Michael A. Cohen reports that "By July [1968] violence had become the norm at virtually every one of Wallace's public appearances. . . . Indeed, cries of 'Sieg Heil,' and 'kill the n*****s became staples at Wallace rallies."[8] The routine nature of violence and threats of violence underpinned both the Wallace campaign and the vision of a white nation that it advocated.

Yet it was possible to argue that Wallace, as presidential campaigner chronicler Theodore H. White put it, was "'a segregationist, not a lyncher,' as if that distinction offered some exoneration for his racial politics. Wallace is infuriated by the epithet of Nazi or Fascist hurled at him in the North. If George Wallace hates anything, it is not Negroes—it is the Federal government of the United States and its 'pointy-head' advisors, the 'intellectual morons,' the 'guideline writers' of Washington who try to upset the natural relation of races and force Negroes and whites to live together in unnatural mixing."[9] For White, it was possible to resent the federal government for implementing desegregation without necessarily hating Negroes. This is the key to conservative politics during these years, a sleight-of-hand that displaces "race" onto "government overreach." As this example indicates,

Wallace's campaign was grounded in race, but it wasn't confined to race. Wallace also attacked the federal government as the source of the nation's woes and tied federal action to the increasingly divisive politics of culture, explicitly arguing that the national culture was under attack. That culture, presumptively white, was "threatened" by the permissiveness of the courts, the emphasis on gun control that followed the assassinations of King and especially Robert Kennedy, the demonstrations, rising crime rates, and a generalized fear that somehow, something had broken.

As the Wallace example indicates, the conservative strategy in general throughout the 1960s was about exacerbating those fears. It wasn't just Nixon, although his campaign became the focal point for these arguments. For example, Representative William G. Bray (R-IN) wrote Nixon, arguing in part that "there is an increasing amount of opposition to Fortas' nomination; not so much against him, but rather the attempt by the Executive to exert control over the Court, even after he is gone." Bray also noted that "the gun control bill is becoming increasingly unpopular," while "your recognition of the middle class—the class that pays the bill, loves the country, obeys the laws and does not demonstrate—is very popular."[10] The arguments that "they" were installing permissive judges, coming after the nation's guns, and disrespecting the middle class were resonating with a developing constituency.

The people to whom this language appealed were moved by the rhetoric of restoration. As one florid note to Nixon during the 1968 campaign argued, "You are going to win! Therefore we are all going to win. And with the dawn of this bright new era, America will once again rise to the proud and beautiful, hopeful land our forebearers envisioned; a country free of crime, of hate, of poverty, of bitterness, of hopelessness, and of despair; a nation fuller of promise, of confidence, of faith, of self-respect, of poise, of realization, and of equality."[11] This letter and others like it equated Nixon and his campaign with both a new beginning and a return to better days. This author saw in Nixon's campaign a real effort to make the United States great again, a return to former glory and a means to an idealized future.

The connection between these ideas is critical to how despicable discourses developed in the 1960s and beyond. That connection depends on a set of assumptions, rooted in the idea that there was an ideal past that has somehow been taken away. The perpetrators of this theft are also those who are understood as unfairly benefiting from a new and debased situation.

The nation's greatness has been diminished by a racialized "them," and "they" are reaping unjust rewards as a result. Both the nation and its most deserving citizens are therefore suffering. Restoration demands purification. Once those elements are removed or returned to their appropriate place in the national hierarchy, the nation will once again be great.

Many important things happened in 1968. In terms of understanding the historical arc of deplorable elections, the most important of them was the defeat of the moderate wing of the Republican Party. That defeat had been years in the making, and this chapter puts that defeat at its center. Unlike the other chapters in this book, this one largely ignores one of the major parties—in this case, the Democrats. I do this for two reasons. First, I want to spend considerable time on the development and use of the Southern strategy. The employment of this strategy, which, as we will see in the next chapter, eventually migrated across party lines, changed American politics in important ways. Second, the Southern strategy signaled a change in despicable discourse. As has been amply displayed in previous chapters, earlier iterations of exclusionary language were generally lacking in subtlety and they were usually brief eruptions rather than sustained political practices. The success of the Southern strategy, on the other hand, required two things: a speaker willing to talk in code and the acquiescence of other elites who allow the coded language to go unaddressed. By refusing to label coded language as despicable, by declining to call its exclusionary and racist elements what they are, these elites enabled the adoption of its fictions. Lacking elite pushback, these discourses became part of the national vocabulary. In 1968, Richard Nixon relied heavily on coded language, a fact that has been well documented. Less well understood is the second piece of this process, the enabling of the implicit racism by Republican moderates like Nelson A. Rockefeller. This chapter tells that story too.

In 1968, this is largely a conservative and Republican story. The Democrats, wounded by the Johnson administration and reeling from the assassinations of Martin Luther King Jr. and Robert F. Kennedy, met for their convention in Chicago, where protests were met by police violence. Their nominee, Vice President Hubert Humphrey, floundered in the early campaign but made a recovery when he broke with Johnson over Vietnam. It was enough to worry the Nixon camp, but it was too little too late, and despite his resurgence in the polls Humphrey ended with 42.7 percent of the vote and 191 electoral votes. George Wallace managed a disturbing 13.5 percent of the national vote and 46 electoral votes, all in the Deep South, winning Arkansas, Louisiana, Mississippi, Alabama, and Georgia. Nixon won with 43.4 percent of the popular vote and 301 electoral votes. This chapter is Nixon's story. It is also the story of how despicable discourse took a longstanding and uninterrupted hold on our national politics. It's a story that neither begins nor ends in 1968, or even with Richard Nixon. To get there, we need to go back to where it started, with Barry Goldwater, in 1964.

A BRIEF PROLOGUE: 1964

Republicans in 1964 were uncertain how best to recover from their narrow defeat in 1960. That election saw the beginnings of the split between moderate and conservative Republicans, a split made most apparent in the person of New York's liberal governor, Nelson A. Rockefeller. For conservatives, increasingly hailing from the South and West, Rockefeller embodied the detested monied interests of the East. Conservatives also hated Rockefeller personally, in part for what has become known as "the Compact (sometimes the Treaty) of Fifth Avenue."[12] In 1960, presumptive Republican nominee Richard Nixon, feeling that he needed the support of the party's moderate wing, visited Rockefeller's Fifth Avenue apartment. During a lengthy meeting, the two hammered out a set of agreements on the party platform. Those agreements included positions on national security, economic growth, and, significantly, a commitment to "remove the last vestiges of segregation or discrimination." During the meeting, Rockefeller turned down Nixon's offer of the vice-presidential slot on the ticket. Conservatives objected to the agreement in principle, railed against many of its specifics, and resented Rockefeller for his refusal to run with Nixon. Goldwater, for example, called it "the Munich of the Republican Party," implicitly likening Rockefeller to Hitler.[13] Eventually, conservatives blamed Rockefeller for not campaigning hard enough for the Nixon-Lodge ticket, contributing to if not causing the Republican defeat. That defeat left Republicans deeply divided, and following the 1960 election Rockefeller became, for party conservatives, the epitome of the hated Eastern establishment.

Rockefeller wanted the party to act decisively against what he understood as its "extremist" elements. He asked convention delegates to include this language in their platform: "The Republican Party fully respects the contribution of responsible criticism, and defends the right of dissent in the democratic process. But we repudiate the efforts of irresponsible extremist groups, such as the Communists, the Ku Klux Klan, and John Birch Society, and others, to discredit our Party by their efforts to infiltrate positions of responsibility in the Party, or to attach themselves to its candidates."[14] This was a remarkable request on many levels. It lumped the Klan and the Birchers together; it labeled them as functionally the same, as equally "extremist"; it positioned the Klan and the Birchers as moral equivalents of Communism, and thus as equally detestable; it declared that all these groups equally merited repudiation; and it charged Birchers and the KKK with tactics similar to those of Communists, including attempts to "infiltrate" the Republican Party and to "attach" themselves to its candidates. Rockefeller insisted that "the time has come for the Republican Party to face this issue realistically and take decisive action." Delegates reacted with rage, catcalling, booing, and hissing.

The taunting of a prominent member of the party was bad enough. Much worse was the overt hostility faced by the convention's African American delegates. Rockefeller delegate Jackie Robinson reported seeing cigarettes being put out on one black delegate, others had their credentials revoked, and one man tried to get in a fight with Robinson, who later wrote that the convention gave him "a better understanding of how it must have felt to be a Jew in Hitler's Germany."[15] One Rockefeller biographer reports that one speaker argued that "'forces are at work to expel Negroes from positions of leadership in our party' . . . 'Yeah,' snarled an opponent in an unmistakable Dixie drawl, 'and next time there won't be no n*****s to expel!'"[16] It's hard to imagine an uglier contemporary convention. Documentarian Ken Burns identifies the convention as "the moment when the Republican Party made a pact with the Devil for which they are still paying."[17] Republican support for Goldwater and resentment toward Rockefeller were not entirely about race. But they were unmistakably about race.

In 1964, Rockefeller lost many of the battles he fought with his fellow Republicans—he lost the nomination to Goldwater and he lost the platform fight. But he succeeded in ensuring that the public saw those he considered extremists for what they were and consequently helped undermine the Goldwater campaign, which lost in a landslide. Rockefeller's success, to the extent that it could be called success, was a short-term phenomenon. He helped defeat Goldwater, but the conservative movement continued to gain strength. In part, that growth was a response to the cultural upheavals of the 1960s generally, but two issues increasingly dominated the national agenda: Vietnam and race.

INTO 1968

Between 1964 and the 1968 election, the Civil Rights Act (1964) and Voting Rights Act (1965) were passed. Johnson escalated the war in Vietnam and the Credibility Gap, as the distrust for the Johnson administration was labeled, became a chasm. The largely African American Los Angeles community of Watts erupted in flames and so did Black neighborhoods in other cities. Students on college campuses opposed the war and demonstrated for a variety of objectives, including civil rights, women's rights, and other causes. But two issues created more conflict than any others, the war and race relations. Together, they posed what whites tended to see as the problem of order, a breeding ground for Nixon's despicable discourse.

Vietnam

Whatever else can be said about Vietnam, the prosecution of that war ruptured the post–World War II consensus on American internationalism. In part, this was because there was no agreement on the causes or aims of the war. Lacking agreement on the nation's purpose in being in Vietnam, it became impossible to create a consensus about what victory looked like or how to achieve it. The war split an already fragile Democratic coalition, as LBJ demanded loyalty to what was increasingly seen as "his" war, and other candidates, most notably Minnesota senator Eugene McCarthy and Robert F. Kennedy, demanded an end to the war. Republicans were more steadfast in their commitment but were also seeking exit strategies.

Nixon's public facing strategy was to rely on ambiguity while proffering the impression that he had a strategy to escape the quagmire in Vietnam. He did indeed have a plan, but it wasn't one that he wanted publicly known. Anna Chennault, a prominent participant in the DC social circuit, maintained connections in Hanoi as well as Washington. During the campaign, Nixon used her to make it clear to Hanoi that they should not consider any offers made by the Johnson administration at the ongoing Paris peace talks—that they would do better under a Nixon administration. Undercutting administration foreign policy is, at the very least, illegal; at worst, Nixon's actions were treasonable. Moreover, delaying peace meant the deaths of US and Vietnamese soldiers. Upon hearing the details of Nixon's connections with Chennault, Johnson privately told Nixon to stop but decided not to make the information public.[18]

While working to undermine the Paris Peace Talks in private, Nixon was saying this in public:

> The more we conduct this war, as long as the war has to be conducted, with less men, the better. I think what is something that must be avoided, however, is to give any indication to the enemy that the United States is cutting back its forces before there is a clear indication that the enemy is ready to negotiate. If we cut back our forces in advance of that time, it will mean that the negotiations, I think, will be delayed because the enemy is going to negotiate when it is convinced that it cannot win militarily in Vietnam. . . . Let me make one thing very clear. I will not during the course of the campaign while negotiations are going on in Paris—I will not indicate what I would be willing to do if I were negotiating or if these negotiations fail, because if I do that, obviously the men in Hanoi will be listening.[19]

Publicly, Nixon was acting prudently. Privately, he was undermining the nation's foreign policy and potentially prolonging the war. Nationally, the controversies over the war continued, with escalating waves of protests. The Tet Offensive, mounted by the North Vietnamese, was a military failure but a public relations success, and it convinced CBS news commentator Walter Cronkite that the war was unwinnable; Cronkite helped convince the nation. But the war continued, contributing to the overall chaos in the Democratic Party, which was also tearing itself apart over the connected issue of race.

The Politics of Race

Initially, it appeared that after the 1954 landmark *Brown v. Board of Education* decision mandating desegregation in public schools, the nation was headed in a direction of increased equity and inclusion, but the dictates of white supremacy proved too strong. The basic assumption of the white supremacist argument is that any gains made by African Americans or members of other marginalized and disenfranchised groups can only come at the expense of white people. It is impossible for anyone to accrue rights and privileges, this thinking goes, without taking rights and privileges away from those who already have them. This belief posits political and social rights as a finite resource, which means that they are always at risk and must be defended, a formulation that runs directly counter to the universalistic premises of US democracy, which insists that all people are created equal and are equally guaranteed rights, a fact that has little to no effect on the political power of this argument.

Those arguments gained strength after the Watts riots broke out less than a week after the signing of the Voting Rights Act, as what little optimism the act generated rapidly dissipated in the aftermath of violence. Whatever optimism remained continued to erode as whites in the South continued to resist civil rights and as the civil rights movement, under internal and external pressure, fractured. White dedication to the cause of civil rights was simply not strong enough to overcome the force of backlash—in a pattern that recalls the response to Reconstruction in the 1860s and 1870s, the energy required to keep fighting resistance to African American equality was greater than the national commitment to that equality. As John Hope Franklin put it, "In their struggle for complete equality blacks, whether in the South or in the North, could be fairly certain to receive northern white assistance in matters of transportation, voting, education in general, and in the enjoyment of places of public accommodation. They could not be nearly as certain of such support in matters of employment, housing, security of their persons, and equal education in the urban ghetto. In that sense the resistance to significant change in race relations could be as vigorous in the North as in the South."[20] Nationally, whites were concerned with protecting their own positions and were only willing to go so far in advancing the interests of African Americans, especially as those interests were seen as potentially threatening to white privileges.

Several things animated Southern resistance to civil rights. Ideology was the first and most important; the doctrines of white supremacy had and continue to have deep roots. Economic anxiety was also a factor, as was fear of losing political power. As the rural South continued to decline economically, its urban centers began growing and gaining in political power. And those urban areas were also becoming Black, meaning that African Americans were also gaining political power. White attitudes in opposition to civil rights fell along a continuum between outright white supremacy and a more implicit desire to preserve national hierarchies by arguing that progress was happening "too fast," or that African Americans were asking for "too much." People adopting the more explicit forms tended to favor Wallace's candidacy. Those adopting subtler forms of racism increasingly found a home in the Nixon campaign. That campaign, rooted in the promise of restoring "law and order," thrived on the national sense of disorder and impending chaos.

The Problem of Order

As protests for civil rights and against the war in Vietnam escalated, white fears about the nation's ability to maintain order also escalated. As the nation's cities burned and its campuses convulsed, it increasingly appeared as if things were coming apart. The campaign itself only heightened the sense of confusion and disorder as incumbent Lyndon Johnson decided to end his campaign in the wake of the McCarthy insurgency. Martin Luther King Jr. was assassinated, and shortly thereafter, so was Robert Kennedy. The nation was caught up in a maelstrom of violence: police violence against African American citizens, civil rights activists, and antiwar protesters; rebellions in the cities and on college campuses; the assassinations of political leaders; and, of course, the war in Vietnam.

The political moment was dominated by a fight over resources as butter increasingly gave way to guns. The demands of the war displaced the Great Society and Johnson's ambitious domestic program. Additionally, concerns over personal security—over housing, finances, jobs, the environment, the exploding crime rate—all escalated, driven in part by increasingly frenetic media coverage. All of this led to a desire among the nation's white middle class for "law and order," a phrase with plenty of racist elements, but not confined to racism. Those citizens wanting more "law and order" wanted a return to the quieter, more predictable days of the 1950s, when things, for those citizens at least, seemed increasingly comfortable, increasingly stable. The appeal of law and order was an appeal designed for a specific subsection of the American electorate, those Americans worried about the security of their nation and fearful in their own personal lives and willing to endorse politics that promised security, willing to overlook the consequences of that security for other Americans. Those worried Americans were at the core of Nixon's electoral strategy, the target of his despicable discourse.

THE NIXON CAMPAIGN

As the 1968 campaign developed on the Republican side, the main contenders were initially Ronald Reagan, whose meteoric rise to the California governor's mansion in 1966 came in the wake of his strong support for Goldwater in 1964, Midwestern moderate and Michigan governor George Romney, and Richard Nixon. Rockefeller lurked as a possible contender as well. Reagan was undone by his unwillingness to declare an open candidacy and the news that he had "tolerated" a "homosexual ring" in his gubernatorial office. Romney, reasonably popular, first broke with the party line by calling Vietnam a "tragic mistake" and then offhandedly remarked that he had been "brainwashed" by US military officials into supporting the war, effectively ending his candidacy. That realistically left Republicans with a choice between Nixon and the on-again, off-again candidacy of Nelson Rockefeller, with Reagan's shadow looming on the right of both men.

Once Lyndon Johnson left the Democratic race, however, things seemed to shift in Rockefeller's favor, as it was possible to argue he was the better candidate against either McCarthy or Kennedy. That feeling sharpened after King's assassination because of Rockefeller's commitment to racial justice. Nixon went in an entirely opposite—and to Republicans, much more persuasive—direction, increasingly staking his campaign on issues of "law and order." Unwilling to credit the possibility of bringing African Americans back into the Republican fold, Nixon jettisoned their votes in favor of trying to capture those of Southern conservatives. He looked to the West and to conservatives there rather than to the East for his support, assuming Wall Street would come back to him in the general election, preferring his candidacy to that of any Democrat. The politics of his coalition meant that he needed to take an exclusionary stand on race relations.[21] Goldwater's defeat in 1964 and Reagan's victory in the California gubernatorial election in 1966 both taught that this stance had to be taken carefully.

In contrast to the half-hearted efforts displayed by Reagan and Rockefeller, Nixon campaigned hard. He spent the years between 1964 and 1968 on "the rubber chicken circuit," speaking at civic and partisan venues around the country, making connections and friends. He also changed his media strategy, hiring network executive Roger Ailes, who spearheaded a strategy designed to keep Nixon both in front of the public and insulated from it. This allowed his campaign to present a polite, professional, mannered Nixon, one whose politics appealed to conservatives but whose presence didn't frighten away moderates. Their goal was to circumvent the print media with an astute use of television, to control the media message through paid media.[22] His campaign was, in fact, cloaked in a veneer of control and civility.

As Nixon reported, "In June 1967 Bob Haldeman gave me a memorandum on the use of the media in a modern presidential campaign. He stressed that creative thought had to be given to developing ways to use television."[23] Nixon connected with the common person in a way that no Republican had before, and his campaign demonstrated a clear understanding of the logics, demands, and potential of television. According to Nixon:

> The goal was to match the candidate with the medium, to determine exactly what manner of presentation would be most effective. They analyzed each performance and decided that the more spontaneous the situation, the better I came across. This insight led to the decision that I would use the question-and-answer technique extensively, not only in press conferences and public question sessions with student audiences but also in my paid political programming. . . . In the campaign this evolved into the "man in the arena" concept, in which I stood alone, with no podium, in the center of a stage surrounded by an audience in bleacherlike tiers. In this setting I was asked questions by a panel of private citizens, sometimes joined by local reporters.[24]

The campaign relied on "spontaneous" formats, in which the candidate could be shown as personable, responsive, and caring. But it was a façade.

Unsurprisingly, after his disastrous debate with John Kennedy in 1960, Nixon refused to debate in 1968. He also refused to visit college campuses or to go places where that façade might be threatened. Nixon went only to places where he could be assured of a positive reception—which made for a reassuring backdrop on the evening news.

As is so often the case with despicable discourse, in 1968 Nixon's was associated with changes in media technology. Through television and ads, Nixon created a particular kind of image of himself, a "New Nixon," one that was less overtly abrasive, more controlled, better able to manage the nation in a time of turmoil. Campaigns always depend on images and all candidates create images of themselves that they think will move the voters. In this case, television helped Nixon invent and circulate a set of fictions that were aimed at a very particular slice of the electorate. He chose to appeal to those people by walking a careful line between the overt racism associated with George Wallace and the politics of inclusion increasingly associated with the Democrats. At stake were the votes of whites who could not countenance Wallace's performance of racism but who were considerably more comfortable with the policies he espoused. As Ibram X. Kendi notes:

> Richard Nixon and his team of aides had carefully studied George Wallace's presidential campaigns. They realized that his segregationist banter made him attractive only to "the foam-at-the-mouth segregationists." Nixon decided to appeal to these Wallace-type segregationists while also attracting all those Americans refusing to live in "dangerous" Black neighborhoods, refusing to believe that Black schools could be equal, refusing to accept busing initiatives to integrate schools, refusing to individualize Black negativity, refusing to believe that Black welfare mothers were deserving, and refusing to champion Black Power over majority-Black counties and cities—all those racists who refused to believe they were racist in 1968.[25]

Nixon could not use overt appeals to the white backlash for at least two reasons. First, Republican moderates saw such appeals as distasteful at best and morally repugnant at worst. Overtly appealing to white backlash voters meant risking the votes of mainstream Republicans. Second, Wallace was a master of the politics of subtle racism, and to compete with him Nixon decided he had to use the same tactic.[26] So he subtly indicated to Wallace voters and potential Wallace voters that he was in basic agreement with their politics while also arguing that a vote for Wallace was a wasted vote, because as a third-party candidate he couldn't win.[27] Voting for Nixon, he constantly implied, would put an ally in the White House; voting for Wallace would put liberal Democrats there.[28]

Nixon thus had three goals concerning the 1968 election. He needed to appeal to enough Wallace voters to minimize the damage caused by Wallace to his electoral coalition, he needed to defeat the moderates in his own party while also maintaining their allegiance, and he wanted to reshape the Republican Party in a way that would make it a dominant force for the foreseeable future. The Southern strategy was his way of accomplishing these things and, incidentally, establishing his own political primacy in the process.

THE SOUTHERN STRATEGY

The Southern strategy was well understood at the time, both by Nixon and by others. In the Rockefeller archive, for instance, there is an eighty-nine-page memo detailing the Southern strategy—by that name, and in great detail—complete with Nixon's views on open housing, busing, riots, "exploiting the riots," "rebuilding the ghetto," and a "general position paper."[29] There are discussions about Nixon's intended audience and the effects of the Southern strategy on that audience, specifically connecting it to "white backlash" and noting its appeal in both the North and the South.[30]

The memo begins by defining the Southern strategy: "Displaying extraordinary political sensitivity, Nixon has developed a civil rights posture which—on its surface—is as politically appealing in the North as it is in the South. It appeals to segregationists, and yet is so hedged and ambiguous a commitment as to fend off strong criticism by civil rights advocates. It is clever, on the verge of duplicity, but tight enough to be fairly well immune from political criticism."[31] The memo's author astutely analyzes the details and aims of the Southern strategy, right down to the rhetorical mechanisms through which it works: "Nixon's words often suggest secondary meanings or include qualifying addendums."[32] The author notes Nixon's "mastery of double talk"[33] and is very clear about the purposes of such maneuvering: "During the 1964 election debacle, the Republican Party watched while the Negro vote abandoned it en masse. Nixon, apparently resigned to this alienation, appears to be subtly riding the white backlash. He shows little sympathy to the problems of the Negro Americans or to other minority groups. Instead, he exploits opposition to government programs which are directed at solving minority unrest."[34]

Rockefeller understood the Southern strategy, knew of its connection to the tactics and strategies Goldwater and his supporters had attempted in 1964, and grasped the fact that in a changed political context and with a different messenger, it might prove effective. And yet he did not make the kind of overt argument opposing the Southern strategy that he had made against those he considered extremists in 1964. He and other moderates effectively ceded the party to the very elements he had opposed four years earlier. They—and the nation—would reap the consequences of that in 1968 and in years to come.

The Southern strategy was designed to stave off the Wallace challenge, defeat Republican moderates, and reinvigorate the Republican Party's national presence. To understand how these three things worked together to forge a coherent set of arguments, I address each goal in turn, associating each with a specific element of the overall strategy. The Southern strategy relies on racial and racist appeals to whites, especially those deemed "white ethnics." Nixon used it as a way of forestalling Reagan's candidacy during the primaries and, more importantly, stemming the loss of those voters, especially in the border South, to Wallace during the general election. Its second pillar is undermining the federal government as a positive force in US politics and a reliance on individualism in its place. That appeal was aimed directly at moderates like Romney and Rockefeller, who accepted in broad terms the goals of the New Deal and the Great Society and was particularly appealing to Western conservatives. The final pillar is what I am calling the politics of polarization, in which he made arguments about the nature of national politics and who merits its benefits, depicting politics as a zero-sum game in which any gains made by the minoritized poor are given at the expense of others—namely the new constituency he wants to develop under the Republican Party umbrella. It was on these grounds that he hoped to build a new majority for the Republican Party. Obviously, all of these elements worked together; the groupings and divisions I propose here are analytic tools, through which I am trying to make the case that as despicable discourse, the Southern strategy had specific kinds of consequences for American national politics.

This rhetoric is, in its broad strokes and in its particulars, exclusionary. It is thus what I call despicable discourse. But it is implicit, not overt, and pretends to be inclusive. Its success requires two things: a speaker willing to engage in this kind of despicable discourse and a party willing to embrace it. In 1968, Nixon was willing to circulate it. Despite his knowledge of exactly what this discourse entailed, how it was being accomplished, and what its consequences would be, Nelson Rockefeller chose to remain silent, allowing this discourse to circulate unchallenged. The consequences of that, for the Republican Party and the nation, continue to reverberate.

The Short Term: George Wallace and the Politics of Race

Wallace's campaigns indicated, if such indications were needed, the political power of those who were becoming labeled "white ethnics"—working-class Irish, Italians, Greeks, Poles, and others who were feeling displaced by the advances made by African Americans and afraid that their neighborhoods and schools would be the first ones—and maybe the only ones—to feel the disruptions associated with integration. A Nixon aide underlined a key sentence in a Gallup poll:

> A significant shift in attitudes has occurred in the areas outside the South over the past year regarding the speed of integration. *"In August of last year, 36 percent of white people living outside the South said that the present Administration is pushing integration 'too fast.'"* In the latest survey, almost one year later, the figure has increased to 44 percent, a rise of 8 percentage points. In the South, a contrary trend is noted. A year ago, 69 percent said the Administration was pushing integration "too fast." Today, the figure is 62 percent, a decrease of 7 percentage points.[35]

As Wallace had noted as early as 1963, whites across the whole country opposed integration; resistance to integration was growing nationally, even as it was decreasing in the South.

Even so, the naked racism of the early 1960s was less politically possible in the context of 1968, and the same Wallace who in 1963 proclaimed "segregation forever" was in 1968 "very grateful for the fact that in 1966 my wife [running as his surrogate] received more black votes in Alabama than did either one of her opponents. We are proud to say that they support us now in this race for the presidency, and we would like to have the support of people of all races, creeds, religions, and national origins. . . . The overwhelming majority of all races in this country are against this breakdown of law and order . . . it's a few anarchists, a few activists, a few militants, a few troublemakers, a few communists."[36] Note here the way that he made racialized claims while defusing them through phrases like "people of all races." If he could plausibly claim that African Americans and members of other marginalized groups shared his beliefs, then exclusionary elements are less easy to spot and more difficult to label as "racist." He placed African Americans and members of other marginalized groups with him in the majority, and placed "anarchists, a few activists, a few militants, a few troublemakers, a few communists" as the minority—there are only "a few" of them. He also conflated anarchists, activists, militants, troublemakers, and communists, rendering them all part of the same unsavory group, each equally dangerous, each equally worth opposing. It is hard to spot this as racism (although it is). It is also despicable discourse, for it pits an "overwhelming majority" of citizens against a carefully defined minority who are depicted as worthy of exclusion in terms that provoke outrage without providing evidence. Entire classes of people were threatened with exclusion.

Wallace was good at subtly racist rhetoric, but he also staked out overtly exclusionary positions on racial politics: "Mr. Nixon and Mr. Humphrey, both three or four weeks ago, called for passage of a bill on the federal level that would require you to sell or lease your own property to whomsoever they thought you ought to lease it to" and "Not one dime of your federal money is going to be used to bus anybody any place that you don't want them to be bussed."[37] He argued here that it was not merely the goal of racial integration he opposed but also the means liberals were using to accomplish that goal—he made arguments against the actions of the federal government as part of the same case against racial equality. Federal action couldn't be trusted because the ends that government was pursuing were wrong, and they were wrong because they required federal, rather than local action. Each position required the other. He said, "Now what are some of the things we are going to do when we become president? We are going to turn back to you, the people of the states, the right to control domestic institutions."[38] Wallace was opposed to federal action and to government in general—here he was securely in the tradition of Barry Goldwater, and his appeal was to Goldwater voters. Wallace made connections between "white interests" and disdain for the actions of the federal government. So long as that government was defending white supremacy, it could be tolerated. But as soon as federal action turned toward civil rights, those actions became delegitimated.

Note also that he claimed there is such a thing as "white interests." The interests Wallace delineates here could easily be understood as economically rather than racially based. But the key to the Southern strategy as practiced by both Wallace and Nixon is that racial interests trump economic ones. They assert that gains made by people of color necessarily come at the expense of whites. This depiction of politics as zero-sum is a feature of despicable discourse because it pits some citizens against others for control of finite resources and does so on the basis of ascriptive traits.

Faced with both the explicit and implicit exclusion of the Wallace campaign, Nixon ceded the explicitly racist vote to Wallace. He did not seriously contest the states of the Deep South. But he was unwilling to cede the implicitly racist vote, and so, like Wallace, he sought ways to make his positions on race clear but did so in ways that would not upset moderates. He declined explicit rhetoric in favor of implicit appeals, leaving explicit exclusion to his surrogates.

Rather than talking about race directly, Nixon displaced racial conversations onto arguments about crime, especially urban crime. He depicted American cities as centers of crime and violence; they were also, of course, loci of African American life. Nixon painted a bleak picture of the nation's cities, stressing, in one statement, the situation in the nation's capital, in which the "Federal Government is wholly responsible for law enforcement," and where

> since the April riots, more than one thousand felonies are being committed every week . . . [since the removal of federal troops] arson has increased 700 percent. Roving gangs have begun the

> collection of extortion from downtown businessmen with threats of looting or arson. . . . Nor is the fear confined to those who live or work in Washington. The school children who used to flock to Washington by the thousands in the spring and summer to visit the monuments of American democracy and to view the machinery in motion—are now kept away by parents and teachers out of a justified fear for their welfare and safety.[39]

A lot of things are happening in this statement. First, note that the problems of the nation's capital are, if not the fault of the federal government, at least not being solved by it. The current administration is failing the nation. Second, the problem has been getting progressively worse. Federal troops were once required to maintain order, and since their departure, the city has been victimized by "roving gangs," who commit looting, arson, and extortion. The members of these gangs are of course people of color, who are preying on other people of color. Even worse, other innocents also suffer—the nation's schoolchildren, once happy to roam the capital and enjoy its museums and monuments, are being deprived of those experiences because of the reasonable fears of their parents and teachers.

Nixon conflates both the disorder of the riots and the uptick in national crime and racializes both problems. In this instance, this was dramatized by his use of the capital, but he considered race and its attendant violence a national problem, a claim he made in a campaign pamphlet titled "Toward Freedom from Fear": "In the last seven years while the population of this country was rising some ten percent, crime in the United States rose a staggering 88 percent. If the present rate of new crime continues, the number of rapes and robberies and assaults and thefts in the United States will double—by the end of 1972. . . . If we allow this to happen, then the city jungle will cease to be a metaphor. It will become a barbaric reality, and the brutal society that now flourishes in the core cities of America will annex the affluent suburbs."[40] The pamphlet title itself evokes one of FDR's famous Four Freedoms, but to a completely different end, as Nixon was instigating rather than meliorating fear, and was racializing both fear—caused by African Americans and felt by whites—and its location—the city in his telling is a "jungle." By implication, Nixon was also telling audiences that integration was dangerous—by letting the jungle into the "affluent suburbs," a "barbaric reality" would also be allowed in.

Crime and race became markers of each other, and both threatened the affluence and security of white people. According to Nixon, that threat was enabled by the Democrats, who, by advocating for civil rights, were understood as abandoning white interests. A Nixon pamphlet on the economy, for example, reads:

> We look to our government, first of all, for the creation of a climate in which our common ideals and objectives are secure, so that each of us can be free to pursue his individual goals. Such a climate does not exist in America today. The Johnson-Humphrey administration has failed in its first and most basic responsibility—the preservation of order in society. . . . The rise of a climate of fear and uncertainty, of crime and anarchy, can be traced partly to a vacuum of leadership at the center of our federal government. Under our system, there must be a continual dialogue between the people and their leaders, a healthy exchange which insures government truly representative of the popular will. Today, there is no such dialogue. Today, there is a sad estrangement between the people and their government.[41]

This pamphlet asserts that by upsetting the nation's long-emplaced hierarchies, the Democrats had opened the door to all kinds of disorder. By continuing to advocate things like busing and other forms of social integration, they were ignoring the will of the presumptively white "people," leading to estrangement. That estrangement was at the heart of the nation's problems, and it could only be eased by a different kind of administration under a different kind of president.

In a speech broadcast over the radio, Nixon argued, "The next President must unite America. He must calm its angers, ease the terrible frictions, and bring the people together once again in peace and mutual respect. He has to take *hold* of America before he can move it forward. This requires leadership that believes in law, and has the courage to enforce it; leadership that believes in justice, and is determined to promote it; leadership that believes in progress, and knows how to inspire it."[42] Nixon was arguing here for a strict enforcement of the law, promising that he would "take hold" of the nation and return it to an ordered existence. This inevitably meant sanctioning many and varied forms of violence against African Americans, who were consistently made the scapegoats for national disorder.[43]

But this argument was not the explicit white supremacy we have seen in earlier chapters. It's white supremacy as code. Codes, Sarah Churchwell argues, "create plausible deniability, and not merely in public. They can also give people who use them a way to evade their own cognitive dissonances. The codes are there to muddy the waters, to keep people from seeing their own faces in the pool."[44] That is, Nixon's language was not necessarily designed to mask overt racism, to sneak it past nonracists. It was designed instead to appeal to those who didn't want to recognize their racism or the ways in which white supremacy was embedded in national political structures. It was racism light, allowing white Americans to engage in racist practices and endorse racist policies without having to admit to themselves or to anyone else that this was what they were doing.

Nixon did not argue against civil rights. Instead he argued for those whose interests he claimed were being displaced by the national focus on civil rights. In this, he followed Goldwater's lead, and relied on the trope of the "forgotten American." For Franklin D. Roosevelt, who popularized the phrase, it referenced (white) people at the bottom of the nation's economic pyramid. But for Goldwater and then Nixon, the Americans they were trying to reach were those fearing displacement in the national hierarchies, not those who found themselves perennially at the bottom of those hierarchies. He phrased it this way:

> In this year of violence and turmoil, the capacity of the American people to govern themselves is being questioned as never before. Terrible and tragic events have thrown a dark cloud of self-doubt across our society. At home and abroad, voices are heard castigating America as "sick." Many are ready—even eager—to write the epitaph of the world's oldest republic and to write off mankind's greatest experiment in democratic self-government. I reject the false argument that all Americans are somehow responsible for the evils that have befallen us and the grave dangers we face.

> We are a nation made up, not of a faceless mass, but of 200 million individuals. In recent months, in a thousand different conversations, people across the country have opened their hearts and minds to me. These Americans have not given up on themselves. These Americans are vital, hopeful, and idealistic—they still dare to believe in the triumph of dreams in a time of nightmare.[45]

This passage relies on the passive voice—the ability of Americans to govern themselves is being questioned by unknown agents who also castigate their society as "sick," and who are willing to write off the national experiment in democracy. These agents are contrasted to exemplary citizens, those who recognize that the key to national greatness lies in the embrace of individualism, not governmental action, who continue to believe in the national dream, and who are not responsible for the problems the nation is facing. This last is so important because it lies at the heart of how the Southern strategy as despicable discourse works—it is the essence of a denial of complicity.

The argument that politics is zero-sum, that African Americans can only make gains at the expense of whites, is disingenuous precisely because of its refusal to admit that this means that any gains white people have made depends on the exclusion of people of color. This argument wants to accept only the first premise—that the extension of rights to African Americans and other people of color damages white interests. It elides the implication that white interests lie in the suppression of the rights of others and that white people are willing to accept that suppression. And it ignores completely the possibility that political life does not have to be zero sum. This rhetoric absolves white people of the responsibility and the guilt, and, by associating it with individualism, implicitly claims that any structural inequality is the fault not of individual white people but of the people who suffer most from it.

Nixon's rhetoric, then, racialized crime and disorder, blamed it on the collective actions of African Americans, and absolved white people of responsibility for either the causes or the consequences of African American disenfranchisement and exclusion. It argued for strong presidential leadership as a means to restore and maintain national hierarchies in the name of "order," a process that was clearly associated with heightened policing of black bodies in order to prevent the threat that they posed from spreading to the nation's affluent suburbs. But in case Wallace voters might be swayed to his side, he also endorsed more explicitly exclusionary and despicable discourse through his surrogates.

None of Nixon's surrogates spoke more loudly or did more to activate resentment than his running mate, Maryland governor Spiro T. (Ted) Agnew.[46] Agnew called an Asian American reporter "a fat Jap" on a campaign trip to Hawaii, asserted that Democratic nominee Hubert Humphrey was "squishy soft on Communism," and claimed that "if you've seen one slum, you've seen them all."[47] There seemed to be no end to the list of people he was willing to offend. In fact, offending some voters as the price of appealing to others was exactly the point. Other surrogates were equally blunt: "'The ideas expressed by George Wallace are the ideas a great many Republicans espouse,' as Nixon's campaign coordinator in the South, Howard ('Bo') Calloway, plainly put it."[48] Both subtly and blatantly, the Nixon campaign dedicated itself to creating race-based appeals and siding with white voters against people of color. In response, African Americans deserted the Republican Party. But Nixon thought that would happen anyway, and he jettisoned their votes for the richer pastures of whites disaffected with the Democratic Party on the issue of civil rights. He wrote, "I was reaping the harvest of the Goldwater campaign. In 1960 I had received 32 percent of the black vote; in 1964 Goldwater received only 6 percent. I was able to increase that Republican share of the black vote to 12 percent in 1968 but the false impression that Goldwater was a racist was still too prevalent for an easy relationship to exist between the black community and a Republican administration. I regretted this fact, but I knew that there was nothing I could say that would change it."[49] Nixon's claim that he was powerless to do otherwise was both false and essential to the masking function of the Southern strategy. This choice was a critical pillar of the Southern strategy's structure, and it helped Nixon fend off the challenge posed by George Wallace. But he had other challenges, and one of them came from the moderates of his own party, who had very different views on how the Republican Party should move forward.

The Middle Term: Republican Moderates

As he campaigned in the Republican primary, Nixon took a middle road between Rockefeller on his left and Reagan on his right. Of the two, he clearly considered Reagan more of a threat. Contrasting himself to Reagan, Nixon positioned himself as a moderate, later writing, "It was Ronald Reagan who set the hearts of many Southern Republicans aflutter. He spoke their conservative language articulately and with great passion, and there was always a possibility that Southern delegates could be lured at the last minute by his ideological siren song. Until I had the nomination, therefore, I had to pay careful attention to the dangers of a sudden resurgence on the right. Equally dangerous would be a serious intraparty split that would deliver the Reaganites into Wallace's camp."[50] The files at the Nixon Library contain considerable evidence that Nixon took a potential Reagan candidacy very seriously. The Nixon team collected opposition research, transcripts of Reagan speeches, and exemplary quotations. They clearly thought they could hurt Reagan with the issue of housing discrimination—they amassed a series of quotations in which Reagan advocated open housing.[51] Rhetorically positioning Reagan as dangerously conservative, promulgating an "ideological siren song," Nixon was ready to claim that Reagan was too liberal on the issue of race for the needs of the contemporary party.

Reagan was adored by the right, but Republican moderates had traditionally controlled the nomination, and so Nixon had to guard his left flank as well. The most prominent contender there was New York governor Nelson A. Rockefeller. Whether as a declared candidate or not (and he undermined his own campaign by his on-again, off-again status as an official candidate[52]), Rockefeller spoke often throughout 1968, offering an alternative to Nixon's Southern strategy. His speeches were designed to appeal to the moderates, whom he saw as the real heart of the Republican Party, and to Democrats disaffected with the Johnson administration. First, Rockefeller spoke in defense of US political institutions, offering a politics of optimism opposed to a politics of fear. Second, he opposed Nixon's theme of "law and order" with "freedom and law."[53] He also offered a vision of a Republicanism dedicated to racial justice, but he generally chose not to expose the Southern strategy for what it was. By stressing his own progressive position on race but failing to overtly attack Nixon's, he allowed conservative Republicans to maintain the fictions inherent in the Southern strategy.

Rockefeller's vision of the nation was an optimistic one. He rejected the politics of fearmongering and argued consistently that "the deeply disturbing problems we face are not the result of a failure of institutions, they are failures in human judgments."[54] Once those humans (clearly Lyndon Johnson and Hubert Humphrey) and their poor judgment were removed, he implied, robust national institutions would once again be responsive and respected. By expelling the Democrats from the White House, he argued, "we can turn a time of political crisis into a time of political creation."[55] Rockefeller was invariably upbeat, arguing, "We have no reason to lose confidence in ourselves or our institutions. Complex and overwhelming as our problems at home and abroad may seem, we have no reason to be discouraged. These problems can be solved. They can be handled. The necessary actions are doable."[56]

On the one hand this is exactly the kind of rhetoric one expects from presidential candidates—they don't normally inveigh against the very institutions they hope to occupy, and they generally argue that they can bring stability to the presidency and the nation. On the other hand, the conservative wing of the party had been arguing against national political institutions for years. A large part of their platform was based on rejection of the federal government's increased role in general, and they specifically railed against the courts. Rockefeller was unlikely to gain their support by arguing that these institutions were sound but needed to be run by Republicans—that was precisely the kind of thinking that they resented from party leaders like Eisenhower. Conservatives wanted a candidate who would push back against the federal government, not one who would endorse its power.

Rockefeller's disagreement with Nixon extended to race relations. He consistently stressed the importance of racial progress.[57] But he never made the comparative argument; he never directly contrasted his views on race to Nixon's. He did not do so in any of his meetings with delegates or in his public speeches. He made it clear that he was more progressive on race than was Nixon, but he did not go further. He made the argument by indirection, but he didn't make the same kind of direct case he had made four years earlier.

For example, Rockefeller supported, if not the riots, then certainly the right to protest: "First of all, let me state my enduring conviction that protest and dissent—the vigorous advocacy of change—are a recognized part of a true and living democracy."[58] For Rockefeller, the disorder caused by dissent was a necessary, even a valuable part of democracy. He argued specifically against Nixon's claim that without order there can be no progress. He told students at the University of Minnesota, "I cannot agree with those who say that we must have order or we shall have no progress. For without progress, and without justice, there will be no order."[59] This was a tacit argument in favor of those who were protesting the war on college campuses and racial inequities in the cities and is, at least potentially, a robust rhetoric of inclusion. It was a long way from this position to Nixon's view on law and order. But the argument remained tacit. He did not challenge Nixon's views directly.

Nixon responded by arguing that moderate positions—in both the Republican and the Democratic Parties—were not actually progressive; they were in fact outdated. His solutions were more able to "speak to the time." A campaign pamphlet published during the general election read, in part, "In the ruins of Detroit and Watts and Newark lie the ruins of a philosophy of government that outlived its origin and no longer speaks to its time."[60] Rather than existing government programs, the better solution is to use the government to create incentives for private investment. "If black and white are to be brought together, indeed, the light of hope has to be brought to the ghetto. If we are to bring this light of hope to the ghetto, we have to show by example that American opportunity is neither a black nor a white opportunity but an equal opportunity—and to make this opportunity real, we have to begin in the ghetto itself, where the people are and where the need is."[61] Consistent with Nixon's rhetoric on race generally, the ghetto is here depicted as a dark place, in need of the light that can only be brought it by a commitment to individualism in the form of free enterprise—a commitment the pamphlet clearly makes. Government programs were part of the problem, not solutions to them. Here, he is taking on the Great Society. But this language also undermined Republican moderates, who were comfortable with many Great Society assumptions and programs. Unlike Eisenhower, who accepted the fact of New Deal liberalism and largely worked within its parameters, Republicans in the 1960s were increasingly challenging those precepts; moderate Republicans who accepted them were increasingly imperiled.

He also made his challenges to moderates in his own party in other ways. As Lawrence O'Donnell put it, "The Republican Party turned away from its liberals in Miami Beach in 1968 and never looked back."[62]

O'Donnell's point is clearly illustrated in Nixon's acceptance speech. That speech both contained apocalyptic rhetoric and offered a way to stave off impending doom. First, Nixon depicted the nation under a Democratic president: "As we look at America, we see cities enveloped in smoke and flame. We hear sirens in the night. We see Americans dying in distant battlefields abroad. We see Americans hating each other; fighting each other; killing each other at home."[63] Democratic governance, in this depiction, had led to violence, division, and war. "America," he said, "is in trouble today not because her people have failed, but because her leaders have failed."[64] Democrats had gone astray and were paying too much attention to the wrong voices, which were providing the wrong answers to the questions facing the nation. There was another set of voices, ignored by the Democrats, that needed to be heard amid the national uproar:

> It is another voice, a quiet voice in the tumult of the shouting. It is the voice of the great majority of Americans, the forgotten Americans, the non-shouters, the non-demonstrators. They're not racists or sick; they're not guilty of the crime that plagues the land; they are black, they're white; they're native born and foreign born; they're young and they're old. They work in American factories, they run American businesses. They serve in government; they provide most of the soldiers who die to keep it free. They give drive to the great spirit of America. They give lift to the American dream. They give steel to the backbone of America. They're good people. They're decent people; they work and they save and they pay their taxes and they care.[65]

These good people, depicted as neither racists nor sick, are the backbone of the nation, exemplifying its rich diversity. They do not protest or demonstrate but go quietly about their jobs and their lives. They accept the nation as the exemplar of democracy and do not question its underlying hierarchies. These fine people were being unjustly attacked and judged: "And to those who say that law and order is the code word for racism, here is a reply: Our goal is justice—justice for every American. If we are to have respect for law in America, we must have laws that deserve respect. Just as we cannot have progress without order, we cannot have order without progress."[66] This last was a direct rebuke to moderates like Nelson Rockefeller, whose campaign had placed progress before order, as well as justification for his own campaign.

He further rebuked Republican moderates, who were adamant internationalists, by stating that his "first priority foreign policy objective of the next Administration will be to bring an honorable end to the war in Vietnam."[67] Beyond this rather vague promise, a more interesting claim lurked: "I say the time has come for other nations in the free world to bear their fair share of the burden of defending peace and freedom around the world. What I call for is not a new isolationism. It is a new internationalism in which America enlists its allies and its friends around the world in those struggles in which their interest is as great as ours."[68] This argument is of a piece with his rhetoric on domestic politics in that he is claiming that there are unequal balances to be made more equitable—that some are unfairly profiting at the expense of others, again depicting politics as a zero sum game in which citizens are pitted against one another. This is the overarching claim of the Southern strategy, and the rock upon which the new Republican coalition is going to be formed. This is also foundational to the capture of the right by despicable discourses.

The Long Term: A Republican Majority

Richard Nixon wanted to both win the presidency himself and secure the White House for Republicans for the foreseeable future. One analyst describes Nixon's view of the new majority that would facilitate those goals this way: "The groups that constituted the majority interest in the new alignment built on the base of traditional Republicans, who emphasized the importance of free enterprise, to include sections of the population whose needs and expectations differed specifically from the Republican core of support, such as 'new liberals,' who emphasized participatory democracy; the 'new South,' interested in 'interpreting the old doctrine of states' rights in new ways'; most surprisingly, black militants, rejecting welfarism in favor of self-help; plus the 'silent center.'"[69] Nonmilitant African Americans and the poor were conspicuously absent.[70] Poor and Black people were, for Nixon, the province of the Democratic Party. He wanted to capture the electoral benefits of disaffected whites who were amenable to the politics of polarization. Those politics were based largely on claims that some people were being unjustly benefited by government programs, and that those benefits came at the expense of other, more deserving, Americans. He said, "For the past five years we have been deluged by Government programs for the unemployed, programs for the cities, programs for the poor, and we have reaped from these programs an ugly harvest of frustrations, violence, and failure across the land. And now our opponents will be offering more of the same—more billions for Government jobs, Government housing, Government welfare. I say it's time to quit pouring billions of dollars into programs that have failed the United States of America."[71] According to Nixon, Democrats were wasting public money on programs that had only short-term consequences and that had consequently contributed to the disaffection and violence now engulfing the country. By conflating the beneficiaries of these programs—the unemployed and the poor—and then locating them in the cities, Nixon implicitly racialized them. Having done so, it was then easy to accuse them collectively of frustration, violence, and failure. This is also an implicit argument that government programs disproportionately benefit people of color, who are receiving money denied to the hard-working but struggling, presumptively white citizens who do not receive such benefits.

In this formulation, not only is the money wasted, but it is money that African Americans themselves do not want, because it came with the debilitating consequences of dependency. Nixon promised to liberate African Americans from their dependence on the national government. He said, "Black Americans—no more than white Americans—do not want more Government programs which perpetuate dependency. They don't want to be a colony in a nation. They want the pride and the self-respect and the dignity that can only come if they have an equal chance to own their own homes, to own their own businesses, to be managers and executives as well as workers, to have a piece of the action in the exciting ventures of private enterprise."[72] This rhetoric relies on the assumption that government programs primarily serve Black people, that they by definition create and maintain dependency, that they do not help those who are struggling, even temporarily, and that they cannot help impoverished people. Any benefits such programs might provide are subsumed under the claim that "dependency" is created and that it is bad. This rhetoric relies on individualism and ignores communitarian elements of politics—it ignores the possibility that in a democracy citizens might conceivably have responsibilities toward one another. Instead, they are competitors for scarce resources.

Exploiting age-old arguments about the deserving versus the undeserving poor, Nixon argued in a campaign pamphlet during the general election that government resources were going to those who did not merit aid. "The role of poverty as a cause of the crime upsurge in America has been grossly exaggerated—and the incumbent Administration bears major responsibility for perpetuation of the myth."[73] It was really about an overly permissive judicial system. The pamphlet continues, "There is another attitude that must be discarded if we are to wage an effective national war against the enemy within. That attitude is the socially suicidal tendency—on the part of many public men—to excuse crime and sympathize with criminals because of past grievances the criminal may have against society. . . . No criminal can justify his crimes on the basis of some real or imagined grievance against his society."[74] Nixon explicitly argued that some Americans are not equal citizens but are "the enemy within," they are among us but are not part of the polity. They are instead a threat to it.

The argument is based on the idea that some people are getting more than their fair share. It further depends on the idea that the grievances they express are not real but are largely imaginary, and even if those grievances were once real, they now lie firmly in the past. Contemporary Americans bear no responsibility. Those claims were made both by minimizing the grievances themselves and by charging that they were being exploited by unnamed others for nefarious purposes. In a memo offering a speech excerpt for use in Fresno, Nixon is advised to first praise the leadership of California's farmers before arguing:

> This leadership, the envy of the world, has made them a target of third party interference in the orchards and fields and in the vineyards. California is out in front in producing the best wages to agricultural workers in the world. It is out in front in housing and working conditions. California farm workers are sheltered by nine of ten of the major social and protective legal provisions suggested by the US Department of the Department of Labor. It is this leadership by California farmers that has made them the target of those who would tear the fabric of our society.[75]

Note the stakes at play here—it's not a state's agricultural or labor policies, it's the "fabric of our society." That fabric is threatened by "third party interference" in the routine of California farm life. The implicit claim here is that prevailing structures and ways of doing business are equitable and fair. Unnamed others, with bad intentions, have been exploiting innocent but naïve farm workers into believing otherwise. And this, not structural inequalities, is at the root of the national disruptions.

There are at least three elements of the Southern strategy: the use of coded language that allows white Americans to pursue racially inflected policies without acknowledging their racism, a reliance on the politics of individualism that denies the communitarian elements of national politics while privileging a zero-sum understanding of those politics, and an insistence that the least deserving Americans are those who are receiving disproportionate benefits from the system. These elements each helped Nixon with some aspect of his campaign, and each reinforced the others, creating a coherent appeal that was used to separate some white voters from the New Deal coalition and the Democratic Party. None of them are explicit arguments in favor of racial hierarchies. All are implicit arguments for them, a fact that marks them as a new kind of despicable discourse. Equally despicable is the way that they all allow adherents to deny the exclusionary potential that inheres in each argument by endorsing a kind of plausible deniability, permitting voters to deny racist intent while advocating racially exclusionary policies. This plausible deniability is only possible when other elites accept the fictions inherent in these arguments and do not challenge them as examples of discourse and politics that lie outside the permissible limits of our national politics. In 1964, Nelson Rockefeller labeled the extremists in his own party as such and contributed to their decisive defeat. Eight years later, faced with the same choice, he remained silent and engaged in the politics of pretense. The consequences of that choice continue to haunt the Republican Party and the nation.

THE POLITICS OF PRETENSE

In 1964, Rockefeller took a principled stand against the extremism and the overt racism of the conservative movement, epitomized for him in the actions and ideology of members of the John Birch Society and the Ku Klux Klan. Four years later, even with an extraordinary amount of data on the nature and probable consequences of Nixon's Southern strategy, faced with a very different context, he argued for and enacted politics that spoke to the old Republican coalition. But that coalition was no longer willing to listen. The West had changed, the South was in play, and Goldwater conservatives wanted Rockefeller's blood.

In 1964 Rockefeller stated that there were people with ideals wholly alien to Republican tradition trying to capture the party; that they were willing to use any tactics, including intimidation and threats, to do so; that in order to preserve the party and the nation these people had to be repudiated and read out of the party; and that the consequences of failing to do so would be dire for both the nation and the party. Rockefeller argued that "the Republican party is in real danger of subversion by a radical, well-financed and highly disciplined minority."[76] For those as deeply embedded in the language of the Cold War as Republicans in the early 1960s, these phrases would have immediately connected the threat Rockefeller perceived to the machinations associated with Communism. Marking these subversives as akin to Communists also marked them as profoundly un-American and therefore dangerous. They did not deal in open debate in the valorized "marketplace of ideas"; they worked in stealth and were dedicated not to democratic interchange but to the imposition of their ideology on an unwilling and unsuspecting people. In both their tactics and in their goals, Communists and Republican infiltrators were, in Rockefeller's rhetoric, disturbingly alike.

Those tactics were worrying indeed. They "ranged from cancellation by coercion of a speaking engagement before a college audience to outright threats of personal violence." He added that he and "countless others" had experienced anonymous late-night and early-morning phone calls, threatening letters, "smear and hate literature," unspecified "strong arm and goon tactics," "bomb threats and bombing," and methods he "associated with Communist and Nazi" actors. These claims rely on the power of testimony; Rockefeller here bears witness, an act that Bradford Vivian calls a specifically democratic kind of public argument.[77] Witnessing testifies to an event and requires public participation in determining its meaning.[78] Rockefeller relied both on his authority as a prominent party member and on his authority as a witness to define the actions of the extremists. His immediate audience denied both kinds of authority and thus the message based on it.

That reaction, though, bolstered Rockefeller's claim that these tactics had consequences. He said, for example, that the purposes of the "extremist minorities" were "wholly alien to the sound and honest conservatism" he associated with the Republican Party. These extremists, he claimed, "feed on fear, hate, and terror . . . they spread distrust, they engender suspicion, they encourage disunity." He argued that "they have no solution for our problems of chronic unemployment, or education, or agriculture, or racial injustice, or strife." For Rockefeller, politics was driven by policy; legitimate voices were policy advocates. Listening to the voices of these "extremist minorities" meant, first, that the party and the nation would be weakened by distrust and disunity. Second, nothing about that would lead to better policy, for these people had no policy agenda.

Rockefeller argued that evidence for this tendency to spread distrust and disunity lay in the people extremists attacked. Their fulminations weren't directed at Rockefeller alone but extended to party luminaries like Dwight Eisenhower and John Foster Dulles. By seeking to drive moderate and pragmatic voices out of the Republican Party, extremists were, in Rockefeller's view, weakening the party both intellectually and electorally. Thus, for both moral and pragmatic reasons, Rockefeller insisted that the extremists be read out of the party. In his speech to the 1964 convention, he stated, "There is no place in the Republican Party for such hawkers of hate, such purveyors of prejudice, such fabricators of fear, whether Communist, Ku Klux Klan or Bircher." He demanded that Republicans repudiate them.

If Rockefeller's speech at the 1964 Republican National Convention is judged on his capacity to move his immediate audience to rethink their political commitments, it was clearly a failure. Goldwater's rejoinder, given in his address accepting the presidential nomination, that "I would remind you that extremism in defense of liberty is no vice," hurled defiance at both Rockefeller and the moderates who agreed with him. It is possible, even likely, that Rockefeller's treatment at the hands of the convention delegates helped create and cement in the minds of the broader public that the Goldwater campaign was in the hands of unruly, even dangerous extremists.

That became one of the themes of the general election and undoubtedly contributed to Goldwater's defeat.

That defeat was understood by Republicans as less a matter of content and more a problem of presentation. Goldwater's brash embodiment of conservatism roused his base but frightened the mass public. Two years later, conservatives found in Ronald Reagan's election as California governor a presentation of the same principles that reassured rather than disquieted. By 1968, Republicans then faced another choice, whether to accept the same principles that animated Goldwater's campaign presented with a glossier finish or to adhere to the principles of Republicanism as understood by the moderate wing of the party. In 1964, that choice had been clear. In 1968, it was equally clear, but the Republicans chose differently.

As we have seen, Rockefeller refused to challenge Nixon's Southern strategy directly, despite the fact that he went to the trouble to amass as great deal of evidence about that strategy. If he wasn't willing to talk about why Nixon was wrong on policy, he was willing to make the case that he was not the right candidate:

> Now, I think we have to be realistic about it. Yes, the Republicans are loyal and enthusiastic about Dick Nixon because he has been a loyal, enthusiastic Republican. He has gone to their fundraising dinners around the country. When he left the navy he went into Congress and from the House went to the Senate and from the Senate he went to the Vice Presidency. And he has been in Washington and in the legislative branch of government all his life. And I think this in wonderful. And he certainly is a brilliant man. He is fully familiar with what's going on. And my only concern, frankly is—and I have to be frank—is what happened in 1960.[79]

He added, "He could not carry the vote in the big cities."[80] More nastily, he quipped, "I hear that Richard Nixon had a nightmare; he was running unopposed and still came in second."[81] Here, despite his implication that he and Nixon had serious policy differences, he stated that his "only concern" with Nixon was not that his policies were wrong, not that the tactics he favored were wrong-headed, but that he couldn't win. The claim that he "couldn't win in the cities" was at least potentially a claim that Nixon would lose the African American vote. Rockefeller's implicit claim was that he could win it. His problem was that Republicans didn't want it.

There was one occasion when Rockefeller did challenge Nixon on the Southern strategy. After Nixon campaign aide Bo Calloway made his comment connecting Nixon voters to Wallace voters, Rockefeller said that Nixon ought to "disassociate himself" from both that comment and from Wallace as well. He said, "In my opinion Mr. Wallace, George Wallace, former Governor of Alabama, is appealing to the racist instinct of the American people; that it is not the course to follow for this country, he does not reflect the thinking of the Republican party, and the Republican party cannot win in November with that philosophy . . . and Mr. Nixon, for his own good and for the party's good, must deny this recommendation by his campaign chairman."[82] The argument here is not only a moral one, as he had made in 1964. It was a pragmatic one. Rockefeller was arguing that the strategy was wrong for the country but also would lose Republicans another national election. As pallid an argument as this is, it is as close as Rockefeller got to bringing up the Southern strategy. Sometimes despicable discourse is a matter of what political leaders say and sometimes it is a matter of what they decline to say. Both speaking and silence were critical in 1968 because Nixon's discourse was quiet, understated, and subtle. Challenging its despicable elements required the kind of clear and even courageous opposition Rockefeller offered in 1964 when faced with overt examples of exclusionary rhetoric. In 1968, the rhetoric was less overt, and Rockefeller offered no real rebuttal, allowing its fictions to go unchallenged. That discourse took hold in our national politics, becoming not episodic, as in earlier examples of such discourse, but a continuous element of national campaigns.

CONCLUSION: THE POLITICS OF SUBTLE RACISM

The politics of 1968 were characterized by a sense of grievance. Richard Nixon as a candidate and as an elected official never relinquished his grievances. He taught other Americans to share his sense that others were being given what they, who worked so hard, were denied. What Jeremy Engels calls the "politics of resentment," took firm hold in 1968 and has yet to let go of our national politics.[83] Those politics are, as we have seen throughout this chapter, based on issues of race, of resistance to the various incursions of the federal government, and of a fear that a putatively white national culture was being eroded. The despicable discourse circulated by Nixon and other conservatives depended on a veneer of civic language. Because the fictions perpetrated by this discourse—that some (racialized) Americans are less deserving than others, that those others are the ones receiving an unfair proportion of societal benefits, and that politics in an individualistic, zero-sum game in which the community is composed not of companions but of winners and losers—became the electoral logic governing Republican Party politics. Both Nixon and his party tied their political futures to despicable discourse.

Race was a key factor in the election. Ninety-seven percent of African Americans voted for Humphrey; fewer than 35 percent of whites did.[84] This racial division was not inevitable. As the 1960s progressed, resistance to integration increased in the North but decreased in the South.[85] Had Southerners received encouragement to accept racial progress as inevitable, enough of them might have done so to make it possible. As two experts on the Southern strategy argue:

> There was a much larger group of troubled white Southerners, men and women who were frustrated and uneasy at the rapid pace of social change over the past decade. They had come to believe that such change was inevitable, that it must be faced with as much grace as could be mustered. But Richard Nixon, the thirty-seventh president of the United States, gave them reason to hope that the clock could be turned back, that at the very least the *direction* of change could be somewhat altered, the movement of it slowed down, that quite possibly, for instance, some form of token integration might satisfy the laws and the courts.[86]

Nixon encouraged resistance to racial change as a means of attaining the White House; he was followed by a series of Republicans who became increasingly locked into that electoral logic.

Race infused the 1968 election in indirect ways as well. Republicans, Nixon among them, continued to tie amorphous "government programs" to race, and white voters increasingly turned against many of those programs and the government that offered them. Even as they endorsed programs like Medicare, they resented the "big government" that made them possible. That distrust of the federal government and the certainty that it distributed benefits inequitably characterized much of the politics of the Reagan era and contributed to the gutting of the safety net in the 1980s.

Nixon helped teach Americans to distrust one another and their government. He did so on the basis of what has come to be known as the "culture wars," or the fear, prevalent among some white citizens, that "their" culture is under attack by a determined coalition of anti-Christian, anti-family, even anti-American leftists. As Kevin Phillips put it, "The emerging Republican majority spoke clearly in 1968 for a shift away from the sociological jurisprudence, moral permissiveness, experimental residential, welfare and educational programming and massive federal spending by which the Liberal (mostly Democratic) establishment sought to propagate liberal institutions and ideology—and all the while reap economic benefits."[87] Nixon and his campaign helped exacerbate fears that cultural power was being lost. This fear, based on the idea that the loss of total control is the same as the loss of all control, also continues to fuel significant fear and anger on the American right.

Overall, the 1968 election was characterized by a fear that the country was undergoing rapid and drastic change and that, as a result, it was falling apart. Some citizens saw the potential of those years while others focused on the losses. While in general, people writing about the 1960s use the theme of breakdown and coming apart, Michael Nelson argues that the system was resilient.[88] I disagree. As civil rights icon and Member of Congress John Lewis notes, in many ways, "the election of 1968 set in motion all the wrong things."[89] In the next chapters, I examine many of those things set in motion in 1968.

CHAPTER 5

THE SOUTHERN STRATEGY GOES BIPARTISAN, 1992

The story of despicable discourse in 1968 was a Republican and a conservative story. By 1992 that story became bipartisan. Democrats, tired of their exile from the White House, nominated Bill Clinton whose "third way" attempted to thread the political and rhetorical needles of maintaining African American allegiances while seeking to restore party strength among members of the white working class. This effort recalled Nixon's endeavors to secure white ethnic voters while holding on to Republican moderates in 1968. In some ways Clinton's rhetoric on race made similar moves, adapting elements of the Southern strategy for a Democratic audience. At the same time, Democrats tried to fend off the right with an ambiguous and often contradictory treatment of women. Republicans, for their part, were increasingly forsaking subtle exclusions for overt ones. In 1988, for example, Ronald Reagan's vice president and presidential candidate George Herbert Walker Bush made Willie Horton, whom we will discuss in more detail shortly, a staple of his campaign discourse. By 1992, the right wing was demanding ever more attention to the "culture wars," and the Republican convention was an explicit display of exclusionary politics. To be clear, I am not arguing that 1988 was not a deplorable election—there is much in that election that qualifies it as such. But I am focusing on 1992 because I want to point specifically to the ways in which despicable discourse was becoming bipartisan. When Democrats took on some elements of subtle racism, they encouraged the Republicans to move farther toward explicitly racist appeals. The assumption of despicable discourse was and is more prominent on the right. But Democrats did not choose to fight it explicitly and therefore abetted its adoption into the cultural mainstream.

The 1988 campaign is widely judged as being vapid and devoid of issue content, a context that all too often opens the door for despicable discourses. In all its emptiness and negativity, it was a harbinger of things to come: Jesse Jackson's campaign indicated the importance of African American voters to the Democratic coalition and the ways in which white presidential candidates sought to maintain their allegiance at the least possible cost to their campaigns. Colorado senator Gary Hart's rendezvous with Donna Rice on the yacht *Monkey Business* provided evidence that candidates were going to be under increased scrutiny from a wider variety of news media and demonstrated the ways scandal would drive news coverage. The Bush campaign's unrelenting attacks on Michael Dukakis's patriotism and positions on cultural politics indicated how the "culture wars" were helping Republicans solidify their presence among the white working class, even while pursuing policies that undercut the economic position of those voters.

The 1988 election is epitomized by the image of Willie Horton that appeared in a campaign ad.[1] Horton, an African American imprisoned for life in Massachusetts on a murder charge, was released on a weekend furlough. While at liberty, he committed a series of crimes, including armed robbery and rape. Picking up on a charge first made in the primaries by Senator Al Gore (D-TN), George H. W. Bush used Horton as a frequent example in his speeches of the crime problem in Massachusetts during Democratic presidential candidate Michael Dukakis's term as governor. This use echoed the "law and order" element of Nixon's Southern strategy, racializing crime and blaming its worst aspects on Democratic leadership. So persistent was Bush's use of Horton as a campaign trope that campaign strategist Lee Atwater remarked, "By the time we're finished, they're going to wonder whether Willie Horton is Dukakis' running mate."[2] Dukakis's countercharge accusing Bush of racism didn't have much sticking power—by 1988, conservative whites were no longer ashamed to admit they were afraid of African Americans, especially when they were positioned as criminals.[3] Conservative whites were becoming more comfortable with their racism and according to journalist Jeremy D. Mayer, the Bush campaign "deliberately racialized the election to hold the Reagan electoral majority together."[4]

Republican strategists Lee Atwater and Roger Ailes were important in turning politics in a negative direction and exploiting race while they were doing it. Ailes, of course, had developed the media strategy behind Nixon's 1968 campaign. He was joined in the Reagan administration by Lee Atwater, and together they ran Reagan's reelection campaign before agreeing to work for Bush. Atwater was known for updating the Southern strategy to appeal to a younger generation of conservative voters. Between them, Ailes and Atwater crossed generations using racialized appeals.[5] By 1988, Republicans had fully committed to the implications of the Southern strategy.

Having won the 1988 election, Bush governed in a context of widespread disaffection with politics. Americans were increasingly alienated by politics and politicians, a phenomenon at least some analysts attributed to the increasing importance of cable television, which relied on segmenting rather than uniting audiences; an increasing reliance on polls and polling, which placed often-uninformed public opinion at the center of the day-to-day business of governing and campaigning; and an increasing reliance on candidate-centered politics, which promoted individual candidates at the expense of political parties.[6] The Gulf War, which at one point seemed to make Bush invulnerable to electoral and political challenge, temporarily masked a weakened economy that eventually contributed to his political undoing. These factors posed problems for a president who preferred governing among elites to communicating with the public and who had no real program he wanted to advance beyond continuing the policies of the Reagan administration.

Walter Dean Burnham thus calls Bush "a third-term understudy," arguing people wanted more of the kind of governance they experienced during the Reagan years.[7] But, Sidney Blumenthal argues, "Reagan's policies had set a trap for his successor."[8] Voters worried about the economy; about the United States' place in the world, given the end of the Cold

War; and about division at home. Bush's governance did little to assuage these fears. He seemed to ignore the problems with the economy, and economic matters worsened in the wake of the savings and loan crisis as real estate prices dropped. On matters of race, he continued Republican policies of appeasing white voters. Bush signed a crime bill that added considerable resources for judges and prosecutors and significantly fewer for public defenders. He attacked the Civil Rights Act of 1990 as a "quota bill," maintaining the fiction that the real victims of oppression in the United States were white males. With language like this, he joined the conservative backlash against multiculturalism as "political correctness." He did sign the 1991 Civil Rights Act, but it was seen as too little too late to make any difference with Black voters. He might have made some progress there when civil rights icon Thurgood Marshall announced his retirement from the Supreme Court in 1991, but Clarence Thomas, Bush's choice as Marshall's successor, was quickly embroiled in a confirmation fight centering on accusations of sexual harassment made by Anita Hill. Making bad matters worse, after police officers were found not guilty of police brutality in the 1991 beating of construction worker Rodney King, violence broke out in Los Angeles on April 29 and lasted for four days.[9] Bush decided that if he visited LA, his presence would lend itself to the accusation that the White House was politicizing the riots, so he stayed away. His absence led to criticism that he was uninterested in race relations or the problems besetting majority-Black communities and contributing to the conditions that caused those problems.

National division centered on but was not restricted to race. Vice President Dan Quayle, chosen for the ticket in 1988 because of his allegiance to the party's right wing, created a stir when he began an argument with the fictional newscaster, Murphy Brown, over her equally fictitious decision to keep and raise a child as a single mother. On its face, the controversy was both trivial and ridiculous, but it revealed much about the importance of the culture wars to the conservative faithful. Bush spokesperson Marlin Fitzwater said, for example, "Our concern and society's concern should be television networks, production and writers and their glorification of social situations. And for years we were very concerned with the glorification of drug use on television. And the concern now is that in the glorification of life as an unwed mother does not do good service to most unwed mothers who are not highly paid glamorous anchor women. . . . We are certainly concerned about family values and the breakup of the American family."[10] For the right, even fictional portrayals of "social situations" were deadly serious.

The acrimony over civil rights and cultural politics was just one example of Bush's contentious relationship with Congress and its increasingly right-wing membership. His decision to support a tax increase after promising not to raise taxes meant that members like House minority whip Newton (Newt) Gingrich (R-GA), already frustrated by Bush's inability to be Reagan, began to question his leadership. He managed a reprieve of sorts during the Gulf War, but even with high approval caused by the war, neither congressional Republicans nor their constituents really warmed to Bush's domestic leadership.

As a result of these factors, Bush went into the 1992 campaign in a much weaker position than would have been expected given his approval ratings during the Gulf War. Three things dominated the agenda of that election: the national economy, disagreement over national values and how they would be interpreted in national policy, and race. White voters especially tended to feel divided rather than united, unsettled rather than secure. And as always in unsettled times, political authority was challenged, and despicable discourses found room to circulate more widely. Challenges to authority were evident in the presence of candidates like Jerry Brown, California's "Governor Moonbeam," who brought a different sensibility to the national campaign; by eccentric billionaire H. Ross Perot, whose combination of massive resources and homespun folksiness captured the imagination and the votes of millions of Americans; and most ominously, by former Nixon speechwriter and political pundit Patrick Buchanan, who challenged Bush from the right, arguing for "America First" policies that smacked of racism and exclusion. On the state level, the rise of Klansman David Duke as candidate for governor of Louisiana underscored the frightening rise of nationalism, xenophobia, and overt racism in conservative ranks. Despicable discourse in 1992 was obvious, subtle, and pervasive.

It circulated over a variety of media, many of them new or playing newly dominant roles in 1992. The 1992 election was characterized by the rise in cable television, which brought with it a new emphasis on "infotainment," seen in the prevalence of both daytime and primetime talk shows, and "infomercials," which Ross Perot used to much advantage. Howard Kurtz called 1992 the "Talk-Show campaign," and others argued it was characterized by "highly segmented audiences," foreshadowing the growth of hyperpartisan and siloed media audiences.[11] Technologies like fax machines and satellite feeds made responding to other campaigns more efficient, and direct mail allowed candidates to reach their supporters without using the airwaves.

In short, the candidates in 1992 faced an electorate that was high in anxiety, low in political trust, distracted by a variety of media, and uncertain about how to understand their nation and its role in the world without the organizing structure that had been provided by the Cold War. The United States was the world's only remaining superpower, and yet to many white Americans, it felt weaker and more divided than ever before. As always, efforts to unite the country around one candidacy or another were often accompanied by efforts to divide it for electoral advantage. It was a breeding ground for despicable discourse.

In my discussion of that discourse, I focus first on Ross Perot's campaign, because while he did not emphasize despicable discourse, his emphasis on economic issues heightened economic anxiety among many voters and helped further the decline in political trust, both of which are factors in making despicable discourses more likely. I then turn to Bill Clinton's campaign, focusing largely on his use of subtle forms of racism and much less subtle sexism in a campaign that ostensibly featured inclusion. Then I examine the Bush campaign, which was dogged by the increasingly overt exclusionary rhetoric of the Republican right and used subtle and overt forms of exclusionary rhetoric. I conclude with a discussion of how this campaign presages the deplorable election of 2016.

FOSTERING ECONOMIC ANXIETY: PEROT THE POPULIST

Despicable discourse is more likely under conditions of low political trust and high economic anxiety, and the Perot campaign was made possible by both these factors. Perot's campaign also provided evidence of the ways in which presidential politics was becoming unmoored from parties and professional politicians. A candidate with enough money or other kinds of resources could now make a play for the presidency without the support of any party organization. Candidate-centered politics and the changing media environment enabled insurgencies that would have been impossible under different kinds of circumstances.

It was not surprising that Perot's first intimation that he might run for the presidency was made on a popular call-in talk show, *Larry King Live*. As the *Richmond Times* reported:

> Amid reports of widespread dissatisfaction with major candidates of both parties, Texas billionaire H. Ross Perot has launched a presidential bid of his own. On Feb. [*sic*] 20, as a guest on Larry King's call-in talk show, Perot said he'd run for Pres [*sic*] if volunteers in all states put his name on the November ballot. His idea is to step in and run as an Independent after supporters have gathered the signatures needed to put him on the ballot in every state. Almost immediately, Perot's office in Dallas was swamped with calls from supporters, a spokeswoman there said. . . . Perot apparently is tapping a vein of discontent that has shown up this primary season in low turnout and in interviews with voters. Pollsters in state after state have found voters wish there were other candidates.[12]

Perot's campaign revealed many things about the 1992 election: after a bruising primary season that featured a plethora of Democratic candidates and a challenge to the incumbent president, voters were largely dissatisfied with the resulting nominees. They were suspicious of politics, politicians, and the parties that structured elections and governance. But that didn't necessarily lead to a lack of political participation. Perot's campaign was interesting not least because of the massive outpouring of volunteer activity. People were angry and disaffected with politics as usual, but they hadn't therefore given up on politics. But mobilizing citizen volunteers was an expensive proposition. It was not coincidental that Perot was a billionaire. Without a massive infusion of cash, a modern campaign is not sustainable. Only the very rich can afford to stop their careers, forsake the rigors of constant fundraising, and concentrate on their campaign. But even with the volunteers and the self-made organization, a third-party challenge is unlikely to yield much in terms of electoral votes. The system is structured in ways that privilege the major parties. Independent candidacies are expressions of discontent and even optimism; they are not viable roads to the White House.

But they can do significant damage to other candidacies. George Bush, for example, was told to take Perot's candidacy seriously almost from the beginning. A letter to White House political advisor Ron Kaufman from Alex Ray of Chesapeake Media offered this advice:

> As one who witnessed and warned of the rise of Jim Langley in Maine back in the mid-seventies, I could argue that there is too much similarity in peoples' feelings today and Mainers then: a man who apparently had a plan versus someone who is perceived as not having one; frustration and dissatisfaction with both the White House and the Congress that makes people want to strike out for any solution; and a man who apparently sees reform of government as his mission. . . . The constituency for Perot's message would be Republicans and Reagan-Democrats and they are support we can ill-afford to have drained away.[13]

Ray understood exactly the kind of threat Perot posed—he couldn't win himself, but he could siphon enough Republican support away from Bush to make a Democratic victory more likely.

The threat was serious enough to require a response. About a week later, Ray informed Kaufman that "the little Texan has installed 1,600 phone lines and has received over a million calls in the last month. That's serous business." He advised the Bush campaign to "Fill the talk-show, news interview circuit with credible Perot-bashers who can cite some of his more extreme ideas. Perhaps a Perot Truth Brigade made up of some of his disgruntled employees or business partners. General Motors has a strong interest in seeing him out of the picture."[14] Bush's people were unable to take Perot seriously as a potential president, believing him to be too eccentric to make a credible candidate, but his ability to mobilize voters had to be countered. It is instructive that the advice given here was to go negative and to do it quickly. Bush was advised to mobilize "Perot-bashers," to advertise Perot's "more extreme ideas," and to rely on "disgruntled employees or business partners." They were not preparing to take Perot's ideas seriously but to discredit the source of those ideas. They were ready to circulate despicable discourse.

The Perot campaign was attentive to Bush's reactions. A memo to Perot campaign regional directors noted:

> We are picking up strong indications that the White House is planning an assault on Mr. Perot's character. It is our understanding that surrogates will be dispatched throughout major media markets in an attempt to plant scurrilous story's [*sic*] about the boss. Those of us who understand Mr. Perot's unique personality will have to be ready to stand behind our state coordinators to combat the propaganda. Our surveys tell us that such tactics will not work on the educated voters of America. It is the blue collar, ethnic and minority voters who will be swayed by the attacks because they have a hard time distinguishing between the personality of a stern leader and the boss that they so dislike.[15]

Some of the voters referenced here—blue collar, white ethnics—had become the holy grail of major party electoral politics. They had once reliably voted Democratic, had separated from the Democratic Party as a result of the Southern strategy, then became the "Reagan Democrats," and their dwindling support for Bush was causing consternation in mainstream Republican ranks. Perot's ability to speak to and for those voters was a very real coalitional problem for Bush.

How much of a problem Perot posed and for whom was not immediately clear. Political scientist Everett Carll Ladd argued that "most Americans simply haven't thought about the Texan as a possible President. For the vast majority who tell pollsters they are inclined to vote for him, 'Perot' means essentially, 'I'm not satisfied at how things are going, and I'm willing to listen to alternatives.'"[16] The Clinton campaign, worried that Perot would grab the mantle of "change candidate" from Clinton, agreed with Ladd's analysis. One of the campaign's pollsters said:

> We really worked the Perot phenomenon because Perot is very hard to poll on. People are much more willing to talk about it than to answer poll questions, so you couldn't really get at it. And I think

> the most important piece about Perot was not that his appeal was so great, because his appeal helped us in some ways by pulling off Bush voters, but that he provided the context in which voters understood us. So when he was in the race, it would change how they felt about us in terms of change or in terms of the economy or in terms of whether we were a candidate who wasn't going negative or who was going negative.[17]

In a political environment in which polls determined campaign strategy and tactics, the unpollable nature of Perot's support created electoral uncertainty in that he might pull voters away from one campaign or another. But Perot also had a broader, more ineffable effect in that he created an interpretive context to which the other campaigns felt they had to respond.

From a systemic perspective, there was at least one worrying element of Perot's candidacy. Ladd characterized Perot's leadership style as "consistently authoritarian." He wrote, "Americans are dissatisfied with aspects of the way their polity is being run, in some instances for good reason. But nothing suggests they are suddenly inclined to turn away from their historic insistence that their presidents be committed and experienced democrats."[18] Ladd argued that a majority of US voters would not support an authoritarian-leaning candidate. But the presence of such a candidate is a danger signal and a sign of a deplorable election. The right was displaying tendencies that would remain in place and affect the outcome in 2016.

While Ladd may have been correct about the thinking of a majority of (white) American voters, the Bush campaign had reason to doubt Ladd's analysis. In June, Bush aides were arguing, "The Perot problem/phenomenon is so great I doubt it can be overstated. Solid, lifetime Republicans are saying they are considering becoming unaffiliated." They were also worried because Perot seemed to be extending his appeal beyond predictable boundaries: "A small mountain community of a few thousand (Idaho Springs, Colorado) has a Perot store front campaign headquarters on its main street. Hard to imagine Bush or Clinton reaching that strongly into such small communities."[19] Bush aides noted that there was something about Perot's candidacy that was touching a political vein more mainstream campaigns did not reach. Perot had the potential to draw support from places and attract voters major party candidates didn't attract. It signaled the potential of his insurgency campaign but also indicated the weaknesses of the major party campaigns. This kind of gap in later years will be filled by the Tea Party.

Whatever potential may have lurked within the Perot campaign was undermined by the erratic behavior of the candidate. After deciding to run in June, he withdrew in July, citing vague, improbable, and unverified threats against his daughter, only to return in September. On his reentry he told *CBS This Morning*, "I think we made a mistake to step aside in July. Now, see, this will probably cause you to faint because you never heard anybody in public life say they made a mistake."[20] Perot positioned himself as the only honest person in politics. He was also volatile, eccentric, and unpredictable. His ability to be unlike anyone else in politics was his main strength.[21] So great was his impact on the campaign that there was speculation that the election might be thrown into the House.[22] Perot's capacity to draw attention had two components: his medium, and his message.

Perot was a master of the art of the "infomercial," an extended (up to an hour) paid media format in which a speaker offers a lengthy discussion of a product or idea, accompanied by toll-free numbers viewers could call to purchase or donate. In the early 1990s, infomercials generally appeared in the late-night to very-early-morning hours, when buying time is cheaper. Perot used this format very much to his advantage, moving it to prime time and offering homey nostrums accompanied by hand-drawn charts and other seemingly amateur props. Both the format and the props underlined Perot's appeal as a nontraditional, nonprofessional politician, making him appear as a simple citizen, sincerely interested in the public good. Populism oozed from both his medium and his message.

Perot didn't talk like a politician but was full of statements like "The debt is like a crazy aunt we keep in the basement."[23] He wanted politicians to "stay in touch with how normal people live" and suggested that they should fly commercial, get out of Washington more, cut staff, and end congressional privileges.[24] Perot claimed to be running only because the people demanded it and because of the dire nature of the nation's economic problems.[25] He argued that his campaign was derived from popular will, not personal ambition. He asserted his ideas and plans came not from elites like him but from the people themselves: "I listened to thousands of people in and out of government, these people have good, solid, practical ideas about how to solve our country's problems and put it on the right path."[26] He emphasized common sense, and like conservatives Goldwater and Ronald Reagan, Perot insisted that the national government was the source of the nation's most serious problems: "Washington has created a government that comes *at* us instead of a government that comes *from* us."[27] He maintained that political processes in the United States were corrupt and unreliable, arguing that while other countries "made the hard choices, our leaders made the easy ones," and announced that "modern politics has become little more that shirking responsibility and blaming somebody else."[28] Perot promised to be a different kind of leader, one who needed nothing for himself but was there to serve the people.

The Perot campaign, as idiosyncratic and erratic as it was, contributed to the context through which the Clinton and Bush campaigns were understood. Neither major party candidate could risk alienating Perot voters, but neither wanted to endorse his arguments. Clinton appreciated Perot's emphasis on the nation's ailing economy, which helped his campaign. As noted, he worried that Perot would grab the mantle of "change candidate" from him. Bush stood to gain nothing from a Perot campaign—arguments for change and about the economy hurt his electoral efforts. Clinton and Bush both had to scramble to earn the votes of an increasingly angry and disaffected electorate. Clinton chose to do that by appearing on the one hand to offer an optimistic and inclusive vision for the country, while on the other adapting elements of the Southern strategy to a Democratic audience. Bush, faced with an increasingly strident right wing, adopted a more explicit negativity that still stopped far short of the loudly exclusionary politics demanded by Republican conservatives.

THE SUBTLE POLITICS OF RACE: CLINTON'S EXCLUSIONS

In any other media environment, and maybe in any other previous election year, Bill Clinton would not have survived his own campaign, much less become president. He was introduced to the public through scandal, and scandal was the consistent theme of the 1992 election. As soon as he recovered from one scandal—say allegations of an affair with Gennifer Flowers—he was embroiled in another—like the controversy over his actions regarding the Vietnam draft. As soon as he put that scandal to rest, there were questions about his possible drug use and the obfuscation of his response to those allegations. Once the worst of that was managed, there were accusations involving other women and investigations involving his financial dealings while governor of Arkansas. It was campaign by scandal, and while Clinton styled himself the "Comeback Kid" after salvaging his campaign in New Hampshire, voters and the media were more likely to think of him as "Slick Willie."

When he managed to remain on message, Bill Clinton's campaign was compelling to many white voters, some of whom had been voting Republican since the 1980s. His main philosophy was summed up in a speech to the Democratic Leadership Council in 1992, where he said, "Our burden is to give the people a new choice, rooted in old values, a new choice that is simple, that offers *opportunity*, demands *responsibility*, gives citizens more say, provides them with responsive government—all because we recognize that we are a *community*. We are all in this together, and we are going up or down together."[29] Clinton "embodied a different way of talking about political choices."[30] One of the nation's "New Democrats," Clinton was among the younger, largely southern Democratic leaders who were eager to recapture national power, and who believed that the best route to doing that was to also recapture the votes of the Reagan Democrats who had begun forsaking the party in the wake of the civil rights advances of the 1960s, accelerated their defections as a result of the Southern strategy, and completed their transition to consistent Republican voters during the Reagan years. As journalist Bob Woodward put it, "Mostly Southerners, they were trying to convince the middle class that the Democratic Party could be strong on foreign and defense policy, moderate on social policy, and disciplined in spending tax money and taming runaway government."[31] "Middle class" was by 1992 firmly established as shorthand for white voters, the mainstays of the Republican coalition. Perot was appealing to these voters, Bush needed to keep them loyal, and Clinton saw in them an opportunity.

His primary appeal, to the extent that his campaign could focus on a primary appeal in between fending off various scandals, was a simple one:

the economy was broken, it could be fixed, and fixing it required a strong president. He argued that where Bush and the Republicans were loath to act, Clinton and the Democrats would use the power of the presidency to reinvigorate the national economy.[32] By focusing on the economy, Clinton could reach out to the white middle class and hope to extend his reach to the white blue-collar workers he needed in key states. Clinton wanted to define himself as a defender of presumptively white, middle-class values. But unlike the Republicans, who could wield race and overt racism in appealing to these voters, Clinton was constrained by his need to maintain African American allegiances to the Democratic Party and motivate them to show up at the polls on Election Day. Clinton had to motivate Black voters while also reaching out to Reagan Democrats. That imperative led to Clinton's adaptation of the Southern strategy for a Democratic audience.

Communicating Clinton

In his efforts to hold on to African American votes, Clinton had three advantages denied Richard Nixon in 1968. First, in 1968, the Republicans were split on the issue of race, with moderates like Rockefeller wanting the party to maintain its traditional support for civil rights, and conservatives rejecting that position. Democrats in 1992 may not have been consistently committed to civil rights, but they were very aware of the centrality of the Black vote to their electoral coalition. Second, Bill Clinton had a cultural advantage Nixon lacked. He could appear on the *Arsenio Hall* show, leverage his comparative youth, and reach audiences in ways that Nixon simply couldn't have done. While he was displaying facility with African Americans on a cultural level, he was, at the same time, representative of the kind of white voter he was trying to attract. He was something of a "Bubba" and could speak and act in an authentically blue-collar vernacular, while also appealing to more sophisticated audiences.

Third, he could do this in a very different media environment than the one Nixon dealt with, one that took advantage of segmented audiences and allowed for more narrowcasting, so that things said and done before one audience might or might not cross over to another. One campaign analyst writes, "The new media included toll-free telephone numbers, satellite linkups, 'town meetings,' video production and distribution, cable television, and above all the television talk show . . . communication formats and programming providing political candidates with freer, more direct access to the public. What these forums shared was a striking tendency to eliminate the middle man, the journalist, and to close the distance between voter and candidate."[33] Clinton was able to take advantage of this environment in all kinds of ways. The Clinton campaign invested heavily in technology. According to one campaign aide, the campaign "said from the beginning we are not going to get beat like we did in 1988. We're not going to get embarrassed on opposition research. We are going to be ready for this thing."[34] In part, this indicated, according to Deputy Campaign Director for Foreign Policy Bob Boorstin, the ways in which "the entire 1992 campaign was a response to 1988. The entire thing, the press, the campaigns themselves, everybody but [President] Bush caught on. And Bush dug his own grave in 1988, with the campaign that he ran then. He laid the seeds for his destruction," because "his campaign tactics in 1988 were so vicious and so interesting in the way that they used them that they provided a road map to how to prevent the same thing."[35] Bush had to be careful because 1988 had given him a reputation for negative campaigning. That campaign also prepared the Clinton team for how best to respond to the inevitable attacks.

The story of the Clinton campaign and its connection to despicable discourse is a complicated one. He explicitly appealed to members of the white working classes through his persona as a "Bubba," a regular guy ostensibly just like them; he implicitly appealed to those same voters through subtly racist and sexist language. At the same time, he could appeal to more educated liberal Democrats through his history as a serious policy wonk, with Ivy League degrees and a similarly educated, explicitly feminist wife. And he could also appeal to African American voters through the politics of popular culture while relying on their allegiance to the Democratic Party. Overtly exclusionary appeals can be overtly challenged; implicit ones can sneak under even watchful radar; both are dangerous to democracy, albeit in different ways.[36] Clinton used implicit appeals, whose consequences were, by definition, less visible, more adaptable. These shifting personae allowed him enormous flexibility as a candidate. They also underscored his shape-shifting, code-switching political nature, contributing to questions about his integrity and trustworthiness, questions Bush was quick to exploit, about whether he had the character to be president.

The Clinton Campaign

Clinton made two main arguments about why he should be president: he could fix the economy, and he could act in a more generalized sense as an agent of change. He infused both arguments with an overall sense of compassion for the suffering caused by current economic dislocations. An insert crafted by the campaign for a speech delivered to the Boston Chamber of Commerce, for example, offered this text: "I hope and pray that Congress and the President can agree on a way to get this country moving again and lift us out of this recession. People don't want 10-second sound bites and vague promises. They're real people with real problems and they're crying out desperately for someone who can help . . . in the 1980s Washington lost touch with the solid, middle-class values that build [*sic*] this country, and people out here know it."[37] Here, he argued that the economy was in recession, that the current administration and Congress were ignoring that fact in favor of sound-bite politics, and that he understood that this failure to act was causing pain—and that this pain had reached into the middle class. The presumptively white middle class was the bastion of "real" American values, the values that built and maintained the nation. When they hurt, the whole country suffered.

Clinton asserted that the solution was therefore obvious—change was required:

> But it is not enough to change government. We must change the political system altogether. For too long, politicians have been taking care of themselves, the special interests have been getting their way, and no one's been looking out for the people. This is not just a campaign. This is a crusade to restore the forgotten middle class, give economic power back to ordinary people, and recapture the American dream. We have to revolutionize government or we risk losing the democracy we cherish, because people will lose faith in the capacity of government to lead us to a better future.[38]

Here he connected the middle class and "ordinary people" and argued that they were pitted against their own political system. Government officials and special interests were on one side of the equation, and Clinton and those ordinary folks were on the other.

These were, in the context of the 1992 election, potent appeals. Clinton had some difficulty getting these arguments through, however, because of the recurrent scandals embroiling his campaign. In what follows, I first discuss the ways he defended himself against the attacks made on him and the offensive strategies he invoked against others, neither of which involve terribly despicable discourse, but both of which reflect the context through which that discourse circulated during the campaign. I then address what I consider to be the heart of his campaign, the despicable discourses of racial and gendered exclusion, adapted for a Democratic audience.

Playing Defense: "Slick Willie"

Clinton had a continuous problem with scandal, but it wasn't so much the events themselves that generated the most consternation as his response to them. That response never varied—he changed his story, sometimes multiple times, evaded responsibility, and deflected issues onto others. This was evident in his reactions to all his scandals, but never more so than in the case of the draft controversy. That controversy put the character issue in the center of the campaign. Clinton, a student during the Vietnam War, sought, as did so many other white students, to avoid the draft. He signed up for the draft, as required, shortly after his eighteenth birthday and received a student deferment. While in college, he grew to increasingly oppose the war and also earned a prestigious Rhodes Scholarship, which would have continued to protect him from the draft, but the Johnson administration abolished graduate student deferments in 1968, which changed Clinton's draft status to 1-A, making him eligible for induction. He planned to return to the United States and enroll in the University of Arkansas's law school, joining ROTC to avoid induction. Then he discovered that he had a high draft number, making induction unlikely, and so decided not to join ROTC, writing a convoluted letter to that effect to the local ROTC commander.[39] It's a fairly routine story of a privileged young man seeking to avoid military service during an unpopular war. But in a presidential candidate, it was explosive. His seeming inability to tell the truth was even more damaging. In a review of polling data, Clinton confidante and campaign aide Diane Blair noted that "the draft issue is not getting better; it's getting worse. It is not the patriotism issue but the honesty/inconsistency issue—and it's drowning out the economic message."[40] Later in the campaign, facing repeated instances of his prevarications and exaggerations, Blair was even more direct with the candidate himself, writing to him: "If we were talking regularly like we used to and I was giving you one of my sermonettes, here's what it would be. The *only* thing that stands between you and the Presidency are doubts about your credibility. Doubts which have been and will be fueled. Please, please, please, in the debates or on the stump or anywhere, do not give them any ammunition by exaggerating any particle of your record. Your record as governor, which I deal with daily, is phenomenal and you should be fiercely proud of it; defend it. But please stick scrupulously to the truth."[41] Throughout the campaign, despite Blair's best advice, Clinton seemed to have an uneasy relationship with the truth.[42] He claimed that he tried marijuana but also said, "I didn't like it. I didn't inhale and never tried it again."[43] Such claims were implausible in themselves, and they increasingly seemed to form a pattern showing Clinton couldn't be trusted. The questionable claims also suggested that Clinton either did not trust the media to convey the facts or that he thought the facts could be hidden from the media. The dubious explanations also implied that he did not trust the voters with the truth or that he thought voters could be manipulated.

If any manipulating was going to be done, the Clinton team wanted it done by them. They had a remarkably effective defensive strategy, which came to be known as the "fax attack." The Clinton campaign responded to everything, letting no accusation, however small, from the Republicans go without a direct challenge. According to Boorstin, this sent "a direct message across the bow of the Bush campaign that nothing they said would go unanswered. The second thing it said to the press, 'Come to us for real information.'"[44] They were justly proud of their response time. In one case, for example, The *New York Times* reported, "On Thursday, Gov. [*sic*] Bill Clinton saw a campaign commercial that made him hopping mad. Today, less than 24 hours later, the Clinton campaign was on the air in 20 states with its own biting rebuttal, accusing Mr. Bush of having the 'worst economic record of any President in 50 years."[45] Clinton's team was determined to counter the negativity they expected—and received—from the Bush campaign.[46] Much of the Clinton campaign's energy was spent on defense. But he spent considerable time on offense as well.

Playing Offense: Attacking Perot and Bush

Clinton hoped to attract many of the same voters who owed allegiance to Ross Perot, and so he was reluctant to make overt criticism of their favored candidate. But the Clinton campaign saw Perot as a threat who could potentially tilt the election to Bush. In public, therefore, Clinton was circumspect when it came to Perot and left him largely alone. But that was in public. Diane Blair, for example, wrote Clinton aide Betty Currie a memo in which she expressed some concern about what the campaign might be doing in private: "At Perot's press conference today he went nearly ballistic over Bush's mountains of operatives working to find some dirt on him (including one 'fruitcake who is trying to find out what's in my mother's will,' etc.). Perot says he gets calls from all over Texas, from courthouses, etc. about people in there trying to find dirt. I just hope that whatever we're doing is deeply deeply covered if we are anxious at this point to leave the impression with both Perot and the public that all the oppo stuff is coming from Bush."[47] Blair clearly was not aware of any opposition research on Perot but knew enough to wonder if it was going on and to sound alarms about the possibility of that fact going public. The campaign did develop negative talking points on Perot, which included noting Perot's support for drilling in the Arctic National Wildlife Refuge, the claim that "he tries to impose his values on others," "supports anti-democratic governments," yet "walks away from the fight when things get tough," and that "he's the slick one."[48] This was pretty mild stuff, and, assuming that this was the extent of their "oppo stuff," it does not rise to the level of despicable discourse. It also reflected the campaign's reluctance to attack Perot, a fact that meant that both Perot and Clinton concentrated attacks on Bush.

Clinton's attacks on Bush were largely standard rhetoric from a challenger. He worked hard, for instance, to turn the victory in the Cold War into a liability for Bush: "At the very moment America's ideas have triumphed and the whole world is rushing to embrace our way of life, our own leaders have been standing still at home and abroad. In the midst of revolutionary change, they have struggled to shore up a status quo that no longer exists. . . . George Bush has invoked a new world order without enunciating a new American purpose."[49] According to Clinton, Bush had created change but was unable to appropriately manage it. Instead, Clinton argued, the Republicans had wreaked havoc on the nation: "The

Reagan-Bush years have exalted private gain over public obligation, special interests over the common good, wealth and fame over work and family. The 1980s ushered in a gilded age of greed, selfishness, irresponsibility, excess, and neglect."[50] He attributed the worst elements of the current political climate to Republican governance in no uncertain terms but did so in ways that are standard kinds of campaign discourse.

The Clinton team accused the Republicans of divisiveness and specifically addressed subtly exclusionary politics. A campaign handbook, *The Clinton Contrast: A Sourcebook*, for example, listed attacks that could be used against the president, which included "George Bush doesn't get it," "George Bush: A Man of No Beliefs," (with subsections on "Lies" and "Flip Flops,") and "The Politics of Divisiveness," in which they charged that "like Lee Atwater taught him, George Bush is more than willing to play to the wedge issues that divide us."[51] He also claimed that "our country is divided by race. Reagan and Bush have played that race card in election after election for twelve years."[52] In other words, the Clinton campaign, which adopted a version of the Southern strategy to woo white voters, was also alerting those voters to the Bush campaign's tendency to do the same thing.

Democratic Exclusions

Clinton's use of subtle exclusion on race was a bit different from the Republican version because his audience was different. He needed to appease racial moderates in his own party, as Nixon had done in 1968, but he also needed to maintain Black loyalty, which Nixon had not tried to do. In addition, Clinton was running at a political moment in which the place of women in politics and in society more generally was a flashpoint, strongly connected to the culture wars that were so central to the 1992 campaign. Consequently, Clinton used subtly exclusionary strategies on both race and gender.

Like many challengers, Clinton argued that the nation under Bush was in a bad way, a situation he laid at the door of the current administration:

> Our people fear that while the American Dream reigns abroad, it is dying at home. We're losing jobs and wasting opportunities. The very fiber of our nation is breaking down: Families are coming

> apart, kids are dropping out of school, drugs and crime dominate our streets. And our leaders here in Washington are doing nothing to turn America around. Our political system rotates between being the butt of jokes and the object of scorn. Frustration produces calls for term limits from voters who think they can't vote incumbents out, resentment produces votes for David Duke—not just from racists, but from voters so desperate for a change, they'll support the most anti-establishment message, even from an ex-Klansman who was inspired by Adolf Hitler. We've got to rebuild our political life together before dangerous demagogues and racists and those who would pander to the worst in us bring our country down.[53]

He gave Bush credit for ending the Cold War and spreading the American Dream abroad. But he undermined that implied praise immediately, arguing that in doing so, he had neglected it at home. He argued in ways reminiscent of Nixon in 1968 that the nation was in a terrible state and that crime and drugs were largely to blame. So dire were things that voters were even willing to entertain arguments for the unacceptable right—arguments propagated by those like David Duke. This is what we now call dog whistle rhetoric, pitched at a level designed for specific voters—white voters were beginning to listen to this extreme rhetoric, white voters who are depicted here as "voters." Operating in a context of decades of rhetoric that racialized drugs and crime more generally, here Black voters are erased at best and are the cause of problems at worst. Rhetoric like this prompted journalist Andrew Kopkind to write that, "in many ways, Bill Clinton is the prophetic candidate of decline" but also that he "offers no evidence that he can reverse the decline of politics in America."[54] As in the Republican version of dog whistling, there are no apparent solutions; the stress is on the nature of the problem. Nixon blamed Johnson, Clinton blamed Bush. In both cases, the coded rhetoric reached out to worried whites at the expense of Black citizens.

The most important example of this kind of coded racializing is his treatment of Reverend Jesse Jackson. Managing Jackson was an issue for the campaign.[55] Showing him too much deference undermined Clinton's ability to attract those important blue-collar white votes. Showing him too little undermined his ability to maintain critical African American support. Clinton chose to show him too little deference, trusting that he could shore up that support in other ways. Several incidents between the two men highlight this tactic.

First, during the primaries, all the Democratic candidates were eager for Jackson's endorsement. While at a campaign event, and on a live mic, Clinton was erroneously told that Jackson had endorsed Iowa senator Tom Harkin. He exploded in rage, and reporters lost no time in circulating his comments widely, causing considerable controversy. An internal campaign memo noted that there would be "no official comment" about the incident but offered some talking points: "Gov. Clinton had a very human reaction upon hearing the news that Rev. Jackson had possibly endorsed Sen. Harkin; at the time, Gov. Clinton did not know that Rev. Jackson had apparently offered to campaign with all the candidates; Gov. Clinton has been in touch with Rev. Jackson; Gov. Clinton has campaigned in the African American community more aggressively than anyone else in the Democratic primary." The memo included a list of endorsements that could be used to fend off charges of racism.[56] They managed to repair the damage for the moment, but more shocks to Jackson's sensibilities would come during the general election campaign.

During that campaign, Jackson invited Clinton to speak at a meeting of his "Rainbow Coalition," an organization Jackson founded to advocate for civil rights and social justice. Clinton appeared shortly after the LA riots sparked by the acquittal of the police officers who had beaten Rodney King and gave a speech that, in part, strongly criticized rapper Sister Souljah for what Clinton called racist remarks. Rather than using the occasion to make arguments in favor of civil rights, Clinton instead criticized an African American entertainer for supposed "radicalism." Immediately after the event, he told Jackson that he was not going to be considered for running mate. There is little doubt that the Clinton team planned the criticism of Sister Souljah as counterprogramming, sending a message to white audiences that he was not overly beholden either to African Americans in general or to Jackson in particular. He baited Jackson in a play for white votes, taking African American support for granted. And he (correctly) trusted that by doing things like appearing on *Arsenio*, he could repair any damage incurred by that behavior.[57]

He continued throughout the campaign to engage in contradictory actions. In the wake of LA riots, for example, where he made a public point of his sympathy with the rioters, Clinton then went golfing an at all-white country club, again obscuring the nature of his racial commitments. When challenged to explain himself, he made implausible excuses, noting he wasn't a real member of the club, that he was someone's guest, that the club was in the process of screening Black members, but still he looked inconsistent if not hypocritical. The inconsistency, of course, was actually the point.

Coding worked its way into policy as well. On welfare, for example, he said, "The new covenant will say to people on welfare: We're going to provide the training and education and health care you need, but if you can work, you've got to go to work. You can no longer stay on welfare forever. . . . The New Covenant can break the cycle of welfare. Welfare should be a second chance, not a way of life. We're going to put an end to welfare as we know it."[58] He argued that, "First of all, we need to reassert the old-fashioned notion that personal responsibility is an important part of public citizenship."[59] In these examples, Clinton was participating in the racialization of certain kinds of government programs for political purposes and he brought subtle racism home to the Democrats as the price of taking back the White House. As is historically the case with arguments grounded in race, these appeals also referenced gender.

Coded Sexism

On an overt level, Clinton was a strongly pro-woman candidate. His wife Hillary was a Yale-educated lawyer who made no secret of her feminism—at least until she moderated that feminism, dropping the "Rodham" from her name, engaging in a cookie bake-off with Barbara Bush (which she won), and essentially downplaying her own ambitions. Hillary posed a constant dilemma for the campaign. She was implicated in scandals of her own, including two important ones concerning Whitewater, a land development deal with which the Clintons had been associated, and the Rose law firm where she worked. A Clinton campaign internal memo reporting polling on Hillary noted, "First, voters need to meet the real Hillary Clinton. They have a distorted, limited, and overly political impression of her. They need to see and hear a broader, more diverse, and more personal portrayal of her character. . . . By focusing on Hillary Clinton's personal life, the campaign can powerfully communicate the values both Clintons share. This message is particularly important given the fact that George Bush's greatest policy strength—and his biggest advantage over Bill Clinton on the domestic front—is family values."[60] The memo also noted that "while voters genuinely admire Hillary Clinton's intelligence and tenacity, they are uncomfortable with these traits in a woman," that "both Hillary and Bill are perceived as being too political," and finally that "less-educated voters are particularly distrustful and resentful of Hillary Clinton."[61] In other words, Hillary needed to moderate her professional persona in favor of representing "family values" in order to attract, or at least avoid further alienating, white voters. Journalists reflected on the "Hillary problem" in more public ways: "Perhaps such criticism illuminates society's ambivalence toward changing roles in this backlash era. Men may be projecting on Mrs. Clinton their hostility toward feminism, while women, overwhelmed by their multiple responsibilities, may be projecting their frustrations."[62] Note the gendered nature of this coverage. Men were depicted as resentful, and women were understood as overwhelmed—as victims, not beneficiaries, of feminism. For both audiences, Hillary was too ambitious, too political, too educated, and too forceful to serve as the kind of first lady Barbara Bush, for instance, exemplified. And the campaign conceded to the demands that she be more like a traditional political spouse. In some ways, of course, this was a concession to the prevailing politics of the presidency, which was (and is) highly gendered. But by conceding so much on the gender front where Hillary was concerned, the Clinton campaign also pointed to a much larger way in which he undermined women—through his own relationships with them and in the ways those women were treated when the relationships became public.

For example, during the Democratic primaries, a story about Clinton's extramarital affairs appeared in the national tabloid the *Star*, causing an enormous uproar and endangering his candidacy.[63] The Clinton campaign generated talking points in response, including the argument that "we believe the American people are more concerned about the stresses and strains that are tearing middle-class families apart—job loss, declining wages, racial tensions, crime—than they are about what problems a political family has overcome in the past."[64] The same memo offered other defenses as well, including the argument that "the Responsible Press is being manipulated by the tabloids," in what campaign strategist Paul Begala called "lowest-common denominator journalism."[65] The campaign's first line of defense was to deflect the issue and to focus on the media—a not unreasonable response to a scandal. But note also the ways in which they focus not on the fact of his womanizing but on the Clinton's joint commitment to their family, a commitment that apparently included her acceptance of his affairs.[66]

When his alleged affair with Gennifer Flowers became public, the Clintons appeared on television's *60 Minutes* and delivered an impassioned defense of their marriage and their privacy. One writer assessed the event in very favorable terms: "Brilliantly, the Clintons had simultaneously exposed their emotional souls, defended their family's sanctity, and turned a debilitating personal weakness into a political strength. Instead of undermining their credibility, the Clintons had enhanced it."[67] There is nothing to criticize here; the Clintons have the right to maintain their marriage on their terms and to argue that their private life is not relevant to his public duties. What is disturbing is the way the campaign encouraged the women associated with Clinton to be demeaned and humiliated in the media. Clinton aide Betty Currie famously referred to news of his various affiliations with women not his wife as "bimbo eruptions," and in order to refute the allegations and limit the damage to their campaign, the Clinton team decided to attack Flowers.

Like Flowers, the women who accused Clinton were treated badly by the national media and fared no better in public opinion.[68] Partly, this was at the instigation of the Clinton campaign. Campaign staffers Loretta Lynch and Nancy McFadden, for example, coauthored a memo that listed "Possible Investigation Needs: Exposing GF completely as a fraud, liar—possible criminal to stop this story and related stories, prevent future non-related stories and expose press inaction and manipulation."[69] When engaged in the politics of self-defense, the Clinton campaign derided the women who accused their candidate, attacked the media who covered their claims, and undermined both the media and the place of women in the political culture in the process. As with the politics of race, when it came to gender the Clinton campaign played one tune very loudly but played another for certain voters, generating a quiet kind of despicable discourse. Unsurprisingly,

Clinton found himself in difficulties with many women voters.[70] This fact reflected a more generalized problem he had with what became known as the "character issue," a major theme of the 1992 general election.

In his overt rhetorical strategies, Clinton did not circulate despicable discourse. He criticized and challenged the president, but he and his surrogates did so in ways that did not significantly exceed the normal boundaries of campaign rhetoric. But he used a kind of implicit discourse that was despicable. On matters of race he looked for ways to demonstrate his independence from Jesse Jackson and African American voters in general and did so by publicly disrespecting Jackson and attacking Sister Souljah. He participated in racializing crime, drugs, and welfare and thus also participated in pitting some citizens against others and doing so on largely racialized grounds. Matters of gender displayed a similar pattern. The Clinton campaign began by valuing Hillary Rodham Clinton as a professional and intellectual equal of the candidate and bit by bit changed her hair, her demeanor, her name, and her public persona, rendering her into a closer approximation of the traditional first lady. More problematic, as a means of defending the candidate from the political consequences of his extramarital behavior, the campaign encouraged the ridicule and humiliation of women with whom he had been intimate. This reinforced strict societal standards about the roles permitted women and damaged the women themselves. The exclusions of the Clinton campaign were pernicious, in part because they were subtle. The exclusions inherent in the Republican campaign, to which we now turn, were considerably more pernicious and nowhere near subtle.

EXCLUSION ON DISPLAY: THE REPUBLICAN CAMPAIGN

In 1968, Richard Nixon courted the conservative right wing in ways that allowed him to maintain the support of Republican moderates. By 1992, the moderates were all but gone and the right was increasingly demanding and increasingly strident. The most vocal of the right-wing Republicans was former Nixon speechwriter, pundit, and gadfly Patrick J. Buchanan, who was both nationalist and isolationist, and whose policy preferences included a drastic reduction in immigration, reform of what he considered unfair trade arrangements, and a two-hundred-mile-long fence along the US-Mexican border. These policies were summed up in his promise to "put America first."[71] Buchanan represented divisive and angry politics as they were increasingly emerging on the right.

Buchanan mounted a challenge to Bush in the primaries, and while that effort was electorally unsuccessful, it did push Bush to the right and influenced both the convention and the platform ratified there. He justified his campaign by declaring:

> Quite simply, our country is careening off course. And neither Mr. Bush nor his advisors have the foggiest notion how to steer her back. . . . Adding to the recession is a hellish social crisis. Crime rates are hitting record highs; test scores of our high school seniors are hitting new depths. Washington D.C. is the murder capital of the nation. Neighborhood datelines from New York, our cultural capitol, say it all: Howard Beach and Bensonhurst, Crown Heights and Central Park. More and more we are behaving like warring tribes, bickering and fighting with one another. Our heritage and traditions are under attack in our schools, our media, our universities, under the rubric of "multiculturalism."[72]

Buchanan, representative of the growing right wing, made economic arguments, but the real thrust of his campaign was cultural—he spoke for white conservatives who feared that "their" culture was being hijacked by permissive liberals and people of color, all of whom were collectively guilty of causing national conflict and debasing national culture and politics.

Bush responded by trying to marginalize Buchanan: "We are in a demagogic year. A lot of people have discovered New Hampshire for the first time, they've never been to this state before, never heard of it, don't know the heartbeat of this state."[73] And "It's a weird year. You've got crazy people running all over, thinking that the way to put the country back to work is to stop exports."[74] Bush claimed that Buchanan's campaign was alien to New Hampshire, "weird" and "demagogic," representative of marginal and extreme elements. His economic policies would do harm. Noticeably, Bush did not challenge Buchanan on values but sought to make the case that he was a better representative of those values.[75] He said in New Hampshire, for example, "Again, I might say that I haven't diverged one inch from my commitment to what I think are New Hampshire values; I know they're Bush family values, in terms of family and neighborhood and community and child care that can be done at the local level and all of this."[76]

Bush also used values against his opposition:

> The next value I speak of must be forever cast in stone. I speak of decency, the moral courage to say what is right and condemn what is wrong. And we need a nation closer to the "The Waltons" than to "The Simpsons"—[laughter]—an America that rejects the incivility, the tide of incivility, and the tide of intolerance. We see this tide in the naked epithet and in the code words that play to our worst prejudices. We see it when people ridicule religion and religious leaders; like the group that desecrated communion hosts on the steps of St. Patrick's Cathedral. We see this tide of incivility and intolerance in bigotry, in discrimination, and anti-Semitism.[77]

The first part of this was defense—he was referencing television families to make cultural arguments about the kind of nation he preferred, represented by the Waltons, not the Simpsons. But he was also making sideways arguments against Buchanan. Bush was not contesting ground over the values themselves—he, Buchanan, and his audience presumably all agreed on those. He was making arguments about how they should be protected—through the kinds of wholesome means represented by the wholesome Depression-era Waltons rather than through the rhetoric of snarky cynicism, which he identifies with the Simpsons. This kind of sideways arguing is leaning toward despicable discourse because it is an attempt to evade responsibility for the accusations he is leveling against a political opponent.

It's also leaning toward despicable discourse because of the indirection of involving surrogates, and Bush surrogates were much more direct than the candidate himself, leading to exchanges like this one with a reporter:

> Q: Mr. President, you said you didn't want to talk specifically about Patrick Buchanan, but your surrogates have called him everything from a fascist to a racist to possibly anti-Semitic.

> Do you endorse what your surrogates are saying? Do you want to rein them in? . . .
>
> The President: I think most fair-minded viewers would feel that I've come under attack from my opponent, so I'm delighted when people defend me.[78]

This is despicable discourse. Bush is happy to have the accusation that Buchanan is potentially a fascist, a racist, or an anti-Semite circulating, but he is trying to evade being attached to those accusations. He seemed to think that if campaign surrogates were doing it, he was not responsible: "I have not been attacking any opponent. I hope you know that. I haven't done it. We've had surrogates trying to put these people into proper perspective, but I have not been engaged in that."[79] Putting Buchanan in "proper perspective" meant leveling charges of fascism, racism, and anti-Semitism, but doing so without wanting to be accused in turn of using negative tactics.

Bush managed to win in New Hampshire, but Buchanan managed about 40 percent of the vote. The signs were ominous for Bush. Buchanan and Perot indicate, in different ways, the ways in which the Republican Party was increasingly angry, increasingly demanding. That anger and those demands took center stage at the party's national convention in Houston.

The 1992 Republican Convention

Conventions are, above all, moments when parties need to reconcile the personal and policy divisions of the primary campaigns and show their unity and sense of shared purpose to the nation. Displays of such unity are especially important in a mass-mediated age.[80] Bush bought the unity of his party at the price of foregrounding its most conservative and its most strident elements: he abandoned centrist positions and gave valuable prime-time slots to some of the party's most extreme members. The resulting spectacle was negative, intolerant, and angry. Bush, who consistently argued against bigotry, ran a convention that put bigotry on display.[81]

The most notable instance of this was Pat Buchanan's speech, which opened with a vituperative assault on the Democrats and the policies they represented: "Like many of you last month, I watched that giant masquerade ball at Madison Square Garden—where 20,000 radicals and liberals came dressed up as moderates and centrists—in the greatest single exhibition of cross-dressing in American political history."[82] Buchanan accused the Democrats of misrepresenting themselves and cast aspersions on their presumed lack of adherence to heterosexual norms, thus implicitly also challenging their suitability as national leaders and representatives. He insisted that "the agenda that Clinton and Clinton would impose on America—abortion on demand, a litmus test for the Supreme Court, homosexual rights, discrimination against religious schools, women in combat—that's change all right. But it's not the kind of change America wants. It's not the kind of change America needs. And it is not the kind of change we can tolerate in a nation that we still call God's country."[83]

Note that this agenda is not Democratic, nor is it the Clinton-Gore agenda. It is held by, confined to, the Clintons. Even if democratically elected, they would impose that agenda on the nation's unwilling populace. It would, he argued, go well beyond what he considered to be the horrors of granting civil rights to gay citizens but would, at the same time, actively discriminate against religious citizens. Buchanan depicted gays (and Democrats) as presumptively nonreligious, and their rights were positioned in direct opposition to those of the religious. Granting rights to gays meant taking them away from Christians. For Buchanan, this invidious agenda was also directly oppositional to "America," a construction that was avowedly Republican in nature. Democrats stood opposed not only to Republicans but to God and country as well. This is despicable discourse at its most obvious.

Buchanan said,

> My friends, this election is about much more than who gets what. It is about who we are. It is about what we believe. It is about what we stand for as Americans. There is a religious war going on in our country for the soul of America. It is a cultural war, as critical to the kind of nation we will one day be as was the Cold War itself. And in that struggle for the soul of America, Clinton and Clinton are on one side and George Bush is on our side. And so we have come home, to stand beside him.

Buchanan made a pitch for a united party, but the unity he demanded was centered on exclusionary claims to national identity. And while the metaphor for campaigning has long been war, few campaigns have offered that metaphor in such stark terms.

Buchanan was not alone in offering those terms. While the convention was notable for its inclusion of a speech by AIDS sufferer Mary Fisher, who made an important case for an empathetic understanding of AIDS,[84] the bulk of the convention addresses tended to conflate godlessness and the Democratic Party, as did Pat Robertson's argument that "George Bush's vision for America, ladies and gentlemen, is one of faith in God, strong families, freedom, individual initiative, and free enterprise. He believes that government should be the people's servant and not their master. The vision of Bill Clinton is a liberal welfare state that dominates every facet of our lives, burdens free enterprise, redistributes wealth, and weakens the family. . . . The campaign before us is not just a campaign for an office, but for the destiny of America."[85] In winning the Cold War, the Republicans had lost a totalitarian enemy; in 1992, they rediscovered it in the Democratic Party.

It wasn't just the assertions the Republicans were making. It was the way in which they were making them that renders this discourse despicable. Robertson's speech, for example, was not all that different from Reagan's—but where Reagan spoke in the often humorous and rarely rancorous way that was his style, speakers at this convention were visibly angry, visibly resentful. The Republicans in Houston claimed, as parties during their conventions always claim, to be speaking for the nation. But in Houston there was a stridency to these claims, an anger underlying them that indicated their exclusionary nature. Republicans were facing a battle for what they called America's soul, but it was easily read as being about American hierarchies and resistance to the ways in which those hierarchies were being upended. They reached not for a new governing consensus but for the reestablishment of an old one.

Republicans lost that round, and the presidency, in 1992. But they had found a set of issues that propelled domestic politics into the next century as the question of American power abroad remained open and the issues surrounding hierarchies at home intensified. At their 1992 convention, Republicans grounded their appeal in overt and exclusionary rhetoric, circulating despicable discourses in which the values of some citizens were assayed above the rights of others. That discourse wasn't confined to the convention but followed Bush as he went negative against Clinton in the 1992 general election campaign.

Bush in the General Election

As the general election campaign began, Bush was in trouble. An internal campaign memo noted, "The mood of the country remains extremely negative. Seventy-five percent (75%) say things in the country are seriously off on the wrong track, up 2% since December. Seventy-six percent (76%) say the country is worse off than four years ago, up 9%. Thirty-nine percent (39%) say they are personally worse off than four years ago, up 3%. . . . Voters are 'hopeful' but also 'worried' and 'frustrated'; a substantial minority (40%) are 'angry.'"[86] The electorate, in other words, was in no mood to reelect the president who had presided over the decline of American prosperity and the ratcheting up of American cultural division. Bush tried to make a positive case for his leadership, one that largely depended on his foreign policy expertise. But foreign policy mattered less and less, and with Perot threatening from one side and Clinton threatening from the other, Bush's campaign went increasingly negative.

The campaign made good use of older forms of media in local markets to make their point. The Bush campaign sponsored a series of negative ad spots with local content, for example. An internal campaign memo observed, "This campaign has been very successful in helping to drive up Clinton's negatives. That his negatives grew dramatically from the last debate to the last weekend is largely a result of the pounding he took from the President, the television, the radio, and an aggressive direct mail program."[87] Rather than making all their arguments national, the campaign made good use of technology to reach niche audiences. Journalist Howard Kurtz writes, "Radio is a stealth medium in politics. Less expensive and less noticed than television, it can be effective in tailoring messages to people who listen to black-oriented stations, religious broadcasts, or country music. Detailed negative criticism often seems less harsh in sixty-second radio spots than on television. The Bush ads, airing in more than a dozen states, attempt to tie his broad-brush attacks to pocketbook issues in each locality."[88] Those local ads brought the down ballot into consideration, telling New Jersey voters, for example, "If you're fed up with Jim Florio, don't let Bill Clinton do the same thing to America," and highlighting local issues like school choice, prayer in schools, and values more generally, connecting the local and immediate to the national campaign.[89] The Bush campaign wielded local events well, but the bulk of their despicable discourse had a national audience. This was particularly apparent in what became known during the campaign as "the character issue."

Trust and the Character Issue

The Bush campaign faced something of a dilemma when it came to circulating despicable discourse in 1992. Because of the 1988 campaign, Bush was sensitive to being accused of negative campaigning, so he didn't want to use rumors about Clinton's sex life or the draft in the campaign.[90] In fact, he made a point of refusing to campaign on "sleaze," telling reporters in April 1992, "I have made specific instructions in writing to our people to stay out of the sleaze business."[91] But his campaign was not reluctant to take advantage of the never-ending scandals that seemed to engulf the Clinton campaign and so argued to the Republican's strengths: "This election is about trust. Trust and taxes."[92]

A representative ad from the general election, for example, asserted, "He said he was never drafted. Then he admitted he *was* drafted. Then he said he *forgot* being drafted. He said he was never deferred from the draft. Then . . . [*sic*] he said he was. He said he never received special treatment. But he did receive special treatment. The question then was evading the draft. Now, for Bill Clinton, it's a question of avoiding the truth."[93] The Bush team emphasized their candidate's trustworthiness and contrasted it to the lack of that attribute in their opponent: "Americans put their trust in President Bush as he led the world through the end of the Cold War. It is no mistake that in ending the Cold War, freedom finished first. . . . Some time in the next four years, a major crisis will break out. When it does, who do you want in the Oval Office?"[94] This is a straightforward, fairly typical comparison ad. But it edges close to despicable discourse because of the scandal-ridden context and the ways in which the Bush campaign was willing to exploit that without involving the candidate directly. On the draft controversy, for example, the Bush-Quayle team issued a press release: "'This is hypocrisy at its greatest height and deception at its lowest depth,' declared Bush-Quayle Deputy Campaign Manager Mary Matalin. 'After months of refusing to tell the truth about his draft record and stone-walling the press about his personal draft papers and now we are beginning to see the full extent to which Bill Clinton was willing to maintain his precious 'political viability.'"[95] They issued talking points that included, "When it comes to the truth, Bill Clinton has lied about his personal life, lied about his record, and lied about raising taxes. That's why the Arkansas *Democrat Gazette* just wrote, 'There is something almost inhuman in his smoother responses that sends a shiver up the spine.' His hometown paper refused to endorse him. Bill Clinton is wrong for you. He is wrong for the country."[96] And they told the press, "'Bill Clinton has sadly come to the conclusion that he can run out the clock without coming clean and releasing his personal papers,' said Bush-Quayle Deputy Campaign Manager Mary Matalin. 'What Clinton fails to realize is that every day he tries to stonewall the American people, he only reinforces the two dominant themes of this campaign: he can't tell the truth, and he lacks the character and judgment to lead the American people."[97] These talking points and press releases are examples of a constant barrage of claims about Bill Clinton's tenuous relationship with the truth. And because these claims are grounded in actual instances of obfuscation, they could well count as legitimate campaign communication rather than as despicable discourse. But even in that case, they contributed to an environment of overwhelming negativity and made the case that Clinton was unsuited for public office, potentially further damaging public trust in political institutions.

Sometimes the surrogates went well beyond the limits of normal campaign negativity, as when Mary Matalin called Clinton a "sniveling hypocrite." Her comments were disavowed by Bush, and she issued a qualified apology—to Bush, not Clinton. One newspaper report summarized it this way: "Not only did she not apologize to Mr. Clinton, she said, 'I stand by my criticism of the Clinton campaign and the Democratic party for their unprecedented hypocrisy and for daily disparaging, in the most egregious and personal terms, the President of the United States. . . . It was Ms. Matalin's latest volley in a hotly worded exchange she began last week when she said the campaign had avoided repeating accusations that referred to Clinton as a 'philandering pot-smoking draft dodger.'"[98] This kind of language was rare and unwelcome in national campaigns; it was understood as crossing the lines of civility and it certainly edged toward, if not fully constituting, despicable discourse.

Even if the claims about Clinton's veracity are counted as acceptable campaign discourse, the arguments concerning a trip to Moscow questioned his patriotism in ways that were clearly despicable. As a student on a Rhodes Scholarship in England during the Cold War, Clinton made a trip to Moscow. A Bush campaign news release stated, "Clinton was also asked if, on his way to Moscow, a one-day stop in Norway had anything to do with the anti-war movement . . . the evidence suggests otherwise."[99] This is despicable discourse—it implies that Clinton was not only unpatriotic but might also have maintained questionable relations with the USSR. "He says he didn't lead anti-war protests, *but he did*. He said he was not drafted, *but he was*. He says he did not receive a deferment from the draft, *but he did*. He said he never broke the laws of this country by smoking marijuana, *but that was nothing more than a deception*. He said he can remember that he did not inhale, *but he can't remember with whom he met when he traveled to Moscow during the same era*. Once again with Bill Clinton, the issue is trust."[100] The overt issue may have been trust, but the implied argument is that Clinton had something to hide when it came to his visit to the USSR. Rather than running a campaign emphasizing Bush's strengths, the Bush team chose to emphasize Clinton's weaknesses (which is legitimate campaigning) and did so in ways that questioned not his abilities but his patriotism (which is despicable discourse).

Unsurprisingly, news of the Moscow trip created a minor uproar.[101] Clinton lost his temper when questioned about it on the *Phil Donahue Show*. A few weeks later, he again got angry when asked about the trust issue, and replied:

> Anytime you get an incumbent President who will literally say anything—say anything to get elected. He said in the beginning he would say or do anything to get elected. He has put on ads all over America that are lies and that have been roundly rejected by every objective press source and (inaudible). He has made up charge [*sic*] about my record. He will say or do anything to get elected. He has no core. . . . The very idea that the word trust could ever come out of Bush's mouth after what he has done to this country and the way he has trammeled the truth is a travesty for the American political system.[102]

At this point, both candidates were so enmeshed in the negative politics of the campaign that there was overt despicable discourse on both sides. The trust issue cut to the heart of the campaign's despicable discourse. But the hot button in 1992 was race.

Racial Politics

Interestingly, Bush went after Clinton on race. This was probably not because he thought Republicans had any real chance of earning African American votes, but more likely because if he could create suspicion about Clinton's racial politics, that might lead Democrats to stay home on Election Day and/or help woo Perot voters who might be racial moderates. And he tried to maintain the support of conservative whites on racial issues, using both subtle and overt racial appeals. His campaign announced, for example, that Bush was proud of the nation's increased conviction rate under Reagan/Bush: "President Bush believes that the answer to overcrowded prisons is more prison space."[103] Crime had become so racialized that this claim was tantamount to reassuring whites that he had the correct attitudes about incarcerating Black criminals and keeping white neighborhoods safe. In the same vein he argued, "I am for civil rights and I am against quotas," a claim that meant he could support civil rights in the abstract and oppose action instantiating economic equality in more concrete cases.[104] But he also tried to label Clinton as racist, noting, for example, that Clinton had allowed the executions of Ricky Ray Rector, "The first black executed in Arkansas since 1960," and stating, "An Amnesty International spokesman told reporters after a clemency hearing the previous week that Clinton is not 'dying to be president, but he's killing to be president.'"[105] Implying that his opponent sanctioned an execution for electoral gain is clearly an example of despicable discourse.

Racial politics took center stage after the Rodney King verdict, and Bush used that occasion to make his position on race clear while obscuring Clinton's: "After the riots in Los Angeles, Clinton joined the 'blame the Republican' [*sic*] game. Only after the riots did Clinton begin to offer the bulk of his urban affairs agenda. Clinton started to criticize the Bush administration for urban neglect, yet at the same time offered empowerment as the centerpiece of his program. Clinton has no original ideas on urban affairs."[106] Bush implied Clinton didn't really care about African American equality as he claimed but was both an opportunist and a hypocrite.

Bush also relied on subtle racism in his own rhetoric on events in Los Angeles. He responded to the riots by saying:

> A tragic series of events have occurred in Los Angeles that include frustration over a verdict, the wanton destruction of property, and the senseless death of several citizens in the last few hours. I urge all Americans to approach this situation with calm, with tolerance, and with the respect for the rights of all individuals under the Constitution. . . . We are concerned about any question of excessive public violence. The murder and destruction in the streets of Los Angeles last night and today must be stopped. Lootings, beatings, and random violence against innocent victims must be condemned. Society cannot tolerate this kind of behavior.[107]

He later referred to the problems of "mob brutality, the total loss of respect for human life," and called the violence "sickeningly sad."[108] He argued that it "is not about civil rights. It's not about the great cause of equality, that all Americans must uphold. It's not a message of protest. It's been the brutality of a mob, pure and simple."[109] Bush denied that there was any real cause for the riots, claiming they were the actions of a "mob." Society could not tolerate such acts of violence; it could, however, apparently tolerate the actions of the police officers who beat King.

Racism was equally clear in his rhetoric on welfare: "Too often, welfare systems create dependency instead of self-reliance. The President believes *welfare should be a temporary helping hand not a way of life*. And, once on welfare, recipients have responsibilities to taxpayers—to find work, to obey the law, to avoid having additional children, and to keep their children off drugs."[110] The implication here is that welfare recipients were using government money as "a way of life," that they were not already looking to find work or obeying the law, and that they were engaged in ceaseless efforts to enrich themselves by having an endless parade of drug-using children at taxpayer expense. This is despicable discourse, for it relies on false claims to demean fellow citizens while also pitting citizens against one another.

In the end, Bush won 37 percent of the popular vote, Clinton 43 percent and Perot 19 percent. Clinton earned 370 electoral votes to Bush's 168. These results reveal a great deal about the directions the Republican Party and the nation were heading. Americans who voted for Clinton, like those who voted for Perot, wanted something the status quo was not offering. By the end of the 1992 campaign, Bush had lost reelection and the Republican Party had suffered convulsions in its hierarchies and expectations. The Buchanan and Perot candidacies each indicated, although in different ways, that there was an important populist constituency emerging, one that had been listening to subtly racist appeals for decades and was now willing to attend to overtly racist appeals. These white voters were stridently isolationist in foreign policy, were anti-immigrant and anti-minority in domestic politics, and were increasingly the victims of changes in the global economy. These elements all contributed to an increasingly toxic stew of political alienation and anger. It did not bode well for the future of Republican politics or for the politics of the entire nation.

CONCLUSION: LEGITIMATING EXCLUSION ACROSS PARTY LINES

By many measures, George Bush should have won reelection. He was enormously popular after the Gulf War, he had the power of incumbency, and he was reasonably well liked within the moderate wing of the Republican Party. But the moderates were less and less important to the Republican coalition as right-wing party members took control over Congress and fought bitterly within the party and against the Democrats for the soul of the party and the nation. Neither Pat Buchanan nor Ross Perot should have had important effects in 1992, but both grabbed and held a good bit of conservative political attention and loyalty.

Perot and Buchanan had much in common, although Perot lacked Buchanan's nasty ethnocentrism. Both put a lot of emphasis on populist appeals and helped encourage the "revolt against globalism."[111] Buchanan and Perot served as warning signs that would eventually lead the disaffected right within the Republican Party to form the Tea Party, with its calls for economic reform and its racism. The 1992 election signaled the continuing importance of the white South to presidential politics and indicated the ways in which it might be won, as Bill Clinton adapted the Southern strategy to Democratic audiences.[112] Clinton's famous election mantra of "It's the economy, stupid; change versus more of the same; don't forget about health care," makes no explicit mention of cultural politics, but those politics were central to the campaign and inflected the way the "character issue" and issues of gender and race were interpreted by various audiences during the election.

It was also an incredibly ugly election, with all kinds of charges and countercharges feeding on and contributing to a lack of trust in national institutions and the people who occupied them. The media, in the midst of a transition from broadcast to cable, and facing the incursion of new electronic forms of communication, were driven toward the sensational as a means of maintaining all-important ratings, and talk shows amplified the most negative aspects of the campaign culture.

The context in 1992 encouraged the developments and circulation of despicable discourse, and the major party candidates, their parties, and their surrogates used both the dog whistle and the bullhorn to attract the votes of an increasingly alienated, angry, and fearful collection of white voters. Those voters would face increasingly difficult economic times and would react in increasingly ugly ways, until the nation found itself embroiled in an election featuring two of the most unpopular candidates in national history, in what almost everyone at the time recognized as an event that threatened the norms and values of democracy itself.

CHAPTER 6

IT DOESN'T GET MORE DEPLORABLE THAN THIS, 2016

While the 1992 election carried portents for 2016, those portents were sometimes hard to read. The right maintained a strong and visceral hatred of the Clintons, for example, which was kept alive by media—especially Fox News—willing to keep pounding on old grudges for the sake of ratings. The intensifying partisanship of the Clinton years underpinned the bitter fight over the results of the 2000 election, and while the tragic events of September 11, 2001, seemed to unify the country, that unity was soon lost as the wars in Iraq and Afghanistan continued amid evidence that the Bush administration had been, at best, disingenuous in its evidence justifying those conflicts. That administration was further damaged by its feckless responses to Hurricane Katrina, which devastated New Orleans, and to the financial crisis of 2008, which did the same to the national economy. Those events contributed to the election of the country's first African American president, and for a brief moment it was almost possible to believe that the nation had overcome some of the worst elements of its past. But that election only exacerbated partisan and racial anger on the right, and Barack Obama endured a constant barrage of vicious and ugly racial attacks as Republicans dug in on their side of the partisan barricades.

Between 1992 and 2016, then, and especially between 2000 and 2016, there were significant increases in the factors that contribute to deplorable elections. The combined effects of the 2000 election, 9/11, the endless wars in the Middle East, the aftermath of Hurricane Katrina, and the economic crisis meant that national trust in the political system was more fragile than ever. The recovery after the 2008 financial collapse was weak and uneven; large swaths of the country, especially rural areas and inner cities, continued to suffer economically, but even the suburbs felt its effects. As Obama's presidency continued, it became clear that the resistance to him was deeply embedded and attributable to a variety of factors, many of them condensed into the question of race.

The growth of the Tea Party, for example, ostensibly organized around economic issues, had clear racial valences. Its presence meant that Republicans who compromised with Democrats were increasingly seen as apostates by the conservative faithful, and to avoid challenges in their primaries, congressional Republicans were forced to the right. Because of the racial toxicity on the right and the economic distress nationwide, immigration was a potentially important issue, although most Republicans running in the 2016 primaries were hesitant to campaign on it. Cable media were increasingly segmented, with the conservatives in particular dedicating themselves to a single channel, one that was increasingly given over to proselytizing rather than to factual reporting.[1] And the internet facilitated the rapid circulation of ideas and theories, some of them only tenuously connected to reality.[2]

Into this political miasma stepped Donald J. Trump, real estate entrepreneur and reality television personality. Trump was part of a mediated political culture that for decades had been portraying politics as an "insider game played by insider elites" to the detriment of the American (white) middle class.[3] Those citizens were depicted by conservatives as the victims of globalized forces beyond their control, which were manipulated by national elites for personal gain. Trump's brand of populism thus contained appeals to class and through class to race. As is often the case in US politics, those appeals were accompanied by messages that divided, rather than uniting the nation along class lines.

"They" were taking "our" jobs; "they" were invading "our" country; "they" were changing "our" culture and "our" country. Trump's discourse was clear, divisive, and appealing to many white Americans. He lost the popular vote but won the Electoral College and the presidency through a campaign that was mired in despicable discourse from start to finish. With the Trump candidacy, the Republicans gave themselves completely over to such discourse and to the political consequences it entailed. Consequently, this chapter is largely the story of the Trump campaign. In it, I first detail the context that opened the door to this discourse, spend some time with the Clinton campaign, and then concentrate on the more despicable elements of Trump's rhetoric throughout the election. I conclude with some thoughts about what this campaign meant for the nation as it endured four years of a president dedicated to despicable discourse.

A PERFECT STORM: OPENING THE DOOR FOR DESPICABLE DISCOURSE

Two Supreme Court cases were pivotal to the 2016 election: in 2010 the Court determined in *Citizens United* that the federal government could not restrict campaign contributions, facilitating a massive infusion of money into the election process. And in 2013, the Court gutted the Voting Rights Act, allowing state governments more control over voting and leading to vast increases in voter suppression across the country, especially among African American and Latinx communities. These two developments meant that a few people—like the conservative Koch brothers—had a disproportionate influence over party councils and that a large number of people, especially people of color, were unable to exercise their franchise. When added to the increasing use of social media like Facebook and Twitter, which amplified divisive messages, the stage was set for a deplorable election.

The context was rendered more vulnerable to despicable discourse by long-term messaging by the Republicans, who added to the prevailing subtle politics of exclusion an implacable opposition to the presidency of Barack Obama. The rise of the Tea Party brought with it an increasing vitriol and animosity and helped further erode already weakened norms of tolerance and forbearance. As the political parties became more ideologically cohesive, they also became less tolerant of internal dissent. This effect was much more marked on the Republican side, and any compromise with Democrats began to look like disloyalty. This meant that important legislation stalled, while other legislative functions atrophied. Senate Majority Leader Mitch McConnell, for instance, blocked a number of White House initiatives, culminating in his refusal to grant a vote for Obama's nomination of Merrick Garland as a Supreme Court Justice.

As the Tea Party and their Republican allies increasingly prevented legislative action, they also argued that Washington politics was the primary cause of the nation's problems, contributing to public distrust of the government and to the overall fragility of the political system. As Hillary Clinton put it, "For years, GOP leaders had stoked the public's fears and disappointments. They were willing to sabotage the government in order to block President Obama's agenda. For them, dysfunction wasn't a bug, it was a feature."[4] That sentiment was shared by many of Clinton's allies on the left, who thought the right deserved far more than half the blame for the problems in the nation's capital. As David Frum wrote, "Even before Donald Trump thrust himself forward as a presidential candidate, American politics had been veering toward extremism and instability."[5] Both extremism and instability were clear in the rise of the Tea Party.

Race was indisputably a factor in the right's animosity for Obama and in the growth of the Tea Party. Even though "the 'racialization' of partisanship was underway before Obama became a national figure," Obama's presidency made race much more salient.[6] Conflicts over race were about African Americans, of course. But they were also evident in attitudes about Latinx people, Muslims, and immigration more generally. The Republicans had largely given up on trying to recruit African Americans in 1968, and they increasingly seemed to give up on the Latinx vote as well. Every election seemed to harden them further into a position where they had to solidify their base of white voters to have any chance at electoral success. Every election also seemed to include more and more racial toxicity to woo those voters and maintain their allegiance. Republicans began by pandering to racism. They ended up exacerbating it.

Yet white voter allegiance to Republicans was not guaranteed, as about 20 percent of Americans—45 million people—considered themselves supporters of the Tea Party.[7] These voters were drawn disproportionately from Republican ranks. The genius of the Tea Party, according to Arlie Russell

Hochschild, is that it is less of a political organization and more a political culture, a way of seeing and feeling about a place. Those feelings aren't explicitly about race, but race permeates the places in question.[8] The Tea Party grew out of disenchantment with a Republican Party that seemed to talk about economic recovery but not to follow that talk with action. It was also a product of disaffection with the federal government, which Tea Partiers understood as attacking their faith, raising their taxes, and depriving them of honor. Members of the Tea Party favored limited government and lower taxes—positions consistent with the right since the New Deal. Like their earlier counterparts, many Tea Partiers were also firm believers in white supremacy, even if, unlike those earlier counterparts, they were often unwilling to say so publicly.

Racial politics had evolved since 1968, and by 2016 conservative politicians were depicting white people as the victims of racist rhetoric. As Ian Henry Lopez sees it, "The complex jujitsu of racial dog whistling lies at the center of a new way of talking about race that constantly emphasizes racial divisions, heatedly denies that it does any such thing, and then presents itself as a target of self-serving charges of racism."[9] By 2016, the rhetoric of racial exclusion was therefore quite complicated. There were those who used the bullhorn, making overtly racist appeals. There were those who dog-whistled, denied they were doing so, and then decried the tendency among their opponents to see affronts where none purportedly existed, exacerbating the sense of grievance already surrounding issues of race. And there were those who denied any racism at all, operating in the dog-whistle tradition of racializing issues such as crime or the economy, and then relying on those issues without ever having to confront their racial elements directly. Many Tea Partiers fell into this final category. This is how dog-whistle rhetoric works, and it's part of why it's despicable discourse—people can endorse exclusionary politics without having to own them overtly, masking racism with a concern for "culture."

It is thus not a coincidence that the Tea Party would develop alongside a kind of populism both in the United States and in Western Europe. Political scientist Stephen Dyson writes, "Populists and their followers believe themselves to constitute a majority, whether as a matter of fact they do or do not. Populisms of the right, such as Trump and the Brexiteers, see themselves as the guardians of the threatened traditions of the nation. Expertise is regarded with suspicion by populists, who elevate folk wisdom and the general will—all of these being, of course, subjectively defined categories."[10] That is, Tea Partiers and many others on the right understand themselves as protecting not necessarily white supremacy but the cultural and political traditions that have long accompanied it. They argue that they are protecting the traditions, not their racial entailments, and believe those traditions to be threatened, requiring action in their defense. There is in this politics a lurking racism, and also a distrust of political and cultural elites, a distaste for the norms promulgated by those elites, and a disbelief in the efficacy of policies enacted by them.[11] Populism, as Julia Azari notes, is about both "grievance and power."[12] Populists exacerbate the first in order to attain the second, which they understand as possessed by undeserving elites, assisted by their allies in the mass media.[13] The cultural aspects of this cannot be overstated. Elite conservatives, who are philosophically suspicious of the "lower orders," are also aware that they need the support of those orders if they are to remain in power.[14] The trick is to "appeal to the masses without disrupting the power of the elites"; to use mass energy to reinforce elite power.[15] But in 2016, the trick failed, and Republican elites were unable to control the mass energy that went driving toward Donald Trump.[16]

Populism itself is not necessarily problematic, nor does it inevitably result in despicable discourse. But in Trump's case, his populism is overlaid with a strain of authoritarianism that is particularly concerning.[17] Some authoritarian tendencies had been visible in Perot's 1992 campaign. Those tendencies had been nurtured by some on the right in the intervening years and were now bearing noxious fruit. Even so, the trend toward a kind of populist authoritarianism is bigger than Trump and broader than the United States. So in many ways, the context of the 2016 election is international. The same forces that drive a turn away from established liberal institutions elsewhere are driving a similar turn in the United States.

One of those forces is undoubtedly the mass media. Mainstream journalists are disconnected from voters. In the current media ecology, mainstream journalists are also less able to serve as gatekeepers. Social media have become increasingly important, and Trump, among all the candidates in 2016, made the best use of these platforms, which were uniquely vulnerable to his talents. Both directly and indirectly, then, media practices exacerbated distrust and legitimated the populism of the right.

The context of the 2016 election thus lent itself to despicable discourse. The system was fragile and increasingly distrusted by both the left and the right. Both race and immigration were overt issues in the campaign, activating some of the worst instincts of some white Americans. The economic recovery proceeded unevenly, as recoveries do, and disadvantaged precisely those people most vulnerable to racial appeals, giving those appeals a patina of legitimacy and allowing voters to mask the racism of their vote under a façade of "economic anxiety." The newer media technologies were vulnerable both to interference from outside the country and manipulation within it. Given this context, a deplorable election was all but inevitable.

But deplorable elections are never inevitable. Candidates make choices. In this case, candidate messaging contributed to a toxic context, as both Clinton and Trump made questions of identity central to their campaigns.[18] Changing demographics meant that group identities were becoming more aligned with partisanship, making identity an implicit campaign issue. The significance of identity in 2016 may have been facilitated by the fact that Clinton talked about race more than Obama had; stressing race may have increased salience of it as an issue.[19] "Identity politics" as a label is too often associated with appeals to nonwhites or nonmainstream voters, those whose gender, racial, or religious identities mark them as "outsiders" in the American polity. But cis, straight, Protestant, white people have identities that matter politically too, and in 2016, those identities were very important to the Trump vote.[20]

Trump's racism was consistently overt and explicit. Like Pat Buchanan before him, Trump eschewed subtlety for outright exclusion. He made national identity the centerpiece of his campaign, promising to "Make America Great Again," an appeal that said much about who he thought was representative of the nation and who might—or might not—be included within it. Unlike Buchanan, however, Trump's appeals landed in a political culture that had been primed by decades of rhetoric that legitimated his discourse, and he spoke to an audience that was receptive to the appeals, if not always to the candidate who made them.

Candidates made other choices too. Like many other deplorable elections, 2016 was characterized by negativity. Sara Mehltretter Drury and Rebecca A. Kuehl call it "highly divisive and negative," noting that both candidates had higher unfavorable ratings than favorable ones. They call the campaign "bitterly contentious" and argue it "seemed to violate so many traditional norms of political campaigns."[21] Weakened political norms and weakened allegiance to democratic values are characteristics of deplorable elections. This election, fought between two notoriously unpopular candidates, was also marked by some of the ugliest discourse in national history. In discussing that discourse, I turn first to Hillary Clinton, who persisted in acting as if 2016 was a normal election year and adhered to the rules of normal elections, and then to Donald Trump, whose campaign was anything but normal and who relied on a continual flow of despicable discourse.

POLITICS AS USUAL: HILLARY CLINTON

Hillary Clinton was one of the most qualified people to have run for the presidency in modern times. A lawyer and congressional aide, she worked on the staff of the House Judiciary Committee during the Watergate hearings before becoming first lady of both Arkansas and the nation. Her time in the White House was often fraught. She first assumed a policy role, unusual in a presidential spouse, and presided over a failed health care initiative. She was also continually involved in deflecting scandal, undergoing constant scrutiny of her financial dealings in the Whitewater affair. She was steadfastly loyal to her husband during the Lewinski scandal that erupted after revelations that he had a sexual relationship with a White House intern, and that led to his impeachment trial, a fact that garnered her both praise and blame. After leaving the White House, Clinton was elected junior senator from New York in 2000 and reelected in 2006, leaving the Senate in 2009 to become Barack Obama's secretary of state, a post she held until 2013. Her time in the Obama administration was largely successful, but again she spent considerable time defending herself against charges from the right, this time centering on her failure to prevent the attack on the American embassy in Benghazi, Libya. While serving as secretary of state, Clinton relied on a private email server, through which classified material sometimes traveled. The resulting controversy was the single-most-covered story of the 2016 election.

As a consummate politician, deeply embedded in mainstream Democratic politics, it is unsurprising that Clinton would treat the 2016 election as normal, assuming it would follow well-established patterns of political behavior. She relied on party contacts and traditional kinds of messaging and organization and designed a campaign that was more about listening and policy than giving speeches. She had lost the Democratic nomination in 2008 to Obama and for a time it seemed she might lose it in 2016 to Independent Bernie Sanders, the long-time junior senator from Vermont. Clinton herself wrote that she felt Sanders's presence in the primary meant she had "less space and credibility."[22] As she explained, "One of the most persistent challenges I faced as a candidate was being perceived as a defender of the status quo while my opponents in the primaries and the general election seized the sought-after mantle of 'change.'"[23] It is hard to run as a change candidate with a history in the previous administration, especially when party leaders lined up behind her candidacy early. But certainly Clinton, attempting to become the first woman nominated by a major party, could claim that she represented significant change.

That argument was complicated by the fact that she wasn't only campaigning against Sanders; she also had to campaign against decades of history in which she figured prominently as a devil figure for the right. This created two kinds of problems. Most obviously, there was a lot of readily available negative information about her and her husband. Second, the longevity of her political career led to a bit of "Clinton fatigue," the idea that "presidential campaigns, like Christmas, seem to come earlier every year," bringing with them the fact that by the time the event actually arrives, the public is already tired of it.[24] "Clinton fatigue" is the argument that the Clintons had been around for so long, and had for so long been the subject of controversies, that the public was exhausted by the very thought of another Clinton campaign. Like Nixon in 1968 (a parallel they both would detest), Clinton had a difficult time reinventing herself as a new, fresh face capable of forging political change. Nixon had the advantage of running in an election where national turmoil led the country to want stability. Clinton ran in a very different context, one in which politics as usual was perceived as failing and drastic change was required.

Sexism was a constant and significant factor in both the primaries and the general election. During the primaries the hostility of some Sanders supporters, who came to be known as "Bernie Bros," became famous for creating an enormous and vituperative backlash to any criticism of Sanders.[25] The label itself, of course, is pejorative, and was used by Clinton supporters on the internet to accuse both Sanders and his supporters of sexism. But when it came to misogyny and sexism, the Bernie Bros were the least of Clinton's worries.

Her gender presented a double bind—she didn't get unequivocal support from women, but the campaign activated sexism, a powerful predictor of vote choice, especially when it was mobilized by appeals to anger.[26] When it came to gender, Clinton was always facing the fact that it did not seem to provide her with support she would not otherwise have had as a Democrat but always threatened the support she might have garnered had she not been a woman. Women continue to face important symbolic barriers to the idea that as women it is possible for them to be president. Those barriers are not necessarily diminishing over time. Indeed, it is even possible that the sexism overtly displayed by the Bernie Bros in the primaries and by Trump himself in the general election helped rather than impeded those candidacies even while they damaged hers.

Clinton faced three other important challenges in 2016: Russian interference, extensive coverage of an FBI investigation, and a scandal involving her inappropriate use of an email server.[27] There is good evidence that Russia did indeed attempt to influence the 2016 presidential election.[28] While Russian bots circulated negative information throughout the election cycle, attempting to sow animosity within the American electorate, one incident in particular stands out as an example of Russian interference. On October 7, 2016, just days before a presidential debate, a tape from the television show *Access Hollywood* hit the news. The tape contained what in a normal year would have been a disqualifying exchange, ending any normal presidential campaign. The tape was released at 4:03 p.m.; at 4:32 the website WikiLeaks began releasing the text of emails it had obtained from Clinton campaign chair John Podesta's account. Those emails had been obtained from Russian hackers who had been targeting the DNC and the Clinton campaign for months. There was nothing especially damaging in the content of the emails, but as scholar Kathleen Hall Jamieson wrote, "The WikiLeaked material added arguments to Trump's rhetorical arsenal, created a countervailing narrative to the one emanating from the release of the *Access Hollywood* tape, changed the contour of two presidential debates, and, throughout critical weeks of the general election campaign, fostered an anti-Clinton agenda and frame in news."[29] Arguably, then, the Russian-backed WikiLeaks release affected the outcome of the 2016 presidential election. Certainly, the question of Russian influence became an important topic in the last month of the campaign.

That controversy was connected to the furor over Clinton's emails in general. Contrary to best practices, Clinton had relied on a private email server while secretary of state. Her use of a private server was the cause of several investigations and was the topic of more news coverage than any other campaign event—including the *Access Hollywood* tape. FBI director James Comey's announcement of yet another investigation in the campaign's final days may have influenced undecided voters that she was not fit to be president.

Throughout the campaign, the media depicted Clinton harshly, focusing less on her experience and competence and more on her personality and scandal-ridden history. By stressing the details of her supposed scandals, the media helped normalize Trump's more egregious behavior. Those practices also made it appear as if both candidates were equally tainted by scandal and inappropriate behavior. It is no surprise that both candidates were historically unpopular.[30] Despite all of the uproar, the constant barrage of scandal coverage, the emphasis on her emails, and the negative media frames, Clinton continued to campaign as if 2016 was a normal election and to do the kinds of things her extensive experience and considerable political skill had taught her would work. Amid all the chaos of the Trump campaign, she tried to run a campaign that adhered to the norms and values of standard campaign practices.

Clinton constantly stressed the idea that the 2016 election was about what kind of country Americans wanted their nation to be and put all the issues at play into that context. In the third presidential debate, for instance, she said, "You know, when we talk about the Supreme Court, it really raises the central question in this election, namely, what kind of country are we going to be? What kind of opportunities will we provide for our citizens? What kind of rights will Americans have? And I feel strongly that the Supreme Court needs to stand on the side of the American people, not on the side of the powerful corporations and the wealthy."[31] Here, she was making an overt argument based on class—that the election pitted "powerful corporations and the wealthy" against "the American people." This was, on the one hand, an effort to assume some of the support that had gone to Sanders in the primaries, to hold the Democratic coalition together. On the other hand, it was also a bid for the votes of those elusive white working-class voters, whose support was crucial in states like Pennsylvania, Ohio, Michigan, and Wisconsin.

She was trying to earn that support through positive messaging, urging those voters to see the nation as "stronger together," united in its need to build community and overcome division. The whole campaign echoed this message, relying on arguments about national progress through national unity. The problem with this rhetoric in 2016 was that a number of Americans saw the fact of an African American president and a woman nominee not as progress but rather as the opposite, as evidence that their situation was precarious and that under the Democrats it would only become more so. The very things the Democrats saw as worth celebrating could be understood as evidence of increasing peril.

But the Democrats located the danger somewhere else entirely. In her acceptance speech, Clinton said, "America is once again at a moment of reckoning. Powerful forces are threatening to pull us apart. Bonds of trust and respect are fraying. . . . We have to decide whether we will all work together so we can all rise together."[32] For Clinton, the nation was menaced by forces of division, not by the cultural changes that led to Obama's presidency and her nomination. Those forces were most starkly represented by Donald Trump: "He wants to divide us—from the rest of the world and from each other . . . he's taken the Republican Party a long way . . . from 'Morning in America' to 'Midnight in America.' He wants us to fear the future and fear each other."[33] The Democrats offered an optimistic vision of what the nation might become if citizens had the courage to make their vision a reality by uniting and moving forward together.

The vision Democrats offered wasn't entirely optimistic. Clinton also argued that Trump and the Republicans not only appealed to fear and pandered to the nation's worst instincts but were also dishonest and dishonorable: "In Atlantic City, 60 miles from here, you'll find contractors and small businesses who lost everything because Donald Trump refused to pay his bills . . . he also talks a big game about putting America First. Please explain to me what part of America First leads him to make Trump ties in China, not Colorado. Trump suits in Mexico, not Michigan. Trump furniture in Turkey, not Ohio. Trump picture frames in India, not Wisconsin."[34]

Trump was, in Clinton's view, misrepresenting himself, his past, and his beliefs, in what she argued would be an unsuccessful attempt to manipulate his way into office. Here she suggested that Trump has a history of dishonesty and that he would behave dishonestly if elected. In the first debate, she asked Trump, "Do the thousands of people that you have stiffed over the course of your business not deserve some kind of apology from someone who has taken their labor, taken the goods that they produced, and then refused to pay them? I can only say that I'm relieved that my late father never did business with you. He provided a good middle-class life for us, but the people he worked for, he expected the bargain to be kept on both sides."[35] Clinton here made the case that she was from a solid, dependable, middle-class background—she was offering identification with the white voters whose support she hoped to gain and who had been hearing depictions of her for decades as an out-of-touch elitist. She was making implicit claims for her fitness for the office she sought, and for which she found Trump singularly unsuited.

It was an office that in her view he had not earned, did not deserve, and was unprepared for. In particular, she claimed he lacked the temperament to be president, arguing in her acceptance speech that "a man you can bait with a tweet is not a man we can trust with nuclear weapons."[36] Other Democrats underlined this theme as well. Michelle Obama, for example, also stressed the Democratic themes about Donald Trump:

> And when I think about the kind of President that I want for my girls and all our children, that's what I want. I want someone with the proven strength to persevere, someone who knows this job and takes it seriously, someone who understands that the issues the President faces are not black and white and cannot be boiled down to 140 characters. Look because—because when—when you have the nuclear codes at your fingertips and the military in your command, you can't make snap decisions; you—you can't have a thin skin or a tendency to lash out. You need to be steady and measured and well-informed.[37]

This quotation illustrates the kind of comparison the Democrats thought would help them make their case for the White House. Trump was a loose cannon, not the kind of man you wanted to trust with a nuclear arsenal. Clinton was measured, deliberate, trustworthy.

Obama made this point here and elsewhere in her speech through pointed references to children, saying, for instance, "With, with every word we utter, with every action we take, we know our kids are watching us. And make no mistake about it. This November when we go to the polls that is what we're deciding—not Democrat or Republican, not left or right. No, in this election [*sic*], and every election is about who will have the power to shape our children for the next four or eight years of their lives."[38] This claim relies, as did much of the Democratic argumentation, especially during the convention, on gendered discourse. Michelle Obama's speech depended heavily on her role as first lady and on her position as mother of two daughters. Clinton, the first woman nominee of a major party, the argument implied, was better suited to nurture those children, to provide them with an example worth emulating. The focus on children meant also an indirect focus on gender; the Democrats were trying to capitalize on Clinton's gender while minimizing the potential backlash because of it.

The argument that Trump was a bad model for children also depended on the idea of the president as the nation's symbolic representative. Clinton thus expressed concern about Trump's inability to exemplify the nation. In Clinton's view, the president provided a role model for the nation, and especially for the nation's children. She said, "I think it's very important for us to make clear to our children that our country really is great because we are good. And we're going to respect one another, lift each other up."[39] In her opinion, Trump was patently unequal to that role. In the second debate, she said:

> You know, with prior Republican nominees for president, I disagreed with them on politics, policies, principles, but I never questioned their fitness to serve. Donald Trump is different. I said starting back in June that he was not fit to be president and Commander-in-Chief. And many Republicans and Independents have said the same thing. What we all saw and heard on Friday [in the *Access Hollywood* tape] Donald Trump talking about women, what he thinks about women, what he does to women, and he has said that the video doesn't represent who he is. But I think it's clear

> to anyone who heard it, that it represents exactly who he is . . . he has also targeted immigrants, African Americans, Latinos, people with disabilities, POWs, Muslims, and so many others.[40]

Because he was abusive to those with less power than he wielded, because he actively "targets" those people, Clinton argued, he was unfit to serve and a poor example for the nation's children.

The centrality of children in Clinton's argumentation was evident across issues. Defending her immigration policy proposals, she said, "I don't want to rip families apart. I don't want to be sending parents away from children. I don't want to see the deportation force that Donald has talked about in action in our country. . . . So I think we are both a nation of immigrants and a nation of laws and we can act accordingly."[41] She was able to mobilize children as a trope that made her gender potentially less problematic, allowed her to talk about the symbolic functions of the presidency in ways that excluded Trump from the office and enabled her to embrace the "family values" that white Republicans claimed to represent. Here, it was Clinton, not Trump, who wanted to protect families, to keep them from being ripped apart, with parents sent away from children, language that resonated both with that political moment and with the long and painful history of slavery. The problem for her was that the families in question were specifically not the ones the Republicans were interested in protecting. As we will see below, the Republican rhetoric of values was apparently inclusive and universal but in fact applied only to a narrow segment of the population, and immigrants from south of the US-Mexican border were not among those thus favored.

Throughout the campaign, Clinton maintained a dim view of Trump but an optimistic vision of the nation. In the third debate, for example, she argued, "So it's not one thing. This is a pattern, a pattern of divisiveness, of a dark and in many ways dangerous vision of our country, where he incites violence, where he applauds people who are pushing and pulling and punching at his rallies. That is not who America is. And I hope that as we move in the last weeks of this campaign, more and more people will understand what's at stake in this election. It really does come down to what kind of a country we are going to have."[42] She consistently returned to the question of national identity, a question that historically, and in a normal election, might have proved persuasive, as it has been hard in contemporary times to make explicit arguments in favor of exclusion. But 2016 was not a normal election, and by putting national identity clearly at the forefront of her campaign, she also enabled arguments that supported a very different view of the nation from the one she was advocating and that was supported by people who did not find the dark and divisive themes of Trump's campaign problematic.

Clinton clung to this optimistic view of the nation, apparently believing that if enough people understood the depth of Trump's poor behavior they would refuse to vote for him. In the second debate, for example, Clinton responded to Trump's attacks on her by saying:

> So much of what he just said is not right, but he gets to run his campaign any way he chooses. . . . he never apologized to Mr. and Mrs. Khan, the Gold Star family whose son, Captain Khan, died in the line of duty in Iraq and Donald insulted and attacked them for weeks over their religion. He never apologized to the distinguished federal judge who was born in Indiana, but Donald said he couldn't be trusted to be a judge because his parents were "Mexican." He never apologized to the reporter he mimicked and mocked on national television and our children are watching. And he never apologized for the racist lie that President Obama was not born in the United States of America.[43]

This illustrates one of the problems with attempting to counter despicable discourse. If despicable discourse is circulating, failing to dispute it can lead to its acceptance and expansion, as I argued in chapter 4 concerning Nelson Rockefeller's decision not to oppose Richard Nixon's subtly racist politics. But if a speaker wants to challenge such discourse, they have to recirculate it, as Clinton does here, giving the despicable discourse wider circulation.[44] Not only does it recirculate the discourse, but it may also be newly circulating it to audiences that potentially agree with it. It is difficult to discredit such discourse without circulating and recirculating the discourse in question.

In this case, all of Clinton's efforts seemed to result in very little. The election remained close, and as her frustration mounted she vented that frustration and referred to the worst of Trump supporters as a "basket of deplorables,"[45] a phrase that quickly went viral and seemed to confirm claims that she was disrespectful of and out of touch with voters. It appeared that Clinton was trying to place Trump and those who endorsed his brand of exclusionary politics outside the realm of acceptable American discourse. This move resonated with many of her supporters. But to others, it seemed to signal her contempt for those voters, reinforcing her image among them as an out-of-touch, patronizing elitist.

Clinton's image problems, on display in the "basket of deplorables" controversy, were exacerbated by the nature of the news coverage she received. In general, she was treated much more harshly by the news media than was Trump. This was true of debate coverage as well as the regular news cycle. Much of the routine coverage focused on scandals associated with her campaign, which received more coverage than did those associated with Trump.[46] Indeed, the sheer number and variety of Trump's scandals seemed to work to his advantage because it was so difficult to focus sustained attention on any one of them. Because the list of Clinton's problems was shorter and more focused than Trump's, there were two important consequences. First, a shorter list had more potential to break through the noise of the campaign. However little attention voters paid to the election, the chances were good that they had heard of the email scandal, for example. Second, the fact of the coverage meant that she looked to be his scandalous equal—for voters who had been hearing negative information about the Clintons for decades, as well as for voters newer to information about her, the fact of unbalanced negative coverage made it appear that there were no good choices in the election as both candidates were equally tainted, equally awful. Perversely, by choosing to cover "both sides," the news media unbalanced the public view of the candidates.

I am not making the argument that the media lost the election for Clinton. There is also mixed evidence on the question of whether Comey's last-minute announcement of a new investigation into her emails directly led to her defeat. His announcement did have a negative effect on attitudes toward Clinton, and while attitudes do matter in vote choice, there's no evidence of direct effects.[47] Presidential campaigns are complicated, and it is more likely that it was a combination of things. On the list of those things would certainly be Clinton's lack of recognition that politics had changed, the gendered ways the media covered her campaign in general and the way they covered news of her scandals in particular, the fact of "Clinton fatigue," choices made by her campaign about where to concentrate time and other resources, the decision made by both candidates to focus on issues of national identity and belonging, and a political context that lent itself to the widespread acceptance of despicable discourse. Donald Trump prided himself on creating and circulating such discourse, and it is to his rhetoric that I now turn.

"WHEN YOU'RE A STAR, THEY LET YOU DO IT": DONALD TRUMP

Donald Trump was a real estate entrepreneur and reality television celebrity who made his entry into politics as part of the resistance to Obama and his presidency, circulating and promoting claims of "birtherism."[48] Birtherism is a particularly noxious political argument, claiming that the president was neither a "real" American nor entitled to the office to which he had been elected. As David Frum argued, birtherism "revealed that as the country diversified, its conservatives would insist ever more militantly that no matter who might *reside* in the United States, the country's institutions and identity should belong only to those recognizably like them."[49] Birtherism is an explicitly racist discourse, and Trump was one of its earliest proponents. As early as 2011, he claimed variously and untruthfully that Obama's grandmother stated he was born in Kenya, that no hospital had a record of the president's birth, that the document eventually produced by Obama was not a legal record of birth, that this document had no identifying official numbers or signatures, that the newspaper announcements of his birth were probably fraudulent, and that nobody knew Obama as a child.[50] The evidence is overwhelming that Obama was born in the United States, as even Trump himself finally conceded.[51] Even after admitting Obama had been born in the United States, Trump maintained, "I'm the one who got him to produce his birth certificate. . . . And I think I did a great job and a great service not only for the country but even for the president, in getting him to produce the birth certificate."[52] He never backed down from the idea that it was legitimate and even productive to challenge the legitimacy of the nation's first African American president. Trump based his political career on despicable discourse.

Arguments about race and its connection to national identity and belonging permeated the Trump campaign. He was, for example, the only Republican to take a negative view on immigration. In his speech announcing his candidacy for the presidency, he said:

> The U.S. has become a dumping ground for everybody else's problems [Applause]. Thank you. It's true, and these are the best and the finest. When Mexico sends its people, they're not sending their best. They're not sending you. They're not sending you. They're sending people that have lots of problems, and they're bringing those problems with us [*sic*]. They're bringing drugs. They're bringing crime. They're rapists. And some, I assume, are good people. . . . They're not sending the right people. It's coming from more than Mexico. It's coming from all over South and Latin America, and it's coming probably—probably—from the Middle East. But we don't know. Because we have no protection and no competence, we don't know what's happening. And it's got to stop and it's got to stop fast.[53]

Several things are worth noting here: the implication that his supporters are by definition among the nation's "best"; the idea that Mexico was "sending" immigrants in some sort of conscious attempt to infiltrate the country; the notion that they were doing so by sending drugs, criminals, and specifically rapists; and that the president was empowered to stop all of these things. These arguments rest on the long history of racist rhetoric in the United States, in which whites—and especially white women—are imperiled by men of color. Restrictive policies ("Build that wall!") are thus justified because they are required for the protection of those (helpless) white women. Mexico was "sending" unsavory people, including "rapists," and "it's got to stop fast." Trump here was tapping into that long history and the racism that undergirds it and was doing so in a shockingly overt way. At least it was shocking at the time, before the nation got used to his despicable discourse, and long before people started taking it for granted.

His campaign was grounded in, but was not restricted to, racism. In addition to securing the nation's borders through the construction of a wall, he promised to protect Medicare, to prevent upper-class tax cuts, to improve on Obamacare. He was going to protect American gun rights and make corporations return American jobs to the United States. In short, he was going to make the nation safe for the white middle and working classes. He didn't sound like a traditional politician, and he advocated things that were not part of the traditional Republican agenda. From the beginning, his campaign was issue heavy but lacking in both ideology and specifics. His campaign was unconventional in other ways as well. He didn't put money into field offices, paid staff, ads, or message testing. What he did do was to shift the process onto ground where he was infinitely more comfortable than his opponents. His behavior was rude, his language was bombastic and crude, and his demeanor was simultaneously smug and belligerent. His opponents, with considerable experience in politics and none in the genre of reality television, kept assuming the campaign would revert to the former, but it remained persistently in the latter.

Sometimes, those opponents sought to meet Trump on his own ground. Marco Rubio, for example, made a reference to the size of Trump's hands in one debate, somehow assuming implying aspersions on his masculinity would either discomfit Trump or wound him with his audience; it did neither. Mitt Romney made a stronger effort, as journalist Katy Tur reported: "The 2012 Republican presidential candidate took the 2016 Republican frontrunner apart with a hatchet. Romney called Trump a 'con man, a fake.' With a Trumpian flourish he also mocked the candidate's foreign policy as 'very, very not smart.' Then he brought up Trump's many, many failed businesses, too, including Trump airlines, *Trump* magazine, Trump Vodka, Trump Steaks, Trump Mortgage, Trump University. He was not endorsing another candidate. Rather, he was begging voters to choose one of the three *other* GOP contenders. It didn't matter which one, so long as it wasn't Trump."[54] And herein lay the problem: Republicans could not decide on a single candidate who wasn't Trump, so the anti-Trump vote was fractured and Trump, while consistently unpopular, survived. None of the Republican contenders understood Trump's tactics, were willing to engage in them consistently, or were interested in out-Trumping Trump. In the absence of party consensus on someone else, Trump was changing the rules of political engagement and no one knew how to follow those rules. Trump brought with him to politics a new sort of political style.

Trump's Political Style

Trump has his own rhetorical style, one that is particularly well suited to the demands of cable news and especially to the internet—it is loud, bombastic, and changeable. Consistently, Trump created a sensation and then immediately moved on to the next thing, and the media obsessively followed his erratic course. Unlike most campaigns, which are governed by the logic of consistent and coherent messaging, Trump often distracted from his own campaign's messaging. But that didn't matter because his messaging consisted of bullet points rather than arguments. His style depended on barrage. On the campaign trail he was a relentless communicator.

As one might expect given this guerilla style of messaging, Trump's rhetorical style relied on hyperbole. He used multiple adjectives in place of one, repeated words and phrases, and constantly exaggerated. A brief example of this tendency will suffice. After descending the escalator in Trump Tower, he began his announcement speech this way: "Wow. Whoa. That is some group of people. Thousands. So nice, thank you very much. That's really nice. It's great to be at Trump Tower. It's great to be in a wonderful city, New York. And it's an honor to have everybody here. This is beyond anybody's expectations. There's been no crowd like this."[55] Trump commented on the size of the crowd, noted his specific location, the city, and claimed to have exceeded expectations. There is nothing of the accustomed humility or modesty in this speech, nothing of the immensity of the tasks associated with the presidency, none of the standard verbiage about the privilege of campaigning. The focus was on Trump, his abilities, his fame, the attention he was receiving.

He combined this self-centeredness with an ability to speak a language that was, if not "relatable," in the parlance of modern campaigns, intelligible to those he sought to reach. Tur wrote, "Some politicians have a gift for language. Trump is not one of those politicians. His sentences call to mind an aerial shot of a burning, derailed freight train. The syntax is mangled. The grammar is gone. 'Donald Trump isn't a simpleton, he just talks like one,' reads a *Politico* article from last August. 'If you were to market Donald Trump's vocabulary as a toy, it would resemble a small box of Lincoln Logs.'"[56] His language was inelegant to say the least. But he spoke like many Americans speak; he did not talk about issues in ways that were hard to follow; he did not use language that recalled policy talk. As journalist Major Garrett has it, Trump "spoke beneath voters, never down to them. He bypassed political reporters entirely and scorned the process of engagement, disarmament, and flattery. When I say Trump spoke beneath his supporters I mean he met them at their level and then made them feel smarter—as if what they had been thinking was now the truth of our times."[57] He used a plain, uneducated style that conveyed in every sentence his distance from politics as usual in Washington, and especially from the kind of politics typified by Barack Obama. He could speak for his supporters because he spoke like them. They could trust him because his language was straightforward, even awkward, because he risked saying things that no one else would say.

Trump wasn't just a Beltway outsider; he was the kind of candidate who promised to take on Beltway politicians and was abrasive and tough enough to beat them. He constantly emphasized strength and argued consistently for unilateral power in the service of "the people," causing one analyst to consider Trump's public speech a version of populist authoritarianism and strongman rhetoric.[58] Like all populists, he argued that the elite were to blame for the ills besetting the mass public; like all strongmen, he argued that if he were given power, he would restore national greatness, relying on a "strident nationalism."[59] These signature elements of his style have caused scholars to consider Trump a demagogue.[60] That demagoguery was enabled not only by other Republicans and the mass media but by a widespread culture of demagoguery that made a politician like Trump all but inevitable.[61] Many of the conditions for this culture are similar to the ones I identify as connected to despicable discourse. It is not surprising, then, that Trump's 2016 campaign was characterized by such discourse. It was enabled, as despicable discourse often is, by a developing media system that one candidate was significantly more successful at manipulating than their opponents.

Mediating Trump, Creating His Audience

Trump, more than any of his opponents, and more than any other current American politician, has bent the media to his will. He dominates media narratives, deflects media criticism, and commands media coverage. Throughout the campaign he made continuous use of his Twitter account, doing so in ways that confounded existing expectations of how a presidential candidate should behave, but always capturing media—and thus public—attention, contributing to his political success. His style, as Brian Ott has argued, is well suited to Twitter, which "promotes public discourse that is simple, impetuous, and frequently denigrating and dehumanizing."[62] It is catnip to distracted minds, perpetually in search of the next thing. Stephen J. Heidt and Damien Smith Pfister argue that Trump uses Twitter for his "microdiatribes," which "channel affective energies of outrage."[63] Trump used Twitter to constantly stir the pot of electoral discourse, always doing something to draw attention to himself and away from others, winning the battle for the attention economy. Trump on Twitter was a kind of verbal spectacle, a scene from which journalists were unable to avert their attention.

The Trumpian Twitter spectacle meant that mainstream news channels granted him extensive coverage. As of March 2016, he had received $1.898 billion worth of free media.[64] Because it remained focused on the spectacle itself, that coverage wasn't especially negative. His message traveled to rural communities in swing states, embedding itself in "epistemic communities of belief" as a result of our siloed media structures.[65] No outlet was more important to creating those communities of belief than Fox News, which is the dominant channel of choice for conservative Americans, and which has consistently done real damage to the democratic norm of mutual toleration through its vituperative political coverage. Through the process of partisan selective exposure, conservative voters hear only news that reinforces what they already believe, slanted in ways that cater to and exacerbate the worst aspects of those beliefs. Such exposure can energize citizen participation. It can also affect what people know about politics and may influence attitudes and beliefs.

This meant that there was a ready-made audience for Trump's brand of politics.[66] They were ready to hear his appeals to rural resentment, an identity located in place rather than party or ideology but responsive to cultural and lifestyle issues.[67] They were open to his arguments that implicated race, and to his claims that government was the cause of their woes. His appeals resonated among those who felt a strong sense of loss.[68] Trump voters are thus best understood—as are all those swayed by despicable discourses—as motivated both by racism and by economic or social dispossession or the fear of it.[69] Trump appealed to those Americans who were feeling the pressures of a globalized economy and who had been listening to news that encouraged them to place the blame for those pressures on the Democrats, immigrants, and racial minorities. Trump capitalized on those grievances. In doing so, he created a despicable campaign.

A Despicable Campaign

Trump's rhetorical style throughout the campaign was bombastic and vituperative.[70] He demeaned his opponents, he evoked fear, he attacked the political process, and as the campaign progressed, he eventually brought the Republican Party with him, as they endorsed a despicable and dangerous view of the nation at their national convention. In what follows, then, I take events somewhat out of order, focusing on the things he said rather than their chronology, ending this section with the convention and its implications for the party and the nation. Before getting there, however, I first deal with the issues he chose to emphasize, the way he demeaned other political actors and the political system itself, the potential for violence inherent in that tactic, and the various scandals in which he was involved.

Political Exclusion

Like all candidates, Trump sought to highlight the issues that best helped him make his case for the White House and elide those that damaged that effort. Trump saw advantages in stressing issues like the Second Amendment and abortion but relied equally heavily on issues that had more obvious racial valences, like immigration. Trump consistently defended the Second Amendment, arguing in the third presidential debate, for example, "We need a Supreme Court that in my opinion is going to uphold the Second Amendment, and all amendments, but the Second Amendment, which is under absolute siege."[71] Here, he offered some support for "all amendments" but essentially said that in a Trump administration there would be a litmus test for a Supreme Court justice—nominees would have to protect the besieged Second Amendment, the right to bear arms. This amendment, which hasn't faced any real challenge from either major party, is an important issue to many conservatives and to the white, often rural voters who are the mainstays of that party. Something of a condensation symbol, gun rights stand in for all kinds of cultural preferences that those holding them find under assault from the different preferences expressed by "coastal elites." To stand for gun rights is to also stand for the protection of cultural traditions associated with the white national heartland, the home of those whom Republicans deem "real" Americans.

It is not despicable to lay claim to cultural turf. It is not even despicable to distort one's opponents' records on such issues; it isn't entirely ethical, of course, but it is common in campaigns. But here is what Trump said of Clinton's position on another hot button issue, abortion: "If you go with what Hillary is saying, in the ninth month, you can take the baby and rip the body out of the womb of the mother just prior to the birth of the baby. Now you can say that's OK, and Hillary can say that's OK. But it's not OK with me."[72] He was referring here to the misnamed "partial birth abortion" policy and misstated both the policy and Clinton's position on it and did so in the most inflammatory way possible. Such inflammatory rhetoric is common on Fox News, and its audience—Trump's audience—was primed to be accepting of such speech without registering it as inappropriate in a presidential campaign.

He was equally inflammatory on the issue of immigration. In the third presidential debate, for example, he said, "In the audience tonight, we have four mothers of—I mean, these are unbelievable people that I've gotten to know over a period of years, whose children have been killed, brutally killed, by people who come into the country illegally. You have thousands of mothers and fathers and relatives all over the country. They're coming in illegally. Drugs are pouring in through the border. We have no country if we have no border. Hillary wants to have amnesty. She wants to have open borders."[73] Here as elsewhere, Trump focused on the few immigrants with violent records and used them to represent the entire immigrant population. Here as elsewhere, he exaggerated Clinton's position. Here, as elsewhere, he used tropes of disaster—drugs "pour" into the country in an unstoppable flood. This is all antidemocratic and thus despicable discourse. These tactics were clearly related to his general tendency to rely on the politics of fear.

The Politics of Fear

As I noted in the introduction, fear appeals can be valuable—it is useful to be alerted to danger. And to incite fear in order to assuage it has long been a tendency among leaders.[74] That tactic is generally associated with more normal rhetoric; it is a tactic, not the primary means of communication.

Trump's rhetoric is unusual—and despicable—in that, in the 2016 election, he relied heavily on fear appeals. He placed frequent emphasis on "radical Islamic terrorism," for example, arguing that it posed an omnipresent danger to the United States.[75] Domestically, he encouraged Americans to fear racial minorities. Asked a question in the first presidential debate about how to heal the racial divide, Trump replied:

> Well, first of all, Secretary Clinton doesn't want to use a couple of words, and that's law and order. And we need law and order. If we don't have it, we're not going to have a country. . . . We have gangs roaming the street. And in many cases, they're here illegally, illegal immigrants. And they have guns. And they shoot people. And we have to be very strong. And we have to be very vigilant. We have to be—we have to know what we're doing. Right now, our police, in many cases, are afraid to do anything. We have to protect our inner cities, because African Americans are being decimated by crime, decimated.[76]

This sounds confused, but in fact Trump encapsulated many of his most important themes into one short answer. He depicted Clinton as opposed to law and order, marking her as both weak and unable to properly defend the nation and its best interests. Trump, in favor of law and order, claimed that it was a basic requirement of nationhood—without law and order "we're not going to have a country." "Our" security depends on excluding "them." He asserted that gangs currently roam the streets, implying that there is a randomness to their action, and that they thus endanger even the most apparently secure neighborhoods. He insisted that those gangs are "in many cases" composed of illegal immigrants, who, since "they have guns" obviously also "shoot people." No one is safe. As a result, Trump supporters must be both strong and vigilant. He stated that things have gotten to such a state that even the police are afraid to act. He pretended to mask the racism inherent in these claims by maintaining that the most endangered communities are inhabited by African Americans, whose best interests he proclaimed he was dedicated to defending.

Similarly, in the second presidential debate he averred, "We have many criminal illegal aliens. When we want to send them back to their country, their country says, we don't want them. In some cases, they are murderers, drug lords, drug problems, and they don't want them. And Hillary Clinton when she was Secretary of State said, that's okay, we can't force them back to their country. Let me tell you, I'm going to force them back to their country. They are murderers and some very bad people."[77] In Trump's view, immigrants posed a number of different threats—they are bad people generally, murderers, drug lords, undesirable in all kinds of ways. He claimed that Clinton either didn't recognize the extent of the threat or was too weak to act on it. Trump contrasted this to his own assertion of strength; he said he would use force to protect the nation. Trump spent considerable energy on the argument that the greatest threat came from "radical Islamic terrorists," and although he claimed he was not opposed to all Muslims, he still said that "Donald J. Trump is calling for a total and complete shutdown of Muslims entering the United States until our country's representatives can figure out what the hell is going on."[78] It is unsurprising that there is evidence that racial resentment and anti-immigration attitudes were important factors in the decision to vote for Trump.[79] The idea that the country is so severely threatened by immigrants is both empirically false and representative of despicable discourse, for it blames the nation's ills on defenseless others and excludes on the basis of ascriptive characteristics. Trump used immigrants as a foil to argue for his own strength. In a similarly despicable display, he used his political opponents as a foil as well.

Demeaning Opponents

I've already touched on his treatment of his Republican opponents during the primaries, and we saw in the discussion of Clinton's campaign mention of his handling of people like the Gold Star family and others who opposed him. So here I want to quickly mention his comments regarding women in general and Hillary Clinton in particular. He often made gendered references, claiming for example, "I have a winning temperament. I know how to win. She doesn't have it. . . . She doesn't have the look. She doesn't have the stamina. And I don't believe she does have the stamina. To be president of this country, you need to have tremendous stamina."[80] The claim here, of course, depends on the fiction of women's weakness as a reason for excluding them from power. The claim that Clinton doesn't have "the look" means simply that she is too female to be commander in chief.

His attacks on Clinton were relentless, if somewhat scattershot. The media were focused on a fairly short list of her transgressions; Trump was considerably more expansive. He blurted out during one debate that she was "such a nasty woman," as if her behavior was so awful that his reaction to it could not be contained.[81] As in that example, Trump's attacks often mirrored accusations that had been made about him, which served, intentionally or not, to make the implicit case that if he was guilty, she was at least equally suspect. For example, he referred to the Clinton Foundation as "a criminal enterprise," claiming "so many people know it."[82] Baseless charges were thus authorized by assertions of popular knowledge. He constantly challenged her honesty, stating, "Hillary Clinton who, as most people know, is a world-class liar—just look at her pathetic email and server statements, or her phony landing in Bosnia where she said she was under attack but the attack turned out to be young girls handing her flowers, a total self-serving lie."[83] And he challenged her record of accomplishment, arguing, "This is the legacy of Hillary Clinton: death, destruction, and weakness."[84] He was cavalier about these tendencies as well. During the first debate, Clinton remarked, "I have a feeling that by the end of the evening, I'm going to be blamed for everything that's ever happened." Trump replied, "Why not?"[85] He expressed himself willing to blame her of anything and everything; her guilt was the premise upon which he operated. Most of all, he insisted, she was guilty of complicity with a corrupt political system.

Undermining the System

Trump both was a product of and contributed to a weakened political system. Despicable discourse is only possible in a weak system; when the system is resilient, other elites fend off such discourse or relegate it to the margins. But in 2016 the system was fragile and outlets like Fox News helped create an audience receptive to Trump's despicable discourse. His language reinforced that audience's lack of faith in political structures by referring continually to "fake news," and denigrating members of the media, as in his references to the "failing CNN." His very presence as a viable candidate undermined the political system. He also took an active role in that process.

Among his more damaging rhetoric was the claim that the entire political system was both corrupt and inhabited by incompetents. In his announcement speech, he said, "We have all the cards, but we don't know how to use them. We don't even know that we have the cards, because our leaders don't understand the game. . . . We have losers. We have losers. We have people that don't have it. We have people that are morally corrupt. We have people that are selling this country down the drain."[86] It is hard to tell from this which is worse, the fact that our leaders are so incompetent that they don't know a winning hand when they see one, paralyzing action, or the fact that they are so morally corrupt that their actions sell the "country down the drain." These two ideas are internally inconsistent, but Trump was not concerned with consistency. The more charges he spread, and the more widely he spread them, the more appealing his candidacy appeared to those he sought most to reach.

He expressed a visceral distaste for "politics as usual," an appeal that, given the lack of trust in the government in 2016, was likely to resonate. During the first presidential debate, he interrupted Clinton to call her a "typical politician. All talk, no action. Sounds good, doesn't work. Never going to happen."[87] In that same debate he claimed, "We have people that are political hacks negotiating our trade deals."[88] He consistently portrayed standard politics as unequivocally bad; Trump represented anything but standard politics. He claimed to stand apart from the system and from the corruptions it contained and, because of that position, could both more clearly see the problems and more effectively solve them. In his speech accepting the Republican nomination for president, he said:

> Every day I wake up determined to deliver for the people I have met all across this nation that have been neglected, ignored, and abandoned. . . . People who work hard but who no longer have a voice. . . . I have joined the political arena so that the powerful can no longer beat up on people that cannot defend themselves. Nobody knows the system better than me, which is why I alone can fix it. I have seen firsthand how the system is rigged against our citizens, just like it was rigged against Bernie Sanders—he never had a chance. . . . I am your voice.[89]

He had a history of participating in the system's corruption, so he was best positioned to root it out and end it, to "drain the swamp." This kind of rhetoric, which offers to replace a broken system with the rule of one person ("I alone can fix it"), is antidemocratic and despicable.

He consistently claimed that the system itself was corrupt and relied on the rhetoric of purification, arguing that he could cleanse the corruption and return the system to its proper working order. He told New Yorkers, "We will never be able to fix a rigged system by counting on the same people who rigged it in the first place. The insiders wrote the rules of the game to keep themselves in power and in the money. . . . It's rigged by big donors . . . it's rigged by big business . . . it's rigged by bureaucrats . . . it's rigged against the American people. . . . I am running for President to end the unfairness and to put you, the American people, first."[90] That meant, most importantly, finding jobs for those who had suffered the consequences of globalization: "And once you say you're going to have to tax them coming in, and our politicians never do this, because they have special interests and the special interests want the companies to leave, because in many cases they own the companies. So what I'm saying is, we can stop them from leaving. And that's a big, big factor."[91] Trump said that he was "opposed by some of the nation's most powerful special interests" and that Clinton "is their puppet, and they pull the strings."[92] He was strong enough to fight the special interests; in her weakness, Clinton was their tool.

No discussion of undermining the political system is complete without a discussion of Russian influence. Such influence had been the topic of conversation as early as the first debate, when Trump said, "I don't think anyone knows if it was Russia that broke into the DNC. She's saying Russia, Russia, Russia, but I don't—maybe it was. It could be Russia, but it could also be China. It could also be a lot of other people. It could be somebody sitting on their bed that weighs 400 pounds, okay?"[93] Despite this disparaging defense, there is little doubt that there was such influence and that he courted it.[94] He said, for example, "'Russia, if you're listening, I hope you're able to find the thirty thousand e-mails that are missing. I think you will probably be rewarded mightily by our press. Let's see if that happens. That'll be next."[95] Of course it did happen, and WikiLeaks released emails that had been obtained from Russian hacking. When this came up in the third presidential debate, Clinton stated that "the Russian government has engaged in espionage against Americans."[96] This claim prompted one of the more famous—and more contentious—moments in that debate. Trump declared that Putin "has no respect for her. He has no respect for our president," prompting an exchange between Clinton, Trump, and debate moderator Chris Wallace, in which Wallace repeatedly tried unsuccessfully to bring some order to the crosstalk between the candidates. Finally, this exchange occurred:

> Clinton: Well, that's because he'd [Putin] rather have a puppet as president of the United States.
> Trump: No puppet. No puppet.
> Clinton And it's pretty clear . . .
> Trump: You're the puppet.
> Clinton: It's pretty clear you won't admit . . .
> Trump: No, you're the puppet.[97]

This is an unimaginable exchange in any election that is not deplorable. The idea that two candidates for the American presidency were locked into an argument as to which of them was the puppet of a foreign power is remarkable. It is unthinkable that a presidential candidate would even potentially be subordinate to another country. The 2016 election was full of such unthinkable moments.

When asked if he would accept the results of the election if he lost, for instance, Trump said:

> I will look at it at the time. I'm not looking at anything now. I'll look at it at the time. What I've seen—what I've seen is so bad. First of all, the media is so dishonest and so corrupt and the pile-on is so amazing. The *New York Times* actually wrote an article about it, but they don't even care. It's so dishonest. And they've poisoned the mind of voters. But unfortunately for them, I think the voters are seeing through it. I think they're going to see through it. . . . So let me just give you one other thing. So I talk about the corrupt media. I talk about the millions of people—tell you one other thing. She shouldn't be allowed to run. It's crooked—she's—she's guilty of a very, very serious crime. She should not be allowed to run.[98]

In yet another Trumpian mash-up of assertions, here he claims variously that he may or may not accept the outcome of the election in the event of his defeat, that the electoral system (presumably) is bad, that the media are corrupt and biased, that voters will see through their machinations, and that his opponent is a criminal who should be barred from the campaign. These statements are at the very least irresponsible. They tend toward a dangerous degree of authoritarianism. He engaged in other overtly authoritarian behavior as well, leading crowds at his rallies in chants of "Lock her up," and stating in the second presidential debate, "If I win, I'm going to instruct my attorney general to get a special prosecutor to look into your situation."[99] This behavior marks the election as dangerously despicable, in which his opponents and the system itself is threatened.

Another, less obvious way in which he undermined the system was through the encouragement of violence and near-violence at his rallies. This was itself a disturbing development, not always seen even in the most deplorable modern elections, and the tendency toward violent action is one of the most despicable elements of his rhetoric. During the campaign, Trump proudly proclaimed that he could shoot someone on Fifth Avenue and voters would continue to support him.[100] He managed throughout the campaign to avoid committing outright violence, but he didn't object when his supporters did. On March 9, 2016, in the middle of a Trump rally, for example, "Quick Draw" John McGraw, an older white man, assaulted a young Black man named Rasheem Jones. In an interview following the event and before his arrest, McGraw was asked what he liked about the rally. He replied, "Knocking the hell out of that big mouth." He continued, "We don't know who he is, but we know he's not acting like an American. The next time we see him, we might have to kill him."[101] Trump noticeably did not condemn the violence. In another example, after a Black Lives Matter activist was attacked at a Trump rally in Birmingham, Trump said, "Maybe he should have been roughed up because it was absolutely disgusting what he was doing."[102] Trump exhorted his supporters to "knock the crap out" of protesters[103] and said of at least one that he'd "like to punch him in the face."[104]

Like all elections, deplorable elections both persuade and mobilize people. They can persuade people to adopt despicable beliefs, but they can also mobilize people to act on those beliefs. And in this election, there was no shortage of such mobilization. One journalist covering Trump wrote, "The thing is they don't look like cruel people. They look like they're in their forties. They're wearing designer jeans and nice boots. They seem healthy and comfortable, and it's hard to imagine them acting this way at home or in the office. . . . But inside a Trump rally, these people are unchained. They can drop their everyday niceties. They can yell and scream and say things they'd never say out loud on the outside."[105] This kind of mobilization is damaging to democracy, because whether or not the behavior recurs outside of the rallies, the attitudes thus reinforced are not ephemeral. Participants may or may not look like cruel people (whatever that might mean), but their cruelty has consequences.

Trump's behavior, like that of his supporters, did not pass unremarked. But it became normalized, accepted as routine, at least in the context of Trump's campaign. But his campaign faced a number of less routinized challenges as well, as the election itself was mired in scandal.

Surviving Scandal

There is some irony in the idea that Donald Trump survived more political scandals during his campaign than any other modern politician; the closest contender for this shameful title would be Bill Clinton in 1992. *Politico* created a list of thirty-seven events during the campaign that would have ended any normal campaign, providing evidence, if any evidence was needed, Trump was not running a normal campaign.[106] By far the most potentially damaging Trump scandal of the election was the *Access Hollywood* tape. In early October, tapes including the following excerpts hit the national news:

> Unidentified voice: She used to be great. She's still very beautiful.
> Trump: I moved on her actually. You know she was down on Palm Beach. I moved on her and I failed. I'll admit it. I did try and fuck her. She was married.
> Unidentified voice: That's huge news there.
> Trump: No, no. Nancy. No this was—And I moved on her very heavily. In fact, I took her out furniture shopping. She wanted to get some furniture. I said, "I'll show you where they have

> some nice furniture." I took her out furniture—I moved on her like a bitch, but I couldn't get there. And she was married. Then all of a sudden I see her, she's now got the big phony tits and everything. She's totally changed her look.
>
> . . .
>
> Bush: It better not be the publicist. No, it's her. It's her.
>
> Trump: Yeah, that's her, with the gold. I've got to use some Tic Tacs, just in case I start kissing her. You know I'm automatically attracted to beautiful—I just start kissing them. It's like a magnet. I just kiss. I don't even wait. And when you're a star, they let you do it. You can do anything.
>
> Unidentified voice: Whatever you want.
>
> Trump: Grab them by the pussy. You can do anything.[107]

The tape was released just a few days before the second debate, and it was the subject of the first question at that debate. Trump replied:

> This was locker room talk. I am not proud of it. I apologize to my family. I apologized to the American people. But this is locker room talk. You know, when we have a world where you have ISIS chopping off heads. Where you have them, frankly, drowning people in steel cages, where you have wars and horrible, horrible sights all over and you have so many bad things happening, this is like medieval times. . . . Yes, I am very embarrassed by it, and I hate it, but it's locker room talk and it's one of those things. I will knock the hell out of ISIS.[108]

This appears to be another example of random, if not incoherent language. But it is noticeable that Trump still managed to make all his key points: the conversation itself was not worth discussing, as it was just an example of standard male conversation, "locker room talk." Even though it was a minor incident, it was embarrassing, as things that happen in the locker room are not meant for public spaces. Consequently, apologies were called for, and most unusually for Trump, were also given. Trump then jumped without even a minor segue to the claim that ISIS has been doing "bad things," chopping off heads and drowning people in cages. He promised to "knock the hell" out of them in return. This appears incoherent, but the subtext is a particular kind of masculinity, one that takes whatever advantages it can of whatever women are placed nearby, that spends time in locker rooms and engages in the sorts of manly conversations that occur in that space, and that therefore has the strength to not only defeat but to "knock the hell out of" ISIS. For Trump, then, the tape provided another way of displaying the kind of masculinity he would bring to the office as president.

Trump defended himself in less direct ways as well. He brought four women (Paula Jones, Kathleen Wiley, Juanita Broderick, and Kathy Shelton) to that debate, all of whom had accused Clinton of sexual impropriety, even rape.[109] During the debate itself, he sought to make Hillary Clinton complicit in those improprieties. He said, "If you look at Bill Clinton, far worse. Mine are words and his was action. His words, what he has done to women. . . . There has never been anybody in the history of politics in this nation that has been so abusive to women. . . . Hillary Clinton attacked these same women, and attacked them viciously, four of them are here tonight."[110] As with his other accusations against Clinton, the rhetorical work being done here is less about making him look innocent or engaging in actual self-defense and more about making her look equally distasteful. As Clinton put it in her book on that campaign, it often seemed as if "for Trump, if everyone's down in the mud with him, then he's no dirtier than anyone else."[111]

It is hard to imagine any presidential candidate surviving direct evidence of sexual misconduct, expressed in such offensive terms. But Trump did. In part, this was because it was news, but it was also not news—it was no surprise to anyone paying attention that Trump was prone to such behavior. The fact that WikiLeaks began to release emails stolen from the Clinton campaign distracted the media as well. But it is only in the most deplorable of elections that a person who said the things in this example could maintain a viable candidacy. This was possible because the damage to the electoral system went well beyond the single case of Donald Trump.

It's Bigger Than Trump: The Republican National Convention

The Republican Convention was not the star-studded affair that one might expect, given the nomination of a Hollywood personality. It featured B-list celebrities like Scott Baio, best known for his work on *Happy Days* and *Charles in Charge*, and *Duck Dynasty*'s Willie Robertson. But if Hollywood

A-listers were absent, Republican Party members were there, all hitting the same themes of angry nostalgia and resentful responses to cultural threats. Republicans had long relied on increasingly overt exclusionary appeals. In 2016, that rhetoric was applied to external as well as internal threats under the larger rubric of the need for security. This relied on arguing that Americans were not safe from one another or from those who sought to do the nation harm. New York's 107th mayor, Rudy Giuliani, for instance, said, "I am here to speak to you about how to make America safe. The vast majority of Americans today do not feel safe. They fear for their children, and they fear for themselves."[112] The premise here is not about whether Americans are actually safe; it is not about the actual crime statistics in most American neighborhoods. It's about instilling and evoking fear. Suitably for Giuliani, who was New York's mayor on September 11, he located that fear precisely: "We must not be afraid to define our enemy. It is Islamic extremist terrorism. I did not say all of Islam. I said Islamic extremist terrorism."[113] For Giuliani, the nation had been attacked by terrorists on 9/11, and it was still threatened by them. He implied that the Democrats were unwilling to respond appropriately to that threat, but Republicans would. This kind of fearmongering spread throughout the convention as other speakers made the case that Clinton was a poor choice for president because she was incapable of protecting national security.

In one of the convention's more infamous moments, retired lieutenant general and former director of the Defense Intelligence Agency Michael Flynn opened with a chant of "lock her up." He said, "I use #neverHillary; that's what I use. I have called on Hillary Clinton to drop out of the race, I have called on Hillary Clinton to drop out of the race because she put our nation's security at extremely high risk with her careless use of a private email server . . . lock her up. Lock her up. If I did a tenth of what she did, I'd be in jail today."[114] This is despicable and dangerous discourse. It is an example of the kind of rhetoric that led observers to worry about the authoritarian strains becoming more evident in Republican circles since the Trump campaign. It is bad enough to delegitimate political opposition instead of merely opposing it. Threatening to jail political opponents crosses a line that separates despicable discourse from antidemocratic action.

Flynn continued: "She needs to go. Before—before I end—before I end, I will repeat my belief that American exceptionalism is very real. Let—let us not fear what we know to be true. Let us not fear what we know to be true. Instead, we should always remember that our country, our country, was built on Judeo-Christian values and principles and instead, instead, let us remember the sacrifices of those who have gone before us. America is unique. America is the greatest country in the history of the world."[115] It is certainly neither unusual nor despicable to offer praise for the nation at a national nominating convention. But here, Flynn specifically associates national greatness with "Judeo-Christian values and principles," which also specifically excludes everyone who does not adhere to those values as Flynn understands them. He is also implying that those values are under attack, because arguing for them requires courage. Those responsible for these attacks should be not disagreed with but jailed.

This reliance on the need for incarceration was connected, of course, to the long-time Republican theme of "law and order," with all of its racial and racist connotations. Trump himself, for example, opened his acceptance speech by saying, "Together, we will lead our party back to the White House, and we will lead our country back to safety, prosperity, and peace. We will be a country of generosity and warmth. But we will also be a country of law and order."[116] Republicans had come full circle back to Richard Nixon in 1968, calling for law and order as a means of consolidating the party around an unpopular candidate in order to win an election. But Trump was no Nixon. He had no experience, little knowledge, and no interest in attaining either. His goals as president were exclusionary: to ban Muslim immigration, to build a wall on the nation's southern border, to keep the nation safe from external threats. He promised to protect the American safety net and to provide American jobs. But he meant those benefits to accrue to those he deemed "real" Americans, the Americans who constituted his base. His campaign offered little in the way of unifying rhetoric; he expressed no intention of being president of all of the American people. His campaign relied on despicable discourse from start to finish and was unquestionably deplorable.

CONCLUSION: LIVING IN DEPLORABLE TIMES

The conduct of the 2016 campaign was unusual, to say the least. Two historically unpopular candidates faced off in a contest that featured normal practices on one side and consistent disruptions of normality on the other. Not only did Trump eschew routine campaign practices concerning staff, organization, and so on, but he was unusual in both the style and content of his messaging. He offered bombastic, inflammatory, divisive, and exclusionary rhetoric. He undermined other political actors, political processes, and the political system as a whole. He appealed to the nation's worst instincts and validated ideological strains associated with its ugliest past.

Trump's victory was variously attributed to the media, the failure of the GOP leadership to stop him, the faults of the Clinton campaign, the pervasiveness of misogyny and sexism, the intervention of James Comey, and the skill of Donald Trump. It is possible to read the election as an example of "negative partisanship," the notion that people voted against Clinton and the Democrats rather than for Trump and the Republicans. Trump was elected in 2016, but the issues at play in the 2016 election go well beyond Trump. His kind of campaign was possible because of a political culture that primed audiences to be receptive to his style and to his arguments. Neither those audiences nor the conditions that created them and that sustain them are going away.

The considerable scholarship that has already gone into determining the causes and consequences of Trump's elections paints a bleak picture. Trump voters were motivated by anger and resentment toward their fellow citizens, by a sense of loss, by economic dislocations, and by the fear of upending national hierarchies. Republicans leaders, many of them once "never Trumpers," conceded the party to him. Nelson Rockefeller implored the Republican Party to expel right-wing conservatives from the party in 1964, fearing where their continued presence would take the party of Lincoln; this is an extreme version of what he feared.

American politics had been heading toward this deplorable election for a long time. The animosities that were apparent in 1968 were fed by decades of Republican rhetoric, nurtured by Fox News, accentuated by the routines of news coverage throughout the mainstream media, and exacerbated by the ways in which information—and especially bad information—is promulgated through the internet. The very real economic dislocations, and demographic and cultural changes, have increased the precarity and the fears of precarity among many citizens whose lives are demonstrably worse off with every national election. But choices are being made to blame other citizens, especially those whose economic travails are added to by the deeply embedded racism facing their communities and the ideological and material consequences of that racism.

And yet, a majority of voters in 2016 rejected the racism, xenophobia, and authoritarianism represented by Trump and Trumpism. It's important to recognize that he lost the popular vote. This election was not a national endorsement of Trump or Trumpism. It was the antiquated machinations of the Electoral College that elected Trump, after what was the most deplorable election in US history. Until, that is, the election of 2020.

AFTERWORD

Or Maybe It Does—A Few Words About 2020

Standing in front of a largely unmasked crowd in Waukesha, Wisconsin, Donald Trump delivered the closing argument of his 2020 campaign: "I had it, here I am," he said. "Here I am in Wisconsin."[1] Referring to his recovery from a bout of COVID-19, Trump told an enthusiastic crowd that his campaign was on track, that a vaccine was imminent, and that Democratic nominee, former vice president Joe Biden, was using the virus to scare voters into voting for him. That day in Wisconsin, and during the final days of the campaign, Trump consistently sought to minimize the deadly consequences of the coronavirus in an endeavor to also minimize its consequences for his reelection efforts. Two days after his Wisconsin speech, he tweeted, "The Fake News Media are riding COVID, COVID, COVID, all the way to the Election. Losers!"[2] Despite his claims that the nation had "turned a corner" on containing the virus, it continued to rage through both his White House and the country.

The pandemic was only one reason why the 2020 election season was anything but normal. The pandemic created a global financial crisis, affecting the nation's economy as well as its health. Both the president and Senate Republicans were more committed to confirming a nominee to the nation's highest court than addressing either the pandemic or its economic consequences, and millions remained jobless as the virus raged through the country. Complicating matters, the police murder of George Floyd in May touched off a series of protests that engulfed every state and expanded to include the destruction of statues and other memory sites relating to the Confederacy and other figures with racist histories and, in several instances, led to violent clashes with the police. The first debate could only be described as chaotic, as Trump repeatedly violated the rules—interrupting, blurting, and distracting. CNN's Jake Tapper called the debate "a hot mess inside a dumpster fire inside a train wreck."[3] He said, "That was the worst debate I've ever seen. It wasn't even a debate, it was a disgrace. And it's primarily because of President Trump."[4] The second debate was canceled due to the president's illness; the candidates appeared instead on separate networks in an odd sort of duel of town halls. The third debate featured a mute button, allowing the debate moderator to cut off the candidates' microphones as required to provide some level of civility, and it did seem to restore some decorum to the process. The final days of the election were conducted amid accusations of systematic attempts at voter suppression, record numbers of early voters, and threats of violence against both elected officials and voters.

It took sixteen days for the final results to be reported: Trump won 46.9 percent of votes, garnering 232 electoral votes while Biden earned 51.3 percent of votes and 306 electoral votes and the White House. Democrats retained control of the House, although Republicans picked up eleven seats. Following a runoff in Georgia, in which Democrats won both contested Senate seats, they controlled the Senate. Trump lost, but many Republicans further down the ballot won; the 2020 election was a rejection of Donald Trump, but it was not necessarily a repudiation of his politics or his rhetoric.

As the final vote counts continued after Election Day, Trump and his allies attempted to stop the count, tried to block votes, and consistently alleged that the election had been stolen. The rhetoric reached a fever pitch as the states each certified their votes, and finally, in an attempt to prevent congressional certification of the Biden victory, Trump supporters, encouraged by the president himself, attempted a violent takeover of the Capitol building, leaving a trail of destruction in their wake. In the days between the election and the inauguration, the Capitol was enclosed by fencing; private citizens and members of state legislatures were arrested for their participation in the attack on the Capitol; there were calls for the resignations of members of Congress and senators like Ted Cruz (R-TX) and Josh Hawley (R-MO), who were seen as complicit in those attacks. The president himself, who had encouraged the violence, was unrepentant and continued to incite his followers, causing social media platforms such as Twitter to ban him permanently from posting on the site. In the week following the attack, Trump, having resisted calls for his resignation, was again impeached by the House.

The inauguration itself was conducted amid heightened security. If democracies are characterized by a peaceful transition of power, the United States lost its claim to that distinction in 2021. The most expensive political campaign in history (estimates begin at $14 billion) remained close, however, and on Election Day, with the outcome still in doubt, Trump declared that continuing to count votes constituted a "fraud on the American public" and falsely stated that he had won the election.[5] His son, Donald Trump Jr., went so far as to claim his father would declare "total war" to keep the White House, drawing backlash from both the right and the left.[6] As the election turned inexorably against the president, he and his family engaged in ever more despicable discourse. This time, however, the media—including Fox News—covered it as despicable, and many Republicans also condemned it.

Trump's 2020 campaign was remarkably similar to his campaign in 2016—including attacks on Hillary Clinton. In 2020 as in 2016, Trump led his audiences in chants of "lock her up," frequently referred to Hillary Clinton's emails, and brought out the same themes of American decay he relied upon four years earlier. But in 2020 he was running against Joe Biden, not Hillary Clinton. Biden lacked Clinton's history of antagonism with the right and was not subject to the same sexism and misogyny Clinton faced. This time, too, Trump was the incumbent not the challenger; if the nation was decaying, it was doing so on his watch and was therefore his responsibility. Despite these different circumstances, Trump continued to rely on familiar tactics. He circulated despicable discourse, he railed against the Democrats, and he played the victim card, insisting that the "Chinese virus" had unfairly damaged his presidency. These tactics helped Trump maintain much of his previous support; some 74 million Americans, the vast majority of them white, voted to keep Trump in office.

As president, Trump encountered and contributed to events that encouraged a deplorable election in 2020. Trump tended to undermine the already fragile political system, insisting that he endured a constant barrage of the "most unfair" treatment any president ever received at the hands of the "deep state" and other various political foes, an argument that grounded his rhetoric during his impeachment and reached a crescendo after the election as he fomented violence and insurrection. His signature achievement, a massive tax cut passed in 2017, provided considerable assistance to the wealthy, while doing very little to advance the economic interests of the middle and working classes. The economic effects of the pandemic were dire, even for the relatively well-off, and were worse than dire for those on the economic edge. Trump supporters thus continued to feel economically disadvantaged and continued to worry about their status vis-à-vis other groups; both economic stress and status anxiety remained potent motivators for many on the political right. The racism that is so hard for the media to distinguish from such anxiety remained potent as well, and that, along with racist and anti-immigrant rhetoric and policy characterized much of the Trump administration, ensured that those issues would be prominent items on the national agenda heading into the 2020 election. He continued to rely on social media, telling *60 Minutes* journalist Lesley Stahl, for example, that even as president, if not for social media, he would not be able to get his message out, given the biases of the mainstream media.[7] And he continually delegitimated his opponents, consistently condemning Democrats for treating him unfairly and characterizing his impeachment as an "attempted coup."

Having won the White House by circulating despicable discourse, Trump as president seemed dedicated to ensuring that the 2020 campaign would be equally deplorable. To understand 2020, therefore, I briefly review some of the major events of the Trump administration and quickly outline the 2020 campaign. I follow those sections with a discussion of what earlier deplorable elections teach us about the effort to conduct two equally deplorable campaigns back-to-back, before concluding with some thoughts about the future of deplorable elections and the US political system, in light of the attack on the Capitol and the nation's response to that insurrection.

A BRIEF OVERVIEW OF THE TRUMP ADMINISTRATION

Trump's management of the pandemic caused by COVID-19 encapsulates much of the Trump administration in general, whose actions brought the country to a tense and deplorable election characterized by despicable discourse. Unlike most presidents elected after deplorable campaigns, Trump made no effort to broaden his appeal after the election. He made no pretense of attempting to govern as "president of all the people," choosing instead to appeal entirely to his base.[8] His animosity toward his former opponents was matched only by theirs for him. His election was greeted by bitter determination on the part of his opponents to resist any and all action by his administration. Democrats in Congress vowed to obstruct him, and many members of the mass public marched in unprecedented numbers after his inauguration and in response to various policy proposals. His inaugural crowd was comparatively small; the protests that emerged after it were among the largest in history.

Trump's unwillingness to even attempt to govern from the center of American politics is typified by his response to events in Charlottesville, Virginia, shortly after his inauguration. On August 14, 2017, a group of white supremacists, loosely organized under the umbrella of "Unite the Right," led a torchlight parade in Charlottesville. The event was specifically intended to invoke the marches of the Hitler Youth in the 1930s, although the immediate exigency was the proposed removal of a statue of Confederate general Robert E. Lee.[9] Chanting "Jews will not replace us" and "White lives matter," some 250 young white people marched through the University of Virginia. Counterprotesters also showed up, and that night and over the next day, fights broke out. The next day a rally was planned, and white nationalists, accompanied by a civilian self-styled militia, and counterprotesters all appeared. The white supremacists became violent. The police failed to step in until too late, and in the ensuing chaos, James Alex Fields Jr. drove his car into the crowd, killing Heather Heyer and wounding two others.

Asked about the events in Charlottesville during a press conference, the president said, "I think there is blame on both sides. You had a group on one side that was bad. You had a group on the other side that was also very violent. Nobody wants to say that. I'll say it right now."[10] He defended those who opposed the removal of Lee's statue, saying, "I've condemned neo-Nazis. I've condemned many different groups. Not all of those people were neo-Nazis, believe me. Not all of those people were white supremacists by any stretch." When pressed by the media, he continued to defend the protesters, saying, "Many of those people were there to protest the taking down of the statue of Robert E. Lee. So this week, it is Robert E. Lee. I noticed that Stonewall Jackson is coming down. I wonder, is it George Washington next week? And is it Thomas Jefferson the week after? You know, you really do have to ask yourself, where does it stop?" Trump here defended neo-Nazis, a previously unthinkable position for an American president to take; he placed those dedicated to attacking US democracy on the same plane as those dedicated to defending it, and he asserted that those who took up arms against the United States were the moral equivalents of the Founders. In making these arguments, the president authorized a certain kind of citizenship—he made room in the polity for white supremacists and neo-Nazis while marginalizing those citizens whom members of these groups most frequently attack.

As during the 2016 campaign, Trump's rhetoric as president often relied on tropes of association and dissociation. He distinctly demarcated those who are welcome—both materially and rhetorically—in his polity and those who are relegated to the margins or the outside of that polity. All presidents, of course, do this. In recent iterations of the presidency, however, these demarcations tend to be ideological—those who are unwelcome or uninvited are excluded based on their practices (say, terrorism) or their beliefs (say, white supremacy), which are deemed threatening to the nation and its democratic project. Thus, there is always hope that the excluded can become included. Trump more specifically defines the nation's friends and enemies and does so on racialized terms—it is not what people believe or do that excludes them but their ascriptive characteristics. They are Mexican; they are Muslim; they are African Americans. The dangers of this rhetoric are clear—the president not only divided Americans, but he did so in ways that are not attributable to national goals and ideals unless those goals and ideals are the sustenance of racial hierarchies. The exclusions he prefers are not remediable by changes in behavior or belief; they are not remediable at all. Those who are excluded are excluded indefinitely.

Unsurprisingly, therefore, neither the bitterness nor the determination to resist subsided as Trump presided over an administration that was remarkable for its contentiousness as well as its inability to enact policy through the legislative process. He relied on the unilateral presidency, governing through administrative mechanisms rather than through Congress, and even those efforts were frequently delayed and prevented by actions in the courts. Adept at cultural politics, Trump was markedly less successful at governance.[11] He managed an attention economy that kept people—whether willing or not—focused on his every tweet, but he got little done. His White House was in constant turmoil, characterized by a revolving door of appointments, confrontations, and resignations.[12] There was continuing controversy over his immigration policies, including his "Muslim ban," the policy of family separation that led to the incarceration of children, and allegations of abuse in detention facilities. He was plagued by scandal, involving both his campaign and his administration, and never managed to generate any governing momentum.

The scandals culminated in early 2019 when he was impeached on charges of abuse of power and obstruction of Congress. In the first instance, Trump was accused of withholding financial aid to Ukraine until they agreed to announce an investigation of Trump rival and former vice president Joe Biden. In the second, he was accused of failing to cooperate with a congressional investigation into the first. He was acquitted by the Senate on a party-line vote, with all Republicans voting to exonerate the president except former presidential candidate Mitt Romney (R-UT).

In late December 2019, the first case of what would become known as COVID-19 was reported in Wuhan, China. Within the month, cases of the virus were being found in other countries, which, by the end of January 2020, included the United States. The Center for Disease Control began to issue warnings in early January, but the Trump administration, which had eliminated the public health position in China dedicated to the detection of health crises there, and which ignored the "pandemic playbook" left by the Obama administration, was slow in responding. While participating in the World Economic Forum in Switzerland in late January, Trump was asked if the United States had a plan to address the spread of the coronavirus. He stated that there was a plan and that the crisis "was going to be handled very well."[13]

The virus continued to spread, and the Trump administration continued to insist that it was under control. The president declared a national emergency in March but soon reverted to earlier claims that it was at best a minor matter as the death toll mounted. The administration was soon involved in disputes with his own administration over how to handle both the crisis and the messaging related to it.[14] By the end of the summer, Trump's management of the crisis and its effect on the nation's economy began to dominate the presidential campaign to the president's increasing fury.

In early September, journalist Bob Woodward revealed that he had tapes demonstrating that the president knew about the severity of the virus and lied to the public about it as a conscious strategy. These revelations deepened anger among both his opponents and, increasingly, his supporters about his handling of the virus.[15] On the defensive about the virus, Trump's problems were compounded in late September, when the *New York Times* revealed the results of months of investigative reporting and announced that Trump, despite his claims to the contrary, had paid only $750 in taxes in 2016, the year he won the presidency.[16] At practically the same moment, Trump's former campaign manager, Brad Parscale, was arrested on charges of appropriating campaign funds; that arrest took place amid allegations of spousal abuse and as he threatened to harm himself.[17] Trump, seemingly impervious to scandal throughout his first campaign and his presidency, now seemed to be drowning in unsavory revelations.[18]

The first days of October continued to be bad ones for the Trump administration. The month began with continuing coverage of a scandal involving Donald Trump Jr.'s girlfriend, Kimberly Guilfoyle, now working for the Trump campaign. She had been fired from Fox News in 2018 amid accusations of sexual harassment, and increasingly distasteful details emerged, keeping the issue in the news.[19] Then CNN's Anderson Cooper played tapes dating back to 2018, in which First Lady Melania Trump was heard ranting about the expectation that she decorate the White House for Christmas, and venting her ire about media coverage of immigrant children being incarcerated at the border.[20] The language was obscene and the contrast between that and her image for grace and style among many conservatives was extreme. The idea that the "war on Christmas" was arguably coming from inside the president's house was greeted with glee by the

Democrats as yet another instance of conservative, and specifically Trumpian, hypocrisy.

The administration was so determined to ignore the virus that upon the death of Supreme Court Justice Ruth Bader Ginsberg Trump held a reception in the White House for his controversial nominee as her replacement, Amy Coney Barrett. Despite longstanding medical advice to avoid large gatherings and to wear masks, these protocols were not followed. That reception unsurprisingly turned out to be a "super spreader event," in which large numbers of people were infected by the virus, including members of the White House staff, top Republicans like former New Jersey governor and Trump confidante Chris Christie, the first lady, and the president himself.[21]

The president, visibly unwell, was flown to Walter Reed for treatment for the coronavirus. The White House refused to reveal even the most basic information about the president's health, such as when he was infected, and the information they did offer was conflicting and contradictory. As he recovered, Trump continued to ignore health and safety advice, taking a ride in the presidential limousine to wave at his supporters near the hospital, a trip that endangered his Secret Service detail; removing his mask once back at the White House, even though he was potentially still contagious; and even hosting another large rally at the White House.[22] The spread was so serious that *Time* magazine's October 8, 2020, cover depicted the virus billowing out of the White House. The president was briefly hospitalized, and upon returning to the White House to continue his convalescence, he sent out a wide variety of tweets that were inconsistent, rambling, angry, and potentially evidence of the medical effects of his steroid treatments.[23] Concerns deepened after an appearance on conservative commentator Rush Limbaugh's radio program, during which even Limbaugh seemed disconcerted by the president's behavior.

Trump's performance in the second presidential debate allayed many of these fears, however, as the debate, while contentious, was at least reasonably well-mannered. He continued to mock those taking the virus seriously, maintained that its effects were not serious, and insisted that the media coverage of the pandemic was "fake news." He continued to campaign, hosting large events during which masks were noticeably absent, and he asserted at those events, on Twitter, and in other forums, that the effects of COVID-19 were being exaggerated by a partisan and unfair media. He ended his campaign by offering increasingly agitated and disjointed appeals, wandering away from the text of one speech, for example, to remark on the size of Joe Biden's trademark sunglasses.[24]

By Election Day, 233,000 Americans had died. Trump continued to raise concerns about his willingness to abide by the election results unless they provided him with a second term, and he continued to endorse the violence and threats of violence by his supporters. He initially refused to concede the election, he offered baseless claims of election malfeasance, and, in short, he continued during and after the election not only to circulate but to emphasize and depend upon despicable discourses, which resulted in a violent attack on the Capitol and the nation's elected officials.

THE 2020 CAMPAIGN: TRUMP'S DESPICABLE DISCOURSE REDUX

For the Democrats, the 2020 campaign began normally enough, with a number of Democrats poised to challenge the president, and with his predictable tendency to demean them all. According to the nation's chief executive, his putative challengers included "Sleepy Joe" Biden and "Pocahontas," the racial epithet he used to reference Massachusetts senator Elizabeth Warren's misleading claim to indigenous identity. Trump's insults notwithstanding, the Democratic primaries were peaceable and even often amicable, with the various candidates avowing themselves to be more dedicated to Trump's defeat than to their own candidacy. As each candidate dropped out of the race, Democratic unity became increasingly apparent. There were no repeats of the Clinton/Sanders race, no difficult reconciliations. Eventual nominee Joe Biden pledged to nominate a woman as his vice president and settled on California senator Kamala Harris, the first woman of color to be on a major party presidential ticket. The Democrats ran a campaign that followed traditional forms, was attentive to the requirements of public health and safety given the pandemic, and was otherwise unexceptional. Biden argued for national unity, promised to be president of all the people, "whether you support me or not," and was, in general, sincere, decorous, and conventional. He did offer some despicable discourse by emphasizing his claim that the campaign was a contest over the fate of the American soul, which delegitimated his opponent and his supporters, an appeal that contributed to the deplorable nature of the campaign.

Biden could choose to remain largely above the fray in part because there was so much animosity toward the president from so many different directions. He had many surrogates, both Democratic and Republican. In addition to predictable support on the left, Biden benefited from several endorsements from the right, including a number of retired military officers, political officials, and members of the national security and diplomatic corps. Newspapers from around the country also endorsed Biden, including the staunchly Republican New Hampshire *Union Leader* and the equally conservative *Economist*. Other endorsements included the American Association for the Advancement of Science and a variety of other organizations, many of which did not make political endorsements part of their normal practice. He was also assisted by the ad campaign managed through the Lincoln Project, a group of Republicans dedicated to Trump's defeat.[25] The Lincoln Project published op eds, engaged in other kinds of public-facing communication, and, most famously, produced a series of devastatingly nasty ads that picked up on moment-to-moment events and parodied, criticized, and condemned Trump and his administration as incompetent, antidemocratic, and even fascist.

As is always the case when an incumbent is in the race, in 2020 the line between the Trump administration and the Trump campaign blurred. Next then, I want to quickly review the kinds of antidemocratic appeals Trump used in 2020, which were notable both because they were substantially similar to his 2016 tactics and because they resonated less widely the second time around. Three elements of Trump's campaign are particularly notable in this regard: his overt racism, his tendency to undermine the political system, and his efforts to delegitimate his opponent.

Racism on the Campaign Trail

Conversations about systemic racism were an important part of the context for the 2020 campaign, as the police murder of George Floyd set off a variety of protests around the country and around the world. Following the initial protests, Trump gave a brief speech.[26] He opened that speech by declaring, "My first and highest duty as president is to defend our great country and the American people," signaling that those people were somehow in need of his protection and defense and declaring that he understood this was his responsibility. This is a typical presidential address. He also gestured toward an inclusive understanding of "the American people," stating, "All Americans were rightly sickened and revolted by the brutal death of George Floyd. My administration is fully committed that, for George and his family, justice will be served." This from Trump is a rare and potentially unifying, if somewhat awkward, opening, as the president affirmed that the circumstances of Floyd's death were sickening and required justice, a return to national health.

But then the president reverted to type, saying, "He will not have died in vain, but we cannot allow the righteous cries and peaceful protesters to be drown [*sic*] out by an angry mob. The biggest victims of the rioting are peace-loving citizens in our poorest communities and as their president, I will fight to keep them safe. I will fight to protect you. I am your president of law and order and an ally of all peaceful protesters. But in recent days, our nation has been gripped by professional anarchists, violent mobs, arsonists, looters, criminals, rioters, Antifa, and others." Here, the president relied on differentiation, separating "good" protesters from "bad" ones. "Good" protesters issue "righteous cries" and engage in protest peacefully. Their legitimate actions, however, were in danger of being drowned out "by an angry mob." The victims in question were not delineated by any of the terms they were themselves using. In Trump's formulation, they were not suffering from the disproportionate effects of the coronavirus on their communities or from the disproportionate effects of the ensuing economic difficulties caused by the virus. They were not victimized by disproportionate police surveillance, incarceration rates, or police violence. Trump argued they were best understood as the victims of "bad" protesters, who included "professional anarchists, violent mobs, arsonists, looters, criminals, rioters, Antifa, and others." These "bad" protesters were imposing their own dangerous agendas on otherwise peaceful African Americans.

This language racialized the protesters. Trump said he was dedicated to protecting "you" through "law and order." That has long been a racialized phrase, strongly associated with Richard Nixon and the Southern strategy. It clarifies just who is going to be protected and from whom.

However, despite Trump's implication, while the protests were driven by African Americans, they were also multiracial. In fact, one of the most important elements of these protests was that participants came from all demographics. But for Trump, the victims were from "our poorest communities," language that operates in this case as code for "Black." According to Trump, African Americans were victimized not by police violence or by governmental policies but by the protests against those things. For Trump, the status quo was benign. The threat emanated from those advocating change and challenging that status quo.

These are examples of the presidential power of definition, as Trump named the cause of the unrest and, in so doing, also named the problem (bad protesters), the victims (Black people), and the solution (the use of force). "These are not acts of peaceful protest," Trump insisted, "these are acts of domestic terror. The destruction of innocent life and the spilling of innocent blood is an offense to humanity and a crime against God." The president claimed the protesters in question were not seeking justice. According to Trump, they were committing offenses against both the nation and God. They were, in Trump's view, "terrorists." It is worth noting as well that Trump defined these protesters as terrorists, a label he refused to assign to white supremacists.

On another occasion, in the middle of (misleading) remarks about the economy, Trump said that George Floyd was "hopefully looking down and feeling good." He continued, "Hopefully George is looking down right now and saying, 'this is a great thing that's happening for our country.' This is a great day for him. It's a great day for everybody. This is a great day for everybody. This is a great great day in terms of equality. . . . It's really what our Constitution requires, and it's what our country is all about."[27] These remarks can most generously be described as tone deaf. To assume that a person who died from police violence that was contemporaneously being associated with racism and the inequalities caused by it would be lauding a president often criticized for racism is boggling. Remarkably, Trump then worsened the situation by retweeting an interview in which Candace Owens, a conservative activist, made derogatory remarks about George Floyd's character in an apparent effort to exonerate those who murdered him.[28]

These remarks had consequences. Police continued to act violently toward protesters; white supremacists continued to threaten and engage in violence, in one case hatching a plot to kidnap the Democratic governor of Michigan and in another to kidnap the Democratic mayor of Wichita, Kansas. Trump's response to these events was to continue the same kind of rhetoric that many believed had led to them in the first place.[29] In a more symbolic but also disturbing kind of uptake, Trump supporters at one of his rallies replaced an American flag with the "blue line" flag, indicating disdain for the claim that "Black Lives Matter" and a preference for "blue lives."[30] This act proclaimed, as nothing else could, loyalty to white supremacy rather than to the nation.

Whether or not the president was, as he claimed in the second debate, ignoring the presence of a woman of color as the debate moderator, "the least racist person in this room," there is no question that his rhetoric throughout his administration and the campaign emboldened racists and white supremacists. As in 2016, in 2020 Trump circulated despicable discourse, enabled its circulation by others, and seemed to thrive on such circulation. His overt racism was again accompanied by efforts to undermine the system and to taint his opponent with accusations of scandal and corruption.

The Process Presidency

Trump's tendency to alter and ignore prevailing political processes, norms, and values, is one of the most frequently deplored elements of his presidency.[31] Susan Hennessey and Benjamin Wittes observe that previous administrations have relied on what they call the "process presidency," which entails the decision-making operations within the executive branch that afford the president advice. The bureaucracy is often frustrating, if not maddening; Trump's tendency to elide and ignore the civil service is, to some of his supporters, deeply satisfying.[32] Trump's rejection of the process presidency is connected to his rejection of expertise.

Trump not only undermined his own bureaucracy but undermined the public perception of it as well, often arguing that its actions are either the product of the "deep state" or of pernicious partisanship, most notably accusing Democrats of engaging in "deranged partisan crusades" during the first impeachment hearings.[33] In 2016, Trump had promised to "drain the swamp," to clean up the corruption that characterized national governance. But his administration had been mired in scandal, and only his strongest supporters could seem to convince themselves that he was making any progress toward more honest government. Indeed, it was sometimes hard to imagine why Trump had decided to run for reelection at all. It was, for example, difficult to argue that there was an important policy agenda awaiting his attention—the Republicans declined to write a new platform and simply reissued the platform from 2016. It was hard to believe that he found in the Democratic nominee a singular and important threat to the American polity—both he and Fox News focused an inordinate amount of attention on the "issue" of Hillary Clinton's emails. Rather than moving into the election with an energized argument for a second term, in other words, Trump seemed mired in the past, wanting to replay 2016. But he was now president, and an insurgent campaign was not among his options.

Yet during the campaign he continued to try to delegitimate the government he was now heading. Accepting the Republican nomination at the White House—a clear violation of the Hatch Act, which prevents political activity on the part of federal employees and in federal buildings—Trump dismissed the contributions of "career politicians," argued against "the political establishment," claimed to have "ended the rule of the failed political class," made plain his disagreements with "Washington insiders," lauded his various victories over "Washington special interests," and railed against the crime and violence he associated with "Democrat-run cities."[34] These are not the words of a person who trusts the political process or who has faith in national political institutions. The difference between 2016 and 2020, however, was that in 2020 Trump was head of the political establishment he was actively undermining. In undermining federal institutions, he was also undermining arguments that he was capable of leading those institutions. Given the way COVID-19 continued to ravage the nation, this was a particular problem. Trump endeavored to solve it by focusing attention not on controlling the virus but on attacking his opponent.

"Lock Him Up"

During the four years between 2015 and 2019, former vice president Joe Biden's son Hunter was a board member of Burisma Holdings, a Ukrainian gas company. Several of the company's executives were investigated for corruption, and at one point during the Obama administration, the senior Biden made it clear that he had been influential in administration efforts to fire Prosecutor General Victor Shokin. Right-wing news sources have long argued that this is evidence of efforts by Biden to hide misconduct, but the evidence indicates that the Obama administration wanted this prosecutor fired because he was not doing enough to fight corruption. Nonetheless, Trump has sought criminal investigation of both Bidens, and the Senate released a report in September 2020 that Democrats claim exonerates them and Republicans argue provides evidence of malfeasance.[35]

The Biden family has been marked by tragedy. Biden lost his first wife and one of his children in a car accident; his son Beau died more recently from brain cancer. Hunter Biden has had his troubles, including drug addiction. His father has stood loyally by his son, and in the wake of Trump's attacks on his family, emails surfaced that included loving messages between the father and son. Apparently happily married to his second wife, Dr. Jill Biden, Joe Biden appears to be the kind of family man long treated as politically untouchable. This did not stop Trump from attacking Biden's sons and his relationship with them in an effort to claim that Biden is a career politician, with all the implied corruption that entails, and to mark himself as an outsider by comparison.[36]

Like his appeals to racism and his tendency to undermine governmental legitimacy, this tactic is reminiscent of his 2016 efforts to discredit Hillary Clinton. But Biden is not Clinton. He does not have a history of investigation, and his family lacks the taint that followed the Clintons through their entire political careers. His loyalty to his son plays very differently than Hillary's loyalty to her husband Bill, and it is much more difficult to read it as the product of naked political ambition. The "damning" photograph of Biden kissing Hunter revealed a great deal about how the US political culture relies on specific versions of masculinity, but it is hard to read evidence of deep paternal affection as a political negative.[37] In 2016, Trump was able to deflect news of his scandals with constant reference to Clinton's, real or imagined. In 2020, facing a different kind of opponent, those efforts had less traction.

In addition, Hillary Clinton was trapped by overt misogyny that limited her rhetorical options. As an older white male, Biden had more rhetorical choices. In the first debate, for example, moderator Chris Wallace quickly lost control of the debate amid Trump's continual interjections, interruptions, and refusal to obey the previously agreed upon time limits. A frustrated Biden asked, "Folks, do we have any idea what this clown is doing?" and finally said, "Would you shut up, man?" before exhorting Trump to "keep yapping, man."[38] Biden could mock Trump in ways that Clinton could not, could point to Trump's tendency to undermine the system in ways that were perceived as less self-defensive and more defensive of norms and values.

In 2016, Donald Trump dominated the nation's attention economy. He continued to do so over the following four years. But in the wake of the protests following the murder of George Floyd and especially in the context of the global pandemic, Trump lost control of the narrative. He had not used his time in the White House to expand either his constituency or his rhetorical repertoire, and so he had few options when it came to running for reelection. The explicit nature of his racism as it had developed into political policy meant that white voters had a much more difficult time ignoring those elements of Trump's administration; they were increasingly faced with a choice between supporting nakedly exclusionary politics or forsaking the president. His constant undermining of the political system disturbed some white Americans, who were increasingly being told by members of the media, by Democrats, and by some Republicans that the very nature of their democracy was at risk. His attacks on Biden and his family lacked the same traction as his attacks on Clinton. Trump needed to be able to adapt his campaign to the facts of his presidency and to the changed context of 2020. He could do neither, and his circulation of despicable discourse proved inadequate to the task of reelection, while also demonstrating the staying power of many of his policies. The nation's political commitments shifted just enough in enough states to cost Trump the White House. There was, however, no widespread repudiation of Trump and no evidence that his despicable discourses were proving less attractive to many white Americans. It is possible to read the results of the 2020 election, however, as an indication of the potential perils of governing through such discourse.

THE PERILS OF REPETITION

Despicable discourse is more likely to circulate when the system is fragile and when the economy is weak, because those structural elements allow appeals that scapegoat both people of color and immigrants to resonate more widely among white people. Because the normal systemic brakes on such behavior are not in place, those conditions also make it more likely that candidates will seek to win elections by not merely opposing but delegitimating their opponents. When those appeals are circulated by the media, when they take hold among enough voters, the odds of a deplorable election increase. Such elections are often preceded in time by an election that has some of these elements; when those elements are not quickly and decisively opposed, then a deplorable election becomes more likely. For example, the centrality of the "Willie Horton" ads in 1988 provided an indication that 1992 was potentially deplorable.

As that example indicates, despicable discourse has an additive quality. Since 1968, as the "Southern strategy" has gained an increasing hold on a Republican Party ever more committed to the politics of exclusion, deplorable elections have increased both in number and in intensity. That is, since there have not been interparty efforts to quash such discourse, and indeed, since the Democrats have also moved cautiously on matters of racial and other exclusions, such discourse has taken a firm grip on the nation's politics, making political appeals like those that characterize Donald Trump's campaigns more likely.

This happens because white voters can deny their complicity, because they can be shielded from the exclusionary consequences of the policies they support. Because it is possible for white voters to claim that they are not individually racist and that they do not support the racism of specific candidates, those voters can hide behind the supposition that the exclusion is an unintended consequence of their support, not a direct outcome of it. In 1992, Pat Buchanan sought to make that denial impossible; his appeals were directly and intentionally exclusionary. He lost the Republican nomination, but in many ways he won the party. In 2016, Donald Trump won the nomination, the presidency, and the party on appeals that Buchanan would have approved.

But in 2020 those appeals were slightly less appealing to white Americans in key states. Partly, this was because of the nature of elections. In 2020 Trump was an incumbent, not a challenger. Partly, it was a result of the abnormal conditions contextualizing the election. Trump's failure to respond to the exigencies posed by COVID-19 surely did not help his reelection efforts. Partly, it was because of his opponent. In 2020 Trump ran against a mild-mannered, older white man with many friends inside the Republican Party and not against a woman who had for decades been demonized by members of that party. Biden had the strong and committed support of the Democratic Party and of Senator Bernie Sanders. And he had Kamala Harris, a woman of color as his running mate, a fact that galvanized communities of color. Trump was unable to gain the kind of leverage against the Biden/Harris team that he had against Clinton/Kaine four years earlier. Partly, too, it was because of the nature of his governance. Trump's administration was divisive and fractious; members of his party seemed determined to avoid compromise and to antagonize Democrats on every front. Trump refused to reach across the partisan aisle or to reach out to the public beyond his base, and so those who might have merely opposed him became committed to his defeat. Trump's loss thus may also be because of the nature of despicable discourse when it becomes the discourse of governance.

Despicable discourse sometimes—but not always—contributes to electoral victories. But most presidents who win after circulating such discourse have historically made efforts to govern, at least ostensibly, as presidents of all the people. Trump made no such pretense. He spoke to his base; he enabled the worst elements of that base. And despite revelations and events that might well have destroyed any other president, his base remained loyal. But it did not expand because politics based on exclusion are, by definition, unable to expand, unable to accommodate, unable to adapt. Despicable discourses are sometimes effective when applied to the narrow context of a campaign. At least since the 1960s, previous presidents who have relied on such discourses have generally realized, consciously or not, the limitations of such discourses, understood their inappropriateness and inapplicability to the unique office of the presidency, and have eschewed them once in office, even if their policies fell far short of inclusion.

Because they have governed from an ostensibly expansive space, these presidents added to their rhetorical arsenals. They developed ways of appealing to those voters who may not have initially supported them. They developed administrative tools of incumbency, with all the power that implies, to craft governing as well as electoral coalitions. Trump made other choices. He was left in 2020 with only a limited rhetorical vocabulary, a limited number of appeals. This is why he sometimes seemed to be still running against Clinton in 2020; he never moved forward as president and so was stuck in an old pattern.

But that pattern was one that in 2020 just enough white Americans found unacceptable. As he became ever more obviously committed to despicable politics as a matter of policy and not just electoral politics, it became harder for many white voters to hide behind the pretense that these policies were incidental rather than integral to Trump's political project. Even those who could accommodate those policies were sometimes unsettled by the sheer chaos that surrounded the president. Approve of him or not, few presidents have proven to be as exhausting as Donald Trump. In the end, he became one of the very few presidents to lose the popular vote twice, and also one of the few incumbents to lose his bid for reelection. He is the only president to have been twice impeached. Trump was defeated in 2020. But as the attack on the Capitol so horrifyingly illustrates, his despicable discourses linger and may be reinvigorated by a candidate with a less abrasive personal style and a less chaotic mode of behavior. Those discourses did not originate with Donald Trump and will not go away on their own.

CONCLUSION: IN SEARCH OF POLITICAL HOPE

Donald Trump's election in 2016 was made possible by weak institutions and a political culture that had been feeding on despicable discourses—primarily from the right—for decades. That discourse resonated amid the changes caused by a globalized economy, causing many white Americans to search for a scapegoat. They blamed the federal government, they blamed people of color, and they blamed immigrants. Trump articulated those fears and the anger that accompanied them, and without ever having the support of a majority of Americans, he nevertheless became their president. There is evidence that substantial numbers of white Americans may have been troubled by the deportment and inefficiency of the messenger during the Trump presidency; there is much less evidence that the message itself bothered them to the same degree. It is notable, for example, that Marjorie Taylor Greene, who supports the conspiracy theories of QAnon, won a congressional seat in Georgia, even as the state turned blue.

Trump was a product of and affected the system and the political culture in which it is embedded. He aligned issues with how many white Americans think about national politics along at least three dimensions: political inclusion, political institutions, and political processes, all of which are relevant to the nation's ability to stave off future deplorable elections. The 2020 election was deplorable, and it signaled the likely continuance of bitter partisanship and division. It also indicated the places where change is necessary.

Political Inclusion

First, Trump's brand of overtly exclusionary politics forced at least some white Americans to acknowledge the structural biases inherent in the US political system as those exclusions galvanized people of color to act in their own defense through peaceful demonstrations. The string of well-publicized police murders of Black people and the resulting marches and protests, the publication of *The 1619 Project*, and the continuing evidence of economic inequality all forced attention on the ways in which some Americans have been and continue to be excluded. Joe Biden's ability to take second chair to an African American president and his choice of a Black woman as his vice-presidential running mate are powerful symbols of the possibilities of inclusion. But that inclusion needs to extend deeper and more broadly into the US polity. White Americans must interrogate national history and learn from the work of people like Ibram X. Kendi; to strive not to be less racist but to be actively antiracist.[39] It means that white people have to engage with enough "intelligent self-interest" to stop consuming and circulating racist ideas and engaging in racist practices.[40] This is not a matter of "better education," although education on such matters must also be improved, but a question of changing patterns of racial discrimination and of reforming political institutions. White Americans have long claimed that equity and social justice lie at the heart of their national politics. White Americans should put them at the heart of national policy making.

Despicable discourses are in some ways quite alluring. The world is a complicated place, and being able to place praise and blame in simple terms and on clearly identifiable sets of people is singularly satisfying. Appeals based on blaming, resenting, and excluding others validate feelings of being embattled and fears of loss. There is comfort here, even as it ratchets up anger and bitterness. But these politics are inimical to democracy. By creating anger and resentment against government, government is less able to help those in considerable need.

Hyperpartisanship is also appealing. As institutions, for instance, the political parties may be weak, but as ideological structures, they remain important guides to attitudes and action.[41] The danger of this hyperpartisanship is that it delegitimates the opposition, as voters are quick to see the members of the opposite party not as wrong but as evil. Partisan feelings tend to tilt more toward the negative than to the positive, and it becomes more important to oppose the other party than to support the goals of one's own. Voters don't necessarily listen to elites, and elites can afford to ignore one another.[42] This means that the political process itself becomes less stable, more susceptible to despicable discourses. This will not be remedied unless white Americans both think and act based on a meaningful consideration of inclusion.

The sharp distinctions between the way law enforcement handled the January 6, 2021, assault on the Capitol and its previous treatment of protests involving people of color rendered systemic discrimination appallingly visible. Biden's appointment of Merrick Garland as attorney general, his other appointments in the Department of Justice (DOJ), and his assertion of commitment to civil rights as central to the DOJ's mission are encouraging signs.[43] Attitudes follow policy; putting more equitable policy in place is imperative.

Political Policy

A focus on inclusion means that different kinds of issues need to be placed at the center of political debate. Questions about the role and duty of government are always on the table, but in the aftermath of the pandemic and the resulting economic dislocations, and especially given the attack on the Capitol, they take on new urgency. Policies such as a guaranteed basic income, more widely available health care, and so on have attained a primacy they should not lose. The long history of deplorable elections indicates the ways in which white Americans need to feel secure. All citizens want to feel a certain economic security, but the nation's history of genocide, colonialism, racism, slavery, and patriarchy has created a complicated web of hierarchies and entitlements. When one's position on those hierarchies is threatened, people can become more open to the lure of despicable discourse. Class is always present in American politics but is rarely overtly acknowledged.[44] Making deplorable elections less likely means disentangling those webs of social, political, and economic hierarchies and focusing attention on the structures of power rather than the competing claims of groups who are fighting for small slices of access to it. Despicable discourses reside in the exploitation of that competition and the masking of those structures.

The analyses of the book and the specific example of Donald Trump indicate the ways in which nostalgia is pernicious and memory is perilous. Despicable discourses often harken back to other days, when the nation was more united, less troubled, when politics was less divisive, and when all Americans enjoyed the fruits of prosperity. These days never actually existed, and yearning for them is only possible if the pain and suffering of many people is erased or ignored. "National" prosperity has always centered on a relatively few Americans, and others have borne the brunt of its costs. Refusing to acknowledge those realities means that white Americans misunderstand national history and are unable to build on it.

The assault on the Capitol on January 6, 2021, demonstrated again that aggrieved entitlement is not necessarily a product of actual economic deprivation but derives from a belief that one's place in the cultural hierarchy is threatened. It also demonstrated again the power of appeals to such aggrieved entitlement. Those demonstrations have made the actual inequities of the system broadly visible; it is important to continue to make those inequities visible and the subject of political action. Neither of these things are likely within existing institutional conditions.

Political Institutions

Political structures themselves must change. Those structures have lost a great deal of legitimacy. In 2020 concerns emerged over whether the US Senate or the Electoral College can ever be made equitable, over which political party is more responsible for "packing" the nation's courts, over institutionalized voter suppression and gerrymandering, over whether to instantiate term limits, reform the Senate, expand the House of Representatives, or increase the number of states. Those concerns and others like them indicate that the crisis of legitimacy will only deepen. To restore faith in the political system, reforms must be extensive. Providing equality of individual voters needs to be the guiding principle of our politics. The Voting Rights Act should be restored; the drawing of legislative districts should be turned over to bipartisan commissions; the Electoral College needs to be eliminated; campaign reform is needed, and *Citizens United* should be overturned; internal processes within the Senate and House may need to be rethought. The system as a whole needs to be protected from foreign and domestic manipulation. These reforms can also be focused on the local, changing politics in the places and through the institutions that have the most effect on the most people.

Consideration about the extent and nature of presidential power is also important. Presidential elections are consequential. But concentrating on the presidency is contrary to the constitutional design of the political system, which requires a strong legislative body. To the extent that the federal political system is broken, part of that brokenness lies at the door of those who would grant unilateral power to the chief executive. Trump's example indicates the dangers of reliance on a too-personalized presidency. If checks and balances are to work, there needs to be a strong and an ethical Congress, one that is willing to defend its prerogatives.

The US media bear no small part of the responsibility for the current state of the nation's politics; the tendency toward "both-sidesism" and the reluctance to label despicable discourses for what they are, on the part of some media, allowed those discourses a foothold in the polity. The fact that social media platforms only banned Donald Trump after he overtly colluded in insurrection is telling. The journalistic commitment to covering the horse race rather than policy commitments and their consequences has contributed to a cynical and poorly informed mass public. And the pernicious reporting of Fox News, with its willingness to support and circulate the most despicable and misleading versions of political events, is answerable for much of the dysfunction on the right. That it is one of the more temperate outlets now developing on the right is disturbing. That ecology has to be disrupted as a precondition for meaningful political change.

As national institutions are imperiled, and voters are increasingly siloed and unwilling to talk to one another, much less compromise with one another, as the uneven effects of the economic downturn and recovery continue to cause real material harm and foster status anxiety, and as elites, especially those on the right, remain willing to offer despicable discourses that divide the nation, creating breaches that become ever more difficult to repair, as aggrieved citizens on the right are willing to commit violence rather than concede defeat, it is hard to see where the nation might find political hope. In a very different context, Cheryl Glenn follows Cornel West in arguing that hope is different from optimism.[45] Optimism, both scholars argue, is based on available evidence that things are actually likely to get better. Hope, on the other hand, is based on the commitment to creating new possibilities in the face of evidence that things are not, in fact, likely to get better. While Glenn does not say so, there is an implied argument here that optimism is easy; hope, on the other hand, is hard. It requires facing the difficult truth that your actions may not make a difference and that the world may remain unyielding. And it requires the commitment to act, and to act ethically, anyway.

There is evidence that cultural predispositions, once formed, are very difficult to alter. Alterations are, however, most likely to occur when the culture hits a crisis point.[46] Deplorable elections contain entailments that may pose just such crisis points. This means that in the period immediately following such an election, change may be possible. The United States is, Nancy Isenberg writes, "a country that imagines itself as democratic and yet the majority has never cared much for equality."[47] That truth undergirded the January 6 insurrection, and if the nation is to continue, it will have to change. No nation has ever successfully constructed a polity based on multiethnic democracy, but if the nation is to survive, white people will have to commit to that endeavor.

In 2020 the United States did not choose a path that unequivocally endorsed systemic change on the valences of political inclusion, governmental policy, or institutional structures. Many white Americans again endorsed the politics of exclusion, and the politics of the Electoral College nearly allowed for yet another election in which the winner of the popular vote lost the White House. Just enough of those citizens were disenchanted just enough with the messenger to remove him from the White House. But the power of despicable discourses and partisan commitments to those who purvey them continues to exercise a strong hold on the politics of the United States. If there is to be political hope, it will originate not in the nation's capital but in the nation's citizenry and in the politics they demand.

NOTES

INTRODUCTION

1. Jon Meacham makes a similar point; see Meacham, *Soul of America*, 5.

2. Katie Reilly, "Read Hillary Clinton's 'Basket of Deplorables' Remarks About Donald Trump's Supporters," *Time*, September 10, 2016, https://time.com/4486502/hillary-clinton-basket-of-deplorables-transcript.

3. On the role of race in US history, see Kendi, *Stamped from the Beginning*.

4. On Trump and the media, see Azari, "How the News Media Helped"; Kellner, *American Nightmare*; Wells et al., "How Trump Drove Coverage."

5. For an evocative and painful discussion of race prior to the founding, see *The 1619 Project*, https://www.nytimes.com/interactive/2019/08/14/magazine/1619-america-slavery.html. For a discussion of the Founders and race, see, among many others, Franklin, "Moral Legacy."

6. Stuckey, *Defining Americans*.

7. Kendi, *Stamped from the Beginning*, 9.

8. Isenberg, *White Trash*, xv.

9. Ibid., xxii.

10. For more on these myths, see Stuckey, *Political Vocabularies*, chapter 4.

11. Isenberg, *White Trash*, xxvi–xxvii.

12. For a discussion of this point, see Engels, *Politics of Resentment*.

13. Gordon, *Second Coming of the KKK*, 4.

14. Didion, *Political Fictions*, 1.

15. Robin, *Reactionary Mind*, 23.

16. Meiley, "Agency Panic," 62.

17. Robin, *Reactionary Mind*, 100.

18. Anderson, *White Rage*.

19. Hochschild, *Strangers in Their Own Land*, chapter 9.

20. Weston, *Political Brain*, 3.

21. For work on how this works regarding race, see Entman and Rojecki, *Black Image in the White Mind*.

22. Franklin, "*Birth of a Nation*," 21–22.

23. Weston, *Political Brain*, 219–26.

24. Burke, *Rhetoric of Motives*, 187.

25. Robin, *Reactionary Mind*, 7.

26. See Young, *Irony and Outrage*.

27. Cisneros, "Contaminated Communities"; O'Brien, "Indigestible Food."

28. Acharya, Blackwell, and Sen, *Deep Roots*, 5.

29. Ibid., 25.

30. See, for example, Browne, *First Inauguration*; Hoffman, *Popular Leadership in the Presidency*.

31. For discussions of his celebrity, see Donald, *Lion in the White House*, 237–38; O'Toole, *When Trumpets Call*, 16–18; Thompson, *Theodore Roosevelt Abroad*, 27.

32. Wright, *Star Power*.

33. Jarvis and Hahn, *Votes That Count*.

34. On the argumentative structure of threat appeals, see Dillard and Shen, "Threat Appeals as Multi-Emotion Messages."

35. See Tannenbaum et al., "Appealing to Fear." See also the literature summarized in Shen and Dillard, "Threat, Fear, and Persuasion." See also Dillard, "Rethinking the Study of Fear Appeals."

36. See Dillard and Li, "How Scary Are Threat Appeals?"

37. See, for example, Kam and Estes, "Disgust Sensitivity."

38. On Trump and the politics of fear, see Stephanie Ann Martin, "In the Wake of Tragedy, Trump Takes Rhetoric of Fear to a Whole New Level," The Conversation, June 15, 2016, https://theconversation.com/in-the-wake-of-tragedy-trump-takes-rhetoric-of-fear-to-a-whole-new-level-61069.

39. The appellation is a nod to the power of white supremacy. See Coates, "It Was No Compliment."

CHAPTER 1

1. See Geggus, *Impact of the Haitian Revolution*.

2. Franklin, "Moral Legacy," 161.
3. Durden, *Self-Inflicted Wound*, 1–3.
4. See Dahl, *Empire of the People.*
5. Acharya, Blackwell, and Sen, *Deep Roots*, 25.
6. Ferling, *Adams vs. Jefferson*, 14–15.
7. Larson, *Magnificent Catastrophe*, 10.
8. Ekrich, *American Sanctuary*, 112.
9. Ibid. See also Sharp, *Deadlocked Election*, 21.
10. Alexander Hamilton, "The Reynolds Pamphlet," July 1797, in Freeman, *Essential Hamilton*, 293.
11. Ekrich, *American Sanctuary*, 111–12; Sharp, *Deadlocked Election*, xi.
12. Ekrich, *American Sanctuary*, 168.
13. Larson, *Magnificent Catastrophe*, 21.
14. "Political Miscellany: To the Republican Citizens of the State of Pennsylvania," *The Bee* 111, no. 144 (September 17, 1800–October 8, 1800): 1–2.
15. Cunningham, "Election of 1800," 45–46.
16. Alexander Hamilton to Theodore Sedgwick, February 2, 1799, in Freeman, *Essential Hamilton*, 321.
17. Ibid.
18. Freeman, "Introduction," xiv.
19. Larson, *Magnificent Catastrophe*, 74.
20. Cunningham, "Election of 1800," 47.
21. Ekrich, *American Sanctuary*, 119.
22. All thirteen Assembly seats went to Republicans in an upset. Larson, *Magnificent Catastrophe*, 87–104.
23. Cunningham, "Election of 1800," 50.
24. Laracey, *Informing a Nation*, 4.
25. Sharp, *Deadlocked Election*, 105.
26. "To the People of New Jersey, Friends, Countrymen, and Fellow Citizens," *Centennial of Freedom* 5, no. 3 (October 14, 1800): page supplement, 1.
27. Ferling, *Adams vs. Jefferson*, 140.
28. Larson, *Magnificent Catastrophe*, 216.
29. Quoted in Ferling, *Adams vs. Jefferson*, 140.
30. Alexander Hamilton to Theodore Sedgwick, May 10, 1800, in Freeman, *Essential Hamilton*, 327.
31. Ibid.
32. Sharp, *Deadlocked Election*, 104.
33. Ibid.
34. Dickerson, *Whistlestop*, 289.
35. On the first point, see Cunningham, "Election of 1800," 54; on the second, 55.
36. "Thomas Jefferson," *Maryland Herald and Hagers-Town Weekly Advertiser* (published as the *Maryland Herald and Elizabeth-Town Advertiser*) 4, no. 184 (September 4, 1800): 1.
37. Ibid.
38. Ibid.
39. Ibid.
40. "Political Miscellany: To the Republican Citizens of the State of Pennsylvania," *The Bee* 111, no. 144 (September 17, 1800–October 8, 1800): 1–2.
41. Laracey, *Informing a Nation*, 9–10.
42. Ibid., 8–9.
43. Quoted in Laracey, *Informing a Nation*, 22.
44. Sharp, *Deadlocked Election*, 3–4.
45. Ibid., 92.
46. Alexander Hamilton to Gouverneur Morris, December 26, 1801, in Freeman, *Essential Hamilton*, 331.
47. Alexander Hamilton to John Rutledge, Jr., January 4, 1801, in Freeman, *Essential Hamilton*, 333.
48. Ibid., 334.
49. Ibid.
50. Alexander Hamilton to James A. Bayard, January 16, 1801, in Freeman, *Essential Hamilton*, 336.
51. Ibid.
52. Ibid., 337.
53. For more detail on the Panic of 1837, see Cheathem, *Coming of Democracy*, 122–25.
54. Heale, *Presidential Quest*, 35.
55. O'Reilly, *Nixon's Piano*, 31.
56. For details on the *Amistad* case, see https://www.archives.gov/education/lessons/amistad.
57. Takaki, *Different Mirror*, 82–83.
58. After commenting on the numbers of Indians already removed west of the Mississippi, he noted in his fourth annual message that, "The emigration of the Seminoles alone has been attended with serious difficulty and occasional bloodshed, hostilities having been commenced by the Indians in Florida under the apprehension that they would be compelled by force to comply with their treaty stipulations . . . having been defeated in every engagement

[the Seminole] dispersed in small bands throughout the country and became an enterprising, formidable, and ruthless banditti." Martin Van Buren, "Fourth Annual Message," December 5, 1840, 602–20, in Richardson, *Compilation*, 616–17.

59. Kendi, *Stamped from the Beginning*, 171.

60. Martin Van Buren, "To the Senate of the United States," January 13, 1840, 561–66, in Richardson, *Compilation*, 561.

61. See among many others, Dippie, *Vanishing Indian*.

62. This "two-thirds rule" led to serious problems for the Democrats in several elections and was finally abolished in 1936.

63. Cheathem, *Coming of Democracy*, 128.

64. Ibid., 2.

65. The platform can be found here: https://www.presidency.ucsb.edu/documents/1840-democratic-party-platform.

66. Many members of the Liberty Party became first Free Soilers and then Republicans, illustrating how political systems disintegrate and reform.

67. Cheathem, *Coming of Democracy*, 134.

68. Ibid., 2–3.

69. Heale, *Presidential Quest*, 106.

70. Cheathem, *Coming of Democracy*, 1.

71. Ibid., 154.

72. Ibid., 164.

73. "Great Meeting of Merchants," *Commercial Advertiser* (New York), April 9, 1839, 2.

74. "New Jersey Convention," *Centinel of Freedom* (Newark, NJ), November 19, 1839, vol. 43, no. 20, p. 1.

75. Quoted from the New Orleans *Sun* in "Harrison and Clay," page [2] iss. 17, vol. 10, June 12, 1839, *Indiana Democrat*.

76. Van Buren, "Fourth Annual Message," 602.

77. Cheathem, *Coming of Democracy*, 175.

78. Franklin, "As for Our History," 60–61.

79. Address of the Republican Convention, to the People of Virginia, page 1, 2, March 23, 1839, *Enquirer*, Richmond, Virginia. All quotations in this paragraph come from this source.

80. Franklin "Southern Expansionists," 104.

81. Isenberg, *White Trash*, 1.

82. Ibid., 129.

83. Skowronek, *Politics Presidents Make*, 177.

84. For a thorough discussion of his administration, see Gara, *Presidency of Franklin Pierce*.

85. Kendi, *Stamped from the Beginning*, 187–88.

86. Isenberg, *White Trash*, 136.

87. Ibid., 143.

88. "Presidential Speculations," *New York Daily Times*, March 25, 1852, 2. Articles from the *New York Daily Times* and *New York Times* have been accessed through the ProQuest Historical Newspapers database.

89. Ibid.

90. Ibid.

91. "Presidential—The Whig Nomination," *New York Daily Times*, May 7, 1852, 2.

92. "Presidential," *New York Daily Times*, June 8, 1852, 2.

93. Henry J. Raymond, "The Campaign Times: A Cheap Whig Paper for the Presidential Canvass," *New York Daily Times*, June 8, 1852, 3.

94. "The Whig Platform," *New York Daily Times*, July 1, 1852, 2.

95. "Southern Rights," *New York Daily Times*, April 10, 1852, 2.

96. "Southern Fanaticism," *New York Daily Times*, April 15, 1852, 2.

97. Ibid.

98. "Washington: Calumnies Against General Scott—Billy Bow Legs and the . . . Correspondence of the *New-York Daily Times*," *New York Daily Times*, September 21, 1852, 6.

99. Ibid.

100. "Presidential: Eloquent Letter from Senator Badger," *New York Daily Times*, September 30, 1852, 6.

101. "Irish Voters for Scott and Graham," *New York Daily Times*, October 11, 1852, 1.

102. Ibid.

103. Skowronek, *Politics Presidents Make*, 181.

CHAPTER 2

1. Morris, *Fraud of the Century*, 5.

2. Polakoff, *Politics of Inertia*, x–xi.

3. Broomall, "Personal Reconstructions," 112.

4. Lee, "Antithesis," 152.

5. Durden, *Self-Inflicted Wound*, 107.

6. Fitzgerald, *Splendid Failure*, 46.

7. Quoted in Wilson, *Reconstruction Desegregation Debate*, 47.

8. Langguth, *After Lincoln*, 108.

9. Ibid., 276.

10. On the *Slaughterhouse Cases*, see Labbe and Lurie, *Slaughterhouse Cases*. On the *Santa Clara* case, see Winkler, *We the Corporations*.

11. Wilson, *Reconstruction Desegregation Debate*, 13.

12. Woodward, *Reunion and Reaction*, 15.

13. Beatty, *Age of Betrayal*.

14. For a history of the first KKK, see Parsons, *Ku-Klux*.

15. Morris, *Fraud of the Century*, 33.

16. Beatty, *Age of Betrayal*, 212.

17. Ibid., 114.

18. Holt, *By One Vote*, 46.

19. Ibid., 47.

20. Woodward, *Strange Case of Jim Crow*, 33.

21. Axelrod, *Gilded Age*, 8; Beatty, *Age of Betrayal*, 25.

22. See, among many others, Dunbar-Ortiz, *Indigenous Peoples' History*.

23. His image has, however, been at least partly redeemed. See Chernow, *Grant*.

24. Langguth, *After Lincoln*, 297–99.

25. Polakoff, *Politics of Inertia*, 180.

26. Ibid., 15.

27. "The Political Situation," *New York Times*, February 22, 1876, 2.

28. "Indiana Politics: The Approaching Campaign, Failure of the Greenback," *New York Times*, February 20, 1876, 1.

29. "National Colored Convention," *New York Times*, April 8, 1876, 1.

30. "Republican Reformers," *New York Times*, June 7, 1876, 1.

31. Ibid.

32. Ibid.

33. The *New York Sun* headline read, "Blaine Feigns a Faint." See Morris, *Fraud of the Century*, 56.

34. Robert Ingersoll, Nomination of James Blaine, https://www.bartleby.com/268/10/8.html. All quotations from the speech come from this source.

35. Blaine moved from the House to the Senate in 1876; he served five years there before leaving to become secretary of state in 1881. He continued to seek the presidency, winning the nomination in 1884 and losing in that year to Democrat Grover Cleveland.

36. Editorial article 1—no title, *New York Times*, January 14, 1876, 4.

37. "The Political Situation," *New York Times*, February 22, 1876, 2.

38. "Address of Frederick Douglass: Further Protection Demanded," *New York Times*, June 15, 1876, 2.

39. "Address of Theodore M. Pomeroy," *New York Times*, June 15, 1876, 2. All following quotations are from this source.

40. "True Republican Manliness," *New York Times*, June 17, 1876, 1. See also "Response of the Country," *New York Times*, June 17, 1876, 1.

41. "Nomination of Rutherford B. Hayes," *New York Times*, June 16, 1876, 3. There were also biographical sketches of the Republican nominees: "The Standard Bearers: Biographical Sketch of the Republican Candidates," *San Francisco Chronicle*, June 17, 1876, 3, accessed through the ProQuest Historical Newspapers database.

42. "The Press Response," *New York Times*, June 18, 1876, 7.

43. "Gov Hayes: How He Was Received," *Chicago Daily Tribune*, June 20, 1876, 3, accessed through the ProQuest Historical Newspapers database.

44. "The Wife and Children of Gov Hayes," *Chicago Daily Tribune*, July 1, 1876, 6, accessed through the ProQuest Historical Newspapers database.

45. Polakoff, *Politics of Inertia*, 34.

46. Ibid., 61.

47. This cut both ways. Supporters of Tammany Hall disapproved of Tilden because of his attacks on the machine. Its detractors disapproved because his attacks didn't come soon enough. See "Tilden and Tammany," *New York Times*, November 3, 1874, 5; "Mr. Tilden and the Tweed Ring," *New York Times*, October 24, 1874, 6.

48. For a brief overview of Tilden's career, see Morris, *Fraud of the Century*, 94–107.

49. Ibid., 125–26. "Copperheadism" refers to "Copperheads," Northern Democrats

who opposed the war and wanted a settlement with the South.

50. "The St. Louis Convention: Fierce and Riotous Contests," *New York Times*, June 26, 1876, 1.

51. "The St. Louis Convention: New York the Pivotal Point," *New York Times*, June 27, 1876, 1.

52. Ibid.

53. "The Wrangling Factions: Rough Words and Acts," *New York Times*, June 28, 1876, 1.

54. "Tilden Nominated," *New York Times*, June 29, 1876, 1.

55. "How the Thing Was Done," *New York Times*, June 29, 1876, 1.

56. "Speech of Hon. S. S. Cox," *New York Times*, June 28, 1876, 2. All quotations come from this source.

57. Ibid.

58. The Battle of the Greasy Grass, also known as "Custer's Last Stand," took place a few days before this speech.

59. Polakoff, *Politics of Inertia*, 89.

60. Holt, *By One Vote*, 124.

61. "Address of Col. Ingersoll," *New York Times*, September 12, 1876, 1.

62. "The Republican Party: Speech of Hon. Stewart L. Woodford," *New York Times*, July 1, 1876, 2.

63. "Speech of Hon. Chauncey M. DePew," *New York Times*, November 5, 1876, 5.

64. "Tilden's War Record," *New York Times*, July 6, 1876, 5.

65. "Mr. Tilden as a Secessionist," *New York Times*, July 11, 1876, 5. All quotations come from this source.

66. Quoted in Woodward, *Reunion and Reaction*, 23.

67. "Address of Col. Ingersoll," *New York Times*, September 12, 1876, 1.

68. "Tilden and Hendricks," *New York Times*, June 30, 1876, 4.

69. *Carnival of blood! Republicans to be massacred at the polls! Secret Democratic circular. Tilden's desparate plan to carry a solid South . . . New York*. New York, 1876. Pdf. https://www.loc.gov/item/rbpe.12804700. All quotations come from this source.

70. "Address of Col. Ingersoll," *New York Times*, September 12, 1876, 1.

71. "How Southern Interests Will Be Advanced," *New York Times*, October 21, 1876, 8.

72. Morris, *Fraud of the Century*, 140.

73. Holt, *By One Vote*, 167.

74. Morris, *Fraud of the Century*, 12.

75. "A Few Plain Words," *New York Times*, November 18, 1876, 3.

76. "Louisiana: The Meeting of the Electoral College Attempt to Bribe," *New York Times*, December 7, 1876, 5. See also Charles River Editors, *The Election of 1876*, paragraph 17.

77. Charles River Editors, *The Election of 1876*, paragraph 18.

78. "The Long Agony: A Review," *Chicago Daily Tribune*, March 3, 1877, 4, accessed through the ProQuest Historical Newspapers database.

79. Axelrod, *Gilded Age*, 2.

80. Beatty, *Age of Betrayal*, 192.

CHAPTER 3

1. Murray, *103rd Ballot*, xiii; for another characterization of the convention as political suicide, see Sobel, *Coolidge*, 292–93.

2. McCoy, *Calvin Coolidge*, 130.

3. Fall became the first cabinet official to go to prison for misconduct while in office.

4. For a succinct account of these scandals, see among many others, Greenberg, *Calvin Coolidge*, 49–52.

5. Kendi, *Stamped from the Beginning*, 313–14. See also Brinkley, *Unfinished Nation*, 628.

6. Kendi, *Stamped from the Beginning*, 323; Anderson, *White Rage*, 3.

7. Brinkley, *Unfinished Nation*, 643.

8. There were actually several pieces of legislation: in 1921, there was the Emergency Immigration Act, the Immigration Restriction Act, the Per Centum Law, and the Johnson Quota Act. Together, they imposed numerical limits and quotas based on national origin on immigration to the United States. The year 1924 saw the passage of the Immigration Act, the Asian Exclusion Act, and the National Origins Act, which together banned immigration from Asia and strictly limited immigration from the

Eastern hemisphere, and provided mechanisms for enforcing these proscriptions.

9. Franklin, "*Birth of a Nation*," 20.

10. Meacham, *Soul of America*, 110.

11. Gordon, *Second Coming of the KKK*, 2. See also Brinkley, *Unfinished Nation*, 645.

12. Murray, *103rd Ballot*, 14. For an example of how this dominance was understood at the time, see "Indiana Swayed Entirely by Klan: Hooded Forces' Domination There," *New York Times*, November 7, 1923, 15; "Klan Candidates Swept Ohio Cities: Lost Only in Steubenville," *New York Times*, November 8, 1923, 1; L. C. Speers, "Klan Shadow Falls on Nation's Politics: Hooded Band Sways Elections," *New York Times*, November 18, 1923, XX3.

13. See Burnham, *Critical Elections*; Sundquist, *Dynamics of the Party System*.

14. Takaki, *Different Mirror*, 307.

15. On the speculation surrounding his campaign, see Richard Barry, "Ford's Presidential Plan Defies Political Canons," *New York Times*, October 28, 1923, XX1.

16. McCoy, *Calvin Coolidge*, 244; Sobel, *Coolidge*, 285. Leopold and Loeb were two University of Chicago students who kidnapped and murdered a fourteen-year-old boy in an effort to commit the "perfect crime." Clarence Darrow was their attorney. For details, see Baatz, *For the Thrill of It*.

17. "Republican Platform to Be Long Document," *New York Times*, May 30, 1924, 17; "Klan and Dry Issues Worry Republicans," *New York Times*, June 8, 1924, 1.

18. "Text of the Keynote Speech by Representative Burton at Cleveland," *New York Times*, June 11, 1924, 6. All following quotations are from this source.

19. "Wet Democrats See Big Chance in 1924," *New York Times*, April 13, 1923, 1; "Democrats Face Two Big Issues: Klan and Prohibition Are Expected," *New York Times*, May 19, 1924, 19.

20. The intraparty differences were noticeably difficult to reconcile. See, for example, the letter written to Al Smith from Franklin R. Patterson, of Florence Alabama, dated June 10, 1924, which praises the governor for his anti-Klan stance, and offers hopes that an anti-Klan plank will be adopted by the convention. It also, however, notes that the author "cannot support you in your drive against Prohibition." Franklin D. Roosevelt, Campaign of 1924, Comm. For Smith Nom., Alabama-Maryland, Cont. 1, "Alabama," Franklin D. Roosevelt Presidential Library, Hyde Park, NY.

21. See, for example, "Anti-M'Adoo Block of 400 Is Claimed," *New York Times*, May 25, 1924, E1.

22. "Two-Thirds Rule to Stand," *New York Times*, June 19, 1924, 1.

23. As one scholar puts it, "Each candidate had support other than the Tammanies and the Klansmen, but to the Klansmen it seemed that Smith, the Roman Catholic, was the candidate of the big cities and to Smith's supporters McAdoo represented the bigotry of the anti-Catholic, anti-Jewish, and Prohibition forces. White, *Puritan in Babylon*, 307.

24. Letter from John J. O'Connor to James J. Hoey, May 28, 1924, Franklin D. Roosevelt, Campaign of 1924, Comm. for Smith Nom., Alabama-Maryland, Cont. 1, "DC," Franklin D. Roosevelt Presidential Library.

25. Telegram from Jos Johnson to James J. Hoey, undated, Franklin D. Roosevelt, Campaign of 1924, Comm. for Smith Nom., Alabama-Maryland, Cont. 1, "Florida-Georgia," Franklin D. Roosevelt Presidential Library.

26. Oscar Underwood, "Underwood Sees Klan as Chief Issue: Urges Democrats to Fight Invisible Empire and Asks Party to Re-enact the Platform of 1856 Denouncing Racial and Religious Intolerance," *New York Times*, June 8, 1924, Franklin D. Roosevelt, Campaign of 1924, Comm. for Nomination of Smith for President,—Corres. "Delaware and Dist. Of Columbia," Franklin D. Roosevelt Presidential Library.

27. Oscar W. Underwood, senator from Alabama, "Underwood Sees Klan as Chief Issue," *New York Times*, June 8, 1924, XX4.

28. Underwood retired from the Senate in 1926 and died in 1929.

29. In fact, they tried to keep the convention from being held there. See "M'Adoo's Backers to Bar New York as Convention City," *New York Times*, January 14, 1924, 1.

30. "Text of Senator Harrison's Keynote Speech Before the Democratic Convention," *New York Times*, June 25, 1924, 6. All following quotations are from this source.

31. Elmer Davis, "Outburst Beats M'Addo's," *New York Times*, June 27, 1924, 1.

32. M'Adoo to Fight Anti-Klan Plank," *New York Times*, June 20, 1924, 2.

33. Richard V. Oulahan, "Storm Over Klan Menacing," *New York Times*, June 28, 1924, 1; for details on the platform, see "Text of Platform as Presented to the Democratic National Convention," *New York Times*, June 29, 1924, 4.

34. For the full text of that speech, see "Text of W. J. Bryan's Speech That Aroused a Great Storm: Stenographic," *New York Times*, July 3, 1924, 1.

35. Quoted in Boyle, *Arc of Justice*, 9.

36. Murray, *103rd Ballot*, 159; see also "Burst of Night Activity Rouses Delegates from Inertia of Day . . ." *New York Times*, July 4, 1924, 1.

37. The final vote on that plank was as close as math could make it: 542.15 in favor, 546.15 opposed (the fractions are the result of severely split state delegations). Gordon, *Second Coming of the KKK*, 169. See also "Anti-Klan Men Lost by 4.30 Vote Margin," *New York Times*, June 30, 1924, 1.

38. "Democratic Convention to Be Radiated by Twenty Stations," *New York Times*, June 22, 1924, XX16.

39. FDR seconded Smith's nomination with the famous "Happy Warrior" speech; see Franklin D. Roosevelt, "Placing in Nomination for the Presidency of the United States, Governor Alfred E. Smith," Democratic National Convention, Madison Square Garden, New York, June, 1924, Vertical File, 1924 Convention, Franklin D. Roosevelt Presidential Library.

40. "Negroes Are Disappointed: National Association Wanted Klan Denounced by Name," *New York Times*, June 30, 1924, 4.

41. "Leaders Acclaim Choice of Davis: See Party United," *New York Times*, July 10, 1924, 1.

42. Robert W. Bonynge, "Election by the House," *New York Times*, April 2, 1924, 18.

43. "Coolidge or Deadlock, Says an Observer," *New York Times*, October 5, 1924, 7; "Coolidge or Bryan Is the Real Issue, Hughes Declares," *New York Times*, October 14, 1924, 1.

44. "Third Party Launched: La Follette Is the Favorite of the New Progressives," *New York Times*, March 19, 1924, 5.

45. "Wheeler with La Follette," *New York Times*, July 21, 1924, 10.

46. Ibid.

47. On his indifference to the Klan, see Murray, *103rd Ballot*, 241. On his opposition to it, see "La Follette Replies to Question of Jews: Restates Opposition to Klan," *New York Times*, September 16, 1924, 2.

48. Murray, *103rd Ballot*, 250.

49. Sobel, *Coolidge*, 300.

50. "Labor Endorses La Follette Ticket but Not the Party," *New York Times*, August 3, 1924, 1.

51. "Third Party Chief Predicts Victory," *New York Times*, August 5, 1924, 1.

52. "La Follette Flails Both Old Parties," *New York Times*, October 9, 1924, 3.

53. "Full Text of La Follette's Speech Attacking Supreme Court," *New York Times*, September 19, 1924, 2. All following quotations come from this source.

54. Murray, *103rd Ballot*, 251.

55. "Big Foes Gone 'Mad,' Wheeler Declares," *New York Times*, October 6, 1924, 3.

56. Murray, *103rd Ballot*, 211.

57. Ferrell, *Presidency of Calvin Coolidge*, 111.

58. This characterization of Coolidge is attributed to Alice Longworth Roosevelt. Sobel, *Coolidge*, 236.

59. "99 Delegates Already Chosen for Coolidge," *New York Times*, March 10, 1924, 2; "Coolidge Has Won Nomination Fight," *New York Times*, April 14, 1924, 1.

60. "Coolidge as Candidate," *New York Times*, June 13, 1924, 18.

61. Coolidge, *Autobiography of Calvin Coolidge*, 189.

62. "Coolidge Decides to Limit Speeches," *New York Times*, September 3, 1924, 3; "Coolidge Rejects Pleas for Speeches," *New York Times*, October 14, 1924, 3.

63. Palmer, *Calvin Coolidge*, 124.

64. Frank R. Kent, "Mr. Coolidge," *American Mercury*, August 1924, Vertical File, Campaign Lit. 1924 Dem "1924 Dem

(3)," Franklin D. Roosevelt Presidential Library, 5.

65. Ibid., 8.

66. "Text of Mr. Coolidge's Address Accepting Party's Nomination," *New York Times*, August 15, 1924, 1. All following quotations are from this source.

67. "Coolidge Assails La Follette Views on Supreme Court," *New York Times*, September 7, 1924, 1; "Stone Dissects La Follette Aims," *New York Times*, October 25, 1924, 8.

68. "Text of Gen. Dawes's Speech Accepting Nomination," *New York Times*, August 20, 1924, 2.

69. Murray, *103rd Ballot*, 238; "Coolidge Plans Campaign by Radio," *New York Times*, July 18, 1924, 3.

70. Ferrell, *Presidency of Calvin Coolidge*, 111.

71. Sobel, *Coolidge*, 303.

72. Ferrell, *Presidency of Calvin Coolidge*, 59.

73. O'Reilly, *Nixon's Piano*, 98.

74. "Negroes Threaten to Bolt on Klan," *New York Times*, September 17, 1924, 2.

75. Coolidge, "Progress of a People."

76. Ibid., 31.

77. Ibid., 32.

78. Ibid.

79. Ibid.

80. Ibid., 34.

81. John W. Davis, "Sea Girt Speech," August 22, 1924, Vertical File, Campaign Lit. 1924 Dem "1924 Dem 4(1)," Franklin D. Roosevelt Presidential Library.

82. Davis, "Sea Girt Speech," 3.

83. Ibid., 5.

84. Ibid., 8.

85. "35,000 Hear Jersey Speech," *New York Times*, August 23, 1924, 1.

86. Campaign pamphlet, Vertical File, Campaign Lit 1924 Dem. Franklin D. Roosevelt Presidential Library.

87. "Gov. Bryan Appeals for Farmer's Votes," *New York Times*, September 2, 1924, 3.

88. "Davis Sees Danger in Present Unrest," *New York Times*, October 19, 1924, 3.

89. "Report and Recommendations" of the Joint Committee Appointed by New York Young Democratic Club and the National League of Young Democrats, to Hon. Clement L. Shaver, Chairman, National Democratic Committee, Vertical File, Campaign Lit. 1924 Dem "Elections US, 1924," Franklin D. Roosevelt Presidential Library.

90. Quoted in Sobel, *Coolidge*, 4.

CHAPTER 4

1. The meeting was secretly taped by the *Miami Herald*. See also Farrell, *Richard Nixon*, 328; Mason, *Richard Nixon*, 29; Nelson, *Resilient America*, 130, 145; O'Reilly, *Nixon's Piano*, 282. For Nixon's more sanitized version of the meeting, see Nixon, *RN*, 305.

2. Nixon speechwriter, conservative commentator, and sometime presidential candidate Pat Buchanan argues that Nixon's ability to conciliate the South had much more to do with a shared contempt "for a liberal press and hypocritical Democratic Party that had coexisted happily with Dixiecrats for a century but got religion when conservative Republicans began to steal the South away from them" than with his positions on segregation and civil rights. He is virtually alone in making this argument. See Buchanan, *Greatest Comeback*, 78–79.

3. Farrell, *Richard Nixon*, 198; Cohen, *American Maelstrom*, 23–28.

4. Phillips, *Emerging Republican Majority*, 25; Witcover, *Year the Dream Died*, 11.

5. Anderson, *White Rage*, 100.

6. Quoted in ibid., 101.

7. Jim Keogh, "Memo to Richard Nixon," September 11, 1968, Campaign 1968, Appearance Files (PPP 140), Box 1, Campaign 1968 Collection, Appearance File 1968, September 11, Durham, NC—Correspondence, RNPL.

8. Cohen, *American Maelstrom*, 239; editing mine.

9. White, *Making of the President, 1968*, 428.

10. William G. Bray to Richard Nixon, September 18, 1968, Campaign 1968, Appearance Files (PPP 140), Box 1, Campaign 1968 Collection, Campaign 1968 Appearance File 1968, September 12,

Indianapolis, IND—Correspondence, Richard M. Nixon Presidential Library (hereinafter RNPL), Yorba Linda, California.

11. Marie Scrivanich Blythe to Richard Nixon, September 18, 1968, Campaign 1968, Appearance Files (PPP 140), Box 1, Campaign 1968 Collection, Appearance File 1968, September 21, Philadelphia, PA, Memos, Gen'l Correspondence, RNPL.

12. For details, see Gervasi, *Real Rockefeller*, 238–39. See also Buchanan, *Greatest Comeback*, 22.

13. Critchlow, *Republican Character*, 50.

14. Nelson A. Rockefeller, "Remarks on Extremism at the 1964 Republican National Convention," San Francisco, CA, July 14, 1964, https://www.c-span.org/video/?c3807346/user-clip-governor-nelson-rockefeller-addresses-64-convention.

15. Zirin, "Ken Burns on Jackie Robinson." For Robinson's own account of that moment, see Robinson, *I Never Had It Made*, 169–70. For another account of the indignities suffered by African Americans at the convention and their reaction to it, see Thimmesch, *Condition of Republicanism*, 58.

16. Smith, *On His Own Terms*, xxi; editing mine.

17. Zirin, "Ken Burns on Jackie Robinson."

18. For details on the Chennault affair, see Cohen, *American Maelstrom*, 322–23; Nelson, *Resilient America*, 213–16; Summers with Swan, *Arrogance of Power*, 297–306; Witcover, *Year the Dream Died*, 443.

19. Transcript of Interview of Richard Nixon with Don McGaffin, KOMO-TV, Seattle, WA, September 24, 1968, Campaign 1968 Collection, Tour Office Files (PPS 200), Box 3, Campaign 1968 Collection, Tour Office Files, Press (1 of 4), RNPL.

20. Franklin, "Great Confrontation," 362.

21. See, for example, the analysis by Charles Bartlett, "Threat of Wallace Forcing Nixon to Shadow Box," *Washington Star*, September 14, 1968, Richard Nixon's Prepresidential Papers 1968 Campaign Research File, Box 110, RN News 9/18–14/68, RNPL.

22. Evidence for this is found in both archival and secondary sources. Nixon's campaign refused, for example, to organize an interview with *New York Times* reporter James (Scotty) Reston, fearing that he wouldn't cover Nixon in the terms his campaign preferred. See John Whitaker, "Memo to Herb Klein," September 5, 1968, Campaign 1968 Collection, Tour Office Files (PPS 200), Box 3, Campaign 1968 Collection, Tour Office Files, Press (1 of 4), RNPL. The classic work on Nixon's media strategy remains McGinnis, *Selling of the President*. See also Buchanan, *Greatest Comeback*, 212; Witcover, *Year the Dream Died*, 69–70. For Nixon's own view of this strategy, see Nixon, *RN*, 304.

23. Nixon, *RN*, 303.

24. Ibid., 304. On "the man in the arena" events, see Farrell, *Richard Nixon*, 339.

25. Kendi, *Stamped from the Beginning*, 410.

26. On Wallace's skill with the dog whistle, see, among others, Dickerson, *Whistlestop*, 371.

27. "Memorandum," Campaign 1968 Collection, Office Files (PPS 200), Box 3, Campaign 1968 Collection, Tour Office Files, Propaganda II (4 of 6), RNPL.

28. For evidence of this thinking, see "Tricia Pool Report," October 8, 1968, Campaign 1968 Appearance Files (PPS 140), Box 3, Campaign 1968, Appearance File 1968, October 8, Flint, MI, RNPL.

29. No author, "Nixon on Civil Rights," For Staff Use Only, Answer Desk, 4 July 1968, Rockefeller Papers, 111 4 G, Box 5, DNA, Notebooks, Youth, Miscellaneous Issues, Nixon on Civil Rights, 111 4G Folder 30, RAC. Folders 32 and 33 contain hundreds of pages of similar opposition research on Nixon.

30. Ibid.

31. Ibid., 1.

32. Ibid., 1.

33. Ibid., 28.

34. Ibid., 60.

35. "Gallup Poll, Northern White Opposition to Speed of Integration Grows," July 19, 1968, Campaign 1968, Research Files, Box 11, Budget Eisenhower Civil Rights, Campaign 1968, Research File 10, Civil Rights—Miscellaneous, RNPL.

36. Wallace, "Campaign Speech," 186.

37. Ibid., 187.

38. Ibid.

39. "Statement of Richard Nixon," June 23, 1968, Campaign 1968 Collection, Office Files, (PPS 200), Box 3, Campaign 1968 Collection, Tour Office Files, Propaganda II (3 of 6), RNPL.

40. Richard Nixon, "Toward Freedom from Fear," Campaign 1968 Collection, Campaign Literature (PPS 148), Box 1, Campaign 1968 Collection, Pamphlet Series (1of 3), RNPL.

41. Richard Nixon, "A New Direction for America's Economy," Campaign 1968 Collection, Tour Office Files (PPS 200), Box 3, A Statement by Richard Nixon, Saturday July 6, 1968, RNPL, 3.

42. Nixon, "Campaign Speech," 164.

43. Kendi, *Stamped from the Beginning*, 401.

44. Churchwell, *Behold, America*, 54.

45. Nixon, "New Direction for America's Economy," 1.

46. One analyst writes that the selection of Agnew "revealed Nixon at his worst." Farrell, *Richard Nixon*, 333.

47. O'Donnell, *Playing with Fire*, 389.

48. O'Reilly, *Nixon's Piano*, 281.

49. Nixon, *RN*, 339.

50. Ibid., 304.

51. "Reagan Positions on Civil Rights with Particular Emphasis on Open Housing," Campaign 1968 Collection, Research Files, Special Files, Ronald Reagan (PPS 501), Box 1, RNPL; "Governor Reagan on Open Housing," Campaign 1968 Collection, Research Files, Special Files, Ronald Reagan (PPS 501), Box 1, RNPL; "The Sell Out of Ronald Reagan and Open Housing," Campaign 1968 Collection, Research Files, Special Files, Ronald Reagan (PPS 501), Box 1, RNPL.

52. See his declaration that he was not a candidate, and also his announcement that he was: Nelson A. Rockefeller, "Statement of Governor Nelson A. Rockefeller," March 21, 1968, Campaign Speeches, Series 33, Box 59, 5/2/68, University of Iowa, Iowa City, Iowa, RAC; Nelson A. Rockefeller, "Statement by Governor Nelson A. Rockefeller," April 30, 1968, Campaign Speeches, Series 33, Box 59, 5/2/68, University of Iowa, Iowa City, Iowa, RAC.

53. Nelson A. Rockefeller, "Excerpt of Remarks at the University of Utah," May 29, 1968, Campaign Speeches, Series 33, Box 59, 5/29/68, Salt Lake City Utah, University of Utah Campus Rally, RAC.

54. Nelson A. Rockefeller, "The Building of a Just World Order," Campaign Speeches, Series 33, Box 59, 5/1/68/, Philadelphia, PA, World Affairs Council of Philadelphia, RAC, 1.

55. Ibid., 6.

56. Nelson A. Rockefeller, "Excerpts of Remarks at Kansas State College, Manhattan, Kansas," May 9, 1968, Campaign Speeches, Series 33, Box 59, 5/2/68, University of Iowa, Iowa City, Iowa, RAC.

57. Nelson A. Rockefeller, "News Conference at Duluth Auditorium, Duluth, MN, June 15, 1968, Campaign Speeches, Series 33, Box 62, Press Conference Transcripts, June 1968, RAC.

58. Rockefeller, "Excerpts of Remarks at the University of Utah."

59. Nelson A. Rockefeller, "Excerpts of Remarks at the University of Minnesota," May 8, 1968, Campaign Speeches, Series 33, Box 59, 5/8/68, Minnesota, RAC.

60. Richard Nixon, "Problems of the Cities," Campaign 1968, Collection, Campaign Literature (PPS 148), Box 1, Campaign 1968, Collection, Pamphlet Series (1 of 3), RNPL.

61. Ibid.

62. O'Donnell, *Playing with Fire*, 304.

63. Nixon, "Acceptance Speech," 154.

64. Ibid., 155.

65. Ibid., 154–55. See also "Excerpts of Remarks by Richard M. Nixon, San Francisco, September 5, 1968, Richard Nixon's Prepresidential Papers 1968 Campaign Research File, Box 110, RN News 9/18–14/68, RNPL.

66. Nixon, Acceptance Speech,"159.

67. Ibid., 156.

68. Ibid., 156–57.

69. Mason, *Richard Nixon*, 28; for a similar analysis, see Wills, *Nixon Agonistes*, 72.

70. Godfrey Sperling Jr., "New Voting Coalition Appears," *Christian Science Monitor*, 14/9, 68, Richard Nixon's Prepresidential Papers 1968 Campaign Research File, Box 110, RN News 9/18–14/68, RNPL.

71. Nixon, "Acceptance Speech," 160.

72. Ibid.

73. Richard Nixon, "Toward Freedom from Fear," Campaign 1968 Collection, Campaign Literature (PPS 148), Box 1, Campaign 1968 Collection, Pamphlet Series (1 of 3), RNPL.

74. Ibid.

75. Ross Wirm and Jack Veneman, "Memo," September 18, 1968, Campaign 1968, Appearance Files (PPP 140), Box 1, Campaign 1968 Collection, Appearance File 1968, September 18, Fresno, CA, RNPL.

76. All quotations in this section come from Rockefeller, "Remarks on Extremism," unless otherwise noted.

77. Vivian, "Witnessing Time"; Vivian, *Commonplace Witnessing.*

78. Rentschler, "Witnessing." Witnessing is especially important to the conservative movement, a point Michael J. Lee makes. See Lee, *Creating Conservatism.*

79. Nelson A. Rockefeller, "Excerpts from a Session of Governor Nelson A. Rockefeller at a Breakfast with Delegates in Hitching Post Motel, Cheyenne, WY, May 29, 1968, Campaign Speeches, Series 33, Box 60, Press Conference Transcripts, April 30–May 68, 1, RAC.

80. Ibid.; see also Nelson A. Rockefeller, "Interview with Governor Nelson A. Rockefeller at Station KTVU in Oakland," June 13, 1968, Campaign Speeches, Series 33, Box 62, Press Conference Transcripts, June 1968, RAC.

81. Nelson A. Rockefeller, "Speech Text," Campaign Speeches, Series 33, Box 61, 6/27/68, Sioux City, Iowa, Rally, RAC.

82. Nelson A. Rockefeller, "Q&A with Governor Nelson A. Rockefeller at the DuPont Hotel, Wilmington, DE, June 22, 1968, Campaign Speeches, Series 33, Box 62, Press Conference Transcripts June 1968, 5, RAC. For Calloway's statement on Rockefeller, see Statement by Howard H. ("Bo") Calloway, Atlanta, Georgia, June 24, 1968, Campaign 1968 Collection, Office Files (PPS 200), Box 3, Campaign 1968 Collection, Tour Office Files, Propaganda II (3 of 6), RNPL.

83. Engels, *Politics of Resentment.*

84. Mason, *Richard Nixon*, 35.

85. "Gallup Poll, Northern White Opposition to Speed of Integration Grows."

86. Murphy and Gulliver, *Southern Strategy*, 67.

87. Phillips, *Emerging Republican Majority*, 471.

88. Nelson, *Resilient America*, xiv.

89. Quoted in Witcover, *Year the Dream Died*, 504.

CHAPTER 5

1. For a discussion of the Horton ad and its relationship to the Bush campaign's effort to manipulate white racism, see Kendi, *Stamped from the Beginning*, 441; Mayer, *Running on Race*, 211–14.

2. Roger Simon, "How a Murderer and Rapist Became the Bush Campaign's Most Valuable Player," *Baltimore Sun*, November 11, 1990.

3. O'Reilly, *Nixon's Piano*, 387.

4. Mayer, *Running on Race*, 201.

5. O'Reilly, *Nixon's Piano*, 381.

6. Shogan, *Fate of the Union*, 5–12.

7. Burnham, "Legacy of George Bush," 2–3. See also Brummet, *Highwire*, 7.

8. Blumenthal, *Clinton Wars*, 20–21.

9. For a discussion of the influence of the King case, see Mayer, *Running on Race*, 239–43.

10. Marlin Fitzwater, Media Interview, George H. W. Bush Presidential Record Press Office, White House, Marlin Fitzwater Files, Subject Files, Box 20; Fitzwater, Marlin, Files, Alphabetical Subject Files, "Murphy Brown," George H. W. Bush Presidential Library, College Station, Texas (hereinafter GBPL).

11. Kurtz, *Spin Cycle*, xxiii; Arterton, "Campaign '92," 90, 91; No author, "Couch Potato Campaign: The Screen Testing of the President 1992: Our Guide to Talk Show Politics," *Entertainment Weekly*, July 19, 1992, MC 1632, Series III, Subseries 1, Box 3; 1992 Presidential Campaign, Magazines of the Clintons, January–February 1992, Diane Blair Papers, University of Arkansas, Fayetteville, Arkansas (hereinafter Blair Papers).

12. Martha Mercer, "Callers Prompt Perot to Go for White House," *Richmond Times*, White House Office of Political Affairs, Ron Kaufman Files, Box 3 of 3;

Ronald Kaufman Folder 4: H. Ross Perot [1], GBPL.

13. Alex Ray to Ron Kaufman, March 19, 1992, White House Office of Political Affairs, Ron Kaufman Files, Box 3 of 3; Ronald Kaufman Folder 4: H. Ross Perot [1], GBPL.

14. Alex, no last name, to Ron Kaufman, March 27, 1992, White House Office of Political Affairs, Ron Kaufman Files, Box 3 of 3; Ronald Kaufman Folder 4: H. Ross Perot [1], GBPL.

15. Texas Central, Ross Perot for President, "Memorandum to Regional Directors," March 30, 1992, White House Office of Political Affairs, Ron Kaufman Files, Box 3 of 3; Ronald Kaufman Folder 4: H. Ross Perot [1], GBPL.

16. Everett Carll Ladd, "Thinking About Perot—Part II," *Christian Science Monitor*, June 5, 1992, White House Office of Political Affairs, Ron Kaufman Files, Box 3 of 3; Ronald Kaufman Folder 4: H. Ross Perot [2], GBPL.

17. Celinda C. Lake, Oral History, MC 1632, Series III, Subseries 2, Box 1, Blair Papers, 3.

18. Ladd, "Thinking About Perot."

19. Gil Cisneros, Jim Henderson, "Memorandum to Ron Kaufman," June 15, 1992, White House Office of Political Affairs, Ron Kaufman Files, Box 3 of 3; Ronald Kaufman Folder 4: H. Ross Perot [2], GBPL.

20. H. Ross Perot, "Interview," *CBS This Morning*, September 22, 1992, White House Office of Political Affairs, Ron Kaufman Files, Box 3 of 3; Ronald Kaufman Folder 4: H. Ross Perot [2], GBPL.

21. Baker, "Sorting Out and Suiting Up," 57.

22. Noted in a memo from Saul Benjamin to Mickey Kantor, Eli Segal, David Wilhelm, George Stephanopolous, Stephanie Solien, and Bruce Reed, June 7, 1992, Blair Papers MC 1632, Series III, Subseries 1, Box 1; 1992 Presidential Campaign Correspondence, May–August 1992, Blair Papers.

23. Perot, *United We Stand*, 8.

24. Ibid., 28–30.

25. Ibid., 3.

26. Ibid., ix.

27. Ibid., 4.

28. Ibid., 12, 17.

29. Klein, *Natural*, 39.

30. Chafe, *Hillary and Bill*, 136–37.

31. Woodward, *Agenda*, 3.

32. Ibid., xi.

33. Hayden, *Covering Clinton*, 2.

34. Eric Berman, Oral History, MC 1632, Series III, Subseries 2, Box 1, Blair Papers, 4.

35. Bob Boorstin, Oral History, MC 1632, Series III, Subseries 2, Box 1 Blair Papers, 4.

36. On this point, see Mendelberg, *Race Card*.

37. Speech insert, Chamber of Commerce, Boston, January 17, 1991, MC 1632, Series III, Subseries 1, Box 1; 1992 Presidential Campaign Correspondence, 1991, Blair Papers.

38. Ibid.

39. Bill Clinton, "Letter on the Draft," MC 1632, Series III, Subseries 1, Box 1; 1992 Presidential Campaign, Bill Clinton Letter on the Draft, Blair Papers.

40. Diane Blair, memo to Betsey Wright, September 13, 1992, MC 1632, Series III, Subseries 1, Box 1; 1992 Presidential Campaign Correspondence, September 1992–1993, Blair Papers.

41. Diane Blair, memo to Bill Clinton, September 28, 1992, MC 1632, Series III, Subseries 1, Box 1; 1992 Presidential Campaign Correspondence, September 1992–1993, Blair Papers.

42. Goldman et al., *Quest for the Presidency*, 113; Hayden, *Covering Clinton*, 5; Kurtz, *Spin Cycle*, xxv; Robert Novak, "The Trouble with Clinton," *American Spectator, 18–22*, MC 1632, Series III, Subseries 1, Box 3; 1992 Presidential Campaign, Bill Clinton Newspaper Clippings, April 1992, Blair Papers, 19.

43. Goldman et al., *Quest for the Presidency*, 230.

44. Bob Boorstin, Oral History, MC 1632, Series III, Subseries 2, Box 1, Blair Papers, 14.

45. Michael Wines, "Dueling Commercials: Clinton Pack Bites Back Fast at Bush Advertising," *New York Times*, October 3, 1992. MC 1632, Series III, Subseries 1, Box 5; 1992 Presidential Campaign, Bill Clinton Newspaper Clippings, Blair Papers.

46. The Bush campaign noted their success in this endeavor with regret. See Bill Lacy, memo to Bob Teeter, Mary Matalin, David Carney, November 3, 1992, Robert Teeter Collection, 1992 Presidential Campaign, Box 51; 1992 Presidential Campaign, Line of the Day Backgrounder, etc.—Book Two [3], GBPL.

47. "Worry-Wart Diane," memo to "Betsey," no date, MC 1632, Series III, Subseries 1, Box 1; 1992 Presidential Campaign Correspondence, May–August, 1992, Blair Papers.

48. Perot Talking Points, MC 1632, Series III, Subseries 1, Box 2; 1992 Presidential Campaign, Bill Clinton Talking Points, Blair Papers.

49. Bill Clinton, "Remarks Prepared for Delivery at the Foreign Policy Association," April 1, 1992, MC 1632, Series III, Subseries 1, Box 2; 1992 Presidential Campaign, Bill Clinton Speeches 1992, Blair Papers.

50. Bill Clinton, *The New Covenant: Responsibility and Rebuilding the American Community*, Georgetown University, October 23, 1991, MC 1632, Series III, Subseries 1, Box 2; 1992 Presidential Campaign, Bill Clinton Speeches 1992, Blair Papers, 2.

51. *The Clinton Contrast: A Sourcebook*, DNC Research Draft #1, MC 1632, Series III, Subseries 1, Box 1; 1992 Presidential Campaign, Bill Clinton Campaign Handbook, Blair Papers.

52. Bill Clinton, Remarks at the Association of Democratic State Chairs, Palmer House, Chicago, November 23, 1991, MC 1632, Series III, Subseries 1, Box 2; 1992 Presidential Campaign, Bill Clinton Speeches 1992, Blair Papers, 2.

53. Clinton, *New Covenant*, 1.

54. Andrew Kopkind, "The Manufactured Candidate," *The Nation*, February 3, 1992, 116–18, MC 1632, Series III, Subseries 1, Box 3; 1992 Presidential Campaign, Magazines of the Clintons, January–February 1992, Blair Papers, 116, 118.

55. Bob Boorstin, Oral History, MC 1632, Series III, Subseries 2, Box 1, Blair Papers, 12.

56. Christopher Dorval and Stephanie Soliene, memo to field staff, no date, MC 1632, Series III, Subseries 1, Box 1; 1992 Presidential Campaign Correspondence, n.d., Blair Papers.

57. Wickham, *Bill Clinton*, 47.

58. Clinton, *New Covenant*, 4.

59. Clinton, Remarks at the Association of Democratic State Chairs, 6.

60. Celinda Lake and Stan Greenberg, memo to the Clinton Campaign, May 12, 1992, MC 1632, Series III, Subseries 1, Box 3; 1992 Presidential Campaign, Magazines of the Clintons, January–February 1992, Bill Clinton Newspaper Clippings, April 1992, Blair Papers, 1–2.

61. Ibid., 2, 6.

62. Letty Cottin Pogrebin, "Give Hillary a Break," no paper, no date, MC 1632, Series III, Subseries 1, Box 3; 1992 Presidential Campaign, Bill Clinton Newspaper Clippings, April 1992, Blair Papers.

63. Matalin, Carville, and Knobler, *"All's Fair,"* 100–116; Goldman et al., *Quest for the Presidency*, 89–90.

64. Paul Begala, "Memorandum to all staff, January 24, 1992, MC 1632, Series III, Subseries 1, Box 1; 1992 Presidential Campaign Correspondence, January–April, 1991, Blair Papers.

65. Ibid.

66. Clinton had a long history of womanizing; that history kept him from running in 1988 because he had a "Gary Hart problem." See Maraniss, *First in His Class*, 425, 439. See also Chafe, *Hillary and Bill*, 125. On his history of alleged sexual improprieties, see Maraniss, *Clinton Enigma*.

67. Chafe, *Hillary and Bill*, 146.

68. For discussions of this point, see, most prominently, AETV, "The Clinton Affair"; Megan Garber, "The End of the Clinton Affair," *Atlantic* November 22, 2018; Matalin, Carville, and Knobler, *"All's Fair,"* 114–15; Leon Neyfakh, "Slow Burn: The Clinton Impeachment," *Slate*, https://slate.com/podcasts/slow-burn/s2/clinton.

69. Loretta Lynch and Nancy McFadden, memo to David Wilhelm, February 16, 1992, Paul Begala, "Memorandum to All Staff, January 24, 1992, MC 1632, Series III, Subseries 1, Box 1; 1992 Presidential Campaign Correspondence, January–April, 1991, Blair Papers.

70. Diane Blair, "Serious Problem with Women Voters," no date, MC 1632, Series III, Subseries 1, Box 1; 1992 Presidential Campaign Correspondence, n.d., Blair Papers.

71. For details, see Mulloy, *Enemies of the State*, 121.

72. Patrick Buchanan, "Dear Friend," White House Office of Political Affairs, Ron Kaufman Files, OA/ID 06497; Buchanan and Hardin Campaign Literature, GBPL.

73. Bush, "Excerpted Remarks with Community Leaders," 88.

74. Bush, "Remarks to Liberty Mutual Insurance Employees," 103.

75. See Ron Kaufman, memo to Marlin Fitzwater, January 23, 1992, George H. W. Bush Presidential Record Press Office, White House, Marlin Fitzwater Files, Subject Files, Box 3; Campaign '92, GBPL.

76. Bush, "Excerpted Remarks with Community Leaders," 89.

77. Bush, "Remarks at the Annual Convention of the National Religious Broadcasters," 151.

78. Bush, "President's News Conference," 421.

79. Bush, "Remarks at BushQuayle Campaign Headquarters," 655.

80. For more on conventions of the time, see Davis and Broder, *National Conventions*.

81. Bush made the argument about the need to oppose racism, anti-Semitism, and hatred in general a staple of his campaign discourse, even as he engaged in dog-whistle rhetoric. See, for example, George Bush, Remarks at a Bush-Quayle Rally in Jackson, Mississippi, Online, by Gerhard Peters and John T. Woolley, The American Presidency Project, https://www.presidency.ucsb.edu/node/267035; George Bush, Remarks Accepting the Presidential Nomination at the Republican National Convention in Houston Online, by Gerhard Peters and John T. Woolley, The American Presidency Project, https://www.presidency.ucsb.edu/node/266944.

82. Pat Buchanan, "1992 Republican National Convention Speech," August 17, 1992, https://buchanan.org/blog/1992-republican-national-convention-speech-148.

83. Ibid.

84. Mary Fisher, "1992 Republican National Convention Address," August 19, 1992, American Rhetoric: Top 100 Speeches, https://www.americanrhetoric.com/speeches/maryfisher1992rnc.html.

85. Pat Robertson, "1992 Republican Convention," http://www.patrobertson.com/Speeches/1992GOPConvention.asp.

86. Briefing Book, Political Perceptions U.S. National Survey Results, Robert Teeter Collection, 1990 Census Date Prepared for the RNC and 1992 Election Campaign; 1992 Presidential Campaign Briefing Book—Political Perceptions, GBPL.

87. Bill Lacy, memo to Bob Teeter, Mary Matalin, David Carney, November 3, 1992, Robert Teeter Collection, 1992 Presidential Campaign, Box 51; 1992 Presidential Campaign, Line of the Day Backgrounder, etc.—Book Two [3], GBPL.

88. Howard Kurtz, "Dogfight on the Airwaves: Bush Radio Ads Distort Clinton's Stances," *Washington Post*, October 24, 1992, 1992 Presidential Campaign, Box 52; 1992 Presidential Campaign, Radio Ads [2], GBPL.

89. No author, no date, "Recommendations for Improvement Next Time," Robert Teeter Collection, 1990 Census Data Prepared for the RNC and 1992 Re-Election Campaign Box 1992 Presidential Campaign, Box 52; 1992 Presidential Campaign, Regional Ads [1], GBPL.

90. Meacham, *Destiny and Power*, 500–501.

91. Bush, "Exchange with Reporters," 585.

92. BushQuayle Talking Points, November 2, 1992, Robert Teeter Collection, 1990 Census Data Prepared for the RNC and 1992 Re-Election Campaign Box 51; 1992 Presidential Campaign, Line of the Day Backgrounder, etc.—Book Two [1], GBPL.

93. "Trust," Robert Teeter Collection, 1992 Presidential Campaign, Box 53; 1992 Presidential Campaign TV/Print Ads and Media Markets [1], GBPL.

94. BushQuayle Talking Points, November 2, 1992, Robert Teeter Collection, 1990 Census Data Prepared for the RNC and 1992 Re-Election Campaign Box 51; 1992 Presidential Campaign, Line of the

Day Backgrounder, etc.—Book Two [1], GBPL.

95. BushQuayle '92 Press Release, October 31, 1992, Robert Teeter Collection, 1990 Census Data Prepared for the RNC and 1992 Re-Election Campaign Box 51; 1992 Presidential Campaign, Line of the Day Backgrounder, etc.—Book Two [1], GBPL.

96. BushQuayle Talking Points, October 30, 1992, Robert Teeter Collection, 1990 Census Data Prepared for the RNC and 1992 Re-Election Campaign Box 51; 1992 Presidential Campaign, Line of the Day Backgrounder, etc.—Book Two [1], GBPL.

97. "A Case of Documented Deception," News Release, BushQuayle '92, October 15, 1992, Robert Teeter Collection, 1990 Census Data Prepared for the RNC and 1992 Re-Election Campaign Box 51; 1992 Presidential Campaign, Line of the Day Backgrounder, etc.—Book Two [2], GBPL.

98. "Clippings Compiled by Staff from Dispatches," August 4, 1992, MC 1632, Series III, Subseries 1, Box 3; 1992 Presidential Campaign, Bill Clinton Newspaper Clippings, August–September 1992, Blair Papers.

99. News Release, October 11, 1992, Robert Teeter Collection, 1990 Census Data Prepared for the RNC and 1992 Re-Election Campaign Box 51; 1992 Presidential Campaign, Line of the Day Backgrounder, etc.—Book Two [2], GBPL.

100. Talking Points, October 10, 1992, Robert Teeter Collection, 1990 Census Data Prepared for the RNC and 1992 Re-Election Campaign Box 51; 1992 Presidential Campaign, Line of the Day Backgrounder, etc.—Book Two [2], GBPL.

101. See, for example, the coverage in the *Richmond Times Dispatch*, October 8, 1992; an editorial in *USA Today*, October 9, 1992; a Bush campaign press release, October 7, 1992; and Bush campaign talking points, October 6, 1992, all available in, Robert Teeter Collection, 1990 Census Data Prepared for the RNC and 1992 Re-Election Campaign Box 51; 1992 Presidential Campaign, Line of the Day Backgrounder, etc.—Book Two [3], GBPL.

102. Bill Clinton, Interview with Andrea Mitchell, *NBC News*, October 29, 1992, Robert Teeter Collection, 1990, 1992 Presidential Campaign, Box 52; 1992 Presidential Campaign, Radio Ads [2], GBPL.

103. Briefing Book, Vice Presidential Debate, Georgia Tech, October 12, 1992, Robert Teeter Collection, 1990 Census Date Prepared for the RNC and 1992 Election Campaign; 1992 Presidential Campaign, Debates Briefing, GBPL.

104. Briefing Book, Vice Presidential Debate, Georgia Tech, October 12, 1992, Robert Teeter Collection, 1990 Census Data Prepared for the RNC and 1992 Election Campaign; 1992 Presidential Campaign, Debates Briefing, GBPL. See also "Talking Points," White House Counsel's Office, Nelson Lind Files, Civil Rights File, Box 3; Civil Rights and Campaign '92, GBPL.

105. "Clinton Facts," October 21, 1992, Robert Teeter Collection, 1990 Census Data Prepared for the RNC and 1992 Re-Election Campaign Box 51; 1992 Presidential Campaign, Line of the Day Backgrounder, etc.—Book Two [1], GBPL.

106. Talking Points, October 22, 1992, Robert Teeter Collection, 1990 Census Data Prepared for the RNC and 1992 Re-Election Campaign Box 51; 1992 Presidential Campaign, Line of the Day Backgrounder, etc.—Book Two [2], GBPL.

107. Bush, "Remarks on Civil Disobedience," 669.

108. Bush, "Remarks to the Ohio Association of Broadcasters," 671.

109. George Bush, "Address to the Nation on the Civil Disturbances in Los Angeles, California," May 1, 1992, 685–87, at 685.

110. Briefing Book, Vice Presidential Debate, Georgia Tech, October 12, 1992, Robert Teeter Collection, 1990 Census Date Prepared for the RNC and 1992 Election Campaign; 1992 Presidential Campaign, Debates Briefing, GBPL.

111. Scotchie, *Revolt from the Heartland*, vii.

112. On the politics of the South, see Cochran, *Democracy Heading South*, 1.

CHAPTER 6

1. Brock, *Fox Effect*; Smith, *Foxocracy*.
2. Zimdars and McLeod, *Fake News*.

3. Dyson, *Imagining Politics*, 3.

4. Clinton, *What Happened*, 49.

5. Frum, *Trumpocracy*, vii; Levitsky and Ziblatt, *How Democracies Die*, 146.

6. Sides, Tesler, and Vavrock, *Identity Crisis*, 25.

7. Mulloy, *Enemies of the State*, 149–50.

8. Hochschild, *Strangers in Their Own Land*, chapter 1.

9. Lopez, *Dog Whistle Politics*, 5.

10. Dyson, *Imagining Politics*, 101.

11. Ibid., 102; Lopez, *Dog Whistle Politics*, 31.

12. Julia Azari, "Populism in the United States: Historical Continuities and Contemporary Complexities," presented at the annual meeting of the American Political Science Association, Washington, DC, August 2019, 1.

13. Ibid., 1.

14. Robin, *Reactionary Mind*, 7.

15. Ibid., 55.

16. Levitsky and Ziblatt, *How Democracies Die*, 57; Zito and Todd, *Great Revolt*, 10.

17. Rowland, "Donald Trump," 194; see also Chattopadhyay, "Understanding the Authoritarian Voter."

18. Sides, Tesler, and Vavreck, *Identity Crisis*, 2–5.

19. Ibid., 114.

20. See ibid., 84–87; Lajevardi and Abrajano, "How Negative Sentiment."

21. Mehltretter Drury and Kuehl, "Introduction," 113.

22. Clinton, *What Happened*, 73.

23. Ibid., 195.

24. John Dickerson, "The Danger of Clinton Fatigue," *CBS News*, July 31, 2013, https://www.cbsnews.com/news/the-danger-of-clinton-fatigue.

25. Dara Lind, "Bernie Bros, Explained," *Vox*, February 5, 2016, https://www.vox.com/2016/2/4/10918710/berniebro-bernie-bro.

26. Valentino, Wayne, and Oceno, "Mobilizing Sexism."

27. Warner and Bystrom, "Introduction," 2.

28. Jamieson, *Cyber War*, 5.

29. Ibid., 150.

30. Eliza Collins, "Poll: Clinton, Trump, Most Unpopular Candidates Ever," *USA Today*, August 31, 2016, https://www.usatoday.com/story/news/politics/onpolitics/2016/08/31/poll-clinton-trump-most-unfavorable-candidates-ever/89644296.

31. Hillary Clinton, Third Presidential Debate, October 19, 2016 https://www.debates.org/voter-education/debate-transcripts/october-19-2016-debate-transcript.

32. Hillary Clinton, Acceptance Speech, Democratic National Convention July 28, 2016, https://www.politico.com/story/2016/07/full-text-hillary-clintons-dnc-speech-226410.

33. Ibid.

34. Ibid.

35. Hillary Clinton, First Presidential Debate, September 26, 2016. https://politico.com/story/2016/09/full-transcript-first-2016-presidential-debate-228761.

36. Clinton, Acceptance Speech.

37. Michelle Obama, Speech at the Democratic National Convention, July 25, 2016, https://www.cnn.com/2016/07/26/politics/transcript-michelle-obama-speech-democratic-national-convention/index.html.

38. Ibid.

39. Hillary Clinton, Second Presidential Debate, October 9, 2016, https://www.politico.com/story/2016/10/2016-presidential-debate-transcript-229519.

40. Ibid.

41. Hillary Clinton, Third Presidential Debate.

42. Ibid.

43. Hillary Clinton, Second Presidential Debate.

44. See Butler, *Excitable Speech*.

45. Han, *Hatred of American Presidents*, loc. 8826.

46. Sides, Tesler, and Vavrock, *Identity Crisis*, 107, 147. See also Hillary Clinton, *What Happened*, 43.

47. Thorson et al., "Media Influence in the 2016 Race," 80.

48. Churchwell, *Behold, America!*, 293; Han, *Hatred of American Presidents*, loc. 8761.

49. Frum, *Trumpocracy*, 7.

50. Gregory Krieg, "14 of Trump's Most Outrageous 'Birther' Claims—Half from After 2011," CNN, September 16, 2019, https://www.cnn.com/2016/09/09/politics/donald-trump-birther/index.html.

51. Stephen Collinson and Jeremy J. Diamond, "Trump Finally Admits It: Barack Obama Was Born in the United States," CNN, September 16, 2016, https://www.cnn.com/2016/09/15/politics/donald-trump-obama-birther-united-states/index.html.

52. Donald Trump, First Presidential Debate, September 26, 2016, https://politico.com/story/2016/09/full-transcript-first-2016-presidential-debate-228761.

53. Donald Trump, Announcement Speech, June 16, 2015, https://www.nydailynews.com/news/politics/transcript-donald-trump-2016-presidential-announcement-article-1.2260117.

54. Tur, *Unbelievable*, 145.

55. Trump, Announcement Speech.

56. Tur, *Unbelievable*, 79–80.

57. Garrett, *Mr. Trump's Wild Ride*, 2.

58. Rowland, "Donald Trump."

59. Ibid., 192–93.

60. See most prominently, Mercieca, *Demagogue for President*.

61. See Roberts-Miller, *Demagoguery and Democracy*. See also Skinnell and Murphy, "Rhetoric's Demagogue."

62. Ott, "Age of Twitter," 60.

63. Heidt and Pfister, "Trump, Twitter, and the Microdiatribe," 172.

64. Dionne, Ornstein, and Mann, *One Nation After Trump*, 39.

65. Dyson, *Imagining Politics*, 117. On those media structures, see Stroud, *Niche News*.

66. Stroud and Collier, "Selective Exposure and Homophily," 35.

67. Cramer, *Politics of Resentment*, 5–7.

68. Ibid., 103.

69. Dionne, Ornstein, and Mann, *One Nation After Trump*, 11; Mutz, "Status Anxiety."

70. Stuckey, "'Power of the Presidency to Hurt.'"

71. Trump, Third Presidential Debate.

72. Ibid.

73. Ibid.

74. Edelman, "Language, Myths, and Rhetoric."

75. Trump, Third Presidential Debate.

76. Trump, First Presidential Debate.

77. Trump, Second Presidential Debate.

78. Quoted in Tur, *Unbelievable*, 82.

79. Hooghe and Dassoneville, "Explaining the Trump Vote." See also Setzler and Yanos, "Why Did Women Vote?"

80. Trump, First Presidential Debate.

81. Trump, Third Presidential Debate.

82. Ibid.

83. Donald Trump, Speech in New York City on the Stakes of the Election, June 22, 2016, https://www.politico.com/story/2016/06/transcript-trump-speech-on-the-stakes-of-the-election-224654.

84. Donald Trump, Acceptance Speech, Republican National Convention, July 21, 2016, https://www.politico.com/story/2016/07/full-transcript-donald-trump-nomination-acceptance-speech-at-rnc-225974. See also Trump, "Speech in New York."

85. Trump, First Presidential Debate.

86. Trump, Announcement Speech.

87. Trump, First Presidential Debate.

88. Ibid.

89. Trump, Acceptance Speech.

90. Trump, Speech in New York.

91. Trump, First Presidential Debate.

92. Trump, Acceptance Speech.

93. Trump, First Presidential Debate.

94. Jamieson, *Cyber War*, 6.

95. Quoted in Tur, *Unbelievable*, 188.

96. Clinton, Third Presidential Debate.

97. Clinton and Trump, Third Presidential Debate.

98. Trump, Third Presidential Debate.

99. Trump, Second Presidential Debate.

100. "Trump's Lawyer Argues President Can't Be Prosecuted for Shooting Someone on Fifth Avenue," NBC News, October 23, 2019, https://www.nbcnewyork.com/news/local/Trump-Fifth-Avenue-Shooting-No-Prosecution-563709621.html.

101. Sides, Tesler, and Vavrock, *Identity Crisis*, 1.

102. Colin Campbell, "Trump on His Black Lives Matter Heckler: 'Maybe He Should Have Been Roughed Up.'" *Business Insider*, November 22, 2015, https://www.businessinsider.com/donald-trump-protester-roughed-up-2015-11.

103. Daniel White, "Donald Trump Tells Crowd to 'Knock the Crap out of' Hecklers," *Time*, February 1, 2016, https://time.com/4203094/donald-trump-hecklers.

104. Ben Schreckinger, “Trump on Protester: ‘I'd Like to Punch Him in the Face,” *Politico*, February 23, 2016, https://www.politico.com/story/2016/02/donald-trump-punch-protester-219655.

105. Tur, *Unbelievable*, 243–44.

106. Warner and Bystrom, “Introduction,” 6.

107. “Transcripts: What the Mic Actually Caught Donald Trump Saying in 2005 and What He Said in His Taped Apology,” *Los Angeles Times*, October 7, 2016, https://www.latimes.com/politics/la-na-pol-trump-bush-transcript-20161007-snap-htmlstory.html.

108. Trump, Second Presidential Debate.

109. Tur, *Unbelievable*, 235.

110. Trump, Second Presidential Debate.

111. Clinton, *What Happened*, 46.

112. Rudy Guiliani, Speech at the RNC, July 20, 2020, https://www.c-span.org/video/?c4611718/rudy-guiliani-delivers-remarks-republican-national-convention.

113. Ibid.

114. Michael Flynn, Speech at the RNC, July 22, 2016, http://transcripts.cnn.com/TRANSCRIPTS/1607/18/se.04.html.

115. Ibid.

116. Trump, Acceptance Speech.

AFTERWORD

1. Tom Howell Jr., “Trump on Virus: ‘I Had It, Here I Am,” *Washington Times*, October 24, 2020, https://www.washingtontimes.com/news/2020/oct/24/trump-virus-i-had-it-here-i-am.

2. Donald J. Trump, Twitter, October 26, 2020, 8:58 a.m., https://twitter.com/realDonaldTrump/status/1320711322284281862.

3. John Bowden, “CNN's Jake Tapper Calls Debate a ‘Hot Mess Inside a Dumpster Fire Inside a Train Wreck,’” *The Hill*, September 29, 2020, https://thehill.com/homenews/media/518879-cnns-jake-tapper-calls-debate-a-hot-mess-inside-a-dumpster-fire-inside-a-train.

4. Ibid.

5. Katherine Watson, “Trump Falsely Claims He Won Elections as Millions of Votes Remain Uncounted,” CBS News, November 3, 2020, https://www.cbsnews.com/news/trump-speaks-election-night-live-stream-2020-11-04.

6. Chantal da Silva, “‘Reckless and Stupid’: Trump Jr. Calls for ‘Total War’ over Election Results,” *Independent,* November 6, 2020, https://www.independent.co.uk/news/world/americas/us-election-2020/trump-jr-election-results-war-b1634841.html.

7. He said this immediately before abruptly ending the interview. See *60 Minutes*, October 25, 2020, https://www.cbsnews.com/news/donald-trump-full-interview-60-minutes-transcript-lesley-stahl-2018-10-14.

8. Phillip Bump, “Trump's Inability to Speak Convincingly to Anyone but His Base Is a Unique Liability in the Moment,” *Washington Post*, June 1, 2020, https://www.washingtonpost.com/politics/2020/06/01/trumps-inability-speak-convincingly-anyone-his-base-is-unique-liability-moment.

9. Dara Lind, “Unite the Right, the Violent White Supremacist Rally in Charlottesville, Explained,” *Vox*, August 14, 2017, https://www.vox.com/2017/8/12/16138246/charlottesville-nazi-rally-right-uva.

10. Donald J. Trump, “Remarks on Infrastructure and an Exchange with Reporters in New York City,” August 25, 2017, online, by Gerhard Peters and John T. Woolley, The American Presidency Project, https://www.presidency.ucsb.edu/node/329623. All following quotations are from this source.

11. For the best analysis of this point, see Hennessey and Wittes, *Unmaking the Presidency*.

12. Kumar, “Contemporary Presidency Energy or Chaos?”

13. Donald J. Trump, “Remarks Prior to a Meeting with President Nechirvan Barzani of Iraq's Kurdistan Regional Government and an Exchange with Reporters in Davos, Switzerland,” January 22, 2020, online, by Gerhard Peters and John T. Woolley, The American Presidency Project, https://www.presidency.ucsb.edu/node/335419.

14. On the problems with the president's communicative strategy on the pandemic, see Heith, “Gone by Spring.”

15. Geoffrey Skelle and Amelia Thomson-DeVeaux, "How Americans Are Reacting to Trump's Covid-19 Diagnosis," FiveThirtyEight, October 5, 2020, https://fivethirtyeight.com/features/will-trumps-diagnosis-change-the-way-republicans-think-about-covid-19.

16. David Leonhart, "18 Revelations from a Trove of Trump Tax Records," *New York Times*, September 27, 2020, https://www.nytimes.com/2020/09/27/us/trump-taxes-takeaways.html.

17. Katherine Faulders, Will Steakin, and John Santucci, "Former Trump Campaign Manager Brad Parscale Hospitalized After Threatening to Harm Himself," ABC News, September 27, 2020, https://abcnews.go.com/Politics/trump-campaign-manager-brad-parscale-hospitalized-harm-police/story?id=73283795.

18. See, for example, Nicholas Confessore, Karen Yourish, Steve Eder, Ben Protess, Michael LaForgia, Kenneth R. Vogel, and Michael Rothfield, "Swarming for Favors in a Swamp Trump Built," *New York Times*, October 11, 2020, A1.

19. See, for example, Eric Lutz, "The Kimberly Guilfoyle Sexual Harassment Allegations Get Even Darker," *Vanity Fair*, October 2, 2020, https://www.vanityfair.com/news/2020/10/kimberly-guilfoyle-sexual-harassment-allegations-get-even-darker.

20. See, among many others, Caroline Kelly, "Secretly Recorded Tapes Show Melania Trump's Frustration at Criticism for Family Separation Policy and Her Bashing of Christmas Decorations," CNN, October 2, 2020, https://www.cnn.com/2020/10/01/politics/melania-trump-tapes/index.html.

21. William Cummings, "'The Data Speak for Themselves': Dr. Anthony Fauci Says White House Held a 'Superspreader' Event for Coronavirus," *USA Today*, October 9, 2020, https://www.usatoday.com/story/news/politics/2020/10/09/anthony-fauci-white-house-held-covid-superspreader-event/5940483002.

22. Andrew Solender, "Trump to Hold Rally with Hundreds of Supporters on White House Lawn Saturday," *Forbes*, October 9, 2020, https://www.forbes.com/sites/andrewsolender/2020/10/09/trump-to-hold-rally-with-hundreds-of-supporters-on-white-house-lawn-saturday/#2aaaef8847c9.

23. On the effects of those drugs, see Rhitu Chatterjee, "Trump Was Treated with Steroids: How These Drugs Are Used for Covid-19 Patients," NPR, October 8, 2020, https://www.npr.org/sections/latest-updates-trump-covid-19-results/2020/10/08/921629391/trump-still-on-steroids-how-these-drugs-are-typically-used-to-treat-covid-19.

24. Maggie Haberman, Alexander Burns, and Jonathan Martin, "As Election Day Arrives, Trump Shifts Between Combativeness and Grievance," *New York Times*, November 2, 2020, https://www.nytimes.com/2020/11/02/us/politics/trump-campaign.html.

25. See https://lincolnproject.us.

26. Donald J. Trump, "President Trump's Anti-Riot Speech," *Newsmax*, June 1, 2020, https://www.newsmax.com/politics/riot-anarchists-white-house-speech/2020/06/01/id/970052. All following quotations are from this source.

27. Nicholas Wu, "Trump Says George Floyd 'Hopefully' Looking Down and Saying 'This Is a Great Thing That's Happening,'" *USA Today*, June 5, 2020, https://www.usatoday.com/story/news/politics/2020/06/05/trump-economy-event-george-floyd-hopefully-looking-down/3154495001.

28. Daniel Poletti, "Trump Retweets Interview Trashing George Floyd's Character as He Breaks Own Twitter Record," *Slate*, June 6, 2020, https://slate.com/news-and-politics/2020/06/trump-interview-trashing-george-floyd-breaks-twitter-record.html.

29. Jeff Mason and Michael Martina, "Trump Blasts Michigan Governor Whitmer, Crowd Chants 'Lock Her Up,'" *Reuters*, October 17, 2020, https://www.reuters.com/article/us-usa-election-michigan-idUSKBN27206V.

30. "Controversial 'Thin Blue Line' Flag Replaces America's 'Stars and Stripes' at Trump Rally in Waukesha,' *Milwaukee Independent*, October 26, 2020, http://www.milwaukeeindependent.com/syndicated

/controversial-thin-blue-line-flag-replaces-americas-stars-stripes-trump-rally-waukesha.

31. See, among many others, Frum, *Trumpocracy*; Hennessey and Wittes, *Unmaking the Presidency*; Levitsky and Ziblatt, *How Democracies Die*.

32. Hennessey and Wittes, *Unmaking the Presidency*, 52.

33. On the first of these, see Marshall Cohen and Jeremy Herb, "Breaking Down 'Obamagate,' Trump's Latest Theory About the 'Deep State' and Obama's Role in the Russia Investigation," CNN, May 13, 2020, https://www.cnn.com/2020/05/13/politics/trump-obama-obamagate-russia/index.html. On the second, see "Trump Accuses Democrats of 'Deranged Partisan Crusades' as Impeachment Trial Heats Up," NBC News, January 28, 2020, https://www.nbcnews.com/politics/donald-trump/trump-accuses-democrats-deranged-partisan-crusades-impeachment-trial-heats-n1125271.

34. Donald J. Trump, "Address Accepting the Republican Presidential Nomination," online, by Gerhard Peters and John T. Woolley, The American Presidency Project, https://www.presidency.ucsb.edu/node/342196.

35. For details on this scandal and its aftermath, see Dan MacGuill, "The Republican Senate Report on Hunter Biden, Explained," Snopes, September 29, 2020. The report is archived here: https://archive.vn/l1Bn3.

36. Jonathan Easley and Morgan Chalfant, "Trump Leans into Attacks on Biden's Family, Business Dealings," *The Hill*, October 24, 2020, https://thehill.com/homenews/campaign/522514-trump-leans-into-attacks-on-bidens-family-business-dealings.

37. Aymann Ishmail, "Why It's So Hard for Men to Look at Joe Biden Kissing His Son," *Slate*, October 22, 2020, https://slate.com/human-interest/2020/10/joe-biden-hunter-kiss-masculinity.html.

38. *USA Today* Staff, "Read the Full Transcript from the First Presidential Debate Between Joe Biden and Donald Trump," *USA Today*, September 30, 2020, https://www.usatoday.com/story/news/politics/elections/2020/09/30/presidential-debate-read-full-transcript-first-debate/3587462001.

39. Kendi, *How to Be an Antiracist*.

40. Kendi, *Stamped from the Beginning*, 504.

41. Azari, "Politics in a Polarized Environment"; Schlozman and Rosenfeld, "Hollow Parties."

42. Julia Azari, "Weak Parties and Strong Partisanship Are a Bad Combination," *Vox*, November 3, 2016, https://www.vox.com/mischiefs-of-faction/2016/11/3/13512362/weak-parties-strong-partisanship-bad-combination.

43. The full text of that speech is available at https://www.cnn.com/videos/politics/2021/01/07/joe-biden-entire-justice-department-merrick-garland-nomination-sot-vpx.cnn.

44. Isenberg, *White Trash*.

45. Glenn, *Rhetorical Feminism*, 193–98.

46. Acharya, Blackwell, and Sen, *Deep Roots*, 4–5.

47. Isenberg, *White Trash*, 316.

BIBLIOGRAPHY

Acharya, Avidit, Matthew Blackwell, and Maya Sen. *Deep Roots: How Slavery Still Shapes Southern Politics.* Princeton: Princeton University Press, 2018.

Anderson, Carol. *White Rage: The Unspoken Truth of Our Racial Divide.* New York: Bloomsbury, 2016.

Arterton, Christopher. "Campaign '92: Strategies and Tactics." In *The Election of 1992*, edited by Gerlad M. Pomper, 74–109. Chatham, NJ: Chatham House, 1993.

Axelrod, Alan. *The Gilded Age: 1876–1912; Overture to the American Century.* New York: Sterling, 2017.

Azari, Julia R. "How the News Media Helped to Nominate Trump." *Political Communication* 33 (2016): 677–80.

———. "Politics in a Polarized Environment." In *The Obama Legacy*, edited by Bert A. Rockman and Andrew Rudalevige, 44–70. Lawrence: University Press of Kansas, 2019.

Baatz, Simon. *For the Thrill of It: Leopold, Loeb, and the Murder That Shocked Jazz Age Chicago.* New York: Harper Perennial, 2009.

Baker, Ross K. "Sorting Out and Suiting Up: The Presidential Nominations." In *The Election of 1992*, edited by Gerlad M. Pomper, 39–73. Chatham, NJ: Chatham House, 1993.

Beatty, Jack. *Age of Betrayal: The Triumph of Money in America, 1865–1900.* New York: Alfred A. Knopf, 2007.

Blumenthal, Sidney. *The Clinton Wars.* New York: Farrar, Straus and Giroux, 2003.

Boyle, Kevin. *Arc of Justice: A Saga of Race, Civil Rights, and Murder in the Jazz Age.* New York: Holt, 2005.

Brinkley, Alan. *The Unfinished Nation: A Concise History of the American People.* New York: McGraw Hill, 1993.

Brock, David. *The Fox Effect: How Roger Ailes Turned a Network into a Propaganda Machine.* New York: Anchor, 2012.

Broomall, James D. "Personal Reconstructions: Confederates as Citizens in the Post–Civil War South." In *Creating Citizenship in the Nineteenth-Century South*, edited by William A. Link, David Brown, Brian Ward, and Martyn Bene, 111–33. Gainesville: University Press of Florida, 2013.

Browne, Stephen Howard. *The First Inauguration: George Washington and the Invention of the Republic.* University Park: Penn State University Press, 2020.

Brummet, John. *Highwire: From the Backroads to the Beltway: The Education of Bill Clinton.* New York: Hyperion, 1994.

Buchanan, Patrick J. *The Greatest Comeback: How Richard Nixon Rose from Defeat to Create the New Majority.* New York: Crown Forum, 2014.

Burke, Kenneth. *A Rhetoric of Motives.* Berkeley: University of California Press, 1969.

Burnham, Walter Dean. *Critical Elections and the Mainsprings of American Politics.* New York: Norton, 1970.

———. "The Legacy of George Bush: Travails of an Understudy." In *The Election of 1992*, edited by Gerlad M. Pomper, 1–38. Chatham, NJ: Chatham House, 1993.

Bush, George. "Excerpted Remarks with Community Leaders in Portsmouth, New Hampshire." January 15, 1992. In *Public Papers of the President of the United States: George Bush, 1992–93*, 88–94. Washington, DC: US Government Printing Office, 1993.

———. "Exchange with Reporters, Prior to a Meeting on Welfare Reform." April 10, 1992. In *Public Papers of the President of the United States: George Bush, 1992–93*, 577–91. Washington, DC: US Government Printing Office, 1993.

———. "The President's News Conference." March 11, 1992. In *Public Papers of the President of the United States: George Bush, 1992–93*, 416–25. Washington, DC: US Government Printing Office, 1993.

———. "Remarks at BushQuayle Campaign Headquarters." April 28, 1992. In *Public Papers of the President of the United States: George Bush, 1992–93*, 654–56. Washington, DC: US Government Printing Office, 1993.

———. "Remarks at the Annual Convention of the National Religious Broadcasters." January 27, 1992. In *Public Papers of the President of the United States: George Bush, 1992–93*, 151–54. Washington, DC: US Government Printing Office, 1993.

———. "Remarks on Civil Disobedience in Los Angeles, California." April 30, 1992. In *Public Papers of the President of the United States: George Bush, 1992–93*, 669. Washington, DC: US Government Printing Office, 1993.

———. "Remarks to Liberty Mutual Insurance Employees in Dover, New Hampshire." January 15, 1992. In *Public Papers of the President of the United States: George Bush, 1992–93*, 102–5. Washington, DC: US Government Printing Office, 1993.

———. "Remarks to the Ohio Association of Broadcasters in Columbus, Ohio." April 30, 1992. In *Public Papers of the President of the United States: George Bush, 1992–93*, 671–75. Washington, DC: US Government Printing Office, 1993.

Butler, Judith. *Excitable Speech: A Politics of the Performative*. New York: Routledge, 1997.

Chafe, William H. *Hillary and Bill: The Clintons and the Politics of the Personal*. Durham: Duke University Press, 2016.

Charles River Editors. *The Election of 1876*. N.p.: Charles River Editors, 2018.

Chattopadhyay, Sumana. "Understanding the Authoritarian Voter in the 2016 Presidential Election." In *An Unprecedented Election: Media, Communication, and the Electorate in the 2016 Campaign*, edited by Benjamin R. Warner, Dianne G. Bystrom, Mitchell McKinney, and Mary C. Banwart, 399–418. Santa Barbara, CA: Praeger, 2018.

Cheathem, Mark R. *The Coming of Democracy: Presidential Campaigning in the Age of Jackson*. Baltimore: Johns Hopkins University Press, 2018.

Chernow, Ron. *Grant*. New York: Penguin, 2017.

Churchwell, Sarah. *Behold, America: A History of America First and the American Dream*. London: Bloomsbury, 2018.

Cisneros, David J. "Contaminated Communities: The Metaphor of 'Immigrant as Pollutant' in Media Representations of Immigration." *Rhetoric and Public Affairs* 11 (2008): 569–601.

Clinton, Hillary. *What Happened*. New York: Simon and Schuster, 2017.

Coates, Ta-Nehisi. "It Was No Compliment to Call Bill Clinton 'America's First Black President.'" *Atlantic*, August 27, 2015. https://www.theatlantic.com/notes/2015/08/toni-morrison-wasnt-giving-bill-clinton-a-compliment/402517.

Cochran, Augustus B., III. *Democracy Heading South: National Politics in the Shadow of Dixie*. Lawrence: University Press of Kansas, 2001.

Cohen, Michael A. *American Maelstrom: The 1968 Election and the Politics of Division*. New York: Oxford University Press, 2016.

Coolidge, Calvin. *The Autobiography of Calvin Coolidge*. New York: Cosmopolitan Book Corporation, 1929.

———. "The Progress of a People." In *Foundations of the Republic*, 31–36. New York: Charles Scribner's Sons, 1929.

Cramer, Katherine J. *The Politics of Resentment: Rural Consciousness in Wisconsin and the Rise of Scott Walker.* Chicago: University of Chicago Press, 2016.

Cunningham, Noble E., Jr. "The Election of 1800." In *Critical Presidential Elections in American History*, edited by Arthur M. Schlesinger Jr., 33–66. New York: McGraw Hill, 1971.

Dahl, Adam. *Empire of the People: Settler Colonialism and the Foundations of Modern Democratic Thought.* Lawrence: University Press of Kansas, 2018.

Davis, James W., and David S. Broder. *National Conventions in an Age of Party Reform.* Westport, CT: Greenwood Press, 1983.

Dickerson, John. *Whistlestop: My Favorite Stories from Presidential Campaign History.* New York: Twelve, 2016.

Didion, Joan. *Political Fictions.* New York: Alfred A. Knopf, 2001.

Dillard, James Price. "Rethinking the Study of Fear Appeals: An Emotional Perspective," *Communication Theory* 4 (1994): 295–323.

Dillard, James Price, and Shu Scott Li. "How Scary Are Threat Appeals? Evaluating the Intensity of Fear in Experimental Research." *Human Communication Research* 49 (2020): 509–32.

Dillard, James Price, and Lijiang Shen. "Threat Appeals as Multi-Emotion Messages: An Argument Structure Model of Fear and Disgust." *Human Communication Research* 44 (2018): 103–26.

Dionne, E. J., Jr., Norman J. Ornstein, and Thomas E. Mann. *One Nation After Trump: A Guide for the Perplexed, the Disillusioned, and the Not-Yet Deported.* New York: St. Martin's Griffin, 2018.

Dippie, Brian W. *The Vanishing Indian: White Attitudes and US Indian Policy.* Middleton: Wesleyan University Press, 1982.

Donald, Aida D. *Lion in the White House: A Life of Theodore Roosevelt.* New York: Perseus, 2007.

Dunbar-Ortiz, Roxanne. *An Indigenous Peoples' History of the United States.* Boston: Beacon Press, 2015.

Durden, Robert F. *The Self-Inflicted Wound: Southern Politics in the Nineteenth Century.* Lexington: University Press of Kentucky, 1985.

Dyson, Stephen Benedict. *Imagining Politics: Interpretations in Political Science and Political Television.* Ann Arbor: University of Michigan Press, 2019.

Edelman, Murray. "Language, Myths, and Rhetoric." *Society* 12 (1975): 14–21.

Ekrich, A. Roger. *American Sanctuary: Mutiny, Martyrdom, and National Identity in the Age of Revolution.* New York: Pantheon, 2017.

Engels, Jeremy. *The Politics of Resentment: A Genealogy.* University Park: Penn State University Press, 2015.

Entman, Robert M., and Andrew Rojecki. *The Black Image in the White Mind: Media and Race in America.* Chicago: University of Chicago Press, 2001.

Farrell, John A. *Richard Nixon: A Life.* New York: Doubleday, 2017.

Ferling, John. *Adams vs. Jefferson: The Tumultuous Election of 1800.* New York: Oxford University Press, 2004.

Ferrell, Robert. *The Presidency of Calvin Coolidge.* Lawrence: University Press of Kansas, 1998.

Fitzgerald, Michael W. *Splendid Failure: Postwar Reconstruction in the American South.* Chicago: University of Chicago Press, 2007.

Franklin, John Hope. "As for Our History." In *Race and History: Selected Essays, 1938–1988*, 59–70. Baton Rouge: Louisiana State University Press, 1989.

———. "*The Birth of a Nation:* Propaganda as History." In *Race and History: Selected Essays, 1938–1988*, 10–23.

Baton Rouge: Louisiana State University Press, 1989.

———, ed. *The Essential Hamilton: Letters and Other Writings*. New York: Library of America, 2017.

———. "The Great Confrontation: The South and the Problem of Change." In *Race and History: Selected Essays, 1938–1988*, 351–66. Baton Rouge: Louisiana State University Press, 1989.

———. "Introduction." In *The Essential Hamilton: Letters and Other Writings*, edited by Joanne B. Freeman, viii–xxi. New York: Library of America, 2017.

———. "The Moral Legacy of the Founding Fathers." In *Race and History: Selected Essays, 1938–1988*, 153–62. Baton Rouge: Louisiana State University Press, 1989.

———. "The Southern Expansionists of 1846." In *Race and History: Selected Essays, 1938–1988*, 104–15. Baton Rouge: Louisiana State University Press, 1989.

Frum, David. *Trumpocracy: The Corruption of the American Republic*. New York: Harpers, 2015.

Gara, Larry. *The Presidency of Franklin Pierce*. Lawrence: University Press of Kansas, 1991.

Garrett, Major. *Mr. Trump's Wild Ride: The Thrills, Chills, Screams, and Occasional Blackouts of an Extraordinary Presidency*. New York: All Points Books, 2018.

Geggus, David P. *The Impact of the Haitian Revolution in the Atlantic World*. Columbia: University of South Carolina Press, 2002.

Gervasi, Frank. *The Real Rockefeller: The Story of the Rise, Decline, and Resurgence of the Presidential Aspirations of Nelson Rockefeller*. New York: Athenaeum, 1964.

Glenn, Cheryl. *Rhetorical Feminism and This Thing Called Hope*. Carbondale: Southern Illinois University Press, 2018.

Goldman, Peter, Thomas M. DeFrank, Mark Miller, Andrew Muir, and Tom Matthews, with Patrick Rogers and Melanie Cooper. *Quest for the Presidency, 1992*. College Station: Texas A&M University Press, 1994.

Gordon, Linda. *The Second Coming of the KKK: The Ku Klux Klan of the 1920s and the American Political Tradition*. New York: Liveright, 2017.

Greenberg, David. *Calvin Coolidge*. New York: Henry Holt, 2006.

Hamilton, Alexander. "The Reynolds Pamphlet," July 1797. In *The Essential Hamilton: Letters and Other Writings*, edited by Joanne B. Freeman, 293–320. New York: Library of America, 2017.

Han, Lori Cox. *Hatred of American Presidents: Personal Attacks on the White House from Washington to Trump*. Santa Barbara, CA: ABC-CLIO, 2016. eBook.

Hayden, Joseph. *Covering Clinton: The President and the Press in the 1990s*. Westport, CT: Praeger, 2002.

Heale, M. J. *The Presidential Quest: Candidates and Images in American Political Culture, 1787–1852*. New York: Longman, 1982.

Heidt, Stephen J., and Damien Smith Pfister. "Trump, Twitter, and the Microdiatribe: The Short Circuits of Networked Public Address." In *Reading the Presidency: Advances in Presidential Rhetoric*, edited by Stephen J. Heidt and Mary E. Stuckey, 171–87. New York: Peter Lang, 2018.

Heith, Diane. "Gone by Spring: President Trump, Crisis Communication, and COVID-19." Forthcoming.

Hennessey, Susan, and Benjamin Wittes. *Unmaking the Presidency: Donald Trump's War on the World's Most Powerful Office*. New York: Farrar, Straus and Giroux, 2020.

Hochschild, Arlie Russell. *Strangers in Their Own Land: Anger and Mourning on the American Right*. New York: New Press, 2018.

Hoffman, Karen S. *Popular Leadership in the Presidency: Origins and Practice*.

Lanham, MD: Lexington Books, 2010.

Holt, Michael F. *By One Vote: The Disputed Presidential Election of 1876.* Lawrence: University Press of Kansas, 2008.

Hooghe, Mark, and Ruth Dassonneville. "Explaining the Trump Vote: The Effect of Racist Resentment and Anti-Immigrant Sentiments." *PS: Political Science and Politics* 51 (2018): 528–34.

Isenberg, Nancy. *White Trash: The 400-Year History of Class in America.* New York: Penguin, 2016.

Jamieson, Kathleen Hall. *Cyber War: How Russian Hackers and Trolls Helped Elect a President.* New York: Oxford University Press, 2018.

Jarvis, Sharon, and Soo-Hye Hahn. *Votes That Count and Voters Who Don't: How Journalists Sideline Electoral Participation Without Even Knowing It.* University Park: Penn State University Press, 2018.

Kam, Cindy D., and Beth A. Estes. "Disgust Sensitivity and Public Demand for Protection." *Journal of Politics* 78 (2016): 481–96.

Kellner, Douglas. *American Nightmare: Donald Trump, Media Spectacle, and Authoritarian Populism.* New York: Springer, 2016.

Kendi, Ibram X. *How to Be an Antiracist.* New York: One World / Ballantine, 2019.

———. *Stamped from the Beginning: The Definitive History of Racist Ideas in America.* New York: Random House, 2017.

Kendzior, Sarah. *The View from Flyover Country: Dispatches from the Forgotten America.* New York: Flatiron Books, 2018.

Klein, Joe. *The Natural: The Misunderstood Presidency of Bill Clinton.* New York: Doubleday, 2002.

Kopkind, Andrew. "The Manufactured Candidate." *The Nation*, February 3, 1992, 116–18.

Kornacki, Steve. *The Red and the Blue: The 1990s and the Birth of Political Tribalism.* New York: Ecco, 2018.

Kumar, Martha Joynt. "The Contemporary Presidency Energy or Chaos? Turnover at the Top of President Trump's White House." *Presidential Studies Quarterly* 49 (2019): 219–36.

Kurtz, Howard. *Spin Cycle: Inside the Clinton White House.* New York: Free Press, 1998.

Labbe, Ronald M., and Jonathon Lurie. *The Slaughterhouse Cases: Regulation, Reconstruction, and the Fourteenth Amendment.* Abridged ed. Lawrence: University Press of Kansas, 2005.

Lajevardi, Nazila, and Marisa Abrajano. "How Negative Sentiment Toward Muslim Americans Predicts Support for Trump in the 2016 Presidential Election." *Journal of Politics* 81 (2019): 296–302.

Langguth, A. J. *After Lincoln: How the North Won the Civil War and Lost the Peace.* New York: Simon and Schuster, 2014.

Laracey, Mel. *Informing a Nation: The Newspaper Presidency of Thomas Jefferson.* Ann Arbor: University of Michigan Press, 2020.

Larson, Edward J. *Magnificent Catastrophe: The Tumultuous Election of 1800, America's First Presidential Campaign.* New York: Free Press, 2007.

Lee, Michael J. *Creating Conservatism: Postwar Words That Made an American Movement.* Lansing: Michigan State University Press, 2014.

Levitsky, Steven, and Daniel Ziblatt. *How Democracies Die: What History Reveals About Our Future.* New York: Viking, 2018.

Lopez, Ian Haney. *Dog Whistle Politics: How Coded Racial Appeals Have Reinvented Racism and Wrecked the Middle Class.* New York: Oxford, 2014.

Lozada, Carlos. *What Were We Thinking: A Brief Intellectual History of the Trump*

Era. New York: Simon and Schuster, 2020.

Maraniss, David. *The Clinton Enigma*. New York: Simon and Schuster, 1998.

———. *First in His Class: A Biography of Bill Clinton*. New York: Simon and Schuster, 1995.

Mason, Robert. *Richard Nixon and the Quest for a New Majority*. Chapel Hill: University of North Carolina Press, 2004.

Matalin, Mary, James Carville, and Peter Knobler. *"All's Fair": Love, War, and Running for President*. New York: Simon and Schuster, 1995.

Mayer, Jeremy D. *Running on Race: Racial Politics in Presidential Campaigns, 1960–2000*. New York: Random House, 2002.

McCoy, Donald R. *Calvin Coolidge: The Quiet President*. New York: Macmillan, 1967.

McGinnis, Joe. *The Selling of the President, 1968*. New York: Trident, 1969.

Meacham, Jon. *Destiny and Power: The American Odyssey of George Herbert Walker Bush*. New York: Random House, 2015.

———. *The Soul of America: The Battle for Our Better Angels*. New York: Random House, 2018.

Mehltretter Drury, Sara, and Rebecca A. Kuehl. "Introduction to the Special Issue on the Rhetoric of the 2016 Presidential Election," *Communication Quarterly* 66 (2018): 11–116.

Meiley, Timothy. "Agency Panic and the Culture of Conspiracy." In *The Politics of Paranoia in Postwar America*, edited by Peter Knight, 57–81. New York: New York University Press, 2002.

Mendelberg, Tali. *The Race Card: Campaign Strategy, Implicit Messages, and the Norm of Equality*. Princeton: Princeton University Press, 2001.

Mercieca, Jennifer. *Demagogue for President: The Rhetorical Genius of Donald Trump*. College Station: Texas A&M University Press, 2020.

Miller, Patricia Roberts. *Demagoguery and Democracy*. New York: The Experiment, 2016.

Morris, Roy, Jr. *Fraud of the Century: Rutherford B. Hayes, Samuel Tilden, and the Stolen Election of 1876*. New York: Simon and Schuster, 2003.

Mulloy, D. J. *Enemies of the State: The Radical Right in America from FDR to Trump*. Lanham, MD: Rowman and Littlefield, 2018.

Murphy, Reg, and Hall Gulliver. *The Southern Strategy*. New York: Charles Scribner's Sons, 1971.

Murray, Charles. *Coming Apart: The State of White America, 1960–2010*. New York: Crown Forum, 2012.

Murray, Robert K. *The 103rd Ballot: Democrats and the Disaster in Madison Square Garden*. New York: Harper and Row, 1976.

Mutz, Diana C. "Status Anxiety, Not Economic Hardship, Explains the 2016 Presidential Vote." *Proceedings of the American Academy of Sciences* 115 (2018): E4330–39.

Nelson, Michael. *Resilient America: Electing Nixon in 1968, Channeling Dissent, and Dividing Government*. Lawrence: University Press of Kansas, 2014.

Nixon, Richard Milhous. "Acceptance Speech." Miami Beach, Florida, August 8, 1968. In *Campaign Speeches of American Presidential Candidates, 1948–1984*, edited by Gregory Bush, 153–63. New York: Frederick Unger, 1985.

———. "Campaign Speech." Radio Broadcast, September 19, 1968. In *Campaign Speeches of American Presidential Candidates, 1948–1984*, edited by Gregory Bush, 163–69. New York: Frederick Unger, 1985.

———. *RN: The Memoirs of Richard Nixon*. New York: Grossett and Dunlap, 1978.

O'Brien, Gerald V. "Indigestible Food, Conquering Hordes, and Waste Materials: Metaphors of Immigrants and the Early Immigration Restriction Debate in the United

States." *Metaphor and Symbol* 18 (2003): 33–47.

O'Donnell, Lawrence. *Playing with Fire: The 1968 Election and the Transformation of American Politics.* New York: Penguin, 2017.

O'Reilly, Kenneth. *Nixon's Piano: Presidents and Racial Politics from Washington to Clinton.* New York: Free Press, 1995.

O'Toole, Patricia. *When Trumpets Call: Theodore Roosevelt After the White House.* New York: Simon and Schuster, 2005.

Ott, Brian. "The Age of Twitter: Donald J. Trump and the Politics of Debasement." *Critical Studies in Media Communication* 34 (2017): 59–68.

Palmer, Niall Andrew. *Calvin Coolidge: Conservative Icon.* Corvallis: Oregon State University Press, 2013.

Parsons, Elaine Frantz. *Ku-Klux: The Birth of the Klan During Reconstruction.* Chapel Hill: University of North Carolina Press, 2019.

Perot, H. Ross. *United We Stand: How We Can Take Back Our Country.* New York: Hyperion, 1992.

Phillips, Kevin P. *The Emerging Republican Majority.* New Rochelle, NY: Arlington House, 1970.

Polakoff, Keith Ian. *The Politics of Inertia: The Election of 1876 and the End of Reconstruction.* Baton Rouge: Louisiana State University Press, 1973.

Reilly, Katie. "Read Hillary Clinton's 'Basket of Deplorables' Remarks About Donald Trump's Supporters," *Time*, September 10, 2016. https://time.com/4486502/hillary-clinton-basket-of-deplorables-transcript.

Rentschler, Carrie A. "Witnessing: U.S. Citizenship and the Vicarious Experience of Suffering." *Media, Culture, and Society* 26 (2004): 296–304.

Richardson, James D., ed. *A Compilation of the Messages and Papers of the Presidents, 1789–1902*, vol. 3, *1833–1844*. New York: Bureau of National Literature and Art, 1907.

Roberts-Miller, Patricia. *Demagoguery and Democracy.* New York: The Experiment, 2016.

Robin, Corey. *The Reactionary Mind: Conservatism from Edmund Burke to Sarah Palin.* New York: Oxford University Press, 2011.

Robinson, Jackie, as told to Alfred Duckett. *I Never Had It Made: An Autobiography.* Hopewell, NJ: Ecco Press, 1995.

Rowland, Robert C. "Donald Trump and the Rejection of the Norms of American Politics and Rhetoric." In *An Unprecedented Election: Media, Communication, and the Electorate in the 2016 Campaign*, edited by Benjamin R. Warner, Dianne G. Bystrom, Mitchell McKinney, and Mary C. Banwart, 189–205. Santa Barbara, CA: Praeger, 2018.

Schlozman, Daniel, and Sam Rosenfeld. "The Hollow Parties." In *Can America Govern Itself?*, edited by Frances E. Lee and Nolan McCarty, 12–152. Cambridge: Cambridge University Press, 2019.

Scotchie, Joseph. *Revolt from the Heartland: The Struggle for an Authentic Conservatism.* New Brunswick, NJ: Transaction, 2002.

Setzler, Mark, and Alexandra B. Yanos. "Why Did Women Vote for Donald Trump?" *PS: Political Science and Politics* 51 (2018): 523–27.

Sharp, James Roger. *The Deadlocked Election of 1800: Jefferson, Burr, and Union in the Balance.* Lawrence: University Press of Kansas, 2010.

Shen, Lijiang, and James Price Dillard. "Threat, Fear, and Persuasion: Review and Critique of Questions About Functional Form." *Review of Communication Research* 2 (2014): 94–114.

Shogan, Robert. *The Fate of the Union: America's Rocky Road to Political Stalemate.* Boulder, CO: Westview, 1998.

Sides, John, Michael Tesler, and Lynn Vavreck. *Identity Crisis: The 2016 Campaign and the Battle for the Meaning of America*. Princeton: Princeton University Press, 2016.

Siskind, Amy. *The List: A Week-by-Week Reckoning of Trump's First Year*. New York: Bloomsbury, 2018.

Skinnell, Ryan, and Jillian Murphy. "Rhetoric's Demagogue: Demagoguery's Rhetoric." *Rhetoric Society Quarterly* 49 (2019): 225–32.

Skowronek, Stephen. *The Politics Presidents Make: Leadership from John Adams to George Bush*. 2nd ed. Cambridge, MA: Belknap Press, 1997.

Smith, Richard Norton. *On His Own Terms: A Life of Nelson Rockefeller*. New York: Random House, 2014.

Smith, Tobin. *Foxocracy: Inside the Network's Playbook of Tribal Warfare*. Reading: Diversion Books, 2019.

Sobel, Robert. *Coolidge: An American Enigma*. Washington, DC: Regnery, 1998.

Stroud, Natalie Jomini. *Niche News: The Politics of News Choice*. New York: Oxford University Press, 2011.

Stroud, Natalie Jomini, and Jessica R. Collier. "Selective Exposure and Homophily During the 2016 Presidential Campaign." In *An Unprecedented Election: Media, Communication, and the Electorate in the 2016 Campaign*, edited by Benjamin R. Warner, Dianne G. Bystrom, Mitchell McKinney, and Mary C. Banwart, 21–39. Santa Barbara, CA: Praeger, 2018.

Stuckey, Mary E. *Defining Americans: The Presidency and National Identity*. Lawrence: University Press of Kansas, 2004.

———. *Political Vocabularies: FDR, the Clergy Letters, and the Elements of Political Argument*. East Lansing: Michigan State University Press, 2018.

———. "'The Power of the Presidency to Hurt': The Indecorous Rhetoric of Donald J. Trump and the Rhetorical Norms of Democracy." *Presidential Studies Quarterly* 50 (2020): 366–91. https://onlinelibrary.wiley.com/doi/abs/10.1111/psq.12641.

Summers, Anthony, with Robbyn Swan. *The Arrogance of Power: The Secret World of Richard Nixon*. New York: Viking, 2000.

Sundquist, James L. *Dynamics of the Party System: Alignment and Realignment of Political Parties in the United States*. Washington, DC: Brookings, 2011.

Takaki, Ronald. *A Different Mirror: A History of Multicultural America*. Boston: Little, Brown, 1993.

Tannenbaum, Melanie B., Justin Hepler, Rick S. Zimmerman, Lindsey Saul, Samantha Jacobs, Kristina Wilson, and Dolores Albarracín. "Appealing to Fear: A Meta-Analysis of Fear Appeal Effectiveness and Theories." *Psychological Bulletin* 141 (2015): 1178–204. doi:10.1037/a0039729.

Thimmesch, Nick. *The Condition of Republicanism*. New York: W. W. Norton, 1968.

Thompson, J. Lee. *Theodore Roosevelt Abroad: Nature, Empire, and the Journey of an American President*. New York: Palgrave Macmillan, 2010.

Thorson, Esther, Samuel M. Thorn, Weiyue Chen, and Vamsi Kanuri. "Media Influence in the 2016 Race: The Debates, Trump Groping Tape, and the Last-Minute FBI Announcement." In *An Unprecedented Election: Media, Communication, and the Electorate in the 2016 Campaign*, edited by Benjamin R. Warner, Dianne G. Bystrom, Mitchell McKinney, and Mary C. Banwart, 61–86. Santa Barbara, CA: Praeger, 2018.

Tur, Katy. *Unbelievable: My Front-Row Seat to the Craziest Campaign in History*. New York: Dey Street Books, 2017.

Valentino, Nicholas A., Carly Wayne, and Marzia Oceno. "Mobilizing Sexism: The Intersection of Emotion and Gender Attitudes in the 2016

Presidential Election." *Public Opinion Quarterly* 82 (2018): 799–821.

Van Buren, Martin. "Fourth Annual Message," December 5, 1840, 602–20. In *A Compilation of the Messages and Papers of the Presidents, 1789–1902*, vol. 3, *1833–1844*, edited by James D. Richardson, 561–66. New York: Bureau of National Literature and Art, 1907.

———. "To the Senate of the United States," January 13, 1840. In *A Compilation of the Messages and Papers of the Presidents, 1789–1902*, vol. 3, *1833–1844*, edited by James D. Richardson, 561–66. New York: Bureau of National Literature and Art, 1907.

Vivian, Bradford. *Commonplace Witnessing: Rhetorical Invention, Historical Remembrance, and Public Culture.* New York: Oxford University Press, 2017.

———. "Witnessing Time: Rhetorical Form, Public Culture, and Popular Historical Education." *Rhetoric Society Quarterly* 44 (2014): 204–19.

Wallace, George. "Campaign Speech." New York City, October 24, 1968. In *Campaign Speeches of American Presidential Candidates, 1948–1984*, edited by Gregory Bush, 185–93. New York: Frederick Unger, 1985.

Warner, Benjamin R., and Dianne G. Bystrom. "Introduction: Understanding the Unprecedented 2016 Campaign; Two Historical Coincidences Yield an Unexpected Result." In *An Unprecedented Election: Media, Communication, and the Electorate in the 2016 Campaign*, edited by Benjamin R. Warner, Dianne G. Bystrom, Mitchell McKinney, and Mary C. Banwart, 1–17. Santa Barbara, CA: Praeger, 2018.

Wells, Chris, Dhavan V. Shah, Jon C. Pevehouse, JungHwan Yang, Ayellet Pelled, Frederick Boehm, Josephine Lukito, Shreenita Ghosh, and Jessica L. Schmidt. "How Trump Drove Coverage to the Nomination: Hybrid Media Campaigning." *Political Communication* 33 (2016): 669–76.

Weston, Drew. *The Political Brain: The Role of Emotion in Deciding the Fate of the Nation.* New York: Public Affairs, 2007.

White, Theodore H. *The Making of the President, 1968.* New York: Athenaeum, 1969.

White, William Allen. *A Puritan in Babylon: The Story of Calvin Coolidge.* New York: Macmillan, 1938.

Wickham, Dewayne. *Bill Clinton and Black America.* New York: Ballantine, 2002.

Wills, Garry. *Nixon Agonistes: The Crisis of a Self-Made Man.* Updated and expanded ed. New York: Mentor, 1979.

Wilson, Kirt H. *The Reconstruction Desegregation Debate: The Politics of Equality and the Rhetoric of Place, 1970–1875.* East Lansing: Michigan State University Press, 2002.

Winkler, Adam. *We the Corporations: How American Businesses Won Their Civil Rights.* New York: Liveright, 2019.

Witcover, Jules. *The Year the Dream Died: Revisiting 1968 in America.* New York: Warner Books, 1997.

Woodward, Bob. *The Agenda: Inside the Clinton White House.* New York: Simon and Schuster, 1995.

Woodward, C. Vann. *Reunion and Reaction: The Compromise of 1877 and the End of Reconstruction.* 1966. Repr., New York: Oxford University Press, 1991.

———. *The Strange Case of Jim Crow.* 2nd rev. ed. New York: Oxford, 1966.

Wright, Lauren A. *Star Power: American Democracy in the Age of Celebrity.* New York: Routledge, 2020.

Young, Dannagal Goldthwaite. *Irony and Outrage: The Polarized Landscape of Rage, Fear, and Laughter in the United States.* New York: Oxford University Press, 2019.

Zimdars, Melissa, and Kembrew McLeod, eds. *Fake News: Understanding Media and Misinformation in the Digital Age.* Boston: MIT Press, 2020.

Zirin, Dave. "Ken Burns on Jackie Robinson and the Republican Party's 'Pact with the Devil.'" *The Nation*, April 11, 2016. https://www.thenation.com/article/ken-burns-on-jackie-robinson-and-the-republican-partys-pact-with-the-devil.

Zito, Salena, and Brad Todd. *The Great Revolt: Inside the Populist Coalition Reshaping American Politics*. New York: Crown Forum, 2018.

INDEX